# ∼ Prelude to a swindle ∼

Just outside his hotel room in Orlando, Florida, a British tourist is shot to death while on his way to visit Epcot Center.

A week later, another foreign visitor to Epcot is killed during a similar robbery, marking the ninth murder of foreign tourists in Florida during a twelve-month period.

Next, a pair of tourists from Ohio are robbed at gunpoint in Kissimmee, not far from Disney World.

Florida's department of commerce responds to the escalating violence against tourists by cancelling its multi-million-dollar "Come on Down!" visitor promotional program.

Meanwhile, CBS television's *48 Hours* program reports that security is generally inadequate at most American hotels.

And a few days later, as if the event had been forecast, a beautiful young woman dials "911" from her hotel room at Disney World and hysterically reports she has been brutally beaten, robbed and raped by an intruder.

Then another young woman is murdered in Florida when six shots are fired at her from point-blank range, and the primary suspect is a police officer she had accused earlier of raping her.

These seemingly unrelated events are brought together to form the focal points of SCAM!, a true-life story of swindles, family betrayal and murder that reveals, for the first time, the unbelievable lifestyles of America's most secret crime families.

## DEDICATION:

To Pam, my love.
and
To Jimmy Burke, with the hope he's found peace.

# SCAM!

*by Don Wright*

**COTTAGE PUBLICATIONS**
P.O. Box 2427
Elkhart, IN 46515-2427
**1-800-272-5518**

# SCAM!

## Inside America's Con Artist Clans

### By Don Wright

First printing 1996

Printed in the United States of America

SCAM! -- *Inside America's Con Artist Clans*

ISBN 0-937877-18-2

**COTTAGE PUBLICATIONS**
**P.O. Box 2427**
**Elkhart, IN 46515-2427**
**1-800-272-5518**

# The Burke Family

James William "Jimmy" Burke

Jimmy's parents: Edward T. and Wanda Mary Johns Burke

### Edward and Wanda Burke's children:
Edward Thomas Burke (wife Elizabeth)
Patrick Paul "The Viking" Burke (wife Rose Mary)
Wanda Mary "Jessee" Burke O'Roarke (husband Billy O'Roarke)
Michael Burke (deceased at the age of 12)
Catherine "Cathy" Burke Robertson (husband Tony Robertson)
Theresa Margaret "Peggy" Burke
Paul Burke
Winifred Ann "Winnie" Burke
Wanda Mary Burke Normile, adopted (husband John Normile)

### Jimmy's aunts and uncles (his father's siblings):
John Burke, deceased (wife Winifred)
- Daughter Peggy Marie (husband Tom Riley)
- Daughter Beatrice Ann "Bridget" (husband Floyd)
    - Sons Lloyd and John Compton
- Son John Burke Jr. (wife Margaret)
James Burke (wife Kathleen)
Mickey Burke (wife Tillie)
- Son Mickey Jr.
- Son John (wife Margaret Daley)
Winifred Ann Burke Young Cleveland
- Daughter Peggy Ann (husband Matt Carroll)
- Son John Young
- Twin daughters Shelly and Kelly Gorman
- Daughter Wanda Mary (later adopted by Jimmy's parents)

### Jimmy's uncles (his mother's siblings):
Douglas (last name kept confidential)
Buddy (killed in the 1950s)
Ronnie (last name kept confidential)

# CONTENTS

# INTRODUCTION

This book required sixteen years to be written. Research for it began during the late winter months of 1980, and it is now February 1996. Although initial investigations were done for a series of articles in *Trailer Life* magazine, it was clear from the outset that the full story of the Travelers needed to be told in book form.

During the first six years, the story of the Travelers was my obsession. Similar to a recurring fever, it blazed like an uncontrollable flame and required nearly constant attention. It stole focus from my family and, at times, threatened to engulf them in its heat. For several years, the fever was nearly dormant, although never quite gone. It flared anew early in 1995, and I realized that only by finishing this book could I ever hope to conquer it.

Over the sixteen years, I tape-recorded interviews with hundreds of people. I collected police reports, court documents and newspaper articles. Wherever I traveled -- and I traveled quite extensively during most of those years -- I searched for Travelers, or evidence of them.

In the course of the research, I became as well known to the Travelers -- particularly to the Irish Travelers -- as they were to me. I began to develop personal contacts within the clans and, as the years passed, one Traveler would introduce me to another, and that one would pave the way for me to speak with one or two more.

As a result, I was able to view their activities -- their scams -- from three unique perspectives: A Traveler would tell me about his swindles; his victims would tell me how they were swindled, and investigating police officers would provide their own analyses of what took place.

The Travelers are a fascinating people.

I particularly like the Irish Travelers. I enjoy being with them and talking with them. And I'm not alone in that regard. Every police officer I've ever known who has become well informed about Travelers feels the same way about them. A few cops -- one in Florida and one in Indiana, for example -- have even become so involved with the Travelers that they've lost their careers because of it.

I can understand that. On several occasions, Travelers invited me to hit the road with them so that I could observe their lifestyles and watch them operate their scams. I was tempted to do it, but I knew enough about the legalities involved to realize if I did that, I would put myself in a position of having prior knowledge about criminal activities and therefore would be open to arrest and prosecution.

This book is about the Travelers and their scams. It is impossible to write about one and not the other.

I won't waste your time trying to convince you that not all Travelers swindle, cheat or steal. The Travelers themselves are quite adept at communicating that; when talking with non-Travelers, they insist that only a few "bad apples" actually engage in criminal activities.

I would like to believe that not all Travelers are con artists. What you believe is up to you.

My purpose here is not to expose the Travelers, but to tell their story by focusing primarily upon the activities of one family. At the outset, let me make it clear that I do not believe that family -- the Burkes -- are necessarily representative of all Travelers. They are the most dysfunctional family I have ever seen. But the scams in which they are engaged -- and the skills they use to plan and execute their scams -- are, indeed, representative of the Travelers.

Jimmy Burke, to whom this book is dedicated, became a friend, and we maintained a unique relationship for most of the last sixteen years. One of the most intelligent, skillful con artists I have ever known, Jimmy was the pillar upon which this book was built. He provided me with the invaluable opportunity to know a career con artist as he developed from a teenager into a mature adult, and he allowed me to see his warts as well as his warm good nature.

Jimmy had an uncanny memory, and he could recall events, details and actual conversations that occurred years earlier. Some of the dialogue you will read in these pages is the result of Jimmy's phenomenal memory. Other conversations were taken directly from legal documents such as police reports, court transcripts or taped interviews with at least one of the persons involved. I took very few liberties with those conversations.

Every event, every crime, every arrest and every investigation is fully documented either by official paperwork or by taped interviews. The contents of this book are true, although individual viewpoints of specific events may differ.

In most cases, individuals have been identified by name. Where a fictitious name has been used, I have made note of that. Some identities were kept confidential for obvious reasons: to protect them from criminal prosecution or unnecessary attention and ridicule.

I readily admit there is one obvious omission within the pages you are about to read: I have avoided discussing, in depth, the companies that supply Travelers with products. There are several reasons for avoiding that discussion, but the primary reason is that no one has yet proven those companies are operating illegally, and until such time as that proof is provided -- not by me, but by someone else -- I cannot justify identifying either the companies or their products by name. I have used the names of companies that are no longer in business, but I have assigned fictitious names to other products and suppliers.

Thus, the firm that supplies Travelers with most of their lightning rods is called Roberts Lightning Protection Company. The three primary producers of Travelers' recreational vehicles are called Kentucky Traveler, Renegade Traveler and Federal Traveler. Another company which once supplied RVs to the clans but no longer does so is called Indiana Traveler. Any person who wants to know the real names of the RV companies and their products can learn those names simply by asking nearly any bonafide recreational vehicle dealer in America.

I expect many of my friends within the RV industry will regard my refusal to name those RV companies as a cop-out. My answer to them is simply this: *SCAM* is a book about the Travelers, not about the business practices of RV manufacturers. The RV industry has chosen to set its own standards and regulate itself; it is the industry's responsibility, not mine, to judge its members.

Some of the Travelers, when reading this book, doubtlessly will criticize me for withholding certain information about individuals or for seeming to paint a group of clan members with too broad a stroke. In each case, I had my reasons for doing that, and I would be happy to discuss those reasons with them.

In general, law enforcement officers have been of invaluable assistance in helping me complete my research. Some of those officers probably will believe this book portrays Travelers in a more positive way than it should and that it unfairly criticizes lawmen. The fact is, a few police officers around the country are quite successful at bringing Travelers to justice, but most law enforcement agencies have proven to be inept at dealing with Travelers in any way.

It is impossible for any writer to finish researching the Travelers because their scams are never-ending. It also is impossible to report, in one book, the full extent of their criminal activities. So I ask you, the reader, to recognize that the scams recorded here are being executed every day in virtually every community throughout North America. It matters not whether you live in Chicago or Walla Walla; the Travelers are either in your town now or they will be soon.

# PROLOGUE

History refers to them as the *Tuath Semon*. During peacetime in the Middle Ages, they were rivet-makers and were highly regarded in all of Great Britain for their skills. But in times of war, they were invaluable because it was then that they repaired the swords and pikes used by warriors to defend villages and kill invaders. Legend, however, says that after the fierce Gaels successfully invaded the Tuath Semon's Irish homeland, the rivet-makers switched from weapons-mending to making pots, pans and other tinware, and they never again recovered the respected position in society that they once held.

According to the legend, they became known as Tinkers.

During the next six hundred years, many of the Tinkers indentured themselves to Ireland's landed nobility and lived rather well, but a majority of the tinsmiths roamed the countryside earning their livelihoods trading horses with farmers. When thousands of the landed gentry were dispossessed of their properties following passage of a law converting tithes of the pro-English aristocracy into land rent charges, the more settled Tinkers were forced to rejoin the itinerant bands.

Traveling in horse-drawn bow-topped covered wagons, the Tinkers gained a reputation for being thieves and con artists as well as pot-menders, carpenters, chimney-cleaners and horse-traders. They referred to themselves as The Travelling People, or Travellers. They developed their own secret language, derived from Gaelic, which western Tinkers called Cant and other clansmen called either Shelta or Gammon.

Between 1845 and 1847, when Ireland's economy was virtually destroyed by the potato famine, more than half a million Irishmen fled to the United States. Among them were several families of western Ireland Tinkers led by a strong-willed con artist named Tom

11

Carroll. By the 1850s, Carroll was head of an American-based Traveller clan that included Sherlocks, Gormans, Donahues and Daleys. From Ireland, they brought with them a determination to retain the purity of their Irish Traveller heritage as well as an uncanny ability to swindle the amazingly gullible Americans.

Old Tom Carroll's children -- Bessie, Foozie and Nannie -- did their part by raising huge families, and the rest of the clan members produced offspring at a phenomenal rate too. By the time Old Tom was buried in Atlanta's Westview Cemetery late in the 19th Century, the Travellers had perfected a wide range of con games and swindles. They still traded horses and mules, but they also earned money by cheating merchants with sleight-of-hand tricks and by selling farmers' wives fake Irish lace and cheap "heirlooms from the old country."

After the Civil War reconstruction period, they set up a huge tent encampment on the outskirts of Atlanta. For twenty years, they used the encampment as a base, with individual family members moving off in all directions to trade horseflesh and work various scams and swindles. Living on the fringe of society, their very existence unknown to most Americans, the Irish Travellers were unmatched as con artists.

And then, the Terrible Williamsons migrated to America.


According to popular legend, a band of dark-skin Romanian Gypsies who roamed the Northern Scotland countryside in the mid-1700s was accused of stealing sheep. Outraged shepherds stormed the Gypsy camp and hanged all the men and boys. They spared the Gypsy women, but left them to fend for themselves in the highlands of Inverness County. In order to survive, the women married into Scottish families of Williamsons, Stewarts and McMillans, but they left those families after a few years, taking the children from the marriages with them and forming a new Gypsy band.

For 150 years, the itinerant Williamsons, Stewarts and McMillans traveled Scotland in a manner similar to Ireland's Tinkers. Then, during the 1890s, a young clan member named Robert Logan Williamson crossed the Atlantic to Brooklyn, New York. Like the Irish Travellers before him, he saw America as a great land of opportunity -- especially for an experienced con artist.

Robert wasted no time fleecing those who were gullible enough to be taken in by his charm and his lies. Acquiring cheap, factory-manufactured cloth, he knocked on doors and represented the fabric as imported woolen suit material. He peddled machine-made carpets as Oriental rugs. He sold coats that were made of rabbit fur which he said was sealskin. He forged famous clothier labels and sewed them into cheap garments that he then sold for ten times their value. And, as his successes mounted, he sent money back to Scotland so that others of his clan could join him in America.

By the turn of the century, law enforcement agencies around the country began to put together files on the Williamson clan and their escapades. Newspapers and magazines of the day heralded the family's exploits but, instead of revealing the Scottish rogues as unscrupulous criminals, they tended to picture them as modern Robin Hoods who stole only from the rich.

They became known far and wide as "The Terrible Williamsons."

By the 1920s, the Williamsons had established a sort of base of operations in Cincinnati, due to its central location. It was in Cincinnati's Spring Grove Cemetery that the deceased Williamsons, including old Robert Logan himself, were buried. The clans trekked annually to that Ohio River city to pay respects to their ancestors and to plant recently dead relatives who were shipped to undertakers there and kept in cold storage until immediate family members could gather for the funerals. Several old, retired Williamsons even took up full-time residence in Cincinnati, but gradually, as America's centers of population shifted to California and the Sunbelt, the Williamsons refocused their attention on those areas.

# 1

# Halloween

In Orlando, Florida, during late October, the evening hours just after dark are usually balmy and pleasant, even at the end of hot, humid days. Halloween night on October 31, 1992, was one of those times. A slight breeze cooled the air, promising to provide relief for the thousands of costumed children who would be walking door to door that night asking for treats and threatening tricks.

Orlando had become North America's premier family party town, thanks in large measure to the presence of Walt Disney World, Sea World, the Wet 'N' Wild water park and numerous other attractions that catered to parents and children. That night in particular, events built around the Halloween theme were scheduled throughout the Orlando area at virtually every place people gathered. The festive atmosphere was dampened only a little by an ever-present undercurrent of concern: Central Florida's world-wide reputation as a safe family vacation spot had been tarnished in recent weeks by a sudden outbreak of violent crimes targeted at tourists.

Orange County Sheriff Walt Gallagher had personally been under immense pressure from civic groups and businesses to protect the Orlando area's huge tourist population. Less than a month earlier, a

British man was shot to death outside his hotel room on the Orange Blossom Trail. Within that same week, another foreign visitor to Epcot was killed during a similar robbery, marking the ninth murder of foreign tourists in Florida during a twelve-month period. Then three armed robberies were reported -- one in Kissimmee against two Ohio tourists, a second against a British couple walking near Lake Buena Vista and the Disney complex, and the third against a Florida man following a basketball game. Just two weeks prior to Halloween night, tourism industry representatives and law enforcement authorities met to review those crimes and consider what could be done to prevent similar incidents in the future. Following that meeting, the *Orlando Sentinal* reported, "The officials agreed that the attacks have been statistically rare and said they saw no reason to beef up law enforcement measures to protect tourists."

Despite that public position, the sheriff quietly began restructuring the squad of about twelve officers that had been assigned to the county's tourist district. Gradually, he added nearly 30 individuals, including a bike squad, two gang suppression officers, five mounted patrol officers, more detectives and a motorcycle officer. As part of an agreement with Walt Disney World, five deputies were assigned to that entertainment complex full time, with Disney paying part of their salaries. The increased police presence seemed to have an immediate positive effect. No violent crimes against tourists had been reported in nearly two weeks.

During the few days prior to Halloween night, the central Florida tourist industry prepared for what was expected to be a huge influx of vacationers from all over the world. This year, Halloween night was on Saturday, and predictions were that with the usual Halloween-type festivities taking place on a weekend evening, record crowds could be expected. At Walt Disney World's popular resort hotels, employees were encouraged to observe Halloween by dressing in costumes -- although nothing scary enough to frighten little children.

Twenty-nine-year-old Vicki Aten was dressed like an Indian maiden as she checked guests into their rooms at Disney's Caribbean Beach Resort Hotel. Friendly and outgoing, she took time to chat with the guests, encouraging them to take advantage of the resort's ticket and shuttle services. Two employees of Disney's nearby Grand Floridian Hotel -- David E. Bahler and Richard A. Horton -- chose Dracula costumes, and Bahler was so proud of his appearance that he searched out friends at the Caribbean Beach facility to show off. For both men, their choice of costume that day would prove to be unfortunate.

By 8:30 on Halloween night, the sky was dark and the blistering heat of the Florida sun was gone, cooled by soft breezes blown in from the Gulf of Mexico. Twenty-year-old Wanda Mary Normile and her 38-year-old sister, Jessee O'Roarke, returned to their room in the Aruba section of the Caribbean Beach Resort after having spent the afternoon and evening visiting relatives, exploring the Disney complex and paying their respects at family gravesites near Winter Garden. With the two women was Mrs. Normile's ten-month-old baby daughter, Winifred Ann.

Mrs. Normile, police would learn later, was separated from her husband and, for several weeks, had been living with her sister in Maine. A small, attractive woman who was barely four feet nine inches tall and weighed a mere ninety pounds, she carried herself with the self-assurance of a wealthy society-class princess. Hotel desk clerk Vicki Aten, when questioned later by police, remembered Wanda Mary Normile quite well.

"She looked to be about 24," Aten said. "She was dressed up nice, wearing a navy blue dress with white pattern. She had blonde hair and a fair complexion and was pretty. She wore a lot of jewelry. She had five or more gold necklaces, some with hanging chains. She wore many rings on her fingers. One ring on her left hand was very large;

it had gold interwinding with small stones spread upon the surface of the ring. Each stone was the same size and color. She seemed like a businesswoman when she stepped up, but as the check-in continued, she was not pushy, but actually nice and, if anything, insecure."

Wanda Mary's sister, Jessee O'Roarke, was a widow with two grown children. A self-employed cosmetics consultant, she told police officers that she regarded the trip to Florida as a combination vacation and an opportunity to renew relationships with an estranged uncle who lived in Orlando. Also, she hoped that her sister's husband, who lived in Texas, could be convinced to visit Florida too and reconcile with his young wife.

The sisters arrived at the Caribbean Beach Hotel on Halloween night in Mrs. O'Roarke's GMC truck. In the parking lot not far from their ground-floor room, Jessee said to her sister, "I'm gonna go get something to eat. Do you want to come?"

"No," replied the young mother. "I don't feel good. I have a headache, and the baby is too cranky."

"I'll carry the baby to the room for you."

"No, it's okay. I can manage."

Wanda Mary got out of the truck, and Jessee waited with the vehicle's headlights illuminating the way as her sister walked across the grass toward their room. A person -- Jessee later told police she thought it was a man -- was standing on the balcony above their room near the corner of a stairway. He was leaning over the railing, watching Wanda Mary and the baby as they passed below. Another man and two small boys, all wearing swimming suits and carrying towels, appeared to be returning to their room from the pool area. Wanda Mary and the baby passed out of sight behind a pillar near the hotel room doorway, and Jessee did not see her sister go into the room. Alone, Jessee drove to the Crab House, a nearby seafood restaurant. She was quite hungry, and she was looking forward to a quiet dinner without the presence of a cranky, teething baby.

One hour and twenty minutes later, at 9:50 p.m., the on-duty dispatcher at the Reedy Creek Improvement District Fire Services answered an emergency "911" telephone call from somewhere in the Walt Disney World complex. Here is a partial transcript of that call:

Caller (crying): You gotta help me!

Dispatcher: What's wrong?

Caller (crying): I'm at the motel at Disney World.

Dispatcher: Which motel?

Caller (crying): The Caribbean Resort.

Dispatcher: What's the room number?

Caller (crying): Oh, my God, let me look on the phone. It's there. It's 5315. Somebody was in my room when I came in.

Dispatcher: Did anybody hurt you?

Caller (hysterical and crying): Yes!

Dispatcher: Do you need an ambulance?

Caller: He came and, came in!

Dispatcher: Okay, do you need an ambulance?

Caller: I'm hurt and (inaudible)...He came in and beat me up, and he took my stuff and he raped me!

Dispatcher: Okay...

Caller (hysterical and crying): He told me he was gonna kill my baby if I screamed!

Dispatcher: Okay, okay ma'am...What's your name?

Caller: My...my name is Wanda Normile.

Dispatcher: Okay, and you said somebody came in the room and beat you up?

Caller: Yes.

Dispatcher: Wanda, where are you bleeding?

Caller: Parts of my mouth.

Andrew M. Cohen, an employee of Walt Disney World Security, broke into the conversation and asked, "Do we have a description of the assailant?"

Dispatcher: No, Andy.

Caller: He, he...When I walked in my room he grabbed me from behind, and he beat me up.

The dispatcher informed the caller an ambulance was on its way.

Hotel duty manager James Thomas was the first person to arrive at Wanda Mary's room following her 911 call. He had overheard WDW Security's dispatch of paramedics to the scene. "A white lady opened the door and wanted to know who I was," he told police. "I told her I was the duty manager." He talked with Wanda Mary until security officers arrived, then directed paramedics to the room.

Reedy Creek paramedic Willis M. Jones arrived next, followed by EMTs Steven Maxfield and Pamela F. Lang. Wanda Mary, clothed in a black slip, was crying as she opened the door to let them in. Maxfield reported, "There were no signs of forced entry on the door. The crying and hysterical patient was in a darkened room with only the television on." Obviously still frightened, she backed up against the wall when Jones entered the room. Remnants of duct tape were wound around her head and wrapped around her wrists and ankles. Jones turned on a light between the beds. Wanda Mary seemed to become less frightened when she saw the female EMT. Jones cut a strip of tape that was still wrapped around her eyes. He noted contusions to her face and arms and began removing tape from her wrists because her left hand was turning blue. As he did, he looked at her other injuries: minor abrasions and swelling around her mouth, edema to her cheeks and forearms. Her teeth appeared to be intact. Looking around, Jones noticed that pieces of duct tape sixteen to eighteen inches long were hanging from the bedposts, and the sheet of that bed was spotted with blood.

Pamela Lang, an experienced 26-year-old EMT, was disgusted by what she saw. "He duct-taped her spread eagled on the bed," she reported later. "She said that he beat her with something long and hard. He hit her on the left cheek, her head, her right forearm and both legs around the ankles. He also hit her just below her right clavicle. She said that he made her do things she didn't want to do. She also mentioned that he turned the television up really loud."

Richard Duane Keith, assistant chief of operations for the Reedy Creek fire department, reached the scene. "The room appeared to have been ransacked. The bed closest to the door had what appeared to be the contents of a purse dumped out on it." Walt Disney World Security personnel arrived, and Keith positioned himself outside the door to stop anyone else from entering.

John Slivonik with WDW Security did not see Wanda Mary until she was being taken to the ambulance. "She had tape in her hair and appeared to be extremely upset, crying and visibly shaken."

When Jessee O'Roarke finished her dinner at the Crab House restaurant, she returned to her room at the Disney's complex. She was searching in her purse for her room key when a man approached her. "Are you Miss O'Roarke?" he asked.

Startled, she answered, "Yes."

The man held a two-way radio in his hand. He told Jessee he was with Walt Disney World Security and asked, "Which room are you in?"

She replied, "Room 5315. Is anything wrong?"

"Yes," he answered. "Somebody broke into your room and robbed your sister. She has been taken to the hospital, but she's okay and the baby is okay." He called for a security car to take Jessee to the hospital. Parked off to one side, Jessee saw a single Orange County police car.

At the hospital, she inquired at the information desk about her sister and was referred to a nursing supervisor, who told her Wanda Mary had been raped.

"Oh, no!" she said and began to cry.

The nursing supervisor told her, "You have to be strong for your sister. You need to get yourself together before I take you in to see Wanda."

Jessee wiped her eyes, composed herself and was taken into the room with Wanda Mary and the baby. Wanda Mary was still hysterical. She was crying and screaming, and when she saw Jessee, she sobbed, "Oh, Sissy! Oh, Sissy!"

Jessee went to her, hugged her and stroked her hair. She asked, "What happened?"

"Oh, Sissy. Somebody was in the room when I got there. He grabbed me from the back and told me not to scream. He said if I screamed, he'd kill the baby. It was dark. The lights were off. He must have been behind the door, and he kept telling me, 'If you scream, I'm gonna kill the baby.' I asked him, 'How did you get in here?' and he said, 'A maid will do anything for fifty dollars.'"

Then Wanda Mary began sobbing and said, "Don't ask me any more. I can't talk about it." She pulled the bed covers around her and lay her head back on a pillow, sobbing quietly. Jessee noticed that strips of gray duct tape were stuck to her sister's strawberry blonde hair.

At 10:15 p.m., at least twenty-five minutes after Wanda Mary dialed the emergency 911 number to report she had been raped and robbed, Walt Disney World Security made its first call to law enforcement authorities. Telephoning the Orange County sheriff's office, a WDW Security representative said, "We need an officer to respond to the Caribbean Beach Resort. It's in reference to a Signal 66."

The sheriff's dispatcher asked, "Where?"

WDW Security: "Ah, it's over with."

Dispatcher: "Alrighty, we'll have a deputy over there."

WDW Security: "Okay, do you have an idea how long it will be?"

Dispatcher: "No, I don't know. It's Halloween."

WDW Security: "Yeah, I know (laughs). They're sealing the room off until he gets there."

Dispatcher: "Okay. It'll probably be within an hour."

Three days later, in a copyrighted front-page article, the *Orlando Sentinal* reported that the first person at the rape scene, and the one who initially interviewed Wanda Mary, was a hotel duty manager. WDW Security personnel arrived a few minutes later. The newspaper stated, "Reedy Creek dispatchers believed security workers had called in an on-duty deputy stationed at Disney. When dispatchers realized the deputy was busy elsewhere (and was not notified), they called sheriff's dispatchers."

Three Orange County deputies arrived at the hotel room at 10:42 p.m. -- fifty-two minutes after the original call was placed. The room was a shambles. The bedspread was pulled off one bed and was on the floor. A single pillow spotted with blood was on the bed at the headboard. Remnants of gray duct tape were tied to each of the four corner bedposts. There were blood stains on the sheets. Coins, cosmetics, an empty purse, an empty wallet and personal clothing items were scattered on a second bed. The deputies found a soft drink can that was still cool to the touch. A roll of duct tape and several short cut pieces of tape were on one bed. Two pairs of women's panties were on the floor.

WDW investigator Philip McNab said the cut pieces of tape had been removed from the victim's hands by paramedics. No one seemed to know the origin of the soft drink can.

Later, physical examination of the scene by forensics experts revealed trace amounts of semen on the bedsheet. Forensics also reported finding a 14-inch wood handle with the words "True Burn" on the hand area. Fingerprints were found on three pieces of the tape.

Meanwhile, one of the deputies contacted Orange County's rape investigator, Detective Tom Harrison, who was at the Orlando Regional Health Systems emergency room on another matter. Thirty-six-year-old Harrison had been assigned to the county's sexual crimes unit only two years, but already he had earned the respect of other officers and rape victims alike. Although an imposing figure at six-foot-two and 250 pounds, Harrison possessed a warm, gentle nature that quickly won the confidence of the injured women with whom he came in contact daily. He found Wanda Mary sitting alone in a conference room. Thus, fifty-six minutes after she placed her 911 call, Wanda Mary met the man who would handle her case -- the police officer who should have been contacted immediately after the rape was reported.

"Ms. Normile was sitting in a wheelchair wearing a blue sweatshirt and covering herself with a sheet," Harrison wrote in his investigative report. "She had remnants of gray duct tape stuck in her hair. Kneeling in front of her, I introduced myself and asked her what happened. Ms. Normile's eyes were open, but she had an appearance as if she were asleep. Her eyes were red, and I could see some abrasions about her face. She began to tell me that she and her daughter entered their room. Once inside, she was attacked by a man that was already in the room. The man bound her with the duct tape and hit her repeatedly with something. Through repeated questioning, she indicated that she had been raped."

Harrison ordered deputies to gather fingerprints, secure the room and canvas the hotel for witnesses. He requested a crime scene unit to photograph Wanda Mary's injuries and asked that the county's victim advocate be sent to the hospital immediately. A physical examination of Wanda Mary was ordered; a vaginal smear later revealed the presence of intact spermatozoa, indicating the victim had experienced recent sexual activity. A list of Wanda Mary's injuries was compiled: swelling and bruising of a birthmark on her nose; bruising and swelling of the top of her right forearm; swelling and red mark on her right wrist; swelling at the center of her forehead at the hairline; red marks on her left knuckles; redding discoloration of the top of her left forearm; cuts and bruises on her right breast; red marks and indentations on her feet and ankles where she was bound with tape; strap-like bruises on her thighs.

During the early morning hours of Sunday, November 1, Harrison drove the sisters to the home of their uncle and then went to the Caribbean Beach Resort for his first look at the crime scene. Like the other deputies and the security personnel who had been there earlier, he found no sign of forcible entry.

For two days before police officers could conduct an in-depth interview with Wanda Mary and her sister, deputies talked with dozens of possible witnesses and hotel employees. In asking if those individuals observed anything unusual or anyone who acted strangely around the time of the rape, the deputies were able to piece together an unexpected series of events. First, a tall, casually dressed white man apparently tried to gain entry to Room 5315 during the same afternoon as the crime. Second, that evening a tall white man dressed in a Dracula costume attempted on at least two occasions to convince hotel employees to provide him with access to that room. Third, multiple sightings of a man -- or men -- dressed like Dracula occurred at the hotel between early afternoon and late evening.

Hotel employee Samuel J. Miller described the Dracula he saw at about 12:30 p.m. as "somewhat pudgy" and between five-foot-ten and six feet tall. "His costume was very professional, as was the makeup. His face was entirely unrecognizable because of the makeup." A woman in her early thirties wearing a hotel uniform was introducing Dracula to other people.

About two hours later, hotel housekeeper Delores Cruz was approached by a man asking her to clean Room 5315. She described him as 35-37 years old, about six feet three inches tall, weighing 178-180 pounds and wearing a white T-shirt, blue jeans and sneakers. He spoke English but looked Irish, she said. Since Room 5315 was not in her assigned section, she referred him to the housekeeping supervisor.

Jeffrey K. Lambert, the resort's doorman, told police he observed a man in a Dracula costume twice during the day near the hotel gift shop -- once in the late afternoon and again about 6 p.m. "He was acting very serious, as though he had something on his mind."

Another hotel employee, Todd McCracken, reported that a tall, stocky white man with dark hair dressed as Dracula was in the hotel's 5400 Building for twenty to twenty-five minutes starting around 7 p.m. "The location of stairs in the 5400 Building is not more than twenty or thirty yards from the victim's room," he told investigators. "I thought it was odd he was dressed up so early because I knew of nothing going on at our hotel until later."

Between 6 and 7 p.m., a tall man dressed as Dracula told employees Kerry Bevan and Cynthia Briggs he had left his key and wallet in his room. He asked for a spare key so that he could retrieve his wallet. Bevan refused to give him a key without identification, but the man said his I.D. was in his wallet. Bevan said if the man would describe his wallet, Briggs would retrieve it from the room for him. The man refused, saying he did not want anyone else entering his room. Briggs described him as 40-55 years old, at least six feet tall, with an English accent. Phone room employee Brad Loutsenhizer observed the conversation and said, "The costume was by far the best costume I have ever seen. It seemed to me to be a rental."

About an hour later, Dracula asked a cashier to provide him with a key to the room. The cashier called supervisor Darci Gonzalez for advice. The cashier said the man knew the correct name on the room's reservation, but he was not listed as a guest. "I told the cashier that the only way we could give him a key was if he could tell us the address and phone number that was on the reservation. I don't know the outcome."

Between 8:45 and 9:30, Dracula approached 21-year-old Kristen Heaney, who was working at the front desk. He said he was locked out of his room and had left his wallet, his identification and his key in the room. Heaney telephoned the room, but there was no answer. Then she asked resort manager Dwan-Aleise Sims for assistance. Sims refused to let him into the room without I.D.

"He got a little irate and said all he wanted was to get in the room," Heaney reported. "Dwan asked him to identify his luggage, and he said he thought it was white leather. Dwan asked him if he had a name on the luggage, and he said he didn't think so. She kept repeating that we could help him if he would identify something in the room. But he refused."

Sims told police she asked the man to identify the wallet he left in his room, but he could not do that except to say it was in his trousers on the bathroom floor. She volunteered to send someone to the room to retrieve the wallet if he would describe it, and he said, "I do not want anyone going through my trousers. I will wait for my wife to come back."

"He finally stormed away," Heaney said.

Heaney described the man as about six feet two inches tall with large features, 25-30 years old, dark hair and dark brown eyes. "He was disguising his voice when he talked; it almost sounded like a British accent."

Sims said he was in his late twenties or early thirties, six-foot-three with a stocky upper body, dark brown eyes and black hair. "When he spoke, he pretended to have an accent."

Two days after Halloween, on November 2, Detectives Harrison and Denny Connors questioned the two sisters formally. Jessee reported she had returned to the hotel room in order to determine what the intruder had stolen. Missing, she reported, were $500 in cash that Wanda Mary had carried in her purse, a video camera and Wanda Mary's jewelry, including a Rolex watch, a diamond dinner ring that had been a 25th anniversary present from their father to their mother, a gold bracelet with four diamonds, lion's head gold earrings, and two gold necklaces with Lady Liberty $5 and $10 coins.

Wanda Mary, her bruised and puffy face providing evidence of her ordeal, was still rather emotionally distraught when the officers interviewed her.

"As soon as we got in the room, this man grabbed me," she told Harrison and Connors.

"Was he already in the room?" Harrison asked.

"Yes. He had to have been already in the room because there was nobody behind me. When I opened the door, he was there."

She added, "I remember having tape all over my head and in my hair and on my hands. I remember him hitting me with something, but I don't remember what it was. I remember him hitting me with something. It was really hard, whatever it was. It was really hard. And I really don't remember much, 'cause I don't want to remember it."

Harrison replied, "Well, I'm gonna have to ask you to try to remember as much as you possibly can about this because what you remember is gonna help us catch this guy. When this guy grabbed you, what was your response to that? How did you react?"

"When he grabbed me and put his hand on my mouth, I went to bite him, and he had gloves on." She described them as cloth gloves. "I asked him...I asked him how he got in my room. And he said the maid will do anything for fifty dollars. Then he put tape over my mouth. I think he had it in the back of his pants...And it was a huge roll of tape. And he hit me with it one time. He said, 'If you don't shut up, I'll kill you.' So I shut up. I didn't say anything. And then I started to say something again. I had tape on my mouth, but I was, you know, screaming, and he said, 'If you start to scream again, I'm gonna kill your baby.' So I didn't say anything else."

Wanda Mary said her assailant wrapped tape around her face, covering her mouth and eyes. Later, she described him as rather short, saying his chin reached only slightly above her head. "He was about a foot taller than me, quite broad, with a high-pitched voice, in his twenties or thirties, big hands and very strong." She estimated he was built like boxer Mike Tyson, that he was clean-shaven and his breath smelled of beer.

She said she was certain the man was black because of his body odor: "I don't know if you have ever noticed it or not, but to my knowledge, black people have their own smell."

Wanda Mary asked the man to let her put the baby in her crib, and he answered, "Okay, do it then." As she did, to further ensure the baby's safety, she pushed the crib from its position near the door into the bathroom. She gave the baby a cookie to keep her quiet. "I didn't want her to get hurt," she explained.

"He told me to get on the bed, and he tied me up with the tape to the posts of the bed." She said as she climbed onto the bed, she purposely broke the strands of her necklaces and tossed them under the bed, hoping he would not see her do it.

"What were you thinking at that point," Harrison asked.

"How to get loose."

"Did he ever tell you that he had a weapon?"

"No, he just kept saying, 'I'm gonna hit you with this,' and I never did see what it was. It felt like something hard; I think it was wood because if it was plastic, believe me, it would have broke."

"You mean from the force that he hit you with?"

"Yes. Then he would call me all kinds of names. Just horrible names. And he was beating me up with that thing, whatever it was. He hit me in the face first."

"Did he sound like anybody that you knew?"

"No, he sounded like a black man. He sounded like one of them people that rap." She indicated he sounded uneducated "because he didn't use proper English, for one thing. Like he said, 'da bed' instead of 'the bed.' Sounded like he had mush in his mouth or something when he called me a stupid blonde."

Harrison asked, "Did he ever remove any of your articles of clothing?"

"Yes. He tore my pantyhose off and my slip and panties. He tore up my dress. I kicked him a couple of times; I think I kicked him in the face once. I think I got him pretty good. He told me to stop it

and said, 'Oh, shit. That hurt!" He hit me in the face with his hand
for doing that. And I didn't do it again."

"Was there any kissing or fondling?"

"Yes."

"Which is it? Kissing or fondling."

"It wasn't kissing."

"Did he fondle your vaginal area then?"

She nodded affirmatively.

"Was there any digital penetration at that time?"

"Yes. Then he told me, 'Be still. Don't move. And if you scream,
I'll kill you.'"


Wanda Mary said the intruder tied her legs apart by using the
duct tape and, as he did so, he struck her repeatedly with the wood
rod. While she was helplessly tied to the bedposts, she heard him turn
on a lamp and go through her purse. He took off her bracelet, watch
and ring. He found her necklaces, and she heard the sound of them
when he tossed them on the table. Then the coins jingled when he
picked them up again.

"I heard him pick up something right by the bed, which must
have been my purse, and dump out all the stuff in it, 'cause I could
hear all my change and things falling out. And he took my money. I
could hear him mumbling to himself, 'This ain't no good, this ain't
no good, this ain't no good.'"

Later, she found her wallet torn apart and family photos from it
scattered around the room on the floor. She said at one point she
thought his feet got tangled in her knitting yarn that he had tossed
on the floor. She quoted him as saying, "I don't know why these stupid bitches make this shit, anyway." She said he went through the
clothing and baby's items in her suitcases and kept saying over and
over, "This shit ain't no good."

Harrison asked, "What do you think made him strike you, even after you complied with what he was forcing you to do?"

She answered, "Because I think that's just what he wanted to do. Because he's mean. 'Cause he has something against women. He said, 'All you bitches are stupid.' He would say, 'All you stupid bitches are alike' or something to that effect. And that made me mad."

"What did he say to you when he left the room?"

"He said, 'If I come back here in ten minutes and you've got loose, I'm gonna kill you.' So that's why I still waited a few minutes because I wasn't sure he was still outside or not; I wasn't sure where he had went. I wasn't even sure if he left or if he hit the room next door. I heard the door shut because it has an automatic spring on it."

Wanda Mary said after the intruder left, she waited about twenty minutes before trying to free herself.

"How did you get loose?" Harrison asked.

"I kicked and kicked and kicked until I broke the tape. And I pulled my arms until I broke the tape. That's how I got this bruise. I looked at my hands and feet, and then I went over and I looked at the baby and made sure she was okay. Then I went to the phone and pushed the button for 911 and then got the tape away from my mouth."

Harrison asked, "What do you think should happen to this guy?"

Wanda Mary's eyes narrowed and her lips pursed in anger. "I think somebody should do the same thing to him that he's done to me, and I also would throw him in jail for the rest of his life so he won't do it to nobody else. 'Cause he probably will. He probably has before. It seemed to me that he knew what he was doing."

"What makes you think he knew what he was doing?"

"Because, how could somebody just go in and say at that second, 'I'm gonna go in here, and I'm gonna beat this girl up and do this to this girl' and know exactly what to do, you know? How to put the tape on somebody's head and on their arms and their feet and everything. I mean, there's no way that somebody could just do that without knowing how to do it already."

For a brief period, Orange County police officers focused a great deal of attention on the two young Disney resort employees who had worn Dracula costumes to work. But investigators quickly cleared them of suspicion. Three other suspects also were cleared. Over the next several weeks, Orange County police consumed literally thousands of man-hours during their investigations, but few valid leads developed. The most promising theory appeared to be that a former occupant of Wanda Mary's room -- disguised with a Dracula costume to conceal his identity -- had used a still-valid key card in order to unlock the door and gain entry during the sisters' absence. A supervisor in the Disney system admitted to officers that "it could have been six months or more since the key card for the lock to Room 5315 was changed." The supervisor was unable to provide documentation regarding maintenance of the lock mechanism on that room.

Two anonymous telephone calls to Walt Disney World proved quite interesting, however. The first, on November 3, went to Dwan-Aleise Sims. The caller seemed to be Hispanic. He told her he knew "for sure" the identity of the rapist. "The man who raped the girl on Saturday is a cast member from the Caribbean Beach," he said. "There is a girl who works here also who knows who the person is because it is her best friend, and she does not want to come forward."

The second call was taken November 5 by Cathleen C. Giddens, an employee of Walt Disney World Security's communication center. According to police, the caller sighed loudly and then said, "About that rape that happened. The guy did not break into the room; he was let in! He and Wanda set this up. Wanda is now headed back to Maine, and the guy is..." At that point, Giddens was interrupted by a radio call. She asked the caller to hold. He replied, "No, I can't hold. I just wanted to say that this was all planned," and then he hung up.

# 2
# Con Artists

Wanda Mary Normile was, indeed, correct when she told police officers the crime was meticulously planned. The planning actually began several days earlier, immediately following a *"48 Hours"* program on the CBS television network. That program focused on the inadequacy of hotel security. It was viewed with a great deal of interest by four members of a family who were successful life-long con artists. Those four individuals were Wanda Mary Burke Normile, her cousin Wanda Mary Burke O'Roarke (also known as "Jessee"), Jessee's younger brother James Burke and their younger sister, Winifred Burke. They were sitting together in Jimmy's rented motel room not far from the Orlando tourist center.

Thirty-one-year-old Jimmy, without question the most skilled con artist of the group, immediately saw the possibilities of a major score against a large hotel. And he felt the timing was absolutely perfect for a scam at a Florida-based facility. It was Jimmy, the quartet's handsome 220-pound, six-foot-two-inch leader, who would ultimately confuse both police and Disney World employees by posing as Dracula on Halloween night.

"Look at it this way," he said to the others. "All the hotels are goin' to be paranoid about security after that TV show. And the ones in Florida will be even worse because of all the recent violence here against tourists. So what we've gotta do is set up a scenario in which a couple of us pose as tourists and somebody gets into our room and robs us. Then we threaten to sue the hotel for its poor security. The hotel, which already is under a lot of pressure to protect its guests, doesn't want the publicity of a lawsuit, so it settles out of court, and we walk away with a bundle of money."

The idea received mixed reactions from family members, and an argument appeared ready to develop. Jimmy forestalled that by saying, "Let's not talk about it now. Just think about it. Consider the possibilities. And let's discuss it again at another time. Meanwhile, try to think of reasons it might not work."


Jimmy Burke was barely nine years old late in the winter of 1969 when his parents, Wanda and Edward Burke, dropped him off at his grandmother's house in Orlando, Florida. His parents were going to a big gathering of the Irish Traveler clan, and there would be lots of drinking and dancing. And maybe even some fights. It was definitely no place for a nine-year-old kid, even one as worldly as young Jimmy.

The boy had attended school a couple of months during his family's stay in Florida that winter, but he didn't care much for school, and he was anxious to get back on the road traveling, selling trailers and watching his dad seal roofs and pave driveways. His grandparents couldn't understand any of that. They weren't Irish Travelers. His mother hadn't always been a Traveler either, but she'd learned how to be one quickly after marrying his father in 1946. Now, she was regarded as one of the most skilled shoplifters of the Northern Travelers, and she'd started teaching Jimmy how to shoplift two years ago, when he was seven.

Jimmy didn't sleep well in his grandmother's house that night. Sleeping in a house wasn't as nice as sleeping in a travel trailer. He liked the sounds of birds outside his window in the morning. He loved the patter of rain on the aluminum roof of a trailer, and he missed the muffled woosh of semi tractor-trailer rigs roaring past campgrounds situated close to interstate highways. In the city, there were strange noises -- car horns and ambulance sirens and fire trucks. People in the city didn't talk softly while you were trying to sleep, and they always seemed to be watching television.

Jimmy's eyes were red and puffy when he was awakened for breakfast the next morning. That was another thing about city people -- and the non-Travelers his family called *country folk* or *refs*. They got up too early in the morning. It wasn't civilized. Jimmy was patient about all of it, though.

His mother had explained to him, "Jimmy, your grandparents aren't Travelers. They're American country folks. But I want you to be nice to them and do what they tell you to do. Don't upset them."

Jimmy understood. He'd been acting polite to refs all his life. It was sort of a game, and he liked to play it. Country folk always thought you liked them if you were nice to them. The thing was, Jimmy really *did* like his grandparents. Especially his grandfather. Of course, the man wasn't *really* his grandfather. He was his grandmother's seventh husband. His real grandfather was Paul Johns, the police chief of Wauchula, Florida, but his grandmother had divorced him many years ago after five years of marriage. Jimmy's mother, Wanda, was their only daughter, but his grandmother had three sons by three different husbands. One of his mother's brothers was dead -- he'd been shot trying to escape from a Georgia chain gang -- but the other two had children of their own, and Jimmy knew that his grandmother liked those kids better than she liked him.

Jimmy always felt that no matter where he was, he didn't fit in.

When he was with the Travelers, the other kids picked fights with him because his mother wasn't really a Traveler, and they called him a ref. But when he was with his grandparents, it was worse because he wasn't allowed to touch anything, and when his grandmother was angry with him, she'd call him a dirty gypsy. His grandmother always bought Christmas presents for his cousins, but she never bought any for him.

He wondered why his grandmother didn't like him. He didn't think he was such a bad kid. But maybe he'd try to do something to impress her or his grandfather.

"Hey, Jim," his grandfather called. "I'm going to the store to buy some things for breakfast. Do you want to come along?"

"Sure," Jimmy said.

In the car, his grandfather fished a quarter out of his pocket and gave it to Jimmy. "Here," he said. "Buy yourself something with this."

On the way to the store, Jimmy considered what he'd buy. A candy bar would be nice, but he liked beefstick, and he also loved the taste of Frito corn chips. Inside the market, Jimmy still couldn't make up his mind which item to buy. But for an Irish Traveler kid with his skills, the problem was easy to solve; he stuffed a candy bar and the beefstick in his pants and used the quarter to buy a bag of corn chips. He knew what he'd done would really impress his grandfather!

Their shopping completed, Jimmy and his grandfather left the store, and Jimmy pulled the prizes out of his pants. "Where did you get the money for all that?" his grandfather asked.

Jimmy answered proudly: "I didn't have any more money. I stole it!"

The old man frowned but didn't say anything. He was quiet all the way home, and Jimmy wondered why. Back at his grandparents' house, he took his snacks into the bedroom. He heard his grandmother shout: "Jimmy Burke, you get out here this instant!" He went into the kitchen, and his grandmother stood there with a yardstick in her hand. She made him bend over a chair, and she hit him with it several times, all the while shouting at him that he was a dirty, thieving gypsy and a disgrace to her family. She sent him to his room and told him to stay there all day until his parents came to pick him up.

That evening, when Wanda and Edward Burke arrived, Jimmy's grandmother began yelling at his mother and said, "Get your gypsy kid out of here and don't ever bring him back!"

Ten years later, Jimmy recalled that shameful incident. "That's when I really learned that everybody wasn't like we were. I didn't think, at the time, that I had done anything wrong. I'd been taught to steal. With our people -- the Travelers -- there was nothing wrong with it. From the time a Traveler child is about seven years old, he's told he's different and that he's not to associate with anyone who's not part of *The People* and not to think that anybody is his friend except his own people. You're told that as long as you're in with your own people, nobody's goin' to do nothin' to hurt you, and if you get in trouble, nobody's goin' to go to the cops. They have a bond with each other, and they feel that if you go messin' around outside The People, you're just askin' for trouble. The Travelers are all into the same things -- the same kinds of scams, the same scores -- and one can go to jail for something as quick as the next one can. One don't do nothin' no worse than the one next door, so they have that bond between them and feel they can trust each other."


Jimmy Burke's fraternal grandmother was an Irish Tinker who emigrated to America about 1920. For reasons that are lost to history now, she and her parents settled in Florida, where she fell in love with a young Irishman named Burke who operated a septic tank cleaning service in Orlando. Burke died young, but not before he fathered several children, including brothers Edward, John, James and Mickey and daughter Winifred Ann. Even as youngsters, the children were attracted to the romantic life of the Irish Travelers, and they loved hearing stories their mother told them about the old country. Encouraged by their mother, they gravitated to the Northern Traveler lifestyle and took naturally to the swindles practiced by the clan. Toward the end of World War II, Edward met a cute seventeen-year-old named Wanda Johns. She was petite -- just over five feet tall and only ninety pounds. She had long, black hair that fell to her waist, and she looked so good in a swimming suit that she was selected Miss Florida that year. Wanda worked part-time in a hotel restaurant managed by her stepfather, and the lounge there was a favorite watering hole of several Traveler men while they spent their winters in Florida. Edward and Wanda were immediately attracted to one another. They dated often when Edward was in Florida, although other clan members frowned on his association with a country woman.

In 1946, in direct opposition to Irish Traveler custom, Edward married his *country* sweetheart. Edward's mother and brothers were outraged, and Wanda was shunned by the clan. Wanda didn't care. She had a handsome, rich husband who always owned a new car and a new trailer, and she was happy. She was, that is, until Edward took her to a trailer park to meet his relatives. The young bride was escorted inside one of the trailers, introduced to the women who were there and then left alone with them while Edward went outside to talk with the men.

Wanda was shocked by the display of wealth inside that trailer. The women wore diamond and gold necklaces, earrings and bracelets. They were all quite well dressed, and they were drinking coffee out of china cups that each cost what Wanda regarded as a small fortune. She smiled and tried to join in the conversation, but the women ignored her. She tried again, and the others began talking in a foreign language called Cant, using ancient Gaelic words no longer in use anywhere in the world except among Ireland's Tinkers and America's Irish Travelers. The ostracism served only to make Wanda determined to become a true Irish Traveler, if not in heritage, then in mind, spirit and behavior.

Years later, as her children were growing up, Wanda told them how she was treated by the clan members on that day in 1946, and she was proud of how she had made the transformation from a poor Florida policeman's daughter to a respected member of the Irish Traveler clan. "Now," her son Jimmy said, "she knows the Traveler language as well as or better than the rest of them, and they've all accepted her as one of them. She has completely turned over her life to the Travelers as if she was born and raised with them. One of the reasons why Travelers don't marry out of The People very often is that most country folks could not adjust to the extremely different lifestyle that the Travelers lead. Most people said Mom and Dad's marriage would never last because the differences in their backgrounds were just like day and night. But evidently, Mom was able to make the necessary changes, even though she was raised in a very strict home by parents who were very religious and didn't believe in stealin' nothin' from nobody. How Mom was able to totally change over to the Traveler life, I don't know."

Edward's sister, Winifred Ann Burke, followed Edward's example and married a man named Young who was not a Traveler, but allowed himself to be converted into one. Winifred Ann and Wanda became good friends, and the two couples traveled together for several years. Winifred Ann was an accomplished shoplifter, and not only did she teach her skills to her new sister-in-law, Wanda, but she also tutored her nieces and nephews in the art of stealing expensive items from department stores and then returning them for cash refunds.

The Burke group followed a special routine when they arrived in a town. After either setting up camp in a trailer park or renting rooms in a motel -- depending upon whether they were towing trailers that they wanted to sell -- Edward and Winifred Ann's husband would load up their trucks with driveway and roof sealant materials and cruise neighborhoods looking for work. Winifred Ann and Wanda would take a couple of the Burke children with them and knock off department stores one by one. Wanda and Edward Burke traveled with all ten of their children: Edward Thomas, Patrick Paul, Wanda Mary, Jimmy, Theresa Margaret (called Peggy), Paul, Catherine, Winifred Ann and a son, Michael, who died at the age of twelve. By the time Jimmy was seven and considered old enough to begin learning to shoplift, his two older brothers, Ed and Pat, were working the paving and sealing scam daily with their father and uncle.

"I'd go into the stores with Mom and Aunt Winnie and, while they were takin' things, I'd make sure no one was watchin' them," Jimmy recalled. "My mother and my aunt Winnie would each make $400, $500 or $600 a day in each town shoplifting, and the next day, we'd go to another town so they could do the same thing there. My brothers and sisters and I watched them work stores together from the time we were very little kids, and they taught us how to do it so we wouldn't get caught. Now, if I want to do it, I can steal anything out of any store there is! I know how to get away with it, and I can spot a security guard a mile away."

In 1981, Jimmy boasted, "I have never been arrested for shoplifting, and I have done it as long as I can remember. One of the first things I learned was how to fix the tickets. Certain stores tear their price tickets a certain way, and others just punch them. Some stores even use an alarm device on their tickets. For example, the Zayres stores in central Georgia have them; they attach a big, white plastic thing on the merchandise, and it says, 'inventory control device,' but it's an alarm trigger. If you walk out of the store with one of them on a dress or a pair of pants, an alarm will go off. But all I do is pop it off with a small screwdriver and take the merchandise anyway. Then I fix the ticket however that particular store does it, put whatever I took in a bag, and another member of the family -- usually a woman -- takes it back inside and says it was a gift to her, but she didn't need it, and since she's from out of state, she wants to return it before she goes back home. She always dresses nice so that no one would ever guess by looking at her that she's a shoplifter."

What kinds of merchandise do the Travelers concentrate on stealing from the stores?

"Usually clothing. Mostly women's dresses because they're easy to take, and they have good prices on them, too. Lately, within the past few years, I guess you could say that's gotten kind of worn out, so a lot of Travelers like to take things that look like they couldn't be shoplifted. Like a tennis racquet; it's something that looks like it wouldn't be easy to steal, so it's easy to return. But really, it *is* easy to steal."

When Jimmy was eleven years old, his father decided he was ready to run a scam of his own. Edward bought large quantities of plastic and beaded purses and grilled his son on how to sell them. Jimmy dressed in old clothes and carried an armload of purses into a bar during the early evening hours. He told the gathered imbibers that his mother was a convalescing widow raising eight children by herself, and the only way she could earn money was by making "Naugahyde" purses by hand. The purses, which cost Edward less than $1.50 each, were sold to the drunks for between ten and twenty dollars each. In some parts of the country, Jim told the drinkers he was half Indian and that his mother made the purses by sewing on each of the color beads by hand. As a personal practical joke aimed at his foolish customers, Jimmy also told them that the purses were machine-washable, knowing full well that the beads were glued on and that they would fall off at the first contact with water! For a year, young Jimmy Burke earned between $700 and $800 every night by selling his worthless purses. His little scam added more than $4,000 a week to the family income!

By the early 1970s, the Burke clan was extremely successful. Edward was earning up to $800 a day sealing driveways and roofs with the help of sons Jimmy and Pat. Wanda matched that amount with her shoplifting and by operating "pigeon drop" confidence games in shopping centers. The family averaged selling two or three travel trailers a month at a profit of $1,000 to $3,000 each, and thousands of dollars more were earned in a never-ending variety of scams, frauds and swindles. Sometimes the oldest Burke son, Edward Thomas, and his wife Elizabeth traveled with the family as they rolled north through Ohio, Indiana, Pennsylvania and New York each summer and then returned to Florida each winter. Without one arrest to blot their records, the Burkes were swindling people out of approximately half a million dollars every year! And, of course, they didn't pay taxes on one cent of that income.

The rest of the Burke clan wasn't doing so well. Edward's sister, Winifred Ann, divorced her ref husband after bearing two children -- Peggy Ann and John. Always regarded as an independent spirit and ostracized by the Travelers because of her marriage, she went to Texas and didn't communicate with her relatives for three years. No one knew for sure whether she was dead or alive until she appeared in Florida one winter driving a beat-up station wagon. With her were twin baby girls named Shelly and Kelly by a new husband -- another ref named Cleveland. Within a short time, Winifred gave birth to another daughter that she named Wanda Mary in honor of her sister-in-law. Five months later, Winifred died unexpectedly. Cleveland, an alcoholic, went to the funeral, then gave all five children to relatives and disappeared. Wanda and Edward adopted baby Wanda Mary to avoid the possibility that Cleveland would ask for her to be returned some day; and from that time forward, the family included two daughters named Wanda Mary.

In the 1950s, Edward and his brother Mickey pooled their funds and started a trailer dealership in Radcliff, Kentucky. One day Mickey's wife, Tillie, got so angry at him about something that she left town. But first, she cleaned out the family bank account, including all the money that Edward and Wanda had. Without funds to support it, the dealership failed. A few months later, Tillie reappeared, broke. Relations were never very good between Tillie and the rest of the family after that.

Like many other Irish Travelers, the Burke men were heavy drinkers. They went out together on regular sprees, drinking until they got falling-down drunk. Brothers Edward and Mickey returned home to their trailers very late one night, and Tillie locked the door before Mickey could get in.

"Let me in, you bitch, or I'll tear this door off and beat the shit out of you!" Mickey shouted.

"You can go to hell, you dirty bastard," answered Tillie. "You try comin' through that door and I'll blow your head off with your own shotgun."

Edward called to his brother, "Mickey, I want you to come on inside our trailer. You can sleep with us and let her cool off. Everything'll be okay in the mornin'."

"You keep your fuckin' nose out of this, Ed!" shouted Mickey.

From inside the trailer, Tillie announced, "You better do what Ed said, Mickey, 'cause you're never gonna sleep soundly with me again. If you aren't careful, I'll kill you sometime while you're in bed."

"I'll show her, that bitch!" Mickey said, and stomped away from the trailer. He climbed back into the pickup truck and sped away, squealing his tires and blowing the horn. Three blocks from the trailer park, he ran off the road, hit a tree and was killed. A few years later Tillie married Texas Traveler Bill Riley, and according to other Travelers, she has totally dominated Riley's life ever since.

Mickey left Tillie with two sons, Mickey Jr. and John. Mickey Jr. travels widely in the Northern Traveler tradition, but John settled in Fort Worth and became well known among the Irish Travelers for his big confidence game scores in Texas. He married Margaret Daley, daughter of Pete and Suzy Daley of the Fort Worth branch of the Travelers, and seems to live very comfortably.

Edward Burke's brother, John, married a Traveler named Winnie, whose sister Beatrice Riley became one of the most notorious

Irish Traveler con artists in America. Winnie gave birth to two daughters -- Peggy Marie and Beatrice Ann, whom everyone called Bridget Ann. Bridget was born with only one leg -- not an unusual affliction among the Irish Travelers, who encourage marriage to close cousins in order to keep the Irish bloodlines pure. Always a fat girl, Bridget grew up wearing a wooden leg. She married a man named Floyd -- a ref alcoholic and drug user from the slums of Cleveland whom she convinced to join the Irish Traveler lifestyle. Soon Bridget became an alcoholic herself. In 1972, the highly intoxicated couple and their five children were towing a travel trailer between Miami and Orlando when the rig went off the road and flipped over several times, totally destroying the trailer and the truck that was pulling it. Miraculously, no one was seriously injured.

Edward and Wanda Burke took Floyd and Bridget to the Cleveland area and rented motel rooms for them in Strongsville. That night, Bridget and her husband drank themselves into a stupor. Bridget rolled off the bed in the middle of the night and burned herself badly on a wall heater. The pain sobered her up quickly and, acting with typical Irish Traveler cunning, she set the bedspread ablaze and then began to shout for help, claiming that the bedspread had caught fire from the wall heater and burned her.

Bridget displayed her burned arm to the motel manager and told him, "I'm gonna sue you for everything you have!"

"Oh, my goodness," he said. "I don't understand how this could have happened."

"Well, I don't care if you understand it or not!" Bridget yelled. "I'm gonna sue your ass off!"

The distressed motel owner called an ambulance for Bridget and then, while she was on her way to the hospital for treatment, he phoned his insurance company. An insurance adjuster convinced Bridget to allow his company to pay her medical bills, and he offered her an additional $10,000 if she would change her mind about suing the motel. She accepted the money.

Soon afterward, Bridget joined Alcoholics Anonymous and gave up drinking. Then she added her name to the welfare roles in Cleveland, Baltimore and Alexandria, Virginia, and was able to draw nearly $3,000 a month in welfare checks for several years. Bridget also received a Social Security disability check every month due to her physical handicap, and she also was getting another check to help support a deaf mute son. In Irish Traveler fashion, her husband sealed roofs and paved driveways. Two of their sons became quite well known among Midwestern law enforcement agencies for their home repair scams.

Bridget's sister, Peggy Marie, married her first cousin, Tom Riley, and gave birth to three mentally retarded children.

Beginning when he was eight years old, Jimmy Burke sometimes went with his father in the pickup truck and watched while Edward sealed people's roofs and driveways. When he was twelve, his father allowed him to help spread the worthless sealant material and taught him how to mix ingredients so the completed job would look good for at least a couple of days, until they could leave town.

"There are places all over the country to buy the asphalt sealing stuff," Jimmy explained several years later, "but the Travelers like to use some stuff that looks like driveway sealer but isn't. It's really cheap; it costs only five cents a gallon. We'll buy fifty gallons of it, dump it in a 200-gallon tank and mix it with 150 gallons of water. It looks pretty good for a while, but after a couple months of rains, it'll wash right off the driveway.

"Now, the stuff that the Travelers put on roofs don't do nothin' except just color it. We'll go to the store and buy a five-gallon bucket of the cheapest kind of driveway sealer we can find. We'll dump it in a tank and then pour in twenty-five gallons of water with it and add the contents of a fifty-five-gallon drum of aluminum paste. The paste ain't nothin' but a color. It's really thick, but when we mix it with the sealer, all it does is turn that stuff silver. The mixture is as thin as water, but when it's put on a roof, it dries instantly and looks great. All it does, though, is color the roof. The people get the impression that it's goin' to stop all their leaks, but it don't. It won't seal nothin'."

In 1974, when Jimmy was fourteen years old, he was helping his dad run driveway sealing scams in Asbury Park, New Jersey. By then, he'd learned to drive the family's truck, and he carried a fake driver's license made out to his sixteen-year-old cousin. Not much sealing work was being done, though, because Edward and Wanda were too busy selling one travel trailer after another from in front of the motel where they were living. Aware that the family wasn't earning as much money as possible with the truck sitting idle most of the time, Edward told Wanda, "Jimmy ought to be out workin' the truck by himself. He's old enough, now." For Jimmy, that moment was his personal coming-of-age experience.

Excited, Jimmy took the keys to the truck from his father and, pretending a casualness he did not feel, he asked his 12-year-old brother, "Hey, Paul. Ya wanna come along?" Paul did, so together the two boys climbed into the pickup truck and began what they were sure was going to be more of an adventure than it was a work detail. Jimmy Burke didn't realize it at the time, but his life would never be the same. He gave up his childhood the second he took the keys from his father's hand.

Jimmy recalled: "I worked the truck either alone or with my brother for about six months until we went back to Florida for the winter. I was doin' better than any of the other families in that part of the country. I was makin' $700 or $800 profit every day. And remember, I was only fourteen!"

What could a fourteen-year-old boy do with so much money? "I gave it to Mom and Dad, and they'd hand me about twenty dollars every day."

Even so, that's quite good allowance for a 14-year-old kid.

"Yeah. But not if you figure the amount of money I was bringin' in. Sometimes Dad would call me aside when Mom wasn't around, and he'd slip me another twenty or something."

What did he do with his allowance?

"Nothin'! Absolutely nothin'. I couldn't go nowhere. We had a lot of disagreements about that. The situation was, they'd hand me the keys to the truck and say, 'Here, go to work.' I was man enough to go out and work the truck all day long, but yet when I wanted to use the truck at night to go somewhere like to a movie, I couldn't. I was only fourteen years old again! Occasionally, on a Sunday afternoon, I'd get the truck and go somewhere with my sisters. I had to take them about every place I went. We'd go to an amusement park, or we'd tell Mom and Dad we were goin' to one, but we'd disconnect the odometer and drive down to Pennsylvania where a bunch of other Travelers were camped. We'd stay there all day and then head back at night."

Before returning to Florida to spend the winter, the Burkes wanted to stop a couple of weeks in Akron, Ohio. They'd always been able to sell several travel trailers in that area while staying at the Akron Turnpike Motel. That time, within hours after moving into rooms at the motel and putting "For Sale" signs on the new Kentucky Traveler trailer that they'd parked out front, the Burkes took a $500 deposit from a Cleveland man who said he'd return in a couple of days to pick up the coach. Edward ordered another Kentucky Traveler delivered from the factory in Elkhart, Indiana, but he left the "For Sale" signs on the unit he had just sold in case another buyer wanted one like it.

Wanda was busy cleaning the trailer and making sure her family's personal possessions were out of it when a dark Chevrolet sedan drove into the motel parking lot. A young, tall man got out of the car and walked over to the trailer. He looked it over carefully and then asked Wanda, "May I look inside?"

"Sure," she said, flashing him a warm Irish Traveler smile. She took him through the coach and pointed out its special features to him -- its roof air conditioner, its double-drain stainless steel sink, its gas/electric refrigerator, its rear twin beds, its full bathroom.

"This trailer looks new," he told her.

"It is," she said. "My husband owned an RV dealership, but because of the oil embargo, he had to close down. We still have a few trailers left, though, and we're sellin' them at our cost just to keep our heads above water. This one is already sold, but another one will be here tomorrow. As you can see, it's an $8,000 or $9,000 trailer, but we're lettin' it go for only $6,000. That's a little bit less than we paid for it."

The customer said, "Well, it's definitely what I want, but I don't know a lot about trailers, so before I buy it, I want to bring a friend back to look at it."

"That's okay," Wanda said agreeably, "but I'd better warn you. We've had a lot of people lookin' at this trailer, and we can't hold the other one that's coming in tomorrow unless we get a deposit."

The man expressed disappointment.

"I'll tell you what," Wanda said. "Give me a small deposit -- say, fifty dollars -- and I won't sell the other trailer to anyone else until you tell me definitely whether you want it or not. If you decide you don't want it after your friend looks at it, I'll return your fifty dollars."

Wanda, experienced trailer salesperson that she was, knew if the man left fifty dollars behind, he was much more likely to return, if for no other reason than to get his money back.

"That sounds like a good deal to me," the man said. He gave her the money and, after another quick walk around the outside of the trailer, he left. He returned within an hour, accompanied by another man. Wanda guided both of them through the coach and went over her sales explanation again. The customer suddenly said he'd changed his mind about buying the trailer and asked for his fifty dollars back."

When the two men left again, Wanda went inside the motel and told her husband, "Ed, something's not right about those guys."

Edward responded, "If you feel that way about them, let's follow them and see where they go." The two Travelers got into Wanda's car and tailed the dark Chevrolet until it drove into the parking lot of an Ohio Highway Patrol station. Quickly, the Burkes returned to the motel, and Ed told the children: "Everybody get your stuff together now! We're leavin'."

The Burke youngsters were accustomed to emergency exits from tight situations, so they were packed and the trailer was hitched behind Ed's truck within minutes. As the family left the motel, they saw two state highway patrol cars coming up the road rapidly behind them. Edward looked in his rearview mirror and recognized their *customer* sitting in the front seat of the lead cruiser. He kept on driving, slowly, and began rehearsing in his mind what he would say to the policemen if they stopped him. The patrol cars followed the family onto the Ohio Turnpike and, although Edward and Wanda both drove well below the speed limit, the troopers refused to pass them. The procession of vehicles proceeded east for about 100 miles until the Burkes crossed the Pennsylvania line, and then the troopers slowed to a stop.

Inside the car Wanda was driving, the youngest Burke children began to cheer and shout. Excited now, they even waved goodbye to the police officers. The young man sitting on the passenger's side of the lead cruiser smiled and returned their wave. His name was Wayne Johnson, and he was an investigator with the Ohio Bureau of Motor Vehicles. His first confrontation with the Burke branch of the Irish Travelers hadn't exactly been a rewarding one, but he was glad that at least the family of *gypsies,* as he called them, was out of Ohio. It was not the last time Johnson and members of the Burke family confronted each other, however. During the next few years, Johnson would gain a nation-wide reputation as Ohio's "Gypsy Hunter," and he would personally become a bigger thorn in the side of the Irish Travelers than any other law enforcement agent in America.

Safe in Pennsylvania, Edward Burke realized he had a problem. He knew that it was never easy for police officers to prove fraud against him in connection with his various swindles, but if he didn't return to Ohio, there was a possibility an arrest warrant would be issued for him because he had left the state with a travel trailer that an Ohio resident had already contracted to purchase. He wasn't ordinarily worried about arrest warrants, but he liked doing business in Ohio, and if he planned to return there each year, he had to figure out a way to deliver the trailer to the man who'd agreed to buy it. Wanda had sold the trailer for a good profit, and Ed wanted that money in his pocket! He telephoned the buyer and told him that the Burkes had just been informed about a death in the family, so they had to leave the state suddenly.

"But don't worry," he added. "We'll deliver your trailer to your house tomorrow."

The next day, following secondary highways and country roads, Ed and Jimmy sneaked into Ohio towing the trailer and delivered it to the Cleveland man. They collected their money, returned to Pennsylvania and picked up the other family members. Then they held a meeting and decided to stay out of the state of Ohio for the rest of the year.

# 3

# The Three-Million Dollar Scam

Most law enforcement officers do not realize it, but there are several thousand Irish Traveler con artists operating various scams throughout North America today. They, along with an equal number of lower-profile English Travelers and between 2,000 and 4,000 Scottish Travelers -- the infamous *Terrible Williamson* clan -- earn more than one billion dollars each year with a never-ending variety of swindles and confidence games. During the more than 100 years that the clans have traveled around the U.S and Canada, a few individuals have pocketed remarkably significant financial rewards. But no Traveler score that anyone can remember even came close to matching the potential of the scam that Jimmy Burke planned against Walt Disney World in 1992.

From the outset, Burke had his sights set on an exceedingly big score. His goal was to scam Disney for at least $3 million!

He had good reason to believe he could succeed:

•The prevailing public mood was that tourists visiting Florida were not being protected adequately from violence.

•He was convinced he could mastermind a violent event that

would illustrate a claim that Walt Disney World's hotels were lax in their room security.

•The CBS *"48 Hours"* broadcast had already underscored a general inadequacy of security at America's hotels.

•His scheme would create doubt over whether or not a hotel employee had accepted money in return for allowing an intruder into a room.

•A scam that would not involve forcible entry would lend additional validity to the claim that Disney's room security system had failed.

To make the scam especially effective, Burke had two additional aces up his sleeve. One was that both Wanda Mary and Jessee were intelligent, experienced con artists who could lie convincingly and were able to cry and sob better than most soap opera actresses. The other was that tiny, innocent-looking Wanda Mary was a perfect victim. Who except the world's cruelest person could fail to be touched by the trauma experienced by that young, strawberry blonde mother following a brutal attack in which she was raped, beaten and robbed and the life of her baby was repeatedly threatened?

Ironically, as the scam progressed, other factors came together which strengthened Burke's case against Disney even more: The Disney complex's emergency 911 system was publicly exposed as being inadequate. Police officers lost any chance they might have had in catching the intruder because they were not notified quickly that a crime had even been committed. A serious question was raised, and apparently never adequately answered, about the hotel's system of changing card key codes. The investigation might have been hampered because Disney employees -- not experienced police officers -- initially interviewed the alleged victim. Hotel employees failed to notify police -- or even their security force -- that a man was attempting to gain entry to a room without showing identification or describing the belongings that he claimed were in the room. An anonymous telephone caller reported that the rapist was a hotel employee. And finally, there was some concern whether Disney employees had tainted the evidence in the room by entering it without the presence of police officers; questions about an opened soft drink can that was still cold to the touch when deputies arrived were never satisfactorily resolved.

To claim that Jimmy Burke was a master criminal would be vastly overstating his abilities. But in fact, he was an intelligent, highly accomplished scam artist who had practiced outsmarting and eluding police for more than twenty years. And his accomplices were family members who had received the same kind of training he had since they were small children.

Jimmy believed in order to win a big settlement from Disney, he needed to convince hotel employees to let him into Wanda Mary's room without providing them with clear evidence he was a guest there. His first attempts at that, by asking housekeeping personnel to unlock the room Saturday afternoon for cleaning, failed. His fallback effort was to gain admission to the room while dressed up in a Dracula costume. He regarded the costume as important from two aspects: first, it would hide his appearance and make future identification by witnesses difficult; second, it would help ensure that hotel employees would remember him, especially if he were successful in convincing them to let him into the room.

That plan also failed because hotel workers insisted that he describe a personal item in the room, such as his luggage or his wallet. Doing that would simply underscore the effectiveness of Disney's security system, not illustrate that it was lax. Earlier in the evening, he could have gained access to the room if he had been able to tell a clerk the name, address and telephone number listed on the reservation slip, but he could not remember Jessee's home address and phone number in Maine. Although he did have that information later in the evening, he was not asked for it and did not feel he could volunteer it without being asked.

At no time until just minutes before the fake rape took place did Jimmy consider asking Wanda Mary to let him into the room. He was so confident in his own abilities as a con artist that he was certain he could convince an employee to unlock the door for him.

In spite of Jimmy's eleventh-hour plan modification, the scam scenario proceeded almost without a hitch. Investigators were a little nervous about accepting Wanda Mary's insistence that she was attacked by a black intruder, especially since anecdotal evidence pointed toward the probable involvement of a tall white man dressed in a Dracula costume. Also, they could not understand why, if Wanda Mary had struggled with her assailant as she claimed, the duct tape that was wound around her head was not twisted. The unexplained presence of a relatively cold soft drink can bothered a couple of the deputies, but there was a general belief the can had been carried into the room and left there by a Walt Disney World Security employee who was then too embarrassed to admit that he had taken a soft drink into a crime scene with him.

Based on statements by Wanda Mary and hotel employees, Detective Tom Harrison had a few clues that he felt deserved to be investigated. One was Wanda Mary's comment that her assailant indicated a maid had let him into the room for $50. Another was the suspicious behavior of a tall man dressed in a Dracula costume. Harrison was convinced the man was, in some way, connected to the crime, but investigations of that aspect led nowhere. At least two hotel employees wore Dracula costumes that night, but they were regarded as suspects only briefly because they did not match descriptions of the tall man.

WDW Security offered only one possible suspect -- a former employee who had been fired for entering women's rooms and soliciting them for sex. When Harrison checked that man's whereabouts on the night of the crime, he was immediately eliminated as a suspect.

Two anonymous calls about the crime seemed to offer better possibilities. The first caller had claimed the assailant was a hotel employee and that another employee knew the assailant's identity. Extensive questioning of numerous hotel employees turned up nothing to support the caller's claims, but Harrison continued to regard that tip as potentially important information.

Harrison considered the second call as significantly more credible because the caller provided two details which were unknown to anyone except investigating officers -- that the victim's name was Wanda and that she was on her way back to Maine. That caller had insisted the incident at Disney World was a scam. Harrison, who was already uncomfortable about a few minor aspects of the incident, could have been convinced that a scam had been executed, but all available evidence indicated a crime had, indeed, been committed.

Investigators from the Orange County sheriff's department conducted a deep, intensive search for clues and witnesses. Because members of the Burke family had criminal records, officers might have had an inkling that a scam was underway if they had known any of the Burkes were involved, but the fact that the two principle players were named Normile and O'Roarke prevented anyone from considering the women as con artists.

As Jimmy expected, Wanda Mary proved to be an excellent victim. And the fact that she was brutally beaten added credibility to her statements. Several months later, Orange County Detective John McMahan, who handles his department's criminal investigations involving *Gypsies* and Travelers, reported, "The beating was never a part of the plan. Wanda Mary had never agreed to that. But after James tied her to the bed, he decided it wouldn't look right unless she were messed up a little. So he messed her up pretty good. She had a split lip, and the mouse under her eye covered about half her face. To all outward appearances, it looked very real. And we told Disney,

'When this goes to trial and we get called to the stand to testify, we're going to have to say, "Yes, she showed signs of having been severely beaten. Yes, she showed signs of having had sex during that night; there was sperm present, and the medical examination showed that she had, indeed, had a sexual encounter that night."' Absent any further proof to the contrary, it was a damning thing. And in civil court, all you have to prove is a reasonable expectation of doubt, not proof to the exclusion of any doubt. And our people were convinced that at a trial, the jury would certainly buy into it."

If anything was a master stroke of genius on Burke's part, it was his assertion that Wanda Mary must provide police forensics examiners with proof she was raped. The beating he administered to her was part of that proof, but he also convinced Wanda Mary that she should engage in sex with someone before making her 911 telephone call. Wanda considered several possible semen donors before settling on a young man who was a friend of her uncle's, but whom she knew on only a casual basis.

Less than two hours prior to her Halloween night arrival at the Disney World hotel, she went to the young man's home and seduced him. Later, some of the semen he unsuspectingly provided for the scam was carefully deposited on a bedsheet in Wanda Mary's room.

"The next day," said the young man several months later, "I got the shock of my life. My brother told me that a 20-year-old girl was raped at Disney, and he told me it probably was Wanda Mary. I said, 'No, it can't be.' And he told me to watch the news. So at five o'clock, sure enough, it was on the news." Although Wanda Mary's name was not mentioned -- Florida law prohibits public exposure of rape victims' names -- news report descriptions of the woman attacked at Disney World fit her quite well. At no time did the young man suspect his semen had been used to provide evidence of the rape.

Presence of semen on the bedsheet, and in Wanda's vaginal area, seemed to verify that a rape took place. The semen could have exposed the crime as a scam, however, because there was a single flaw in Jimmy Burke's plan. The panties that Wanda Mary wore following her seduction of the young man were discarded on the floor of the hotel room instead of being removed from the scene by Jimmy. They were the panties Wanda Mary said were ripped from her body by the intruder; clearly, since they were worn prior to the rape, they should have not contained any evidence of semen, but a laboratory examination of them would have determined just that. The panties were retrieved by investigators, along with another pair of underwear, and retained as evidence. Ordered to examine all the evidence, the Florida Department of Law Enforcement was put under immediate pressure to develop leads in the case. Evidence sent to FDLE's crime lab ranged from samples of Wanda Mary's pubic hair and saline swabs from her inner thighs to virtually all the hotel room bedclothes and tubes of Wanda's blood.

A memo that accompanied the evidence instructed the forensics lab to conduct a "standard sexual assault examination" of the items and, "in addition, please sweep the sheets, pillowcases and mattress cover for hairs. Please attempt to determine if hair is human or animal, area of origin and race of suspect. This is a high-profile case, and any information obtained is required for investigative leads. Sexual battery occurred at the Walt Disney World Caribbean Beach Resort."

So convinced were law enforcement authorities that a violent rape had taken place, the panties were not examined closely by anyone, and they were never sent to the crime lab to be tested for traces of semen!

Jessee O'Roarke did not return to the hotel room as quickly as planned because, she admitted many months later, she was beginning to have second thoughts about the scam, and she hoped if she delayed her return, her sister and brother would cancel the operation. The original plan called for Jessee to discover that her sister had been tied, beaten and raped and call the police. In fact, Wanda Mary became impatient when Jessee failed to return as soon as expected, so she broke loose from her bonds and telephoned 911 herself.

Even without Jessee's initial involvement, Jimmy's scheme worked so well that poor little Wanda Mary was given a solid foundation of support from individual Orange County police officers. Detective Tom Harrison and the other deputies involved in the case could not have been more sympathetic or solicitous of the young woman's well-being. Sheriff's office victim's advocate Maria Curtis spent several hours comforting Wanda Mary on Sunday and Monday following the crime, and she conveyed to the public an image of Wanda Mary as a brave young woman trying her best to cope with the most traumatic experience of her life. Questioned by the *Orlando Sentinel*, Curtis said, "She's hanging in there because she's got a very supportive sister."

Jessee O'Roarke was, indeed, supportive by that time. Almost immediately after arriving at her uncle's home following the crime, she took on responsibility for selecting an attorney that could sue Walt Disney World for millions of dollars! Then four days later, she packed Wanda Mary and the baby into her pickup truck and drove home to Maine so that they would not be under the daily scrutiny of police investigators. Her brother Jimmy had left Florida on Halloween night after he had completed his part in the scam.

As the days evolved into weeks, it became clear to Orange County authorities that investigation of the Disney rape case had reached a dead end. Public anger about the rape and its implications, however, were focused not on the police department, but on the security system at Walt Disney World -- America's highest-profile tourist attraction.

With no new information being provided by law enforcement, newspaper reporters began their own investigations, and they discovered that Disney's 911 system was the oldest emergency response system in the state; it had been installed in the mid-1970s. In a copyrighted article, the *Orlando Sentinel* reported, "Disney's property in Orange and Osceola Counties is the only place in Florida not covered by state laws governing the operation of 911 telephone systems." All 911 calls were handled by the Disney-managed Reedy Creek Improvement District Fire Services.

At the time Wanda Mary made her call for help, Reedy Creek's policy was for dispatchers to decide whether or not to involve Orange County police and, if so, to dial the sheriff's office and ask for assistance. Following the public exposure of that policy, Walt Disney World Security modified the system so that 911 calls could be transferred to the sheriff's office with the push of a button. For Jimmy Burke and the attorney representing his sister, Disney's decision to change the 911 system amounted to a public admission that Wanda Mary's emergency call had been handled improperly.

Months passed, and the rape case nearly faded from the public consciousness. But on April 19, 1993, the *Orlando Sentinel* reported, in response to queries from its readers, that no suspects or leads had yet been found by investigators.

Eight days later, Orlando attorney Ernest H. Eubanks Jr., representing Wanda Mary Normile, wrote a letter to Walt Disney World Company demanding payment of $3,000,000 for damages suffered by his client at the Caribbean Beach Resort.

The company apparently did not respond to that demand in any way until June 18, when attorney Eubanks attended a conference in the offices of Disney's law firm, Rumberger, Kirk & Caldwell. Several months later, Disney Assistant Secretary Carol S. Pacula, who was present at the meeting, stated in an affidavit, "At that conference, Walt Disney World Company offered to pay Wanda M. Normile the sum of $200,000 in full settlement of her claim."

Eubanks telephoned Wanda Mary and Jessee in Maine and told them about the settlement offer. "He said he thought it was an unreasonable amount," Jessee said later, "and that it wasn't right, considering what had happened and the way things were. He suggested that Wanda Mary turn it down." The sisters discussed the offer, and they agreed with the attorney. They did not inform Jimmy, whose whereabouts were unknown to them at that moment, partly because they believed he might want to accept the settlement.

They told Eubanks to reject Disney's offer.

Less than a week later, on June 23, Eubanks filed a civil complaint in Orange County against the Walt Disney Company on behalf of a client known only by the initials W.M.N. The suit did not assign a dollar amount to damages, but legal experts at the time estimated it was possible that judgments against Disney could total ten or twenty million dollars.

The complaint cited the entertainment company's negligence in protecting Wanda Mary while she was a guest at the Caribbean Beach hotel. It said Disney's negligence included an inadequate 911 emergency phone system, ineffective security patrols and accounting of room keys, poor screening of employees, and insufficient maintenance of guest room door locks. The suit claimed an adequate 911 system, properly utilized, would have "deterred, prevented or minimized the risk of sexual assault...or other criminal acts to its patrons, guests or invitees," and it stated Disney World did not provide that type of 911 system.

When Walt Disney World Company was served with the complaint on June 24, it also received an offer from Eubanks to drop the suit for $1,200,000. That figure later was adjusted upward to $1,400,000 with Disney's consent.

# 4
# On His Own

Orlando, Florida, has always been the closest the Burke family has ever had to a home town. Born there, buried there and returning there every winter to live, the Burkes are like thousands of other Irish and Scottish Travelers: They swarm into Orlando each fall like swallows returning to Capistrano. There, they work their scams on a relatively small scale, preferring to keep a rather low profile and not attract much attention from vigilant police officers who await their arrival with dread.

For the Travelers, winter is a time of family reunions, parties, anniversaries, funerals and weddings. It's the time pretty young Irish princesses become acquainted with handsome male cousins who will be their husbands a year or two later. To Traveler women, the winter reunions offer an excellent opportunity to show off the diamonds, gold jewelry, new chinaware and Royal Daulton dolls that their successful husbands have allowed them to buy. To Traveler men, there's drinking to be done at favorite Orange and Pinellas County watering holes and plans to be made for next spring's travels and schemes. During the social events, decisions will be made about which families will travel together when the clans leave Florida in March or

April. For example, Johnny Donahue's parents would not consider letting him marry Suzie Rafferty next winter unless the two families could spend some time on the road together first. The Donahues want to see for themselves if Suzie is as good a shoplifter as her mother claims, and the Raffertys insist upon watching Johnny as he negotiates for driveway sealing jobs in Ohio.

And fights. Of course, there'll be fights. One or two of them probably will develop into full-fledged brawls. Some familiar faces will be rearranged, and some brains scrambled, but there'll be no real damage, and likely no one will get killed. But out of those confrontations will come a clear picture of which Traveler families shouldn't be messed with.

The whole Burke family was in Orlando the winter of 1974 -- the same year that Jimmy Burke learned to seal roofs and driveways on his own. Jimmy's parents, Edward and Wanda, had rented rooms at the Realms Apartments on Orange Blossom Trail because they did not want to spend the entire winter in the cramped quarters of a travel trailer with their six youngest children.

Still just fourteen years old, Jimmy spent the first part of the winter hitting central Florida neighborhoods with driveway sealer and roof sealer scams, operating a 1972 Ford pickup truck that Edward had bought for him and equipped with appropriate tanks and hoses. He was still using a driver's license in his cousin's name. "Them and me had disagreements over this and that, and every time they'd get mad at me, they'd take the keys to the truck and the driver's license away from me. About three or four weeks before Christmas, we really got into it one night over something, and Dad took the license. So when nobody was watchin', I put all my stuff behind the seat of the truck, and that night, I snuck out and took off in the truck."

Jimmy drove to Augusta, Georgia, and checked in at the Augusta Hotel downtown. The next day, he sold the truck for $2,000 at a used car lot in South Carolina. "Now, the truck was in my dad's name, and I didn't have no driver's license or no I.D. whatsoever, but I signed my dad's name to the title, and the guy gave me a check without askin' me for any I.D. I took the check over to the bank, and they wanted I.D. before they'd cash a check that large. I had them call the guy at the dealership, and he told them to go ahead and cash it for me."

When he returned to the hotel, he called the apartment where his parents were living and talked with his sister Peggy. "I told her where I was and what I had done. It turned out Mom was listening on an extension phone." Early the next morning, he heard a knock on the door.

"Who is it?"

"It's the police! Open up!"

Panicked, he tried to find a way out of the room, but he was on the fifth floor and there was no fire escape. "They banged on the door a few minutes more, so finally I opened it, and my dad came in ravin' and yellin' about the truck. There was a cop with him, and my mom. I gave Dad the money from the truck, but him and Mom said I couldn't come back home. They knew I wouldn't stay."

The policeman told Ed and Wanda, "If you aren't taking him home, I'm gonna have to take him out to the RYDC (Augusta's Regional Youth Detention Center)."

Wanda said, "No, I don't want him to go to a juvenile home or jail."

Ed slipped the policeman a one-hundred-dollar bill, and the officer left. They gave Jimmy fifty dollars and left too. "I started throwin' my clothes in my suitcase, and there was a knock at the door. I opened it and there was the cop again. He said, 'Get your stuff. I'm taking you over to RYDC.'

"I said, 'Wait a minute. My dad just gave you something to take care of that.'"

"He said, 'I don't know what you're talking about,' and he took me down and put me in a police car and drove me over to the city jail. He phoned Mrs. Dee Hamilton, who was head of juvenile over there. Me and my sister both had been out at RYDC the year before, and Mrs. Hamilton didn't particularly care for either one of us.

"The policeman gave the telephone to me, and she said, 'James, what are you doing back here again? You don't live here. Why do you always want to come back to Augusta and get into trouble?'

"I said, 'Well, I'm tryin' to go home, but they won't let me.'

"She said, 'They told me your mom and dad just left.'

"I said, 'Yeah, they did. But they want me to take a bus home so I can have time to think about things, and they gave me fifty dollars to buy a bus ticket.'

"She said, 'Let me speak to the officer.' I gave him the phone, and she told him to put me on a bus home. So he took me over to the bus station, bought me a bus ticket and waited until the bus left the parking lot. The bus stopped in Jacksonville, so I got off there, cashed in my bus ticket and bought another ticket to Columbia, South Carolina."

Aboard that bus, he met an elderly woman about eighty years old and told her his parents had died when he was younger and he had been living with an evil aunt and uncle who beat him. "I said I didn't have no money or no place to go. She was a retired school teacher who had a home in Camden, South Carolina. Her husband owned a car lot there, and her son ran some sort of carpet mill. She asked me if I would stay with her, and she said she would get me a job either at the car lot or the mill. Well, I had nothin' better to do, so I went with her."

The woman lived in a beautiful home, and she was quite nice to Jimmy. He stayed with her about two months and worked at the carpet mill. "She gave me my own room and fixed meals for me. I didn't tell them anything about my life or who I really was. A lot of people tend to get scared when they find out something like that. I didn't look at it that I was takin' advantage of them, though. I appreciated what they were doin' for me, and I never forgot that they helped me a lot when I really needed it. After I got on my feet, I stopped back there a few times and offered to do their pavin' or anything else I could do to help them. About two years after I left, her husband died, and I lost touch with her when I got in trouble in Georgia."

After two months in one place, Jimmy could not control his urge to travel. "I got the itch to move on. I wanted a lot of things which I couldn't have there. I could have stayed there and earned a living and just got by. But I wanted a new car, a new truck, a new trailer. I told her I had decided to go to Ohio to find a relative and see if I could live there." He had saved nearly $400 which he intended to spend on a car. Instead, her husband offered him a 1969 Pontiac Catalina for only fifty dollars.

Jimmy traveled leisurely around the mid-South for several weeks before checking into a motel at Alexandria, Virginia. "I met a girl in Washington, D.C., and we started goin' around to places in Alexandria and Washington. There must be fifty -- if not more -- Zayres department stores around there, as well as a lot of other stores, and we hit 'em all!" The pair compiled several different I.D.'s and shoplifted successfully all summer and fall, but their earnings increased dramatically as Christmas 1975 approached.

"From about a week before Christmas until a week after, we went back to the stores over and over again, and we saved $3,000. We split up the money, and she went back to Washington. I got the car tuned up and bought new tires and had it painted a tan color. It looked really good, and the guy at the motel where I lived started in on me to sell it to him. The day I was leavin', he offered me $300 for it. But I wouldn't sell it. Then he offered $350, then $400. My grandfather always said, 'If you have a horse and someone offers to buy it from you, sell it or the horse is gonna die.' But I wouldn't sell that car."

In January 1976, he left Virginia intending on driving to Ohio. "I got about fifteen miles and the darned motor blew up. I called a station to tow it in, and the mechanic said it would cost me $400 to fix it. So I just left it there at the station. I bought another '69 Pontiac -- a station wagon -- from the mechanic, and drove to a motel in Strongsville, Ohio, outside Cleveland. I met another girl at a club one night, and me and her started workin' the Cleveland stores together.

"She told me that it was really easy to get on welfare in Cleveland, so we got a marriage license and then went to the welfare office and told them we'd just moved there and didn't have any money or any place to live. They gave us an emergency rent grant of $200 and $200 in food stamps, and they gave us an emergency grant of $200 in cash. We rented an apartment and bought some food. We had some extra money besides that -- about $1,200 or $1,300 each. A check for $240 started coming in every month, so I stayed there for about two months."

In March, he treated himself to a late sixteenth birthday present and traded the car on a 1973 Ford station wagon. "I had a hitch put on the car, and then in the middle of one night, I stole a trailer, hooked it to the station wagon and we left Ohio. We sold the trailer in Pennsylvania for $2,000.

"One night we decided we wanted some more money -- bigger money -- so we went to Elkhart (Indiana) and bought a new trailer, took it down south and made $4,000 on it. Then we split up, and I bought a new truck and a used trailer that I could stay in."

Later in the spring of 1976, Jimmy went to North Augusta, South Carolina, where the Southern branch of the Irish Travelers had settled in a mobile home court called Murphy Village. "My brother Pat lives there in the wintertime and goes off in the summer. He married a girl from there -- Rose Sherlock. I stayed with him and worked with him for a few months. Then I started workin' for myself, sealin' driveways and roofs."

After accumulating enough money to buy another new trailer, Jimmy and a Murphy Village Traveler named Johnny McNally drove to Elkhart to purchase one. "We stopped in Akron to visit Peggy, who was stayin' in a motel there by herself. My cousin, Bridget Ann and her husband Floyd, who lived in Cleveland, came over to the motel drunk one night while we was gone, and she started jumpin' on Peggy. When we came back with our trailer and found out about it, we checked out of the motel, left my truck and trailer down the street at another motel and we piled into Peggy's car and drove over to their house. We hired a girl they didn't know to go up and knock on their door while we hid in the bushes.

"When Bridget's husband opened the door, the girl asked, 'Pardon me, but is that your truck out there?'

"He said, 'Yeah.'

"She said, 'I just seen somebody out there tryin' to break into it.'

"So he came out on the porch, and we all jumped on him. He broke loose and ran inside. He tried to close the door and broke out the glass window. He ran up the stairs and into a bedroom and locked the door. We could hear Bridget Ann inside yellin' and screamin'. We ripped the phone wires out so they couldn't call the cops. We beat on the bedroom door over and over, but they wouldn't open it. We couldn't get at them, so we tore the house up downstairs and busted all their Daulton dolls and everything and then left. Them Daulton dolls are expensive, and The People try to show off with them -- to show, I guess, that they've got money. All the Travelers have them. The cheapest ones are about $75, and they go up over $1,000."

The financial loss to Bridget Ann and Floyd was doubtlessly sweet revenge, but even so, Jimmy would have good reason later to regret he participated in the rampage.

Shortly after that, Jimmy joined his older sister Wanda -- who later would change her name to Jessee -- and worked most of the summer on the road with her husband, Billy O'Roarke. At Lancaster, Pennsylvania, Jimmy hit local department stores quite hard with his shoplifting. "I had a new truck and a little used trailer that I had bought in Elkhart for about $700. Wanda and Billy had sold the Marauder trailer they were livin' in, but they had to wait a week before they could get their money and buy another trailer, so I decided to take off for the weekend and drive to Alexandria, Virginia, to work the stores. Along the way, I stopped in York, Pennsylvania, where I saw a K-Mart. I parked my truck next to the curb at the garden shop, went inside and shoplifted two dresses that cost $24 each and stuffed them in a paper sack I was carryin'. When I came back outside, stacked just ahead of my truck were several bags of fertilizer. I have a habit that, whenever I leave a store and get into my truck, I lock the driver's side door immediately just in case I've been spotted by a security guard and he's followed me outside. It's a good thing I did it that time, because just as I was takin' the dresses out of the sack, two guys came runnin' out of the garden shop. They grabbed the door handle and started bangin' on the window, tellin' me to get out. I started the truck, put it into first gear, and one of the security guys ran over in front of my truck and stood there. I tried to back up, and the other guy was behind me. I rolled down my window a little and shouted, 'You better get out of my way or I'm gonna run over you.' He didn't believe me, so I let the truck roll forward a few inches to scare him, and he jumped up on the sidewalk. When he did that, I took off and knocked down the big stack of fertilizer. I didn't stop until I got into Maryland.

"I went on to Virginia and stayed there a week and then went back the same way -- but I didn't stop at K-Mart that time! I got back to Lancaster, but I had already worked the stores over and over. Lancaster had three K-marts, a Sears, a Penney's and a couple of other stores, but I had been through all those stores so many times that I didn't want to work them again. I had saved $700 or $800 on my trip to Virginia. I put it with some other money that I had saved because I wanted to buy a new trailer when I sold my used one.

"Now, my brother-in-law Billy wouldn't outright go into a store and steal anything, and he wouldn't allow Wanda to do it. But Wanda was used to doin' that when she lived at home, so she told me, 'Let's tell Billy we're going to a movie, and we can go work some stores. If you'll get the stuff, I'll take it back in for you.'

"Sometime earlier, I had bought a small color TV set from a K-Mart in Cleveland, but it didn't work right. I took it back to a K-mart in Lancaster and was gonna exchange it for a new one, but they gave me a cash refund of more than $300 even though I didn't have a box for it or a sales slip. So that started Wanda thinkin', and she told me, 'I've got a TV set I bought at a flea market last year for $25, and it quit workin'. If they carry that brand at K-mart, maybe they'll take it back.' So she brought that TV set with us. The store didn't have a set identical to it, but they had one that looked a lot like it in the same brand. So I took the price sticker off the back of the one in the store, and Wanda put the sticker on the back of her set, and we took it in the store. They paid her $150 refund.

"Then we went to another K-mart and picked up two dresses that cost $30 each, and Wanda took them back in for the refund. She was in there for a long time, so I was startin' to get worried. Finally I seen her walkin' out the front with the money in her hand, so I thought everything was all right. But before she could get out the door, two guys came runnin' out and grabbed her by the arm. One of them saw the truck and came runnin' over to it. I locked my door. He knocked on the window. I started the truck, but I couldn't back up because there was a car behind me. There was room in front for me to pull out, but he did like the other guy -- he walked to the front of the car, thrust out his badge and yelled, 'Get out!' Again, I rolled down my window a little and said, 'You better move out of my way or or I'm gonna run over you.' He wouldn't move, so like before, I let the truck roll forward a little and he jumped up on the sidewalk. I took off.

"I was gonna park my truck somewhere and take a cab back to the campground and tell Billy so he could get Wanda out. I got about two miles down the highway, and a Pennsylvania highway patrol pulled me over. I was using the name Michael Burke at the time --

my deceased brother's name. I was sixteen but I had I.D. that said I was twenty-one.

"The cops pulled me out of the truck and asked me, 'Did you just leave K-Mart?'

"I said, 'No.' But here came another car with the security guard in it, and he said, 'Yeah, that's him.'

"I figured out later that if I had sat in the parking lot at K-mart, they couldn't have proven I stole the stuff because they didn't catch me stealin' it. All they could have done was hauled me downtown and harassed me or questioned me. They charged my sister with theft by deception because the other K-mart found out the TV she had returned was not their TV and that she had glued one of their stickers on the back of it. But they couldn't pin me with nothin'. When they came out to me at the parking lot, they just wanted to talk to me, but I thought they had seen me steal the dresses.

"When it all got done, the only thing they could charge me with was reckless endangerment -- due to threatenin' to run over the security guard. I had a $10,000 bond, and Wanda's bond was $3,000. In Pennsylvania, they didn't have bondsmen, so the state would go your bond, and if you put up ten per cent, you automatically got out. Wanda put up $300 and was out. I had my money in the trailer, but for some reason I misplaced my keys, so Billy had to break into my trailer so he could get my money out and put up $1,000 bond for me.

"That night, I told Wanda, 'I'm blowin' this town. They don't have my real name, and I'm not goin' back to court for that charge.'

"She said, 'Well, if you leave, they'll try to put everything on me, and I'll go to prison.'

"I said, 'No, it'll actually look better for you because you stayed while I blew. Just don't give 'em my real name.' I left that night. I got just a little distance down the road, and one tire blew on the trailer. So I put it in storage in a campground, and then I picked up another trailer -- just hooked it on and drove away with it -- and towed it to New Jersey, where I put it in storage. I drove down to Alabama and got papers on the trailer, came back to New Jersey and sold the trailer in Atlantic City for $6,000 and another trailer on trade. I pulled that trailer to Canton, Ohio, and sold it for $3,500 and then went to Elkhart and bought a brand new Marauder. I changed my I.D. to Daniel Burke and traded my truck on a newer one. So I had a new name, a new truck, a new trailer and different tags on everything."

For several months, Jimmy swindled his way around the Midwest selling travel trailers and working his truck with sealing and paving scams, always using the Daniel Burke I.D.. Even today, the State of Ohio has several outstanding arrest warrants for a tall Irish Traveler con artist named Daniel Burke. He acquired that I.D. earlier when he towed the travel trailer to New Jersey. He explained, "In New Jersey, you can go into the driver's license office and get a learner's permit. They give you a card to fill out with your name, address and date of birth. You put any name you want on it, any address, any date of birth. And then they'll give you a temporary learner's license, but they won't validate it. They won't ask you for any I.D., but they'll tell you to carry it across town to another office and get it validated and take your driver's license test. All I did was get it and leave with it. I didn't get it validated because when you do that, they ask for I.D. I'd take that to another state, and they'd think it was a regular temporary learner's permit; they didn't know it hadn't been validated. They'd accept that as an I.D. so I could take a test and get a driver's license for that state." As Daniel Burke, he took his test and acquired his new driver's license I.D. in Virginia.

During the fall of 1976, the sixteen-year-old returned to Florida to show his parents he had been successful on his own. "I wanted to see the expressions on their faces when I pulled in with a new truck and trailer after they had left me with fifty dollars." He camped that winter in Tampa at the Happy Traveler, a campground near Busch Gardens that has become a traditional winter refuge for both Irish and Scottish Travelers.

There's no other way to say it: From the time she was a little girl, Jimmy Burke's sister Peggy was a real pistol! She marched to a different drummer than the rest of her family, and even as a young teenager, she did not hesitate to tell anyone who asked that she totally rejected the traditional Irish Traveler lifestyle. Blonde and pretty but always a little chunky, Peggy possessed more than her share of the Burke cunning, but she felt none of the family's rules -- nor society's, for that matter -- applied to her. She could -- and did -- charm the pants off a street-smart vice cop, and she could stand toe-to-toe with the ruling queen of a prison ward and trade blows until one of them was down and could not get up again.

Following Jimmy's lead, she ran away from home the first time when she was thirteen by climbing out a bathroom window at night while the family was camped in Neptune, New Jersey. "I went to Cherry Hill, New Jersey, and met up with some Turks," she reported several years later. Travelers refer to Rom Gypsies as *Turks*. Peggy said, "They told me they knew about an old woman who had a lot of money that we could take away from her. So me and three of the Turk women broke into the old woman's house and tied her up in the bathtub. One of the Turks wrote out a check and made the old woman sign it, then we went to the bank and drawed out all the woman's money."

Instead of leaving town with their loot, Peggy and the Gypsy women returned to the motel room where they were staying and arranged a big party. Meanwhile, the old woman's husband returned home, found his wife tied up in the bathtub and called police. Peggy laughed when she recalled what happened next. "Since the cops knew the people who robbed the old lady were Turks, they went to all the motels in town until they found us. When they knocked on the door and said they were police officers, I crawled under a bed and hid there while they hauled everyone else to jail. Then I sneaked out and hitched a ride to Philadelphia."

Peggy met a Puerto Rican family in Philadelphia and convinced them to let her live with them. About three months later, she learned where her parents were and telephoned them, asking if she could return home. During the next two years, Peggy ran away periodically but always returned to her parents, contrite and begging forgiveness.

During the fall of 1976, while Jimmy was camped in Florida at the Happy Traveler, fifteen-year-old Peggy ran away from home again. Not long after that, Edward and Wanda were notified that she was in juvenile detention in Cleveland, so they flew to Ohio after her. She stayed with them only two or three months and split again. By that time, Jimmy had left Florida and was camped near Augusta, Georgia, not far from where his brother Pat was living at Murphy Village. Unexpectedly, Peggy arrived at the Village one morning and asked if she could stay with Pat and Rose Mary. While there, she got into trouble and was again placed in juvenile detention. Her parents retrieved her and took her back to Florida with them, but they could not control her, and they knew it would not be long before she ran away again. They asked Jimmy for help, even though he was only sixteen himself.

"They said they'd rather she was with me than runnin' around by herself," he recalled. "They didn't know what else to do with her." But Peggy was a true free spirit. She traveled with Jimmy only a short while before leaving in the middle of the night. And during the next eighteen years, free-spirited Peggy would suddenly appear at a family member's campsite, stay a few days or a few weeks and then disappear just as quickly.

In late January 1977, a couple of weeks before his seventeenth birthday, Jimmy discovered a minor bonanza in travel trailer sales at Columbus, Georgia. He sold one trailer and took delivery on another, and he drove to downtown Atlanta with his aunt, Lizzie O'Roarke, to register it. He and Lizzie had rented motel rooms in

Atlanta for the night.

"When we got back to the motel, my uncle came out and said, 'Get the hell out of here. The cops have been here lookin' for you.'

"I said, 'What for?'

"He said, 'I don't know, but you better leave.'

"So I threw everything in my truck. My trailer was parked between two semis, so I backed up between them to hook on, but before I could, here came this plain brown Plymouth and tried to block me in. A guy got out, pulled a gun and told me to get out. I maneuvered between the Plymouth and a semi and got past him. I went through a guardrail and onto Interstate 75, and the cop car followed right behind me. And every time I looked in my mirror there'd be two more police cars following. First there was the plain car, then a county car, then two or three more plain cars, a highway patrol, and another county car. There were about ten of 'em behind me on the expressway. I'm ridin' on the side and on the median with my emergency flashers goin' and my hand on the horn, doin' about a hundred miles an hour. They're all flyin' behind me with their lights goin', and I'm sure everybody else on the highway wondered what was goin' on.

"I hopped off an exit and entered another county. I went down back streets, ran red lights and drove through people's yards. I went down one-way streets the wrong way. I did everything. But they were all still behind me. I couldn't lose 'em. And up ahead, I seen that the cops had blocked off the street I was on. So I went down another street the wrong way and then through a woman's yard so I could get around the cops, and the truck got stuck in the mud.

"I hopped out of the truck and took off on foot, but some Clayton County cops pulled up and jerked out their guns. One of 'em said, 'If you move another damn step, we'll blow your head off.' So I stopped. They grabbed me, threw me down on the ground and put handcuffs on me. They said, 'Wait until we get you to the police station. We're going to beat you so bad your mom won't know you.'

"I said, 'What's goin' on?'

"They asked, 'Is your name Michael Burke?'

"I said, 'No it isn't.'

"They asked, 'What is your name?'

"I said, 'Daniel Anthony Burke.'

'Do you have any I.D?'

"I said, 'Yeah.'

"They said, 'If you're not Michael Burke, what were you runnin' for?'

"I said, 'How in the hell would I know who you were? There I was, hookin' onto my trailer, and a plain brown car pulls up in front of me and a guy gets out and pulls a gun on me without flashin' a badge and tellin' me he's a cop. The car don't say you're a cop. I don't know who you are, and I've got over $3,000 in cash on me. So I think that somebody's tryin' to rob me. What am I gonna do except get the hell out of there?'

"He said, 'Well, if that's true, why didn't you stop when you saw the lights flashing on all those police cars?'

"I said, 'I thought they were chasin' the brown car, not me, and that damn brown car kept right on my tail! I didn't know what was happenin'.

"He said, 'Well, we'll see about that.'"

The officers took Jimmy to jail and charged him with attempting to elude the police, reckless driving, running several red lights, going down four one-way streets the wrong way, speeding and several other traffic violations. As he sat in a jail, Clayton County authorities verified his fingerprints and learned he had used the name "Michael Burke" and that he was wanted in Pennsylvania for skipping a bond.

He hired an Atlanta attorney who advised him to admit that his real name was James Burke and that he was only sixteen years old. He paid several hundred dollars in fines and, upon his attorney's advice, agreed to be extradited to Pennsylvania.

The lawyer told him, "When you get back to Pennsylvania and

they find out you're a juvenile, there won't be anything to it." Two detectives from Lancaster County, Pennsylvania, picked him up and took him by commercial airline to Lancaster, where he was placed in the Lancaster County Prison along with convicted felons and others who were still awaiting trial. "I was scared to death," he recalled later.

He told an officer at the prison, "My real name is James Burke, and I'm only sixteen years old. I'm not supposed to be here."

The officer answered, "Yeah, and I'm only fourteen."

"I'm tellin' the truth."

The officer said, "I can look at you and tell you're older than sixteen, and we've got you right here: Your name is Michael Burke, and you're twenty-one."

"That's not me. That's my brother, and he's dead. I was using his I.D. If you'll call Florida, they can verify it."

He said, "No, we're not going for that."

Jimmy was kept there fifty-three days until he could contact a lawyer. The attorney filed a writ to prove Jimmy's real name and age so he could be released, and a hearing was scheduled. "Mom and Dad came up for the hearing. The district attorney was a woman, and she raised a lot of hell. She said, 'Here he is. He was arrested eight months ago under the name of Michael Joseph Burke, twenty-one years old. He leaves town, skips his bond. We find him six months later through an anonymous phone call in Atlanta, Georgia, and there he has a valid driver's license under the name of Daniel Anthony Burke saying his age is something else. Now he says his real name is James William Burke, and he's only sixteen. What are we supposed to believe? Sure, here's a birth certificate that says James William Burke and shows he's only sixteen, but how do we know that's him? Because he also had a valid driver's license saying he is Daniel and he is twenty-three and another one that said he is Michael and he is twenty-one.'"

Fortunately for Jimmy, his birth certificate had his footprints on it, and when prints were made of his feet and compared with those on the birth certificate, they proved his real identity. When the authorities concluded that Jimmy was sixteen, they dropped all charges. However, they also discovered a warrant had been issued for his arrest in York, Pennsylvania, following the shoplifting episode there, so he was extradited to York County, where he had to prove his age and identity again. In the meantime, his sister Wanda, who had also skipped bond in Lancaster County, was arrested in Ohio and extradited to Lancaster. She was fined and sentenced to thirty days in jail.

Jimmy learned later that his arrests and I.D. difficulties were the result of the time he had trashed his cousin Bridget Ann's home in Cleveland, Ohio. An anonymous call to Georgia police alerting them to his whereabouts had been placed by Bridget. "Mom and Dad had been in Akron just the week before, and Mom told her where I was."

After picking up his truck and travel trailer in Georgia, Jimmy drove to Ohio and put the coach up for sale in a motel parking lot near Cleveland. There, he had his first personal encounter with the Department of Motor Vehicle's Gypsy Hunter, Wayne Johnson -- the same man who had followed his family out of Ohio a few years earlier. Johnson told Jimmy he would not be allowed to sell the trailer that he had displayed.

Jimmy asked, "How come I can't sell it?"

Johnson answered, "You're not a dealer."

"I don't care if I'm a dealer or not. I bought it a couple of months ago because I do construction work and travel, and I needed it to live in to save me some money, but now things are rough and I need the cash. I'm not working and I'm about broke."

Johnson repeated, "Well you can't sell it in Ohio."

Jimmy said, "But I ain't got no money to go nowhere else, so I'm gonna have to sell it before I can leave here."

"You'd better get it out of here," Johnson told him. "I'm coming back tomorrow, and it better be gone."

Johnson left, and Jimmy considered what he should do. "I was there by myself and had already placed an ad in the paper. I had Florida tags on my truck, I had matching Florida driver's license and Ohio tags on the trailer, and I said to myself, 'What in the hell can he do to me? I'm not goin' anywhere.'" The next day, Johnson returned and ordered Jimmy to leave, but he refused. "He told me he was coming back later to impound the trailer, but he didn't come back. I stayed there and sold the trailer and delivered it. I didn't go back to that place again, though, because I figured that then they would have something to holler about."

Before he sold the trailer, he opened his motel room door one morning and found his sister Peggy sitting there smoking a marijuana cigarette and casually watching the clouds drift by. She stayed with him a few days and talked him into buying her a Dodge Coronet automobile. She was only fifteen but, like her brother, carried her own forged driver's license. Not many days later, Jimmy and Peggy drove to Richmond, Virginia. "We didn't get into town until about 2 o'clock in the morning, but Peggy wanted to go downtown drinking with a girl she knew there. I told her she couldn't because we were leavin' early the next morning, but she went anyway. About 5 or 6 o'clock, I was awakened by the highway patrol tellin' me she was in an accident down on the highway. I hopped in my truck and followed the cop to the accident scene. They were still tryin' to get her out of the car. There were fire trucks and ambulances all around. She was either drunk or high on drugs, and she ran off the road into a tree. The whole steering column was pushed up against her, and her legs were crushed under it. After they cut her out, they took her to the hospital, where they operated on her and put a rod in her leg and a pin in her hip. She was in the hospital for several months and then had to use a walker for a long time until she could learn to walk again."

The rest of the summer, Jimmy traveled around the Midwest shoplifting, working out of his truck and trying to sell a trailer that he had been unable to move in almost four weeks. At one point, he rendezvoused with Wanda and Billy O'Roarke shortly after she was released from jail in Pennsylvania, and Billy suggested that he try selling the trailer in Jamestown, New York. Billy said he had been in Jamestown the year before and had sold several trailers in a brief period of time.

"I didn't have no other place in mind," Jimmy said, "so I took off up there. I had never been in that particular town before. I set up at a motel in Lakewood, which is just outside of Jamestown. I put the trailer up for sale and ran an ad. The first day, before the ad even came out in the newspaper, some people bought the trailer. So I called the factory that day and had another one delivered. It was the same brand and the same color as the first one, so I just let the ad run, and some more people came out the first day and bought that one. I took off to Indiana and bought another one, brought it back with me and took it to another motel in Falconer, which is the other side of Jamestown. I sold it the first day the ad ran in the newspaper. So I had another one delivered to me at a campground and moved into it. I stuck a for sale sign in the window, and while I was movin' into it, the people who owned the campground came around and asked me if they could look at it, and they ended up buyin' it."

He laughed. "It was just like I couldn't lose. I sold about ten trailers very quickly. Mom and Dad were in Atlanta at the time, and I talked with them by phone and told them I was havin' some luck with the trailers, and they came up there too. They went over to one side of town, and I was on the other side. They were dealin' Jeffery trailers; my uncle, Tommy Jeffery, owned a trailer company in Elkhart, Indiana, at that time. They were dealin' his trailers, and I was dealin' Marauders. Mom and Dad sold five or six within a couple of weeks' time, and I sold another two or three. While I was there, I also started workin' my truck pavin' and sealin' driveways, and was doin' pretty good with that, so I just decided to stay there the rest of the summer. I went out to Elkhart and picked up a 35-footer that I could live in for the summer; I didn't put it up for sale. I was already makin' $500 or $600 a day sealing driveways."

In New York, at the tender age of seventeen, Jimmy Burke was earning at least $3,000 weekly by sealing driveway and roofs six days a week; $600 weekly shoplifting during parts of two days, and $2,000 a week selling trailers, primarily during evenings and on Sundays -- an income that was the equivalent of more than $280,000 a year!

He had both surprised and impressed his parents by his success. But he still had another major surprise in store for them. He had not yet revealed to them that he was a practicing homosexual.

# 5

# Hip Pocket Money

Late one fall night during the middle 1970s, two teenage boys were driving through an industrial section of a northern Indiana community. They pulled into the driveway of a small, obscure travel trailer manufacturing company to turn around. The driver, a sixteen-year-old, slammed on the brakes and said to his fourteen-year-old companion, "Hey Joe. Look there. The door to that plant is open." He pointed toward the building, where his headlights revealed that a large, horizontal sliding door had not been closed completely. The boys grinned at each other.

"Let's take a look," Joe said.

The sixteen-year-old parked his car and shut it off. He retrieved a flashlight from the glovebox, and together the two boys walked cautiously toward the open RV plant. Inside, they searched around for something of value that they could take, but found nothing except a lot of tools, wood and travel trailer parts that they didn't want. A glassed partition separated the plant from an office area, and when the sixteen-year-old aimed his flashlight through one of the windows, he saw a bonanza inside: a large, open snack tray filled with candy bars, peanuts and other goodies. The door to the office was locked, but Joe broke the window with a hammer and unlocked it by reaching through the hole. Once inside the office, the boys stuffed their pockets with snacks and were about ready to leave when Joe spotted a small safe, about three feet tall, sitting on rollers in one corner. The teenagers tried to open it, but couldn't, and the sixteen-year-old said to his companion, "Wait here a minute." He went back into the plant and returned quickly with two sledge hammers and a crowbar. Then together, the boys began beating and prying on the door of the safe.

After two hours of fruitless labor, they gave up trying to open it. Paul, the older boy, rolled the safe out into the parking lot and chained it to the rear bumper of his car. Then cautiously, careful not to attract attention, and timing their movements so that there was no nearby traffic, they towed the safe out of the parking lot, down the street and around a corner to a vacant lot. Paul unchained the safe from his car, and the boys half-dragged it and half-carried it into some weeds. After covering it with brush, they left and returned to their homes for a few hours of sleep before going to school the next morning. That evening, after dark, they returned to the open field and resumed their work on the safe door. About 2 a.m., the door popped open, and out fell a large pack of papers and a shoebox.

Paul and Joe scattered the papers in the wind, angry that they had wasted their time trying to open the safe. As almost an afterthought, Joe lifted the lid on the shoebox and looked inside. "My God, Paul, look at this!" he shouted. He handed the box to his friend. The box was packed with money -- $100 bills!

Paul gasped and his mouth fell open. Then he tucked the box under one arm and said to Joe, "Let's get the hell out of here!"

The boys ran to the car and leaped inside. Paul's hands were shaking so badly he had difficulty starting the old Plymouth. He slammed the car into reverse by mistake, shoved the gearshift the other direction hard and rammed it back into "Park" without knowing it. He revved the engine, but the car just sat there. Realizing what he'd done, he shifted the lever again, and the rear wheels sprayed gravel for twenty feet. Joe shouted, "Jesus Christ, Paul, what're you tryin' to do, get us arrested?"

"Shut up and count the money while I drive," Paul ordered, speeding north out of town toward the Indiana Toll Road.

Joe counted the bills, stopping every few minutes to shout aloud about their good fortune. Paul aimed the car west on the toll road and waited for Joe to finish counting the money. After a few minutes, Joe looked at him and smiled. "Holy shit, Paul! You're not gonna believe this. We've got sixty thousand dollars here. All in one-hundred-dollar bills!"

"Oh, my God!" exclaimed Paul. "What are we gonna do with it?"

"Spend it, of course."

"Yeah, but what on?"

"Damned if I know. Maybe a couple of new cars."

"Naw," said Paul. "We can't do that. If we try to buy cars with hundred-dollar bills, we'll just get arrested. And what're we gonna tell our folks when they ask us where we got the money?"

"Yeah, that's a good point," said Joe. Then his face brightened, and he added, "Let's not tell them. Let's take off someplace."

"Good idea. Where to?"

"I know! Florida."

"Yeah, Florida. Great. Let's go!"

The teenagers drove to the first exit, reversed directions and pointed the Plymouth toward Ohio. At Fremont, they picked up Interstate Route 69 and turned south. For twenty hours, they drove without stopping except to buy fuel and food. Between them, they had enough money for gasoline to drive halfway to their destination before it was necessary to spend one of the crisp one-hundred-dollar bills. Just south of Nashville on Interstate Route 24, they pulled into a Shell service station and ordered a full tank of gasoline. The grizzled, middle-age attendant watched the two boys closely as he pumped gasoline for them. They didn't look very trustworthy to him, young as they were, and he didn't take his eyes off them when they went inside his station to buy soft drinks out of a machine. The pump clicked off just as they were walking back to their car, and he said, "That'll be fifteen dollars."

The older boy pulled a bill out of his pocket and handed it to the attendant. The man looked at it, saw it was a one-hundred-dollar bill and said, "I can't change that. Don't you have anything smaller?"

"Sorry," said the boy. "That's the smallest bill we've got."

"Well, I don't have that much change," the attendant repeated. "Looks like you'll have to wait until my mechanic comes back from lunch and I can send him to the bank for some money."

"How long's that gonna be?" asked the younger boy.

"About an hour."

"Oh, shit!" the older boy said. "We can't wait that long!"

"Hell no," said his companion.

The attendant's eyes narrowed and he asked, "Where did you kids get that hundred-dollar bill?"

A trace of sudden fear showed in the eyes of the older boy, but the younger one just smiled and said boastfully, "Won it last night in a poker game!"

The attendant didn't believe him. He was considering what to do about the boys. Maybe he'd call the police and suggest that a check be made of the Plymouth's Indiana license plate. He was sure the kids would stick around for awhile, since he was holding their hundred-dollar bill. The boys were on the other side of the car from him, whispering, and the attendant considered going into his station and getting a gun he'd hidden there. Then the younger boy got inside the car, and the other boy walked toward him smiling. "Tell you what," the kid said. "We're in a big hurry, so you just keep the whole hundred dollars, and we'll take off."

"Wait a minute!" the attendant shouted. "I can't do that! You've got eighty-five dollars comin'."

The boy waved aside his words, got behind the steering wheel of the Plymouth and drove away. The attendant watched them leave, then ran to his station and dialed the nearest post of the Tennessee Highway Patrol. "This is Jake at the I-24 Shell station. I think I've just been paid for some gas with a counterfeit one-hundred-dollar bill!"

A pair of Tennessee state troopers received a call to watch for a 1964 brown Plymouth sedan just as they left the Stuckey's restaurant where they always ate lunch. One trooper wrote down the description of the Plymouth, and its license plate number, while the other officer drove their patrol car out of the restaurant's parking lot. Neither man spotted the brown Plymouth from Indiana that pulled into the same parking lot just as they were leaving.

An hour later, Joe and Paul finished their first full meal since noon the day before, and Paul pulled a one-hundred-dollar bill out of his shirt to pay the check. The waitress smiled sweetly as she rang up their charges on the cash register, but her eyes widened at the sight of the one-hundred-dollar bill. "I'm sorry, sir," she said in a hill country accent, "but I cain't accept a bill this big. We ain't got that much change in the register."

"Tell her to keep it as a tip," Joe suggested.

"Oh, no sir! I couldn't do that! Why, if I did somethin' like that, I could lose my job!"

"Just a minute, then," said Joe. He took the bill from her hand and told her, "I'll be right back in a minute. I'll get change." He walked over to a booth where a truck driver was sitting, sipping a cup of coffee. He said something to the man, then returned to the cash register and gave the girl a twenty-dollar bill.

She counted out change and thanked the teenagers with a hospitable, "Y'all come back, now, y'hear?"

As they drove out of the parking lot, the truck driver left the booth where he'd eaten his lunch and approached the manager of the restaurant. He carried a one-hundred-dollar bill in one hand. "Pete, you'll never guess what just happened. It was the damndest thing I ever saw. A little runt of a kid just sold me a hundred-dollar bill for twenty dollars!" He laughed, but stopped when Pete made an unpleasant face.

"Are you sure it isn't counterfeit?" asked the restaurant manager, and the smile faded from the truck driver's face.

"Where's a phone?" asked the driver.

Word quickly went out to police officers throughout Tennessee and Georgia to watch for two teenage boys driving a brown 1964 Plymouth sedan with Indiana plates. The boys were wanted for questioning to determine why they were selling one-hundred-dollar bills for twenty dollars each. Two service station managers in Georgia reported to police that they'd exchanged twenties for C-notes but had second thoughts about the transactions when they realized the hundreds might be phony. The Georgia Highway Patrol had tracked the Plymouth through the state as far south as Tifton and had warned law enforcement authorities in Florida that the boys seemed to be headed that direction. But for three days, no one else reported receiving any suspicious one-hundred-dollar bills.

Paul exchanged one bill for a tank of gasoline in Gainesville, Florida, but the service station attendant -- a teenager himself -- didn't report receiving it. A waitress at a restaurant not far from Lake City, Florida, accepted another hundred as payment for two ham-and-egg breakfasts. Joe bought a new $237 wristwatch at a jewelry store in Crystal River, Florida. He paid for the watch with three one-hundred-dollar bills and told the clerk to keep the change; the clerk did. At New Port Richey, the boys were offered a one-hundred-dollar trade-in allowance on their Plymouth at a used car lot, so they switched their Indiana license plates to the rear of a badly scratched old Corvette with a dingy blue paint job and drove away after leaving eighty crisp one-hundred-dollar bills in the hands of a smiling

used car salesman. They worked their way slowly down the western
coast of Florida, sleeping nights in luxurious motels and cruising
beaches looking at bikini-clad girls in the daytime. At Clearwater,
they stopped at a Penney's department store and outfitted themselves
with new shoes, shirts, trousers, socks and underwear. As usual, they
paid their tab with one-hundred-dollar bills -- four of them -- and as
soon as they left, the alert store clerk telephoned the Clearwater
police department.

The Corvette proved to be quite a gas guzzler, and the Hoosiers
left a trail of hundred-dollar bills behind them as they drove down
the coast. A couple of service station attendants phoned police about
the bills, but most did not. Still, the trail they left was solid enough
that Florida state police began closing in on the teenagers. Troopers
throughout the state -- but especially in the south -- were watching
for a light blue 1971 Corvette with an Indiana license plate. The
advice to officers was cautious: "Proceed carefully. The two boys are
wanted for questioning. They may or may not have committed a
crime. The money they have definitely is not counterfeit!"

The teens were traced to Naples, where they seemed to drop out
of sight. Reports of suspicious C-notes being spent suddenly stopped
being phoned in to police stations. Rumors and speculation ran ram-
pant through the ranks of the Florida state troopers. Had the boys
run out of money? Had they gone underground, aware they were
being sought? Or had the money been stolen from them?

For five days, troopers searched fruitlessly for the youths and their
Corvette. They found neither, even though the automobile was
parked all that time not far from East Naples while Paul and Joe were
fishing in the Gulf of Mexico aboard a chartered boat. Five days after
the trail police were following suddenly went cold, the two sun-
tanned boys climbed back inside their blue Corvette and drove east
on the Alligator Alley toll road toward Fort Lauderdale. They left
behind in East Naples a one-hundred-dollar bill that they traded for
a tank of gasoline. The service station attendant didn't report receiv-

ing the bill for two days, and that gave the boys enough time to reach Fort Lauderdale and drive to the booming metropolis of Miami, where hundred-dollar bills were as commonplace as tourists.

Not until nearly two weeks later, when Joe and Paul sold a hundred for twenty dollars in Melbourne did police officers pick up their trail again. Determined not to let the teenagers get away that time, several troopers converged on the Melbourne area from all directions, and the surprised youths were arrested just outside of Cape Canaveral. Questioned by friendly police officers -- and treated almost as if they were famous -- the boys willingly told the whole story of their escapade, leaving out no details as the troopers laughed and joked with them about their adventure. A friendly Florida police sergeant volunteered to call the boys' parents in Indiana and tell them what had happened, and he also made arrangements for an Indiana trooper to fly to Florida and take the teenagers back home for prosecution.

The short, stocky Indiana state police sergeant was excited. It wasn't often, in those days of rising crime rates and public apathy, that a policeman had an opportunity to tell someone that his stolen merchandise had been recovered and would soon be returned. But Sergeant Bill Evans (not his real name) would be able to do that in just a few minutes, and he was pleased. He'd called Carl Johnson (also not a real name), the president of an Indiana travel trailer manufacturing company, for an appointment earlier that morning. When Mr. Johnson asked why Sergeant Evans wanted to see him, the detective had simply said, "I can't tell you over the phone, sir, but I know you'll be pleased."

Technically, Evans was breaking departmental rules by even leaving headquarters with the shoebox of money that sat on the car seat beside him. If his superiors ever found out about his taking the money to Johnson, he'd almost certainly receive a suspension. Evens was willing to risk it. It was all so *damned* exciting! The kids had copped out to everything, and the Florida police had recovered forty-two thousand dollars of the original sixty thousand that the boys had stolen three weeks earlier. Evans parked his car in front of the RV company building, tucked the shoebox under one arm and marched proudly inside. He told the receptionist who he was and asked to see Mr. Johnson. He was ushered into an empty office and sat there a few minutes alone before a middle-age, balding man in a striped shirt and string tie walked in. "I'm Carl Johnson, Sergeant," the man said. "What can I do for you?"

Evans stood up and smiled as he shook hands with the RV company president. "It's not what you can do for me, Mr. Johnson. It's what I can do for *you*. I believe the contents of this shoebox belongs to you. Now, I can't let you have it, because it's evidence against the boys who took it, but I can let you look at it, and I am pleased to report that most of your sixty thousand dollars has been recovered."

Johnson frowned and appeared to be a little upset. "What sixty thousand dollars?" he asked.

The sergeant answered, "Why, the sixty thousand dollars that was stolen from your plant about three weeks ago. We've caught the two teenage boys who broke in here and took your safe with your money in it!"

Johnson said, "I don't know what you're talking about."

Evans smiled patiently. "Sure, you do. Don't you remember? Some kids hauled a safe out of here one night, broke it open and found your shoebox full of money inside. They headed south on a spending spree and bought a Corvette with part of the money, but they were caught in Florida, and we've recovered forty-two thousand of your sixty thousand dollars."

"Sergeant," said Johnson, "I don't know how you got the idea that somebody stole sixty thousand dollars from me, but it's not true. I wish to God it were. I could use the money. But wherever that money came from, it wasn't stolen from here."

Evans was puzzled. "I don't understand. Did you have a break-in here three weeks ago?"

"Yes, we did, Sergeant, but we didn't even bother to report it to the police. Someone broke a door glass, got inside our offices and stole some candy bars and peanuts, but that's all."

"They didn't take a small safe out of here?"

"Why yes, as a matter of fact, they did. It didn't have anything in it, though. It was totally empty, and the door was wide open. It was a worthless old safe, and we were going to have to pay someone to haul it away, so when we discovered that whoever broke in here had taken it, we just counted our blessings. There was certainly no shoebox full of money in it."

More puzzled than ever, Evans asked, "Well, if the money wasn't stolen from here, where did it come from?"

"I'm sure I haven't the slightest idea, Sergeant. Now if you'll excuse me..."

Dazed, Sergeant Evans put the lid on the shoebox and tucked the box under one arm. As he left, he thought of a question he wanted to ask Johnson, and he walked back to the company president's office. Johnson was talking angrily on the telephone to someone. His face was beet-red. Evans changed his mind about asking his question and returned to his car. He took the box of money back to his headquarters, then telephoned the assistant district attorney who was handling prosecution of the case. The assistant D.A. listened to his account of the conversation with Johnson and said, as Evans completed his report, "I'll be damned."

Evans started to ask the prosecutor if any action could be taken against the boys, and the assistant D.A. said, "Hold on a minute. I've got another call." Evens held the silent telephone to his ear for what seemed like a long time before he heard the prosecutor's voice at the other end again.

"Bill," the county attorney began, "are you sitting down?"

"No, but if you think I need to, I'll do it. What's happened now?"

"That other call was from the boys' lawyer. He said his clients want to change their story. He said they didn't break into a factory and steal any money. They won it gambling!"

"Oh, shit!" Evans exclaimed.

"My sentiments exactly," responded the prosecutor. "It looks like we'll have to let the kids go and give them back that forty-two thousand."

Evans was angry. "Where in the hell did that money really come from?"

The prosecutor laughed. "I don't have any doubt at all where it came from, Bill. It was taken from a little safe on wheels by two teenage boys who decided to go on a trip to Florida with it. The question isn't where the money came from; it's how it got there in the first place and why its owner doesn't want to claim it. But I'm pretty sure I know the answer to that, too. A lot of trailer companies had a tough time making it through the Arab oil embargo, and some of them sold trailers secretly to gypsies. My friends in the RV industry call that 'selling out the back door.' The gypsies paid cash for the trailers, and those transactions were never reported to the IRS. So far as anyone is concerned, the trailers and the cash never existed."

Evans was astonished. "You're telling me that those two teenage boys committed a perfect crime, and they're going to get away with stealing sixty thousand dollars?"

"That's right, Bill, but if you ever tell anyone I said that, I'll deny it."

An RV industry leader who asked not to be identified was not surprised when he was told the story about a shoebox full of money. "Frankly, at some point in history, probably every travel trailer manufacturer in the industry has been guilty of selling to the gypsies."

Not only was he right about that, but the owners of several small RV companies have hinted, confidentially, that if financial difficulties ever force them to make a choice between closing their doors or selling trailers to the con artist clans, they'll build trailers for Travelers and, if necessary, sell them "out the back door." During this nation's economic crunches of 1979-81 and 1990-92, more than one long-established RV company did "sell out the back door" to the Travelers.

It's easy for any businessman whose company is in financial trouble to justify selling to the clans in order to keep his operations afloat. There is nothing illegal about doing that, and the profits are usually very good. The clan members pay cash for everything they buy, too, and it is very tempting for a supplier to accept cash for his products and never record the money in his company's books. That practice is called "putting the cash in your hip pocket." Executives of several well known companies skimmed money in that manner during the early 1970s, and especially during the oil embargo of 1973-74 and the Iranian crisis of 1979. Without question, that's why the sixty thousand dollars that the two Indiana boys found in a shoebox was hidden in an old office safe, and why the owner of the RV company refused to admit that the cash even existed.

It was hip pocket money.

Most RV industry executives whose companies build trailers for the Irish and Scottish Travelers don't have to engage in "hip pocket" and "back door" deals in order to earn substantial profits. Those companies apparently operate well within the framework of the law in the ways they build and sell their products. Certainly, they have been criticized severely within the RV industry for allowing the Travelers -- generally but mistakenly referred to as *gypsies* -- to market their trailers, but they have a legal right to sell their products to whomever they wish. Executives of those companies have stated publicly that they regard the Travelers as dealers.

During the 1970s, the primary suppliers of travel trailers to Irish and Scottish Travelers were Marauder Travelers of Wakarusa, Indiana, and a company we'll call Kentucky Traveler of nearby Elkhart. They became so successful that since 1978, at least eleven other trailer manufacturers have tried to imitate them by building trailers for the so-called *gypsy* retailers. Initially, only one of those companies -- the now-defunct Rush Industries, which manufactured Safari brand units -- was able to build much sales volume among the Travelers because of the clans' long-standing loyalty to Kentucky Traveler and Marauder. Two companies, Meck Industries (producer of Regal trailers) and Custom Delux, closed their doors after a few months. In 1982, the Travelers also bought and sold trailers built for them by Skylark Industries, Franklin Coach Company, Stateside Homes, Trophy Travelers and American Travel Trailer Corporation.

Marauder Travelers and Rush Industries ceased operation during the late 1980s, and their absence created a substantial product void that Kentucky Traveler apparently was unable to fill. Almost immediately, two new companies were opened to meet Travelers' demands for a broader selection of travel trailers. Two employees of Kentucky Traveler left that company and set up business under a name we'll refer to as Renegade Traveler, and an employee of Rush Industries formed his own RV company that we'll call Federal Traveler. Within a few years, Federal Traveler's products would dominate the so-called gypsy travel trailer market, and by 1994 the company would be so successful that its owner would build a multi-million-dollar country home east of Elkhart.

From the outset, Federal Traveler and its president -- whom we'll call Rutherford Randle -- produced travel trailers (and later fifth-wheels) that fit the needs of the Irish, Scottish and English Travelers perfectly. Although somewhat higher priced than units built by the Travelers' two other primary suppliers, Randle's various brands had a distinctive, though garish, appearance that RV industry insiders often referred to as "Alabama flash." They were eye-catching, appeared to be of better quality than competitors' units and were available in a wide variety of styles and colors. In addition, Randle offered his trailers under an assortment of brand names and permitted the Travelers to select the brands they liked best.

One of Randle's earliest models was called Coachmaster, and it quickly became his company's best selling nameplate.

A few miles from the Federal Traveler plant near Elkhart, Indiana, corporate executives at one of the nation's largest RV manufacturing companies -- Coachmen Industries -- were quite unhappy with Randle's decision to sell trailers under the Coachmaster brand. They, and their legal advisors, believed the brand infringed upon two of their own trademarks -- the Travelmaster brand and the Coachmen name itself. Also convinced that their own prospective retail customers were confused by the Coachmaster's appearance in the marketplace, Coachmen's executives filed civil action in federal court alleging trademark infringement and unfair competition by Federal Traveler.

Late in 1991, Randle signed a consent decree pledging never to use the Coachmen, Coachmaster or Travelmaster names "or any colorable imitation" of those brands. However, two weeks later, Federal Traveler sold the first of thirty-one Coachmaster trailers to an RV dealership in Warwickshire, England. Coachmen did not learn of those sales for nearly two years.

And in early 1992, Federal Traveler introduced a new brand of trailer it called CoachCraft.

Coachmen Industries, after learning about the new brand from its dealers, notified Federal Traveler that it believed CoachCraft represented another infringement of its trademark. Coachmen demanded that Federal Traveler halt production and sale of trailers with the CoachCraft name. Randle did not respond to Coachmen's demands but, instead, registered the new brand with the U.S. Patent and Trademark Office. Between January 1992 and June 1993, Federal Traveler sold approximately 297 of the CoachCraft trailers.

Meanwhile, Coachmen's lawyers filed a second civil complaint against Federal Traveler, alleging trademark infringement, unfair competition and breach of the consent decree. That action later was amended to include a contempt of court allegation.

In September 1993, Susan and Henry Knox (not their real names) of Fort Wayne, Indiana, began shopping for a larger RV to replace their growing family's old Lark trailer. They were particularly drawn to a thirty-two-foot CoachCraft model being offered for sale in a campground near Decatur. The trailer's owner, who identified himself as Joe Norris and said he was a police officer from Kalamazoo, Michigan, was willing to sell the coach for less than half what he said he'd paid for it.

Susan later said under oath, "He (Norris) told me that it was only nine months old and he had just gotten it out of storage. It was in storage for six months out of the nine, and his reason for selling it was that his wife, after they got it, didn't like traveling around in anything that big."

After walking through the trailer and examining its features, Susan and Henry asked Norris and a woman he said was his sister Dorothy, "What type of travel trailer is this?"

Norris replied, "It's made by Coachmen."

When the Knoxes asked the price of the trailer, Norris told them he had bought it for $24,500, but he said, "I'm asking $12,000 for it."

The Fort Wayne couple offered $9,000 for the trailer, and Norris's sister responded, "What did you say?"

Henry answered, "Nine thousand dollars."

"Oh, no. I can't do that," Norris said.

His sister suggested, "Let the kids have it for $11,000."

Norris pointed a finger at Dorothy and said, "You're going to have me broke." Henry said he could not afford to spend $11,000 for a trailer, and Norris replied, "I'll let you have it for $10,500."

Susan and Henry agreed they would buy the trailer for that price if they could arrange financing, but they refused to pay Norris a deposit. As the Knoxes drove home, Susan told her husband she was uncomfortable about the purchase. "Why would he pay $24,500 for that nine months ago and be willing to let it go for $10,500?" she asked Henry.

Back in Fort Wayne, Susan telephoned a well known Indiana RV dealership, Tom Raper's of Richmond, and asked a salesman for information about the CoachCraft. "He referred to it as a gypsy model, and he did not think that it was made by Coachmen," she reported. "So then we really started becoming more and more suspicious."

The following day, Susan telephoned Coachmen, and she was referred to the company's legal department. She was informed that not only was the CoachCraft not a Coachmen product, but also that Coachmen had filed a legal complaint against Federal Traveler for using that brand name on its RVs. Subsequent research revealed that the trailer Norris offered for sale had a suggested retail price of $14,447 when it was new, not the $24,500 Norris claimed he had paid. Investigations also determined that the home address Norris had given the Knoxes was phony and that no one named Joe Norris had ever been employed by the Kalamazoo Police Department.

Reluctantly, Susan Knox agreed to provide a sworn deposition as a witness in Coachmen's suit against Federal Traveler, and after reviewing the transcript of her testimony which became evidence at the trial, U.S. District Judge Allen Sharp said Susan's story provided "a good example" of how Travelers operated their trailer scams using products supplied to them by Federal Traveler.

Courtroom testimony also was given by a writer who, the judge said, provided "credible evidence" about "the phenomenon of gypsy trailer sellers, who purchase trailers, then immediately resell them using a 'hard luck' story to sell the trailer for well more than its original cost.'"

In his decision on the lawsuit, Judge Sharp added, "It seems obvious to this court that (Federal Traveler) and its officers knew their market and offered (brand) names for their customers to select which aided their underhanded sales techniques." Reinforcing that position, the judge concluded that Federal Traveler "not only manufactured trailers for sale to gypsies, but also provided an assortment of names which the gypsies could choose to put on the trailers, CoachCraft and Coachmaster included in that assortment. And it is apparent to this court that gypsies chose the name CoachCraft in hopes they could palm the product off to their customers as a Coachmen product. Given (Randle's) long-time involvement in the gypsy part of the RV industry, it is highly unlikely that the name was chosen for any reason other than to be used by gypsies to palm off the product."

Judge Sharp ruled that Federal Traveler's attempts to hide its sale of Coachmaster trailers "were in willful contempt" of his court, and the company's failure to comply with the consent decree was "willful and contemptuous." Calculating that Federal Traveler earned at least $1,000 in profits from the sale of each Coachmaster trailer, he ordered the company to pay triple its profits as well as Coachmen's cost of litigation -- a total of $191,369. In addition, the judge said he would reserve judgment on an additional $297,000 in damages resulting from sale of the CoachCraft trailers, hinting that those damages could be awarded to Coachmen if Federal Traveler continued its practice of trademark infringement. Judge Sharp also ordered the U.S. Patent and Trademark Office to cancel its registration of Federal Traveler's CoachCraft brand, and he issued an injunction prohibiting Federal Traveler from using that brand name "or any colorable imitation."


Irish and Scottish Travelers discovered the financial bonanza of selling cheap travel trailers in the early 1960s, when a member of the Northern Irish clan, Tom Jeffery, opened a recreational vehicle dealership in Louisville, Kentucky. Jeffery, without question the most successful Traveler entrepreneur of the period, bought travel trailers from various Indiana manufacturers at that time and sold them at a low price, but with a slight markup, to fellow Travelers. It was apparently a satisfactory arrangement for everyone concerned; manufacturers were able to sell their products to a legitimate dealer at a profit; Jeffery sold the units to the Travelers at a profit, and the Travelers made money by reselling the coaches to retail customers.

Occasional difficulties developed over who was authorized to perform warranty service on the trailers, but generally, Jeffery handled that aspect to everyone's satisfaction. Many of the Irish Travelers -- including young Jimmy Burke -- claimed to be related to Jeffery, although the relationships were always quite vague and tenuous. Before his death in 1982, Jeffery consistently declined requests for media interviews, saying he was in poor health and that he had lost touch with the Irish Travelers during the previous few years.

Prior to Jeffery's death, the Kentucky state fire marshal's office was requested by another state's bureau of motor vehicles to check out the relationship between Jeffery and the Kentucky Traveler and Marauder plants. In answer to that request, Chandler Robinson, then chief of the manufactured housing section of the fire marshal's office, replied: "I have contacted Jeffery Trailer Sales, Inc., and find that Mr. Jeffery is still listed in the telephone directory of Louisville as a trailer dealer. However, he does not maintain a lot nor does he have, at this time, a valid license to transact business within the Commonwealth of Kentucky. In a telephone conversation with Mr. Jeffery, he admitted that he had some interest in Kentucky Traveler of Elkhart and informed me that he had, at this time, a mortgage on the Marauder Travelers, Incorporated. However, he is not actively participating in either, so he claims."

Jimmy Burke, who switched his allegiance to Marauder after initially selling Kentucky Traveler products, typically paid $4,500 for a 32-foot travel trailer during the 1980s, and he nearly always sold it for at least $7,000 or $7,500. In 1995, Travelers reported they bought travel trailers and fifth-wheels for between $9,000 and $17,000 and sold them for $12,000 to $22,000.

Once asked if he ever sold a trailer at a loss, Jimmy replied, "I never did, and I can't say Mom and Dad ever did either. A couple of times, they kept one and lived in it all summer, and by the time the summer was over, it had a few things wrong with it. Maybe the toilet wouldn't work or the air-conditioner quit operating. So, to sell it quickly, they'd let it go for what they paid for it. But they never lost any money on one."

Over the years, Jimmy bought every brand of trailer that he thought he could sell for a profit. He even tried one of the short-lived Custom Delux models. "Those were the worst pieces of junk I ever saw!"

Custom Delux was established in Elkhart by a Traveler named Joe Smith who thought he could follow in Tom Jeffery's footsteps and earn a quick fortune. Jimmy Burke recalled, "The trailer I bought from him was so bad that I returned it to him and demanded my money back. It *looked* beautiful! It was a 32-footer with green shag carpeting all through it, and it even had a bar and a china cabinet. I pulled that thing from Elkhart to Atlanta, and by the time I got to Atlanta, the refrigerator had come off the wall and was layin' in the middle of the floor. The screws in the metal on the outside of the trailer came out, and the piece of metal coverin' one side was flappin' in the wind as I was goin' down the road. Part of the step broke off, and the step just hung there by one side. When I hooked up a water hose at a campground, water poured out of the walls all the way around. I'm not exaggeratin'! I mean, out of the *walls*! And there were several other things wrong with it, too. I just unhooked the water and towed that trailer back to Elkhart. Joe Smith looked at it and said, 'I'll give you another one.'

"I said, 'I don't want another one! I want my money back!' He started givin' me some shit about doin' that, and I said, 'I'll just get in touch with somebody in law enforcement, then.' I was bluffin' him, but he didn't know it, and he bought what I was tellin' him. I guess he figured I could make a couple of phone calls and cause him some problems without involvin' myself too much. But I really wouldn't have done nothin'. All our trailers are paid for in cash up front, you know. And as far as the law was concerned, no such trailer existed. As long as there was no such trailer, no money ever exchanged hands and no one had to give anything to Uncle Sam."

Burke said, "When I buy a trailer from Marauder, the factory gives me a certificate of origin and a bill of sale sayin' what I paid for the trailer. But, you know, the factory also gives me another bill of sale with whatever price I want listed on it. (In actual fact, investigations revealed that the second paper was not a bill of sale; the manufacturer called it a *factory invoice* and claimed it was merely an option list with a *suggested retail price* on it.) I also get a temporary tag to put on the trailer until I get where I'm goin' with it. I'll go into Kentucky, Alabama or Florida with that certificate of origin and get a title. I used to use Atlanta all the time, but they started givin' The People hell about it there, so nobody gets titles in Atlanta any more. In Kentucky, I can get a title off a certificate of origin without payin' no sales tax because the taxes are paid the second year and, of course, by the time the second year rolls around, I've already sold that trailer. In Kentucky, most of the Travelers go to Louisville and to a small town about a hundred miles from there named Hartford. Some towns will give you a hassle, but not those. In Lexington, for example, you're always told to get the trailer inspected. Every town is supposed to require that, but most of the small towns don't.

"In Alabama, the place is Opelika, or maybe Gadsden. At either one of those towns, I believe I could take in a piece of paper that I've written on sayin' that I bought a trailer from someone for any amount of money I wanted to claim; I could even mark out a couple of places and then carry it in, and I could get a license plate from that without any hassle at all. Now, nobody goes to Birmingham or Montgomery for plates any more. The Travelers who went into those towns a few years ago had a lot of trouble and were gettin' harassed by people who said they knew who we were. During the seventies, we got titles very easily in Florida; in Tallahassee, they'd give titles to us right over the counter. Then Florida quit handin' them out like that. The registration people required that we fill out papers and then wait six or eight weeks until they could mail a title to us. That was no good for us, of course, because we wanted to sell the trailers as fast as we could. Then Florida started allowin' titles to be picked up over the counter again, so everybody was gettin' titles in Florida once more. In Florida, they ask you what you paid for the trailer, but they don't put the price on the title."

Is it important to Travelers that prices not be put on titles?

He grinned. "Yeah. See, most of the Travelers say the trailer was a gift so they don't have to pay no taxes on it, or they'll say they paid $500 for it. In Ohio, for example, you pay taxes on the amount you say that you paid for the trailer, and they don't ask you to show them nothin' provin' that's what you paid. But in Ohio, if you say you paid $500 so you only have to pay taxes on $500, the registration people write that price on the title. Then, when you try to sell the trailer, the people who buy it can see that you only paid $500 for it, and that don't look good to them 'cause you've already told them you paid eight or ten thousand dollars for it. That's why, when I get a title in Ohio, I say the trailer was a gift."

How do the Travelers come up with all the different stories they use to explain why they're selling a new trailer?

"I don't never have a story planned. They just come to mind very easily, probably because I was raised knowin' I might have to make up a believable story at any time, about anything. I've told different stories, but I usually say I'm in the construction business, and I bought the trailer because I travel a lot with my work. That explains two things at one time: It explains why I'm drivin' a truck with one kind of tags on it, have a driver's license from another state and a license plate on the trailer from still another state. And, it explains why I want to sell the trailer -- because construction work is slow.

Now that I'm laid off, I'll tell people, I need money badly, and I've got to take a loss on the trailer. Or, I'll say my parents bought the trailer for me because I was gettin' married, but I broke up with my fiance. That one usually works. Or, my wife had a car accident and she's in the hospital in another state, and doctor bills are mounting up, so I've got to sell the trailer to pay the bills."

Jimmy Burke, of course, had never been married. And during his entire life as a con artist, the wife he frequently described in the stories he told to people was never more than a figment of his fertile imagination.

# 6

# The Gay Irish Traveler

When Jimmy Burke practiced his various scams in Jamestown, New York, during the summer of 1977, he was only seventeen years old, but he had been a full-time, self-supporting con artist more than two years. Using a fake I.D. to prove he was much older, Jimmy spent most of his spare time at a bar called Big Mike's Place. There, he quickly became quite popular among the patrons because not only did he flash a lot of cash, but he often spent it buying drinks for everyone. To the local crowd, he was a successful young businessman from Florida who operated his own blacktopping business, and there was no doubt in anyone's mind that the man they knew as James C. Murphy was rich.

At the bar, he met a man we'll call Stinson who, in turn, introduced him to a tall, thin young woman named Diane. "I liked her right off," Jimmy said sometime later. "She was a very cheerful, happy-go-lucky person who liked to have fun and was fun to be around. We talked about me being from Florida, and she said she'd heard a lot about me from Stinson. We hit it right off immediately. She knew I was gay, but it didn't matter to her. She's straight, but she's really open to people and can get along with anybody." Eventually, Diane would become the most important -- and influential -- person in his life.

Five years later, she would say, "He's not really gay, you know. He tried to convince me that he was very gay, but I knew better all along. I just told him he didn't have to convince me, that it didn't really matter."

While operating the business he called Murphy's Paving, Jimmy surprised himself by discovering that from time to time, he was doing good quality driveway and roof sealing work. Although profits were considerably lower on those occasions, he enjoyed the feeling of satisfaction those jobs gave him. The other Travelers would have been appalled if they had known. As always, Jimmy's customers were provided with guarantees that the work would last, and although he regarded those guarantees as simply window-dressing to help with his sales pitch, he responded to complaints by repairing or retouching his work whenever necessary.

It was beginning to appear that Jimmy Burke had found a home.

On the other hand, the open road continued to beckon, so as summer became autumn, he found himself thinking more and more about driving to Florida so he could join his relatives and the other Travelers there. Finally, one crisp day in November, he hitched a travel trailer to his truck and headed for Orlando. "I wasn't there very long -- a few weeks before and after Christmas," he recalled later. He rented an apartment not far from where his parents were camped, and he parked his trailer at a vacant lot with a "For Sale" sign on it. "I didn't work the truck, but I sold a couple of trailers."

In the meantime, his older sister Cathy had married and divorced a non-Traveler during a three-month personal independence period, and Peggy had convinced Cathy to share expenses by renting a mobile home with her just off the Orange Blossom Trail. Sixteen-year-old Peggy and nineteen-year-old Cathy supported themselves, against their parents' wishes, by dancing topless in a go-go club called

Mister Big Stuff's Topless Bedroom. Jimmy recalled, "Mom and Dad gave Peggy a lot of grief about what she was doin', so she quit the job, moved out of the trailer park and came to live with me."

Soon, he would have a second young house guest.

One almost needs a scorecard to follow the exploits of the Irish Travelers. There are so many Travelers, often related, with the same or similar names that maintaining a list of players is nearly impossible at times. Typically, children in one branch of a family are named in honor of adults in another branch; then, in reverse fashion, children in the second branch are named after adult members of the first one. Thus, a family such as the Burkes might include as many as a dozen individuals named Winifred or John.

Jimmy Burke had two aunts named Winifred. One was his father's sister who died. The other Winifred was married to Jimmy's father's late brother, John. The Aunt Winifred who died was Wanda Mary Normile's real mother; she also gave birth to a son named John Young and three other children, all of whom were turned over to relatives after Winifred's death. The other Aunt Winifred was the mother of Jimmy's first cousins, Beatrice Ann (also known as Bridget Ann), Peggy Marie and John Burke Jr.

After the first Winifred died, her teenage son John Young was sent to Fort Worth to live with John Burke Jr. and his wife Margaret. But within six months, the boy had gotten into so much trouble in Texas that John and Margaret decided they could not handle him. They placed him at Boys Town near Omaha, Nebraska. Next, Jimmy's uncle, James Burke, who operates scams out of Cleveland, Ohio, agreed to try raising the boy. He and his wife also gave up after six months and were ready to return him to Boys Town when Jimmy's brother and sister-in-law, Pat and Rose Mary, offered to take him in.

Three months later, when Pat returned home after working out of his truck all day, he found his wife standing outside their trailer, her face red and her eyes flashing. "I want you to get that monster out of here," Rose Mary said. "He's no good, and I don't want him around my kids. If you can't find someone else to take him, you're gonna have to send him back to Boys Town."

When Jimmy heard about Rose Mary's demands, he knew she meant what she said, even though he figured she was exaggerating her complaints about John. "I thought that John had just never really been given a chance." He also felt a debt of gratitude to John's mother, his aunt. "She was a wonderful woman. She was a Traveler, but she wasn't like one. She never lived as a Traveler. She struggled to survive; she never had much, but she never wanted much. She just wanted to be happy. She was the best aunt a kid could want. She did everything she could for us. Even though she had four or five kids of her own, whenever she was around, she'd come and get us. She'd take us to Disney World and on tours.

"I knew none of the other relatives would do nothing for John, and he'd end up back at Boys Town. So I volunteered to help. I talked with John and told him he could stay with me and work for me in the truck." That was a decision Jimmy would regret, and one that would haunt him for years. During the next three months, while seventeen-year-old Jimmy provided food and shelter for his sister and his cousin in Florida, John proved to be more than Jimmy could handle.

"When we stayed at motels, he'd break into the Coke machines and cigarette machines, or he'd call all over the country on the telephone and charge the calls to other people's rooms. Then the manager would come around, and I'd have to pay for the damages or a fifty or one-hundred-dollar phone bill in order to keep John out of jail."

One night, John swiped the keys to Jimmy's truck and took it on a joy ride around Orlando. When he returned, the truck's front end was smashed. "He tried to cover up and said he didn't do it. I started thinkin': He was lyin', but he was doin' it convincingly; maybe he had the makings of a good con artist." However, Jimmy later learned that John had been involved in a hit-and-run accident, and police were searching for the truck and driver. Finally, Jimmy decided that he, like the other relatives, could not control or influence John, so he tracked down the boy's father in Cocoa Beach.

"I told him it was time he did something for that kid, and he came over and picked up John." Exactly three years later, Jimmy would learn that John was using Jimmy's name on an I.D. while he worked a series of scams in Florida that landed him in prison. Not long after being released from a two-year prison stint, John and his girlfriend went to a drive-in theater near Jacksonville. On the way home, John's truck blew a tire, and when he got out to repair it, a semi-truck rig struck him and killed him.

When Jimmy and Peggy left Orlando early in 1978, they drove to New York, where Jimmy sold his trailer, then went to Elkhart to pick up another one and begin traveling with their sister Wanda and her husband Billy. From there, it was on to Charleston, West Virginia, where they visited with Pat and Rose Mary, then back to Elkhart to buy another trailer before going on to Jamestown, New York. In Elkhart the second time, Peggy decided to try shoplifting at the K-Mart south of town while Jimmy picked up his trailer. Never the family's most accomplished shoplifter, Peggy was spotted by a security guard and arrested. The incident was considered her first offense because she was carrying I.D. under the name of Evelyn Hernandez. Jimmy posted bond for her, and they skipped town.

On the way to New York, they stopped near Cleveland at a large department store in Shaker Heights. Jimmy recalled, "She had stole some stuff, but she seen a woman watching her, so she threw it under a rack and left the store. The woman came out and tried to flag us down.

Peggy said, "Keep goin'. Keep goin'."

Jimmy replied, "No, if I keep goin', she's gonna write down my tag number and have us picked up. You didn't get nothin', did you?"

"No."

"Okay, then we'll stop. They can't do nothin' since you didn't take nothin' out of the store."

They stopped and allowed the woman to search both Peggy and the car. Police officers arrived, and they also searched Peggy and the car. "The woman went back inside and found the stuff that Peggy had balled up in her purse before throwing it under the rack, and they still arrested Peggy for shoplifting. I didn't know they could do that. It probably would been thrown out if she'd gone to court, but I posted another $200 bond, and we left town."

Back in Jamestown, Jimmy met and became romantically involved with a homosexual named Buck. He also developed a warm, close relationship with Diane, although she still did not know his background. He told her his nickname was Danny, partly because at the time, he was using the Daniel Burke alias in some of his scams. "She'd come out to the trailer, and we'd have cookouts, or we'd go out and have a good time. She had four kids, but sometimes she'd leave her kids with somebody and we'd take off to New York City for the weekend. We got really close."

Any possibility of a heterosexual romance with Diane seemed destined to fail, however, especially when Jimmy, Buck and a woman named Kathy left Jamestown and rented a house in Cleveland. There, Jimmy supported the trio by selling travel trailers throughout northeast Ohio. Several times, Jimmy joined forces with his brother Edward and his wife Elizabeth, and they enriched themselves with various scams in the Buckeye State.

On May 27, Ed and Elizabeth -- the Travelers call her Betty -- parked a new 28-foot Rogue travel trailer at a motel near Elyria. Ohio, and advertised it for sale in the *Cleveland Plain Dealer.* The ad stated: "Used two weeks, cost $7,975, will sacrifice for $5,200." Immediately, a local resident named Hart offered to buy it and gave them a $100 check to hold the trailer until he could accumulate the $5,000 agreed-upon purchase price. Before he could do that, Elizabeth sold it to another local man, Ora N. Shaw. When Shaw registered the coach with the bureau of motor vehicles, he said he paid only $1,200 for it; he was charged just $48 in state sales tax. Elizabeth mailed Hart's deposit check to him with an explanation that the trailer had been sold. She added that a new 25-footer would be delivered within a week, and she would be happy to sell that trailer to him.

Because the first trailer was supposedly being sold due to the Burkes' financial hardships, Hart suspected a scam, and he complained to the Elyria police department. Officers there alerted Ohio's "Gypsy Hunter," Wayne Johnson. His investigations revealed the Burkes had bought, sold or registered dozens of travel trailers in Ohio during the previous twelve months. Among those was a 27-foot Kentucky Traveler trailer that Jimmy Burke bought new for $3,200. A few days later, he parked it at the Turnpike Motel near Cleveland and advertised it for sale in the local newspaper. Stow resident Paul D. Forquer noticed the "For Sale" sign on it when he drove past the motel, and he stopped to look at it.

"I wasn't really in the market for a trailer," Forquer recalled, "so when the young man told me he was asking $5,595 for it, I told him I couldn't pay more than $4,800. He sounded sorta desperate to sell it so he could get goin' to Florida. Said he'd decided to marry a girl in Florida and had to get down there right away. I said, 'Listen, here's my card. I live around the corner. If you don't get any buyers before you've got to go and you'll accept $4,800, call me.' The next day, he called me. I went up and made the deal. I kept it two years and sold it for more than I paid for it."

One of Ed's customers was Joseph P. Dalonzo of Wellsville. When informed he had purchased his trailer from a con artist and was told about the type of stories the Travelers relate to their victims, he responded, "Yeah, you're gettin' pretty close. You're right around my neighborhood! It was parked on the highway south of here. He said he'd gotten transferred to Florida and had to give up the trailer and sell it right away. I liked it, but took a couple of days deciding to buy it."

Dalonzo explained, "My old lady had been buggin' me about campin', so I said okay. Burke said he paid about $7,000 for it, but I couldn't tell whether that was high or low because I wasn't a camper before I bought it. It looked pretty damned good, so when I got home, I mentioned it to my wife. We took a ride up back there. The price was $5,100, and I told him I couldn't afford that much. So he went down a little bit on the price, and I told him, 'If I can finance it, I'm interested.' He talked to his wife and then said, 'My wife said you can have it for $4,795.'"

Ed promised he would deliver the trailer because Dalonzo did not have a hitch on his vehicle. "He was drivin' a new pickup truck, and there was a lot of new blacktopping equipment -- tanks and a compressor outfit and the like -- in the back end of it. I remember he was a very fidgety guy. He was awful excited about gettin' the money, and he said he preferred cash. In fact, when I handed it to him, he rolled it up in a ball and put it in his pocket and held his hand over it. I said to my wife later, 'Boy, if I didn't know better, I'd say those people were con artists.'"

A few days after Officer Johnson began his investigation, Elizabeth telephoned Hart and told him that the new 25-foot Rogue trailer had arrived, directly from the Marauder Travelers factory in Wakarusa, Indiana. Hart agreed to meet Elizabeth at Sommers Trailer Park Campground near Elyria, and he informed Wayne Johnson about the meeting. Johnson and Elyria Detective Don Waite arrived at the campground while Elizabeth haggled with Hart over the trailer's price. She and Ed were arrested and charged with selling new motor vehicles without a dealer's license and giving false information to a state agency -- Elizabeth had claimed she resided at 800 West Main Street in West Jefferson, a vacant lot. Parked at the campground were new Safari and Rogue travel trailers, one registered to Ed's father Edward and the other, the old man said, owned by his son Daniel, whom Edward claimed was in the hospital at Ashtabula. Ed and Elizabeth posted $200 in bonds and paid $75 in fines. Informed they were being investigated for complaints about blacktopping frauds in Madison County, Ed and Elizabeth immediately left Ohio and did not return for two years.

Ironically, Johnson did such a good job of harassing and arresting Travelers that between 1978 and the mid-1980s, Ohio was given a wide berth by most of the con artist families, and as a result, there was not enough investigative work to keep him busy, so he was reassigned. A few months later, he quit his job with the department of motor vehicles and went to work with a mortgage title service company in Texas.

Still consulted by law enforcement agencies around the country, Johnson offers this advice to anyone considering investigating Travelers: "You've got to I.D. each one. And I don't care how many different names they use. They've always got different driver's licenses, and their driver's licenses never match the registrations, and nothing else ever matches. And none of the stories pan out. Fingerprints and photographs are the only positive I.D.'s that matter. All the registrations and driver's licenses come and go with the wind."

He added, "They've been here since the beginning of time, but they don't exist, especially as far as the federal government is concerned. They don't pay taxes, and most of them don't even have Social Security numbers. They're all pretty flaky, but I'll tell you what; they've all got a pocketful of money. You can never get the truth out of them, but it's easy to get them to contradict themselves. They always give their customers such a good deal. They say, 'You'll only have to pay sales tax on one thousand dollars, even though we're selling the trailer to you for three thousand five hundred. But if anybody asks you any questions about us and what we sold to you, you don't know anything about it.' They cover their corners so well that it's hard to get people to testify against them."

Expressing the same frustration as every other police officer who has tried to arrest Travelers for their vehicle sales scams, "Gypsy Hunter" Johnson said, "Every time I tried to run a title chain, it would always come back with confusing information because the middle name wouldn't be the same or the address would be different or something else wouldn't quite fit. It was something to pull your hair out over."

That fall, Jimmy considered whether it was time to release his homosexuality from the closet. Once again, he was drawn to Florida and the Travelers he knew would spend their winter there. But now he was not living alone; Buck was with him. "I really hadn't broken away from the Travelers much; I still felt an obligation to go to Florida with them every winter. I couldn't go down there with Buck and then take him around to meet my people because they would automatically know what was happenin'. If I had a girl with me who wasn't a Traveler, they might talk about it, but they wouldn't really care; nobody would make a big deal about it. But if I went down there with a guy, and it's not some black guy that I've got workin' with me, they'd know what I was into. Yet, if I didn't take him, what was I goin' to say to him? We'd lived together for several months, and no matter what I said, he would think I was tryin' to get away from him to be with somebody else. So I ended up takin' him down there with me.

"We rented a house about six blocks from my Uncle Doug's house, and I put the trailer out on the road for sale. Buck would sit in the trailer for me in case somebody came to look at it, and I was workin' the truck on and off. About two weeks before Christmas, my Uncle Jimmy Burke -- my father's brother, who I'm named after -- stopped by the trailer to see me one day because he thought I was there. He seen this guy in there, but he didn't know if the guy was a Traveler or not, and when he talked to him a couple of minutes, he figured out the guy wasn't a Traveler. The guy told Uncle Jimmy he was stayin' with me, and my uncle went back to the campground."

Jimmy's mother had harbored suspicions about her son's sexual preferences for many years, but she'd never discussed her concerns with her husband, and Edward was oblivious to Jimmy's chosen lifestyle. Edward was, therefore, astonished when his brother informed him Jimmy was living with a homosexual *country* man.

"By the time I got to the campground that night," Jimmy said, "everybody was askin' Mom and Dad about me. And Dad was just about ready to flip out. Mom asked me about Buck, and I told her the truth. Mom and Dad raved on and on that if any of our people saw me with that guy, who wasn't one of us, what were they goin' to say? It ended up in a big argument with everybody yellin' at everyone else, and Buck and me broke up over it. I got mad and left. I went back to New York, sold my trailer, picked up another one and drove back to Florida again."

Wanda and Billy, camped in Tampa, asked Jimmy to spend Christmas with them. The Travelers in Florida -- Irish, Scottish and English alike -- were planning a huge Christmas Eve dance, and Wanda wanted to attend. An entire nightclub on University Boulevard in Tampa had been reserved, and when Jimmy arrived with his sister and brother-in-law, the place was packed with more than one thousand Travelers.

The mixture of English, Irish and Scottish Travelers, free-flowing booze, loud music and young men on the prowl for eligible women was an explosive combination. There was little doubt in anyone's mind how the evening would end. Ordinarily, Jimmy would have steered clear of that sort of environment, but on that night, he was in a foul mood.

He recalled, "Me and my sister and brother-in-law were sittin' at a table over by the dance floor. I got up and went out to dance, and when I came back to the table, Billy was gone. I asked, 'Where did Billy go?' and Wanda said, 'He went to get us some drinks.' A few minutes later, Eddie McDonald came running over and said, 'Jimmy, your brother-in-law is in a fight out there.' So I went outside. It turned out, some local guy had stumbled in and didn't know it was a private get-together, and he had made a pass at one of our girls. My brother-in-law hit him, and him and Billy had gotten into it."

Billy did not realize it, but the gate-crasher was not alone. Once he and Billy were outside the building, he shouted for help, and half-a-dozen big Florida toughs responded. Together, they all attacked Billy. As Jimmy came outside, he was amazed by the scene. "All the rest of our people -- the Travelers -- were just standin' there," he said, "and I couldn't understand it. You don't just stand there and watch someone beat up on your own people, you know, so I jumped into it and started helpin' out my brother-in-law, and we ended up both gettin' the shit beat out of us while the other Travelers just stood there and watched."

In the distance, police sirens could be heard, so the local toughs ran away into the darkness. Billy's face was a mass of cuts and welts, and blood streamed from his nose and mouth. He spat out two broken teeth. Jimmy's shirt had been ripped from him, and his ribs and kidneys had been beaten seriously. He coughed, spit up blood and then vomited in the grass. With the fight over, the crowd had thinned, but several Scottish Travelers were still standing nearby. Billy yelled at them, "You Scotch bastards! You stood there and watched some of your own people get beat up by the refs!"

The Scottish Travelers shouted back insults and challenges. "There were four or five of them that I had known since I was a little kid who were standin' a few cars over," Jimmy said. "One of them yelled somethin' about the Burkes, and when he did, I jumped across the car on top of him, and two of his friends jumped on me. We was sluggin' each other, and Billy came over and started pullin' 'em off. I was eighteen at the time, and they were boys my own age. Billy was thirty-two or thirty-three. There were only a few Irish around, but they lined up with Billy and me. Things cooled down a little, so Billy and Wanda and I left."

The trio was camped on Route 301 outside Tampa while most of the various Traveler families were gathered in their favorite Florida campground, the Happy Traveler. "Billy kept on drinkin' a lot, and then he decided he wanted to go over to the Happy Traveler and jump on those Scotch. My sister was tryin' to get him to go to bed. She said, 'If you go over there, you're gonna end up spendin' Christmas Eve in jail. If you want to go over there, do it tomorrow.'"

Billy answered, "No, I'm goin' now! Jimmy, are you with me or not?"

Jimmy responded, "All right."

Wanda said, "Well, I'm goin' too," and the three of them drove to the Happy Traveler. There, Billy pulled a baseball bat out of the bed of his truck and walked around the campground banging it on the sides of the trailers, yelling, "Come out here, you Scotch bastards!"

Scottish, English and Irish Travelers alike began appearing outside their trailers. Jimmy recalled, "Billy went to his brother's trailer and drug his brother out of bed so he could help us fight, but his brother said, 'Go home. I'm in bed and my kids are in bed waitin' for Christmas. You better go to bed yourself.' So then Billy got into it with his brother, and me and Wanda had to break that up. We finally got him back over to our campground and put him to bed.

"Then a few minutes later, a truck pulled up in front of Wanda and Billy's trailer, and about five or six Scotch boys got out of it. One of 'em said, 'Jimmy Burke! You ain't nothin' but Irish shit, and I'm Scotch, and I'm gonna beat the shit out of ya, so why don't you come out here?'

"I went out on the road, and I said, 'I'll fight ya, one on one, but

I ain't gonna fight all of ya at one time.' Then here comes my brother-in-law out of the trailer, and he's carryin' his pistol. He goes, 'My brother-in-law will beat any of ya, but you're gonna fight him one-on-one, and if anyone goes to jump in, I'm gonna pull the trigger.' Me and this one guy got into a fight, and I beat the shit out of him, so the others took off runnin'. They didn't even get back into the truck; they just left. The guy I beat up got up and got back in his truck and left then too, so we went inside. We'd hardly gotten to bed when the owner of the campground came runnin' out and told us we had to leave the campground, and she was callin' the police, but we talked her into lettin' us stay the rest of the night. The next mornin', the Scotch boys' mother brought them back over and made them apologize."


For many years, the two oldest Burke brothers -- Ed and Pat -- were well known among all the Travelers for their fighting abilities. But Pat, in particular, was even at that time building the fearful reputation that he would continue to enjoy for many years as a cruel, violent man with a tendency to settle disputes with either a gun or a knife. Blond-haired and carrot-red-bearded Pat, who other Travelers nicknamed "Red Pat," liked to be called "The Viking," and he even had a license plate on the front of his favorite royal blue Ford Ranchero that said "Viking." A few weeks before the Christmas Eve fight, another driver had cut in front of Pat in Tampa and nearly hit his sporty truck, so Pat had pulled the man out of his car and beaten his face bloody before climbing back into his Ranchero and leaving the fellow unconscious in the street. Several witnesses had given his license plate number and description to police, and a warrant was issued for his arrest. Pat had left Florida only minutes before officers arrived at the Happy Traveler with the warrant, and he did not return to central Florida again for sixteen years.

Pat's behavior in public was an absolute violation of the Travelers' code of conduct. Although it was perfectly acceptable to swindle and rob country people, the use of violence against non-Travelers was seriously frowned upon. By assaulting a local citizen, Pat risked focusing unwanted attention on all the Travelers. Word of his actions spread quickly among the Traveler community, and no one would have been surprised if police would have retaliated with raids on the Orlando and Tampa campgrounds.

Years later, Tampa Detective John Wood commented about Pat's reputation: "Now that's a dangerous guy. There are a lot of people in the Traveler community who are considered dangerous -- not necessarily to outsiders, but within that community. But the typical violence that occurs among the Travelers is fistfights and beatings -- maybe even beatings with baseball bats. When knives and guns are involved, that's an aberration. As a matter of fact, they view it that way. They'll tell you they always settle things with their fists. If somebody pulls a knife or goes and gets a gun, that's a whole different world for them. They don't like those people; they don't like to be around them because they attract attention, and they're frightened of them because most of the Travelers, as violent as they are within the Traveler ranks, don't use weapons. And you don't go to a gunfight with your fists or a ball bat. Guys like the Viking are rare in the Traveler community, and the Travelers themselves consider them extremely dangerous."

When the mother of the young Scottish Travelers forced her sons to apologize to Jimmy for their insults the night before, she was not upset that her boys had started a fight; she was worried that Pat might return to Tampa for retribution.

# 7

# Betrayal

Cruel, violent and dangerous Patrick Burke had no involvement with the scam against Walt Disney World Company until July of 1993 -- eight months after Wanda Mary reported that she had been raped at the Caribbean Beach Resort and a couple of weeks after attorney Ernest H. Eubanks Jr. demanded that Disney pay his client a three-million-dollar settlement.

What follows is the official, public-record versions of events. Participants disagree on what actually took place, however, and their versions will be explored later.

After hiring Eubanks to represent Wanda Mary, Jessee took her sister/cousin back to Maine, and Jessee resumed the settled life she had been trying to live for the previous six years. She worked part time for a national cosmetics company and shared expenses with a friend, but she was having difficulty making ends meet. Although she maintained her determination to follow a non-Traveler lifestyle, it was hard to forget the days when she traveled freely and had more money than she could spend -- the days before she changed her name to Jessee, when she was named Wanda O'Roarke, and her husband Billy provided a comfortable living for her and her two children.

But Billy had been dead since 1983, and now her children were grown, off on their own, and she seldom saw them. Now, she could definitely use her share of the Disney scam. Almost every day, Jessee saw opportunities to make considerably more money than she earned by selling cosmetics to suburban housewives. Ideas for swindles, scams and frauds occurred to her constantly; it was difficult -- and sometimes impossible -- to banish them from her mind. But Jessee was determined to lead a straight life. She knew she was not the first Traveler to try that. Her brother Jimmy had tried to break away from the Travelers once, and he had failed. Because Jessee had supportive friends around her, though, she thought she could succeed where the other Travelers had not.

John Wood, an investigator with the Pinellas County consumer fraud office in Florida, has studied Travelers for many years, and he has also observed several clan members attempt to break away from their inherited lifestyle. Had he known the struggle Jessee was facing, he would have sympathized with her.

"People wonder why they don't opt out of the lifestyle," Wood said, "but when you look at the way they live, and because theirs is a closed society -- the wife is a Traveler, the parents are Travelers, their in-laws are Travelers, their kids are Travelers, all their friends are Travelers, all their relatives are Travelers -- if they want to get out, they sacrifice all that. Nobody will have much to do with them after that, and they certainly won't be as closely tied to their friends and relatives as they were. And if they settle down, they'll be alone most of the time because their families are still going to be elsewhere; they're not going to hang around just because one person decides he's going to settle down permanently."

Wood's fellow policeman, Orange County Detective John McMahan, added, "And they're going to make markedly less money, considering the type of work they'll have to do because of their limited education and skills."

Wood nodded agreement. "They don't have education enough to

do anything else, although I'm convinced that the ones I've met could do a really good paint job or paving job if they wanted to; they *know* how to do it right. They don't choose to because it would take too long and their overhead would be too high."

Coupled with Jessee's struggle to earn a satisfactory living was a constant series of disagreements with Wanda Mary. The young mother had no intention of leading the life of a non-Traveler. She was accustomed to complete freedom of movement and to having every luxury she wanted. She agreed to live with Jessee only until the lawsuit against Disney was settled, and then she intended to travel widely and participate more actively in the Irish Traveler lifestyle of her family. Meanwhile, she wanted to party and live independently with no interference from Jessee.

Recognizing she could not support herself as well as her sister and the baby on what she earned, Jessee helped Wanda Mary find a furnished apartment, and then she arranged for her sister to receive welfare payments and food stamps. Jessee told Wanda Mary, "I'll help you all I can, but I can't hand you fifty-dollar bills so you can go out and play at the malls, and I can't come over here and babysit while you run around and do whatever you want to do."

Wanda Mary complained by phone to her brothers, Pat and Jimmy, that Jessee was trying to control her life. Pat sympathized but Jimmy advised her to be patient until the lawsuit could be settled. Pat suggested that maybe he ought to handle Wanda Mary's discussions with the attorney for her. According to police reports filed later, he hinted that she should consider settling for considerably less than the three million dollars that Eubanks had originally demanded. Many months later, Wanda Mary disputed that during a conversation with the writer. She said Pat urged her to drop the lawsuit because he was afraid she would be arrested and sent to prison. He suggested that whatever position she took, Wanda Mary should escape Jessee's controlling influence by traveling with him and his family.

Most of the Burkes believed that if Disney offered a settlement,

Jimmy would insist upon accepting it. What they did not know was that Jimmy had already decided -- for his own private reasons -- that no settlement under a million dollars would be acceptable. He had discussed various options with his sister Peggy and had told her, "I want this score to be the largest ever pulled off by an Irish Traveler."

Waiting for the lawsuit to be concluded was taking its toll on Jessee. From the beginning, she insisted later, she had not been enthusiastic about the scam, and in fact, while Jimmy was in Wanda Mary's hotel room tying her wrists to the bed, Jessee said she was sitting in a restaurant trying to figure out how to convince the others to call off the scheme. As the weeks turned into months, Jessee became convinced that there were too many possibilities the scam could be exposed, and she did not want to risk the new life she had tried to build for herself during the previous six years. Several times, she said, she tried to convince Wanda Mary to drop the lawsuit and forget about collecting money from Disney. But each time, Wanda Mary refused. Later, Wanda Mary would deny that and insist that she, not Jessee, wanted to drop the suit, but Jessee threatened to beat her and have her arrested.

Filling more the role of strict mother than that of an older sister, Jessee also tried to influence Wanda Mary's choice of friends, but she failed. She said she learned Wanda Mary was having an affair with a Portland man who worked at the Salvation Army and boasted he was a member of the Ku Klux Klan. She confronted Wanda Mary with what she knew and said, "I won't put up with it. I won't have you sleeping around with this one or that one. Until you get a divorce, you're a married woman, and I want you to remember that."

Jessee said that when her sister was confronted by evidence of her affair, Wanda Mary fell back on Irish Traveler tradition and lied to her sister. Jessee slapped her. Then slapped her again. And again. Wanda Mary later denied Jessee's allegations and said Jessee did not slap her, but beat her with fists, blacking her eyes and splitting her lip.

Three days later, Jessee said, Pat arrived in Portland with his family, obviously summoned by Wanda Mary.

About that time, Eubanks telephoned with Disney's offer to pay a $200,000 settlement, but following his advice, the family agreed not to accept the offer. Jimmy was not told about the offer because the others mistakenly believed he would have insisted upon accepting it. Excited, Wanda Mary and Pat fantasized about the ultimate conclusion of the lawsuit and potential size of their score. They discussed plans for dividing the money, and during those discussions, Jessee claimed, they decided Jimmy should not be given a share. Wanda Mary later denied that. Jessee said Wanda Mary announced that she intended to give Jimmy's share to Pat. Wanda Mary and Pat promised that Jessee would get part of any settlement, although they were vague about how large her share would be. Jessee said she surprised them by responding, "I don't want any part of the settlement. I just want it to end."

After learning about those statements later, Wanda Mary insisted it was Pat, not Jessee, who did not want a share of the settlement. "Jessee was the one who said we shouldn't give Jimmy his share," Wanda Mary reported.

In any case, the end Jessee wished for was just a few months ahead. After Eubanks formally filed suit against Disney on June 23 and the family read news reports in which legal analysts predicted cash awards of up to $20,000,000 if the case went to a jury, Wanda Mary and Pat sketched out an endless variety of ways they intended to spend their shares. Jessee said Wanda Mary told Pat that Jessee had tried to talk her into dropping the lawsuit. A few days later, Pat and his family left Maine towing a travel trailer. Wanda Mary and her baby went with them.

Over the next three months, family members communicated by telephone, and tentative plans were made to hold a strategy meeting in Florida with Eubanks. Jimmy was not told about the meeting. Jessee said Pat insisted that he would handle all discussions with the attorney from that point forward; Wanda Mary denied that and stated, "Pat wanted nothing to do with the attorney." Convinced there was still an outstanding warrant for his arrest from an assault on a Florida motorist in 1978, the Viking decided that when he visited central Florida for the first time in fifteen years, he would use his brother Edward's identity, complete with a Virginia driver's license, and his wife Rose Mary would carry I.D. in their oldest daughter Winifred Ann's name.

According to police reports filed later, on a Saturday afternoon in September 1993, Jessee checked into the Scottish Inn Motel near Youngstown, Ohio. Her brother Pat and his family were camped in a nearby mobile home park; Wanda Mary and her baby were with them. The family met that evening in Pat's trailer to discuss plans for their trip to Florida. Eubanks had already provided Jessee and Wanda Mary with airline tickets to Orlando.

After dinner, family members discussed their travels and the adventures they had experienced since they were together in Maine, and Pat said he'd had a couple of unpleasant encounters with some members of the English Traveler clan. He told Jessee, "If them English ever threaten me or my family, I'm gonna kill 'em." Jessee laughed, thinking he was joking.

"You think I'm kidding? C'mere, I wanna show you somethin'."

He led Jessee into the rear bedroom of the trailer, where he pulled loose a piece of trim board from the wall near the bed. From behind the trim, he retrieved a Smith & Wesson nine-millimeter semi-automatic pistol. He pulled a clip from the butt of the gun and showed Jessee that it was full of bullets. Then he pointed the unloaded pistol at his sixteen-year-old daughter's head and pulled the trigger. Young Winifred Ann screamed, and the Viking laughed.

The next day, in direct opposition to Pat's instructions, Jessee telephoned her Uncle Doug in Florida and told him that she, Wanda

Mary and Pat would fly into Orlando on Monday to meet with the attorney. She warned him that Pat and Wanda Mary did not want him to know they were coming or that the meeting was taking place because they were concerned he might tell Jimmy or another member of the family. Jessee said if it were possible, she wanted to talk with Doug while she was in Orlando.

Monday, Jessee drove her truck to the mobile home court to pick up Wanda Mary and Pat. The plan was for her to then drive to the airport and store her truck while the three of them flew to Orlando for the meeting with the attorney. When she arrived at Pat's trailer, he was not there; he was getting a haircut. Taking advantage of his absence, Jessee asked Wanda Mary if she could talk with her in the bedroom, and then she appealed once more to Wanda Mary to consider dropping the lawsuit.

Wanda Mary responded with anger. "This is none of your business anymore," she said. "If you don't want to be a part of it, you don't have to go with us. I don't even want you to go! You aren't a part of it anymore anyway, so just go away and forget it, and you won't get any of the money."

Jessee answered, "I'm not out of it. I'm into it up to my ears. But I'm not going on with it any farther, and either you agree to drop the lawsuit, or I'm gonna tell the truth when we get to Florida!" Jessee walked back into the living room, and at that moment, Pat returned. He went into the bedroom where Wanda Mary was, and she told him what Jessee had just said.

He turned and glared at Jessee. His rotund, red-bearded face, always somewhat naturally flushed, was now dark crimson from anger. Pat's wife and children exchanged worried glances and then waited for either Pat or Wanda to react. It was clear to everyone that something bad was about to happen.

Pat rushed forward from the bedroom like a charging bull. He grabbed Jessee and shook her. "Get the fuck out of here!" he shouted. "You ain't goin' to Florida with us!" He raised one huge, beefy fist and hit her in the face. She ducked her head and put her arms up, and he struck her repeatedly on the head.

Jessee responded, "I don't care what you say! I'm goin'!"

Pat continued punching her, then threw her onto the couch and pinned her there. He turned to his son, Sean, and said, "Go get my gun from the bedroom. You know where it is."

Sean ran into the bedroom, found the pistol in its hiding place and returned, handing it to his father. Pat put the muzzle of the weapon to his sister's head and pulled the trigger three times.

# 8

# Insurance

Three weeks after fighting with the Scottish Travelers in Tampa, Jimmy Burke hit the road again. Within a short time, due to a set of fluke circumstance, he would soon stumble onto a new scam. Posing as a self-employed contractor named James C. Murphy, and with excellent credit references from businesses in Jamestown, New York, he bought a new Chevrolet El Camino truck in Atlanta by providing a $2,400 down payment and financing the rest through General Motors Acceptance Corporation. Before he returned to Jamestown, he intended to change his identity again, so he bought the car knowing full well that he would never make a loan payment.

"I had it only a month, and I was on my way to Pennsylvania when some guy in an old truck two cars ahead of me dropped something off it. It was rainin' hard, and the guy in front of me in a Jeep slammed on his brakes, and I rammed into the back of him. His Jeep wasn't damaged, just my truck, and since I was at fault, nothin' was done about it. The truck looked bad, but I could still drive it, and I didn't have enough money at the time to get it fixed.

"Later, I went down to Georgia to be with Peggy, and she had wrecked her car too. She had totalled it. She'd only put $200 down on it and had not yet made a payment, but she had insurance on it, so the insurance company paid her $900 for it. We went to the K-Mart on the Gordon Highway, and in the parking lot, this old guy pulled out in front of me in a little Honda Civic. I started to stop, but I said to myself, 'Hell, let him hit me and maybe I can get my truck fixed.' So I ran into the side of him, and his insurance company paid me $1,000. But even though I had the money, I didn't want to get my truck fixed. I needed the money too bad. So I said to myself, 'I'll do that again and get some more money so I can fix the truck.'"

Jimmy and Peggy drove to Columbus and staged a similar accident. That time, the insurance company paid Jimmy $1,400, partly because the triple-crunched El Camino looked worse each time it was involved in a wreck. Since he had paid very little for the El Camino, he staged several more accidents with it before trading it on a new Thunderbird. He kept the T-Bird a week and traded it for a new red and white pickup truck. Then it was on to Atlanta, where Jimmy arranged for his truck to be struck by an old fellow leaving Piedmont Park.

"He didn't have any insurance or any driver's license," Jimmy said, "but he promised he'd pay for the repairs if I would get an estimate. I got an estimate for a little over $600, but I put a '1' in front of the six and made it $1,600, and he paid me in cash."

In Columbia, South Carolina, another accident netted $900 more. Then Jimmy drove back to Jamestown, and Peggy hitched a ride to Florida. In New York, Jimmy taught the insurance fraud to his seventeen-year-old brother Paul, and for a month, they staged accidents throughout northern Pennsylvania, collecting about $10,000 from insurance companies.

Jimmy's insurance scam quickly became famous among other Irish Travelers, and it wasn't long before variations of it were being used all over America. Here's how the most common variation operates today:

A Traveler selects a town that has a few friendly, low-key automobile dealerships in it. If he does not have a telephone in his RV or at a motel room, he simply memorizes the numbers of a couple pay phones in a location where a member of his family can answer the phones each time they ring, and he orders business cards printed with those telephone numbers on them. Next, he'll drive through residential neighborhoods looking for a home with a driveway that needs to be paved or sealed. He tells the family living there, "I'm Joe Gorman, and I just opened a paving business here in town. I had a business in a town fifty miles away for twenty years, but I just moved here and I'm trying to get my business established. I need something to prove to people I can do the work. So what I'll do for you is put in a whole new driveway for you free. And the only thing you have to do to get it is this: I want to be able to give people your name and phone number, and if anyone calls you, you say, 'Yes, Mr. Gorman does my work, has done it for years and does a real good job. I paid him $3,000 for paving my driveway, and I always give him $300 for sealing it.'"

He convinces the family he will provide them with a few thousand dollars worth of paving work at no charge. And then he'll actually do the work! Next, he'll go to an automobile dealership and tell the salesman he's lived in town all his life and he owns his own business and earns $75,000 a year. He wants to put $5,000 down on a $15,000 car, but he's never financed a vehicle before because he's always paid cash for everything. He wants to establish his credit by purchasing a car now.

The salesman says, "Well, even though you don't have any established credit, with that kind of down payment, if we can verify that you earn the amount of money you say you do, I can get the car financed for you."

The Traveler responds, "Sure. Here's my business card with my office and residential phone numbers; you can call the office to verify employment and income, and here are the names of some people you can call. I do work for them every year."

Supported by the large down payment, verification of employment and income, and the comments of local residents who swear that Gorman has been doing work for them for years, financing of the Traveler's car almost certainly will be approved. But the day after he picks up his new car, he leaves town with no intention of ever making a loan payment on it. He might have to pay $50 or $100 for insurance in order to get the car, but once it's in his possession, he won't pay insurance premiums either. However, he will leave town with an insurance card verifying that he does have insurance in case he's ever asked about it by the police. Then he can stage accidents with the car for a few months and collect $10,00 or $15,000 on it before he abandons it and starts over in another town with another new vehicle.

By the spring of 1979, Jimmy had reconciled with his friend Buck, and they were living together in a house overlooking Lake Chautauqua near Jamestown. Determined to reconcile with his parents too, Jimmy planned a large party to celebrate his father's fifty-fifth birthday. All the family members except Peggy agreed to attend the event; no one knew where Peggy could be found. A few days before the party, Jimmy's friend Johnny McNally called him from Georgia and told him Peggy had been arrested for shoplifting at the Jane Fields department store near Augusta. Her bond -- set for the Peggy McNally alias she was using -- was $500, but she was broke. Jimmy immediately drove to Buffalo, hopped a plane to Augusta and posted her bond, then took her back to New York with him.

When Jimmy's parents arrived for the party, it was clear to them that their son and Buck were living together, but at first Edward remained silent about the issue. Jimmy recalled, "I had the place all decorated real nice and had two big cakes and all kinds of liquor sittin' around. My older brothers kept askin' me what Buck was doin' there. I told them he lived there, and I could hear them talkin' behind my back. My dad was a diabetic and not supposed to drink, but he did, and after two or three drinks, he would sometimes lose control. That time, he had a couple of drinks, and he started ravin' on about me bein' gay."

Edward grabbed Jimmy by the arm and pointed at Buck. He asked, "What are you doin' here with this guy? He's just a piece of trash, a queer, and I expect you to quit doin' whatever it is you're doin' with him."

Jimmy's mother interrupted, "Edward, please shut up."

"Hell no, I'm not gonna shut up. You're a Traveler, Jimmy. You're my son, and you're supposed to be a man, but you're livin' up here with all these refs and queers."

Wanda saw that her son was struggling to keep his anger from exploding at his father, and she told Edward, "Will you shut up? Your son is givin' you a birthday party and tryin' to be nice, but you just have to act up."

Edward looked around and realized the whole family was watching, concerned. He poured himself another drink and slumped into a chair. He was quiet the rest of the day. The next morning Edward and Wanda returned to Florida without telling anyone goodbye.

Irish Traveler Bobby White, for many years regarded as one of the clan's best and most successful con artists, was living at the Southern Sun motel in Orlando that winter, and due to poor health, was slow about leaving Florida when spring arrived. Just after the rest of the clan had dispersed to various parts of the U.S., Bobby had a heart attack and died. It took two weeks for word of his death to be spread among the Travelers, and his body was kept in cold storage until friends and relatives could return to Orlando for the funeral and wake. Jimmy and his younger brother Paul flew to Florida from New York in time to attend services at St. James Catholic Church, where Jimmy had been baptized. Like most members of the Northern Traveler clan, Bobby was to be buried at Woodlawn Cemetery in Winter Garden.

The funeral was attended by about two thousand Travelers. Scottish Travelers from the western states were there, including several individuals from the notorious Williamson contingent. A small group of English Travelers from Wisconsin and Louisiana attended, but kept to themselves somewhat apart from the rest. There were Irish Travelers from Fort Worth -- the so-called Greenhorn Carrolls; Southern Travelers from Murphy Village, the Sorries, were there too, and even several families of seldom-seen Mississippi Travelers from near Memphis made the trip to Florida. Travelers weren't the only ones in attendance, however. Police officers from all over Florida observed the funeral, burial and wake with a great deal of interest. Many of them carried cameras through which they fed dozens of rolls of film, and one central Florida detective said later that he filled an entire stenographer's notebook with automobile and truck license plate numbers. Even law enforcement agencies from Illinois, Ohio and New York sent representatives, and at least two special agents of the Federal Bureau of Investigations were on hand.

The caravan of automobiles and pickup trucks from Orlando to the cemetery was nearly eight miles long, and burial had to be delayed two hours until all the vehicles could be parked within walking distance of the gravesite. Huge floral displays required almost an acre of space around the grave. They included a life-size floral arrangement of a thoroughbred racehorse with a jockey on its back, representative of Bobby White's lifelong interest in the sport of kings; someone estimated that one display cost several thousand dollars. When Bobby's casket was finally carried to the famous con artist's final resting place, eight pall bearers had to be used because of the added weight of the gold and diamond jewelry, as well as large-denomination coins, that had been put into the casket before the lid was closed. An estimated thirty or forty thousand dollars worth of precious metal was buried with Bobby's body.

None of the Irish Travelers could remember a larger, more memorable funeral. The only one that even compared, in fact, was the funeral of Patty Rafferty, who had died a few years earlier. Patty, who emigrated from Ireland and was quite proud of his heritage, was buried in a green suit with shamrocks on it. A large four-leaf clover made entirely of flowers was placed on his grave, and Irish music was played at the wake.

Back in New York, Jimmy's relationship with Buck came to an end. Jimmy had taught Buck the art of writing bad checks, but Buck did not quite understand the principle of it, and he cashed several checks on Jimmy's personal bank account. "He really went overboard," Jimmy reported later. "He had $300 worth of new tires put on his car at Sears and then paid a garage for a new brake system with a $200 check he wrote. He bought a new sound system, with all new wiring, that cost several hundred dollars more. I didn't know anything about all that until I found out there was a warrant for my arrest for passing bad checks." Following an argument, Buck left the state. Six months later, Jimmy would be arrested on the bad check charges.

With Buck out of his life, Jimmy's relationship with Diane started to blossom. Not surprisingly, that relationship -- even though it was with a non-Traveler woman -- received the enthusiastic support of his family. Jimmy's mother met Diane during the summer of 1979 when Wanda decided to visit her son following one of her regular fights with her husband. Unannounced, she arrived at Jimmy's house with fifteen-year-old Winnie and eight-year-old Wanda Mary in tow.

After meeting Diane, she actively tried to fan the sparks of romance between the young woman and her son.

Jimmy said, "She asked me several times what was goin' on between me and Diane and whether we were goin' to get married. Clearly, that would have made her very happy. Me and Diane even started talkin' about it. I cared for her a lot, and she also cared for me, but we really didn't want to make no commitments until I was ready to settle down. I didn't feel I could ask her to marry me while I was runnin' all over the country."

There were other barriers to the relationship: Diane still believed his name was Daniel Burke, and she had no knowledge of the Irish Traveler lifestyle and Jimmy's part in it. Jimmy and Diane dated often, attending movies and going dancing at a new Jamestown disco, but periodically, his Irish Traveler heritage called to him, and he left New York to travel and work his scams.

Within a year, Jimmy's freestyle life would come crashing down around him, but before it did, he was surprised to realize one night while he was in Charleston, South Carolina, that he missed Diane dreadfully. He telephoned her at two o'clock in the morning, talked with her for an hour and, when the conversation ended, he drove to the airport and bought Diane a round-trip airline ticket to Charleston. After returning to the motel where he was staying, he telephoned Diane again and asked her to find someone to babysit her children so she could spend the weekend with him. Later, she told him she could not find a babysitter and could not make the trip.

"I missed her so bad, that really upset me," Jimmy said. "So I ended up flyin' up there and spending the weekend with her instead."

Earlier, following his breakup with Buck, he tried to escape the emotional pain he was feeling by visiting some Irish Traveler relatives in California. "I didn't like it at all while I was there, and I was lonesome. I think I called Diane and wrote to her every day. About a week before her birthday, I asked her what she wanted me to send her, and she said she just wanted me to come back. So the night before her birthday, I hopped on a plane in Los Angeles and flew back to Jamestown. I had some friends wrap me up in a big refrigerator box and put me on her doorstep. A big card was attached to the box that said, 'To Diane From Danny. Happy Birthday.' When she got home from college that night, there I was, a big birthday present. I had a little hole put in the side of the box so I could watch her, and when she unwrapped the box and ripped it open, I jumped out."

At nineteen years old, Jimmy Burke had never experienced sex with a woman, even though there were numerous opportunities for him to do so with Irish Traveler girls who regarded him as a very eligible bachelor. A few of the most aggressive Traveler girls even talked their way into Jimmy's bed, only to discover that he was not interested in anything except sleep. They considered him to be one very shy young man, but Jimmy regarded himself as a homosexual unable to have sex with a woman.

Diane changed all that. He later claimed she seduced him, and she said he initiated their lovemaking, but no matter how it started, the result was a romantic relationship that surprised Jim- my and delighted his family. From that point until a Georgia police officer put an end to his wandering, Jimmy sent special gifts and surprises to Diane no matter where he was. "I'd send her two dozen roses from time to time, or I'd have a six-foot telegram made up and sent to her special delivery."

Jimmy also developed a warm relationship with Diane's four children. During his travels, he made a point of buying special gifts for them, especially toys that he knew Diane could not afford. If she mentioned something that the kids needed, Jimmy bought it. In the Irish Traveler tradition, money was no object.

Asked once how much money he usually earned during a twelve-month period, Jimmy was stumped. He didn't know. "I'll bet not very many Travelers could answer that question," he responded. He laughed and added, "We don't keep records of the money we make, you know. And we make an awful lot of money!"

However, Jimmy did admit that during his month-long trip to California and then the month afterward when his return trip detoured south through New Mexico, east into Florida and then north to New York, he kept track of some expenses. "I recorded the mileage on my truck and how much money I spent on gasoline, restaurants and motels. Not including other expenses such as drinks, movies, clothes, campgrounds, gifts for relatives and the airline ticket to New York and back, those costs came to $20,000. I didn't have much money when I got to California, and I worked stores and the truck while I was there and on the way back. When I arrived back in New York, I had about $700 on me, so I guess during those two months I made about $40,000." That figure translates to $5,000 a week!

Jimmy added, "I couldn't even guess what most Travelers earn in a year. I know that most of them average making $500 or $600 a day, every day, and that's just for work out of a truck or the stores, not includin' whatever they make on the side from sellin' trailers or lightnin' rods or doin' the other things that they all do. But you know, you've got to figure, too, how much a Traveler spends each day. Especially with the price of gasoline being so high. And most of them have large families and eat in restaurants and stay in motels or in campgrounds with full hookups. You have to figure that in, too. It's still a lot of money -- an awful lot of money. A lot more than most people make. But if you compare what Travelers make with the money a doctor or lawyer makes, what we earn over and above what it costs us to live would even out to be about the same thing that a doctor or lawyer has left."

So a typical Traveler, with his fifth-grade education, does not earn much more money, after expenses, than a successful doctor or lawyer?

"Right," Jimmy answered. He did not see the obvious irony.

While Jimmy's romance with Diane blossomed, his sister Wanda called with the news that she was in Aurora, Illinois, for a big fiftieth wedding anniversary party of a popular Irish Traveler couple, Millie and Jimmy Rafferty.

Jimmy recalled, "With our people, you don't miss a weddin' or a funeral or an anniversary of someone who's popular because you know that everybody else will be there, and they'll expect you to be there too. At the time, I wasn't too flush with money, and I didn't feel like goin' up there, so I told Wanda I couldn't make it.

"She said, 'Billy didn't come. I left him in New Hampshire and flew up, and I've got money, so come on up, and if you need anything, I'll take care of it.'

At Aurora, a suburb of Chicago, the Travelers had rented the entire five-story Holiday Inn. All the rooms at the nearby Scottish Inn also were occupied by Travelers, every site at a campground a few blocks away was rented by clan members, and within a 20-mile radius of the Holiday Inn, the parking lots of virtually every small motel was packed with flashy vehicles owned by Irish, Scottish or English Travelers. When Jimmy arrived at the Holiday Inn where he was to share a room with Wanda, he was stopped by two security guards and questioned about his identity before he was permitted to enter the building.

The anniversary party was scheduled for the next night and would be attended by more than 2,000 individuals. And that night, there was a social reunion in the lounge of the Holiday Inn, and Travelers there for the anniversary were invited to stop and meet old friends before dinner. Jimmy said, "When I got there, about 200 Travelers were already in the lounge area, dancin', drinkin', and carryin' on. Two cops came in and one said everybody was goin' to have to keep the noise down or he was goin' to close the bar. One of the Travelers told them to mind their own business because we were all together, that there was nobody else in the hotel, so who else would we disturb? One of the cops walked out, but the other cop decided he was

going to haul that guy in for disturbin' the peace. He started to handcuff the guy, and when he did, three or four Travelers came over and
told the cop, 'You'd better not try to take him anywhere.'

"The cop said, 'Move aside. This man's going to jail.'

"So the Travelers jumped on the cop and beat the hell out of him.
He was layin' on the floor when the other cop came runnin' in to
help him out, and they beat him up too and left him layin' on the
floor. In just a few minutes, the lounge was cleared out except for the
two cops, who were pretty badly beaten. A bunch more cops came in
-- there were about ten cop cars and detective cars there -- and they
started goin' from room to room lookin' for the men who beat up the
cops. Those Travelers were there all the time, too; they'd go from one
room to another. Whenever the cops looked in one room, they'd go
through the connecting door into the next room and then back
again. The cops never did find them."

The next night, a nearby country club was rented for the reception. A full orchestra entertained and provided music for dancing.
The parking lot was jammed full of Cadillacs, Lincolns, Corvettes
and one-ton pickup trucks. Two security guards were parked at the
end of the road leading to the club, and they checked the identities
of those seeking entrance against a master guest list. The reception
lasted until about 3 o'clock in the morning. "The whole time I was
there," Jimmy reported later, "I felt out of place because I hadn't
been with everyone in a group for so long. There were all the boys
my own age that I had grown up with, but I hadn't associated with
any of them for four or five years, and when I would try to get into
their conversations, I felt awkward."

After the Travelers left the country club, they found a reception of
another kind awaiting them. Along every street leading toward the
Holiday Inn, police cruisers were parked with their lights flashing.
And as the Travelers drove past, they were arrested for offenses such
as changing lanes without signaling, underinflated tires, lack of
license plate lights, broken taillights, and carrying too much weight

in their trucks. Those who were intoxicated or did not have appropriate driver's licenses were fingerprinted, photographed and jailed.

In November, about the time the Canadian geese winged their way south for the winter, Jimmy Burke once again felt the uncontrollable urge to visit Florida, and Peggy said she wanted to go with him. They drove to Indiana and picked up a new Marauder trailer and then detoured through Ohio with the intention of selling it. There, Jimmy would have his final encounter with Ohio's "Gypsy Hunter," Wayne Johnson.

The Akron motel where Jimmy parked his trailer and advertised it for sale was just a few blocks from Ohio's largest recreational vehicle dealership, Sirpilla Trailer Sales, and Jimmy figured that the dealership would draw traffic past the spot where his trailer was prominently displayed, increasing his chances of selling it. A few minutes after he put a "For Sale" sign on the coach, a man with a trailer hitch on his car stopped to look at the Marauder.

He asked Jimmy, "Why are you selling it?"

"Well, my parents bought it for me because I was gettin' married, but the weddin' is off now, so I'm just gonna sell it."

The customer asked, "How much do you want for it?"

Jimmy told him and then said, "I notice you have a hitch on your car. Do you already own a trailer that you'd like to trade?"

"No, I have one that I'm going to sell myself. So I'm looking around to find another one."

The man left, and an hour later, he returned with two other men, and they all inspected the trailer closely. Jimmy's suspicions were aroused when they asked him offbeat questions such as where he bought the trailer, why he was in Ohio with it and why he had an Ohio tag on the trailer but Florida tags on his truck. When the three men left, he followed them, and they went directly to the Sirpilla RV dealership. Jimmy went inside and spotted his *customer* sitting behind a desk in an office with "Sales Manager" on the door. He concluded the man was John Sirpilla. He wasn't; his name was Dick Williamson, Sirpilla's sales manager.

"Less than an hour after I got back to the motel, a couple of men pulled up in a plain Plymouth automobile," Jimmy said later. "They knocked on my door and asked if they could see the trailer. Well, I knew there was something funny about them, especially since they were dressed in suits, and then I recognized one of them as the guy who had tried to run me out of town a couple of years earlier -- the same guy who had chased my parents out of Ohio when I was a kid. So I told them that the trailer wasn't for sale."

When one of the trio asked why he had for sale signs on it, Jimmy answered, "I just bought it, and I haven't had time to take the signs off yet. I just picked it up. I don't want to sell it."

Jimmy realized the man he recognized as the "Gypsy Hunter" was looking at him closely. Finally Johnson said, "You look very familiar. Do I know you from somewhere?"

"No," Jimmy answered.

"I could swear I met you somewhere before, maybe a couple of years ago. Were you selling trailers here two or three years ago?"

"Not me. I just moved to Ohio from New York. I've never been in Ohio before."

One of the other men asked, "Didn't you sell a trailer here last week?"

Jimmy answered, "Yeah."

Johnson pressed, "How come you sold one here last week and now you've got this one?"

"Because I wanted to get a new one, and this is my new one that I just bought."

Johnson told him, "We're from the Ohio Department of Motor Vehicles, and we've been having trouble with curbstone dealers."

Jimmy said, "Oh, gosh, I'm not one of them, and I'm leavin' town tomorrow, headin' home to Cincinnati."

Johnson responded, "All right, but we don't want to see that trailer for sale here. If we come back here tomorrow, those for sale signs better be gone."

After the DMV agents left, Jimmy started to take his signs off the trailer, but just then a young family stopped and asked if they could look at the trailer. "They fell in love with it, but they said they had just given Sirpilla a $100 deposit on a trailer they were going to buy from him. Instead, they decided they wanted my trailer. So they went back to Sirpilla's to get their deposit back, and the manager told them the Marauder was a gypsy trailer and it was a piece of junk and that he wouldn't give them their deposit back so they could buy it. They came back and told me that and asked what they should do. Well, I was making about $1,500 on the trailer for the price I was askin' for it anyhow, so I said, 'Don't worry about Sirpilla. I'll knock $100 off my price, and that'll make up for the money you lost.' They bought the trailer off me, and I left town the next day. I haven't been back to Ohio since then."

# 9

# Those Terrible Williamsons

For more than one hundred years, most of the scams and swindles pulled off by Irish Travelers such as Jimmy Burke and his family have been blamed on -- or credited to -- the notorious Williamson clan. The fact is, less than one-third of the scams considered to be the work of the Williamsons -- or, more accurately, the Scottish Travelers -- actually involve them. But the Scottish Travelers, exemplified by the relatively small number of individuals who continue to claim the name of Williamson, are a colorful group. They've been colorful since Robert Logan Williamson immigrated from Scotland in the 1890s and brought with him survival skills developed by that country's itinerant Travelling People, the Tinkers.

During the first half of this century, the Terrible Williamsons, as they came to be called, were the subjects of numerous newspaper and radio articles. Even as they struggled to maintain a low profile and to keep their very lifestyles secret from American *country folk*, the Williamsons were elevated to legendary status. Stories about their exploits spread from coast to coast, and ordinary citizens became intrigued by those devil-may-care adventurers who led lives of total freedom as they searched for foolish victims they could trick.

As the Williamson notoriety grew, it became clear that no one -- least of all law enforcement agencies -- wanted to hear about a bunch of other ethnic con artists who worked the same kinds of scams, but did so even more effectively than the Williamsons! For police officers, slapping a "Williamson" label on every itinerant scoundrel who lived by his wits seemed to be an easy way to categorize the seasonal crime wave that hit virtually every community in America.

And so, even the existence of Irish Travelers and English Travelers remained unknown except to a few policemen with exceptional tenacity and investigative skills. But when those individuals tried to communicate to their superiors and to officers in other law enforcement circles that several thousand con artists no one had ever heard of were responsible for most of the consumer fraud activity in America, no one believed them. That attitude was reinforced -- and in fact is still reinforced today -- by the utterly stupid and narrow-minded belief by many police officers that all the itinerant con artists were Gypsies, no matter what names they gave themselves.

In 1956, the deeds of those Terrible Williamsons became permanently etched in the collective memory of the American public, and any opportunity that existed to reveal the existence of Irish and English Travelers disappeared for another twenty years.

The event which did that was publication of author John Kobler's definitive article, "The Terrible Williamsons," which appeared in the October 27 edition of what was then America's most respected magazine, *The Saturday Evening Post*. A magnificently researched article that gained world-wide attention and is still quoted in books and periodicals, Kobler's piece accurately portrayed the Williamson clan of the mid-1900s and, more than anything else, focused so much public attention on them that many hundreds of them stopped using their real names on driver's licenses and other forms of I.D.

The article is still worth reading.

But in his article, Kobler made a couple of false assumptions and accepted a few inaccurate assertions by his sources as fact. In doing that, he provided a shaky foundation upon which most future evidence about Travelers would be built. He assigned too much credibility to an anonymous informant who claimed to be a member of the Williamson family, and he allowed himself to be duped into reporting that the clan consisted of 75-100 families, all led by a powerful boss named Uncle Isaac Williamson who exacted monetary assessments from the families as tribute. Although there is no doubt Uncle Isaac was an important clan figure during the 1950s, he certainly was not so powerful that any of those highly independent Scottish Travelers would have shared part of their earnings with him! Furthermore, there were considerably more than 100 families, even in the 1950s; today, there are about 4,000 Scottish Travelers.

An unfortunate result of the Kobler article was that for decades, law enforcement officers trying to catch con artists assumed the Williamson clan consisted of a small, highly organized nucleus of families that took orders from a shadowy king-like figure who lived in secrecy somewhere in either Cincinnati or Florida. In actual fact, all the Traveler clans -- including the Williamsons -- are loosely knit, interrelated families without any leaders at all; they operate independently of each other, sharing details about their successes and failures and warning each other about locales that should be avoided. Most of their communications are by telephone, generally utilizing a network of *advisors* who serve informally as message forwarding services.

Unwittingly, and understandably since he clearly did not know about the Irish Travelers, Kobler described in his article a now-famous (among Travelers, that is) Christmas week fight that took place at Miami Beach in 1952. Kobler assumed the participants were all Williamson clan members, but in actual fact seven Scottish Williamsons squared off against three Irish Carrolls in a fistfight that apparently lasted more than one hour. In the end, Irish Traveler Matthew Carroll was rushed to the hospital nearly dead, his right eye gouged out. It was a fight Travelers still talk about today!

Kobler wrote, "The first to cross the Atlantic was Robert Logan Williamson. He resided for a while during the '90s in Brooklyn, New York, took a Scottish emigre wife, who bore him numerous progeny, and embarked upon the itinerant life. Kindred McDonalds, McMillans et al, fired probably by letters Robert wrote home recounting the easy pickings in the Land of Opportunity, began emigrating too. By 1914 the prolific tribe was a fixture of the American underworld. The first Better Business Bureau, which set up quarters in Minneapolis that year, had scarcely installed its telephones before a call came from the anguished owner of a Williamson-sprayed barn."

Kobler also reported, "The Williamsons are proud of their lineage and proud of their traditional guile, with no apparent sense of wrong-doing. The gullible, they seem to feel, were put on earth to be gulled, and they perceive no sin in assisting the operation of what they regard as a natural law. 'We can trace our blood back to the Picts,' a tribal elder once boasted. 'Under the Romans, we were tinsmiths, and for the last two centuries we've been in our present line of business."

Their primary businesses at the time of the Kobler article were peddling cheap products and fabrics sold as handmade imports, painting barns and houses with watered-down whitewash, and installing partial lightning rod systems on farmhouses.

Since the 1960s, the Scottish Travelers and their Irish counterparts have become considerably more sophisticated. Today, their primary day-to-day incomes are from shoplifting, sealing roofs and driveways, and selling cheap travel trailers after misrepresenting them. But they also engage in an almost endless variety of scams associated with termite extermination, home downspout and chimney repair, carpet and linoleum sales, tree trimming, basement remodeling, utility worker or bank examiner frauds, auto insurance fraud, pigeon drop swindles, RV theft, reconditioned automobiles from flood scenes, fake cable TV hookups, lottery ticket swindles, counterfeit money cons, slip-and-fall accident insurance fraud, welfare fraud, quick-change money flimflams, telephone fraud, auto finance swindles, and fake gold bar sales.

Kobler estimated in 1956 that the Williamson scams netted nearly one million dollars per year. Today, the Scottish, Irish and English Travelers are bilking the American public out of more than one *billion* dollars annually! A successful Traveler family earns at least $200,000 each year just from shoplifting and the roofing/driveway scams. Police officers who track Traveler activities estimate there are about 1,500 Scottish families representing up to 4,000 individuals; approximately 2,000 Irish families totaling between 4,000 and 6,000 individuals and nearly 1,000 English Traveler families that include 2,000 to 3,000 individuals. Even assuming that half those families are relatively unsuccessful in comparison with those who are especially successful, when all their various scams are considered, the total net take comes to a minimum of one billion dollars, and perhaps as much as $1.5 billion.

Most of today's Scottish Travelers are not named Williamson. They are named Mesker or Keith, Reid or Stewart, McDonald or McMillan. Family names also include Gregg, Woods, Collins, Young, Callahan, West, Parks, Cooper, Bradley, Bishop, Halliday, Johnston, Ross, Hayworth, Martin, James, Kelby, Holton, Varey and Ford. Several other names are mixed in, by marriage or circumstance, to make identification even more difficult. For example, members of a family named Linzy often socialize and work scams with both Scottish and Irish Travelers. Originally, the Linzys were so-called *road refs* -- that is, non-Travelers who participated in Scottish Traveler scams by handling the manual labor; they have adapted to the Traveler lifestyle so completely that they are now indistinguishable from them.

One of America's best authorities on the Scottish Travelers is John Wood, an intelligence officer with the Pinellas County, Florida, Consumer Affairs Office. "God knows how many Scotch there are because there are almost no settled areas for them," said Wood, who has become so personally involved in investigating Scottish Travelers that he often refers to them as "my guys." He said, "It might very well be that the Scotch are the smallest group of Travelers of all. They travel all over. The only times I've ever heard of when a large group of them would be in once place are the few times a year when they have get-togethers such as Christmas parties, weddings or funerals."

Wood added, "It's bogus to believe they do any real planning as a group, that they actually set out who's going to do what. None of the Scotch Travelers I know would stand for that. They're all going to do their own thing, and if Joe Traveler over here doesn't like it, that's tough."

The Florida deputy has little patience with other police officers who refer to all Travelers as Williamsons. "That's crap! When I do a seminar for police agencies, I say, 'Don't let this Williamson crap creep into your vocabulary.' The Williamsons are only one family, and all the Scotch Travelers aren't even Williamsons. A lot of them have changed their names, of course. The Parkses are all Williamsons. The Holdens are Williamsons. The James family. The Rosses. The Kelbys. The Bishops. The Fords. But McMillan is a real family name, and so is Keith. The way to separate the real names from the fake ones is to visit the cemeteries. The real names will be on the headstones."

Wood emphasized, "When Mary Ross died, her headstone said Mary Williamson. When John Hayworth died, his headstone said Williamson. When George Martin dies, it'll say Williamson on his headstone. When a Parks dies, Williamson is on his headstone. But when a Keith dies, his headstone says Keith. You'll see headstones for the Keiths, the Johnstons, the McMillans, the Hallidays, the Watsons, the Vareys and the Stewarts. No matter what name a Scotch Traveler used all his life, he'll be buried under the name with which he was born, no matter if his father changed the family's name legally to Parks."

Trying to remember which names are real and which are fake is virtually impossible, Wood said. "They get confused about it themselves. At a 1988 funeral in Kissimmee, the guy who died was Jimmy Ford, but the funeral director got calls from all over the country, asking, 'Is this the funeral home where Jimmy Williamson is laid out?' He'd say, 'We don't have any Williamsons here,' and then they'd say, 'Oh, that's right. Jimmy Williamson Ford. Is he there?'"

In central Florida, where most eastern Traveler families headquarter each winter, law enforcement authorities have become quite familiar with individual members of the clans and, generally speaking, understand the differences between a Scottish Traveler and an Irish or English Traveler. Unfortunately, until about 1986, police in the Orlando area tended to refer to all the scam artists collectively as gypsies, making no distinction between traditional eastern European Romanian Gypsies and the white-skinned ethnic Travelers. They warned an unwitting public that the gypsies, with their various scams, had arrived in central Florida, and consumers responded by being wary of all dark-skinned people with foreign accents. Scottish, Irish and English Travelers, not fitting that description, continued to be quite successful, thank you, with their swindles. Around 1987, Florida cops focused attention almost entirely on those Terrible Williamsons, and the result was, scam artists who identified themselves as Gormans, Carrolls, Keiths or McMillans were not suspect -- in the minds of consumers, they weren't Williamsons and therefore must have been legitimate businessmen. During recent years, officers in central Florida have tried to convey more complete and accurate information to the news media and to chambers of commerce, but without much success. Each fall, the same old alarm is still raised: "The Williamsons are coming! The Williamsons are coming!"

In 1991, the *Orlando Sentinel* trumpeted, "The Terrible Williamsons are back, and Orange County deputy sheriffs say the traveling clan of gypsies have one interest in central Florida: getting your money."

Two years later, when the Travelers were once again starting to set up their winter bases in central Florida, police alerted the news media but emphasized that press coverage about the con artists should not be focused on the famous Williamsons. The result was an article in the *Orlando Sentinel* which stated, "The Terrible Williamsons are not the Williamsons anymore. They couldn't take the notoriety, so they changed their names. They continue to be terrible, however, and they continue to plague Florida's weak and elderly. Like migratory birds, the Williamsons and other traveling bands of con artists are swooping once again into Florida. The English, Irish and Scottish groups come from points north to escape the winter cold. They bring with them a battery of home repair and other scams."

It was another case of "The Williamsons are coming!"

Misinformation about the Travelers, and especially about the group known as Williamsons, has been prevalent in America for many years. The Chicago Tribune-New York News Syndicate produced a wordy report in January 1957 that did little except rehash the *Saturday Evening Post* article. However, it also added more incorrect information to the Williamson lore. For example, after citing a couple of inter-family feuds, author Worth Gatewood wrote, "Though no loyal Williamson will reveal the clan's affairs, the feuds might arise from disputes over the allotment of territory -- a prerogative said to belong to the tribal rulers, a mysterious pair known as 'Two Thumbs' and 'Black Queen Jennie.'"

That article was responsible for another major error that also was added to the Williamson legend. Gatewood stated as fact that the bodies of deceased Williamsons were kept "on ice" for weeks or months until Memorial Day, when the entire clan descended upon Cincinnati for the funerals. For thirty years after that article, news reporters and police officers from around the country traveled to Cincinnati on Memorial Days so they could witness the once-a-year funerals. No such funerals were ever held!

Like Kobler before him, Gatewood identified the Irish Carrolls as a "branch" of the Williamson family.

When free-lance writer Jean Carper and Senator Warren G. Magnuson co-authored a book called *The Dark Side of the Marketplace* in 1968, they went to great pains to illustrate how extensively Americans were being swindled in home-repair scams. But they were unable to reveal -- the fact is, they didn't bother to investigate! -- the identities of the shadowy criminal figures who were swindling thousands of people throughout America every day. They simply pointed their fingers at "one Irish family known as the Terrible Williamsons" and stated, "It is said that the clan on the road now numbers at least one hundred."

With news organizations such as the *Chicago Tribune* and authorities such as Carper and Magnuson reporting in an off-hand way that the Williamsons were clearly a minor factor in the nation's alarming flood of home-repair swindles, it was no wonder that consumers and law enforcement officers alike failed to take the traveling con artists seriously. No one in America at that time considered that the same people who were operating home-repair scams were also shoplifting from department stores, engaging in insurance fraud, selling cheap travel trailers on street corners and conning elderly citizens out of their life savings. And certainly no one considered that several thousand individual con artists, not just a few dozen, were involved!

According to the National Association of Bunco Investigators in Baltimore, not until the late 1970s did anyone in American law enforcement recognize that most of the people who had been labeled as gypsies were really distinct clans of Scottish, Irish and English Travelers!

About that time, a book that was purported to be the first complete analysis of American swindles was published. Still occupying shelves on libraries around the nation, that 1976 book, *Hustlers and Con Men*, included a major reference to "The Terrible Williamsons." Unfortunately, it was little more than the rewritten text from Kobler's twenty-year-old *Saturday Evening Post* article.

Charles R. Whitlock at least made the distinction between Gypsies and Travelers in his awkwardly titled 1994 book, *Easy Money: The Truth Behind the Billion-Dollar Confidence Industry and How to Protect Yourself and Your Money.* Not once in the book did Whitlock mention the Williamsons. However, the author apparently was unaware of how extensive the Travelers' scams were; he referred to them only briefly, and then simply in oblique reference to a few home-repair swindles. Erroneously, Whitlock described them as a "group of Deep South residents...typically dwelling close by one another in opulent homes in Georgia and Florida."

Two excellent and, for the most part accurate, articles about the Williamsons were published during the last eighteen years. The first was a 1978 piece in *Free Enterprise* magazine written by Ford N. Burkhart, an associate journalism professor at the University of Arizona; the second, by *Sacramento* magazine Contributing Editor Ginny McReynolds in 1980. Like other writers before him, however, Burkhart mistakenly stated that the clan was "bankrolled from a central fund run by a handful of the mobile clan patriarchs," assuming once again that some authority figure or figures directed the Travelers' activities and exacted tributes from family members.

Burkhart also wrote, "Cash is relayed from the roving teams to the ruling elders by means of secret compartments built into the walls of the travel trailers in which nearly all Williamson families live." For years after that article, police officers who arrested Travelers searched the interiors of their trailers, in vain, hoping to find cleverly concealed compartments in which large hordes of cash were stored! Although Travelers frequently do hide money or cash wherever they can in their trailers, it is ludicrous to presume that secret compartments are built into the coaches, especially since the trailers are sold by the Travelers as quickly as possible as part of their system for earning a living.

Except for being mystified by the clan's simple telephone com-munication system, Burkhart made only one other important error: He said, "Williamson parents forbid their children to attend schools." The fact is, nearly all Traveler children receive a small amount of formal classroom education so they can learn to read, write and do simple mathematics. As traveling business people, they need those skills to survive. Few children in any of the Traveler clans, however, attend school beyond the eighth grade, and much of the schooling the most itinerant children receive is provided during the winter months that their families reside in the Sunbelt.

Significantly, it was Burkhart who revealed publicly for the first time that the Scottish Travelers had started investing heavily in real estate. Afterward identifying a California state police investigator in Sacramento as his source, he wrote, "The clan's assets are huge and seem to be growing fast. Its holdings include an estimated $20 mil-lion worth of real estate and other property, much of it located in the Sun Belt states..." A few years later, CBS television producer Pat Lynch, while researching a segment about the Williamsons for *20/20*, confirmed that family members were, indeed, earning millions of dollars in profit by buying, operating and selling mobile home parks in Arizona. The *20/20* segment was never produced, but Lynch's evi-dence became part of NBC's first *Monitor* news magazine episode in 1983.

In 1995, Florida Detective John Wood said his own research indi-cated that Scottish Travelers currently owned about fifty mobile home parks in and around Phoenix as well as numerous parcels of valuable land in Florida. "A couple of families own six million dol-lars worth of property right here in Pinellas County," he reported. "We have no idea -- not a clue -- as to how much money they've got in investments. Mobile home parks are perfect for the Travelers because they leave a country person at the site as a manager while they go out on the road. He collects the rents and pays the expenses, and they don't have to mess with it. They come back a couple of times a year for conferences with him and then take off again. They keep the park a few years while it appreciates in value and then sell it and make a million or so in profit."

A widely held assumption is that the Travelers, like other Americans, invest as much of their earnings as possible so they can live comfortably when they retire. When asked about that, Wood laughed. "Retire? They don't *retire*! Why would they want to retire? I've seen those guys out there when they're 75 years old, still working. Old Hughy Carroll with the Irish group is out there working right now. So is Tom Ross, and he's in his seventies. What the others do with those guys is make them the hose men. They stand outside the customer's house with a water hose and keep the customer inside while the rest of them are up painting the roof. There are guys who are worth millions of dollars still painting houses, sealing driveways and doing the quick-change money flimflam."

Wood explained, "With all con men, their status within their community depends on the big score they made yesterday, not last year."

Wood's associate, Orange County Detective John McMahan, added, "And also buying the vehicles, the jewelry, the clothes and flashing the money."

Wood nodded, "That's part of it, but they want to be able to brag about scoring against us -- 'us' being anyone other than a Traveler. That's what maintains their status. If they get out of the painting or the seal coating or the lightning rods, there's nothing to brag about anymore. The guys who own the mobile home parks are proving that they're still hard-chargers, big players in the game."

McMahan agreed. "Also, the fact that they're still active, successful people elevates the status of their children and grandchildren."

McReynolds, in her 1980 *Sacramento* article, revealed another fact: Some of the Scottish Travelers had enough money, and enough influence, to hire the best legal advice in America if they needed it. She reported that after Scottish Travelers John and Henry Woods --

also known as John and Henry Williamson -- were arrested in California for fraud, theft, burglary and conspiracy in 1978, they hired nationally famous Texas lawyer Percy Foreman to represent them. Although the case against the brothers was considered quite strong, and police calculated they would serve many years in prison, Foreman plea-bargained their sentences to thirty days in jail and three years' probation, with fines and restitution totaling just over $12,000.

When NBC's Lynch was researching her *Monitor* TV report, she talked with Foreman, and she learned he had provided legal advice to the Scottish Travelers numerous times. "He said they helped him get through the Depression, and he's very devoted to them," Lynch said a few hours after meeting with the famous lawyer.

Fifteen years later, Detective Wood called Lynch's *Monitor* program "the best overall media coverage that's ever been done on Travelers." He said it illustrated some of the reasons law enforcement officers are frequently frustrated in their attempts to put Travelers in jail. "There are a couple of attorneys in the south that are known throughout the Traveler community, and the Travelers use them consistently. There's a guy in Jackson, Mississippi, that the Travelers have nicknamed 'The Fixer.' He cannot practice in other communities, but what he can do is be a negotiator and convince the authorities that a crime was not committed, but the money will be paid back anyway. He'll say, 'As a matter of fact, it's already been paid back by my client, who is a poor itinerant painter that didn't know better.' And that's usually a good sell job because the cops and prosecutors responsible for charging the Travelers don't even know who they've got in custody."

McMahan added, "The Travelers are such great talkers, and they'll talk to their victims when they pay back the money, telling them how sorry they are. So between the Travelers and the lawyers, the victim rolls over and refuses to prosecute, and the cop's case just goes into the toilet. If you don't have a victim, you don't have a case."

"All along the way, every step of the investigation is a sell job," Wood explained. "The investigator or detective has to sell his supervisors on it, and the supervisor doesn't really want to bother with a case like that. Once the supervisor gets past that, he has to sell the case to the prosecutor. And then, if it gets that far, the prosecutor has to sell it to a judge. Even juries aren't as hard to sell as the legal system itself."

Over and over throughout America, there have been instances of a single investigator in a state who develops an interest in the Travelers' scams, tracks them effectively, arrests them and convinces someone in the legal system to prosecute them. As the investigator's successes mount, word spreads quickly within the Traveler community, and Travelers begin avoiding that state. The result is, the investigator's arrests decline sharply, and his supervisors decide he is no longer using his time effectively, so he is reassigned.

"That's exactly what happened in California with Peterson," Wood said. A Department of Justice intelligence officer who accumulated an amazing amount of information about Scottish Travelers during the late 1970s and early 1980s, Peterson (not his real name) shared his data with law enforcement agencies throughout that state. Wood said, "He did such a good job that the Travelers started avoiding California completely. All of a sudden, there wasn't a Traveler problem there, and his boss told him, 'Peterson, this is all a figment of your imagination. We're putting you someplace else.' They reassigned him, and the Travelers found out about it within a year and moved right back into their old haunts. They've been there ever since. There's an enormous Traveler presence in California at certain times of the year, but the people with the Department of Justice don't believe it."

Wood shook his head. "I was in Costa Mesa in 1989 for a seminar. I did a presentation on the Travelers, and the California people told me, 'We don't have any Travelers around here. We drove them out a number of years ago.'"

Historically, the Scottish Travelers have operated their scams year after year in areas of the country where they have been the most successful: Cincinnati, Dayton, Toledo, the Chicago suburbs, Tampa, Minneapolis, Tucson, Sacramento, Kansas City, Omaha, the Rio Grande Valley of Texas, Fort Worth, Phoenix, Salt Lake City, Billings, Seattle, Denver, Madison and Minneapolis.

The *Saturday Evening Post* article especially emphasized the Williamson family's ties to Cincinnati, both for buying their new automobiles and trucks and for burying their dead in Spring Grove cemetery. Author John Kobler wrote, "Unfailingly, every May, the bulk of the clan returns to Cincinnati both to honor their dead and to hold a convention -- a custom which impels the local Better Business Bureau to circulate warning bulletins."

Publication of Kobler's article was reported on the front pages of the *Cincinnati Post* and the *Cincinnati Times Star*. Less than two months later, another brief article in the *Post* noted that three Williamsons -- James, Margaret and Mary Ann -- were questioned and released after being warned to stay out of the city. "It was reported they were soliciting sales of Canadian rugs," the newspaper said.

Mrs. Jean Williamson, then 30, was particularly active in the Cincinnati area. She was arrested in 1947 for peddling without a license and was fined $50. She received a 30-day workhouse term for shoplifting in 1952, and in 1954 she was fined $25 for registering falsely at a hotel. During the late 1950s, while other clan members gathered for a funeral, Jean peddled what she claimed were all-wool fabrics for women's suits in Milford; she sold bolts of the material -- which turned out to be inexpensive rayon -- for $12.50 each, claiming the fabric was imported from Scotland. As police officers searched for her, the *Post* reported, "Mrs. Williamson had her young son with her, teaching him the tricks of the trade early."

Early in 1957, Jean was one of seven Scottish Travelers arrested near Dallas, Texas, and they told officers their homes were in Cincinnati. Police said the seven were involved in robbing an old man of

$300 while two of the women prayed for him. Mary "Granny" Wilson confessed that nineteen-year-old William Williamson dressed like a woman and took the money. William and Granny, then 78, were jailed, and another member of the clan, Charlotte Williamson, elected to stay in jail "to look after Granny." Within a few days, the family had posted $3,000 bond and skipped town.

Exactly three years later, sixty Scottish Travelers gathered in northern Kentucky at Covington's Allison & Rose funeral home near Cincinnati for the funeral of Catherine Williamson. Private security guards cordoned off the funeral home and refused to allow anyone to enter who could not tell them a secret password. The next day, an enterprising reporter from the *Cincinnati Enquirer* said the woman lay in a solid bronze casket valued at between $4,000 and $6,000 -- an enormous amount of money at that time. The newspaper said, "Elaborate floral pieces were stacked to the ceiling in the double-room north parlor, and a number of floral arrangements had to be put in a hallway. An onlooker counted 107 baskets, some addressed to 'Mother,' others to 'Grandmother' and 'Aunt Catherine.'" Burial was at Covington's Highland Cemetery.

In his *Enquirer* article, reporter George Amick wrote, "The Covington services yesterday represent a change of policy. Customarily, the family has patronized a well-known Cincinnati funeral home and has done its burying in a family plot in Spring Grove. An official of the Cincinnati firm said it has been years since a Williamson funeral was held there. Since then, he said, 'We know they have been going somewhere else but have no indication why.' One report was that the Williamsons were unhappy with the firm because of a 'security leak' by which a photographer gained admittance to one of their services."

By mid-1980, a 50-year-old Williamson file compiled by the Cincinnati Better Business Bureau was five inches thick.

Suburban Chicago has been another primary target of the Scottish Travelers for almost 100 years. In 1963, a small band of Williamsons set up camp in the Chicago area. Three of them convinced an elderly man that his basement floor needed to be rebuilt. While two distracted the homeowner, the third poured water into the cracks of his basement's concrete floor and told the old fellow it was evidence that water and sewage had collected under the house and that the whole structure could collapse at any minute because it was sitting on a cesspool. They agreed to repair the damage and rebuild the basement floor immediately. The homeowner signed a contract to have the work done for $9,000, and he paid the con artists $4,500 in advance. The Travelers left the house that day, ostensibly to buy supplies, and never returned.

The same group convinced a Chicago couple who owned an apartment building that the structure was badly infested with termites -- they displayed dozens of dead termites and hole-ridden boards they said were removed from the basement -- and that the building's two chimneys needed repaired. The couple hired the Travelers to do all of the work for several thousand dollars. For three days, the con artists worked in the basement of the apartment building and chipped mortar from the chimneys. Tenants were comforted by the sounds of hammering and banging because they thought their building would be made safer. After three days, the leader of the workmen announced the termites had been exterminated and the chimneys repaired. He collected the agreed-upon fee, then warned the building's owners and tenants not to venture into the basement for about three weeks or they could be asphyxiated by poisonous chemicals used in the termite extermination process.

After three weeks, when the building's owners checked the basement, they discovered that absolutely no work had been done there. And later, a utility company investigator found the chimneys so clogged with bricks and mortar that carbon monoxide was unable to escape, and the tenants could have been killed by the poisonous air!

The Scottish Keith, Reid, Watson, Gregg and Walker families take their scams to the Chicago area every spring, and sometimes they spend all summer and fall there too, traveling from suburb to suburb. In 1981, Catherine Keith and Robert Watson operated their swindles from a campground near Elgin. While Watson scoured neighborhoods for roof and driveway sealing work, Keith shoplifted in department stores and sold Kentucky Traveler trailers. A Naperville resident who gave Keith a $2,000 deposit on a trailer before learning about the RV sales swindles tried to enlist the aid of Illinois law enforcement in recovering his money. He received no assistance from the state attorney general's consumer fraud office, local police agencies or even from a large RV dealership in Elgin.

At about the same time, two Scottish Traveler families named Gregg and Reid started selling Kentucky Traveler, Safari and Vega travel trailers from a vacant lot not far from a Des Plaines RV dealership. Conducting his own investigation, the dealer learned not only that the Travelers were misrepresenting the trailers, but also that they were falsifying registration documents to avoid paying state sales taxes. Delighted to have that evidence, he contacted the Illinois Department of Revenue. An agent named Dan Petty told him, "There's nothing we can do. It's strictly your problem."

Meanwhile, unknown to the dealer, Des Plaines Detective Norman Klopp was being kept busy investigating numerous consumer complaints about travel trailer sales, shoplifting and driveway and roof sealing scams. The operation, he discovered, was being directed by a Florida-based Scottish Traveler named Sam Reid. Several dozen individuals appeared to be involved in the various scams, with home bases in travel trailers that were being offered for sale throughout the area. Front awnings of the trailers identified them as the Travelers' favorite brands, built by Kentucky Traveler, Marauder, Rush Industries and Meck. For several weeks, Klopp gathered evidence and took statements from victims and witnesses. Finally ready to arrest clan members on a wide variety of charges, he was astonished to learn that they had disappeared, apparently having left town in the middle of the night.

A dozen years later, Travelers were as active in the Chicago area as they had ever been. In January 1993, a Traveler man and a teenaged boy knocked on the door of a Hoffman Estates home that was for sale and asked the 44-year-old female owner if they could look inside it. Once inside, the man asked her to lead him to the basement, leaving the boy upstairs. After the pair left, the woman realized gold necklaces and a gold bracelet -- all valued at $1,100 -- were missing.

The following month, a Scottish Traveler named Walker telephoned a 78-year-old Libertyville woman and identified himself as an investigator with First of America Bank. He said evidence indicated tellers were stealing from the bank, and he asked her to help him catch them. She consented. After following his direction, she withdrew $1,400 from her checking account and met the man at a nearby post office, where she gave the money to him. He told her to go home and wait for his partner to return the cash to her. Eventually, after no one arrived at her home, she called police.

In May, Travelers in Crystal Lake and Elgin posed as illegal immigrants who had won $400,000 in state lotteries but were willing to sell their tickets to elderly people they approached in shopping centers. Less than a month later, a middle-age Traveler with a European accent conned a clerk at the Wood Dale Currency Exchange out of $680 in a currency-skimming flimflam. The same individual failed in attempts to flimflam clerks at the Elk Grove Village and Bensenville currency exchanges.

Late in September, two Travelers persuaded a 57-year-old Downers Grove woman shopping in Berwyn to give them $10,000 in cash and $1,500 worth of jewelry in exchange for a share of a $200,000 lottery ticket. After receiving the money, the con artists asked their victim to drive them to a store so they could purchase aspirin. They entered the store by a front door but apparently exited in the rear while the woman waited outside.

In the Libertyville suburb during early December 1993, two women Travelers swindled a Mundelein woman out of $3,000 in a version of a pigeon drop scam. They told her they had acquired tens of thousands of dollars in drug money, and they showed her stacks of $100 bills. Because they could not afford to risk being identified to the drug dealers who owned the money, they said, they asked her to turn in the money at a local bank in exchange for a $15,000 reward. If she would put up $3,000 in good-faith cash, they would give her the drug money and, after receiving the reward, she would split $12,000 of it with them, keeping the extra $3,000 to replace her investment. She withdrew $3,000 from her account at the LaSalle Talman Bank and gave it to the women in exchange for the drug money in a valise, whereupon they asked her to take it back to the same bank and collect the reward from a man named Mr. Goldman. Once inside the bank, the woman learned that no one named Goldman worked there, and when she returned to her car where the other two said they would wait for her, she discovered they were gone and the stacks of $100 bills had been switched to strips of newspaper.

A week before Christmas, two Travelers posing as sidewalk repairmen invaded an 89-year-old Gurnee man's home and took $500 in cash from a bedroom hiding place while their victim was in another room filling a bucket with water for them.

In the nearby Chicago suburb of Carpentersville almost a year later, Howard Williamson walked into the Northwest Bank branch and deposited a credit line check for $60,000. The following day he withdrew $45,000 from the account -- $18,000 in cash and the rest in cashier's checks. When the bank discovered that the credit-line check was bogus, they notified police, who tracked down Williamson and arrested him. Williamson told investigating officers he was broke, that he had lost the entire $45,000 gambling at the area's riverboat casinos. Admitting he was a lifelong gambler, he said he had tried to recoup $60,000 that he had lost earlier.

"We told him maybe he has a problem and that we could put him in touch with some help," said Carpentersville Detective Michael O'Brien. "His response was basically noncommittal."

Early in 1995, thirty-four-year-old Keith Reid used a $20 bill to purchase a cinnamon roll from a clerk at the Sirloin Stockade restaurant in Des Plaines. Then, through a series of sleight-of-hand maneuvers and currency switches, he flim-flammed the clerk out of $80. The store's alert manager notified police, and Reid was arrested a short while after leaving the restaurant.

Known only as "The Williamsons," Scottish Travelers sold fake sealskin coats in Omaha during 1936. They started peddling fake and partial lightning protection systems in 1945 after purchasing equipment from a manufacturer in Maryville, Missouri. During 1954, they were sought throughout Minnesota and Iowa for lightning rod and barn painting swindles. They hit Hartford, Connecticut, and Topeka, Kansas, at the same time in 1955. Some 600 Williamson family members invaded Los Angeles with their scams in 1956. During the 1960s, they earned tens of thousands of dollars by installing worthless lightning protection systems on farm houses and barns throughout Minnesota. A remodeling scam in July 1967 netted several thousand dollars from an elderly couple near Goshen, Indiana. Scottish Traveler Joseph McMillan was arrested near Columbus, Ohio, in 1969 when he tried to pull a home-repair swindle at the residence of a local police officer; fined $25 by a sympathetic judge after he complained about migraine headaches, McMillan immediately left town with his family: father Pete; mother Dorothy Mitchell; brothers Sammy, Blancy and Floyd; sister Janice; companion Ruby Mitchell, and friend Mack Mitchell.

Eighty-seven Williamsons were arrested for various scams in New York during 1969. New York Consumer Affairs Commissioner Bess Myerson credited them with being "the slickest, most successful clan of bunco, flim-flam artists in the United States." A year later, the city's department of consumer affairs estimated that twenty-five per cent of all complaints about home improvement contracts were the result of work by the Williamsons. But in 1972, that same New York department reported 117 family members were legitimately licensed to perform home remodeling work, and a total of only eight complaints were filed against them the entire year. The department boasted, "Today in this city, former Williamsons are successful businessmen giving a day's labor for each contract taken."

Informed of that statement, Miami police Lieutenant Herbert Netsch pooh-poohed it. "There is no Williamson alive who wouldn't bleed the protein out of a biscuit," he told the *Miami Herald*. That year, Scottish Travelers posing as electricians with Florida Light and Power Company told a Dade County woman faulty wiring in her house was causing blackouts in the area. Asking her to hold a light switch with a length of board -- "so you won't get shocked, madam" -- they leisurely walked through her home, pocketing everything of value they could carry away with them. "Williamsons" also were blamed for swindling another widow in the same area three times -- for a total of $2,000 -- with painting, roofing and wall papering scams.

In a special report on "The Williamsons" March 26, 1972, the *Miami Herald* said New York Inspector Adam Tatem "recently completed an exhaustive study of the bloodlines and found 38 families of Williamsons, 18 Stewarts, 11 McDonalds, 6 McMillans, 4 Greggs and 7 Johnstons, at which point he concluded that the bloodlines became hopelessly entangled." This editorial revelation matched, virtually word-for-word, a section of the *Saturday Evening Post* article of sixteen years earlier! Except the *Post* article credited that same bloodline study to Van Miller of the National Better Business Bureau.

Scottish Travelers hit Tucson with a series of swindles in 1957 and 1964. They returned in 1974 with a wide range of home-repair scams. John Jack Stewart, later identified as "an in-law of the Williamsons," was arrested there a few years later after he and two accomplices swindled several widows with a roof sealing scheme.

During the mid-1970s, the Lightning Protection Institute composed a long letter to the president of the Missouri company that was supplying lightning rod equipment to the Travelers. The letter pleaded with him to stop doing business with "The Williamsons." He refused.

On August 8, 1975, Ohio police arrested Martha Parks, one of America's best known members of the Williamson family. Investigations revealed that during the previous twelve months, she and her husband and daughter had titled twenty-three different travel trailers in ten states. Hurriedly charged with a relatively minor offense in order to be brought into custody -- the actual charge was making false statements in order to obtain vehicle titles -- Martha immediately posted $500 bond and left the state. Today, she continues to work a wide variety of scams under the aliases of Mary Ann Brooks, Mary Turner, Joanne Parks, Mary Jane Williamson and Rachel Parks. Police officers all around America tell stories about her almost with affection. They all call her, simply, "Martha."

During the spring of 1980, while members of the Scottish Traveler clan were in Elkhart, Indiana, to pick up new trailers they could sell, they scoured outlying areas for scam victims. An elderly woman east of Elkhart hired three Williamsons to install lightning rods on her house after they warned her it could burn down around during an electrical storm; she paid them $2,300 even though she thought she had been swindled. A farmer near Millersburg hired the same men to repair his lightning rod system for $1,600; a qualified installer later examined the work and determined the Williamsons had done nothing except perhaps tighten a few screws. A man in nearby Marcellus, Michigan, paid $880 for similar repairs. An elderly woman just outside Wakarusa, Indiana, read about those swindles in a local newspaper and called police; the trio had put rods not only on her home, but also on her daughter's house and on the homes of three neighbors.

Several months later, young Scottish Traveler Adam Angelo Halliday was indicted in Indianapolis for a series of insurance frauds. Because he had already served prison time in Missouri and had a prior history of felony convictions, he was one of the first individuals to be convicted under Indiana's new habitual criminal statutes, which required that an automatic thirty years be added to his sentence. Already regarded by other Travelers as a very wealthy man, Adam was a member of a family that had earned huge profits buying and selling mobile home parks near Tampa, Florida.

Early the following year, Scottish Travelers using fake identifications swindled several residents of Marshall County, Indiana, with a lightning rod scam. Investigator Doug Larrimore later admitted, "We're having a difficult time discerning which laws they've broken. We don't know whether it's intimidation, deception, fraud or what."

Chicago area department stores are particular favorite shoplifting targets of Scottish and Irish Travelers. In 1994, a representative of the Illinois Retail Merchants Association estimated that the state's retailers lose about $1.8 billion in merchandise each year to shoplifters. He said that translates into increased retail prices of $600 to $800 a year for the Illinois residents.

Almost proudly, members of the nation's con artist clans openly boast that they shoplift merchandise virtually at will throughout the Chicago area. And, when asked how often they are arrested for those offenses, their individual answers are always the same: "Never!"

Indeed, a quick review of shoplifting arrest reports between 1992 and mid-1995 reveals that not a single Scottish or Irish Traveler apparently was caught shoplifting anywhere in the Chicago metropolitan area during that period. With little hard proof that the Travelers are responsible for a high proportion of shoplifting losses, it is understandable that most law enforcement agencies there believe shoplifting is a crime committed primarily by local residents.

Gradually, however, police departments around the country are beginning to realize that shoplifting for cash is not just a spur-of-the-moment activity of bored housewives in need of a little extra spending money. Between 1987 and 1991, shoplifting increased eighteen per cent nation-wide, according to the FBI Crime Index. The average item stolen in 1991 was worth $104.

In the Chicago suburb of Naperville, police sergeant Lisa Burghardt told the *Chicago Tribune* in early 1994 that almost all shoplifters caught in her town were career thieves who stole as a way of life. Later, she admitted she had no solid evidence to support that statement, but she said her experience clearly pointed toward career criminals such as the Scottish and Irish Travelers as being responsible for a very high proportion of department store shoplifting.

One mistake merchants consistently make about Traveler shoplifting is to assume clan members steal merchandise for their own use. On the contrary, Travelers shoplift items with the sole intention of returning them a few minutes later for cash refunds. The typical Traveler shoplifter earns between $300 and $600 each day by "working the stores," as they call it.

Based simply upon the consistent long-term shoplifting success of the Travelers, it is evident that even the best security systems operated at department stores will not stop them from shoplifting. Not only are they the type of "career criminals" that Sergeant Burghardt described, but they also are life-long experts at avoiding arrest. The only hope department stores have in stemming their financial losses to Travelers is to set tougher policies on paying cash refunds for returned merchandise. Refunds policies at most department stores -- particularly those that pride themselves on their good customer service -- literally invite the Travelers to shoplift.

In the Chicago area, the favorite department stores of Travelers are K-Mart, Marshall Field's, Nike Town, Lord & Taylor, Nordstrom and Saks Fifth Avenue. For years, the stores gave on-the-spot cash refunds for returned merchandise. Except Nordstrom, most of those stores gradually modified their policies to prevent stolen merchandise from being returned. Nordstrom, widely known among the Travelers for its aggressive store security, but also for its liberal returns policy, is regarded as the best shoplifting target in the Chicago area. A highly successful Traveler shoplifter reported, "It's harder to work the Nordstrom stores because of their security, but the payoff is worth it, and no one questions you when you take stuff back in for refunds."

Marshall Field's, like many other upscale Chicago stores, changed its returns policy in 1993, expecting to reduce its alarming rate of shoplifting-for-cash. Utilizing an expensive electronics system at each cash register, Field's began issuing vouchers for its own merchandise instead of making cash payments for returns when no receipts were available. The new system puzzled Travelers for only a short time, but they quickly found an easy solution to it: They used the vouchers to "buy" new merchandise at the store; then, armed with a new receipt, they returned the new merchandise for a cash refund.

The Travelers' least favorite Chicago stores are Bloomingdale's, Carson Pierie Scott and Nieman Marcus. When merchandise is returned to those stores without a receipt, the stores either apply credit to the customer's charge account or mail a refund check within two weeks. Because most Travelers avoid using credit cards and are reluctant to wait around in an area until they can receive checks in the mail, they simply choose to concentrate their shoplifting efforts on easier targets.

Detective John Wood of Pinellas County, Florida, said it is impossible for anyone in law enforcement or retailing to estimate the full scope of Traveler shoplifting. "Nobody has any idea how extensive it is. The Traveler names are, for the most part, common enough that there has been no attempt by anyone to separate out Traveler shoplifters from normal, every-day shoplifters. How many people are named Stewart? Thousands upon thousands that are not Travelers. So if a woman named Mary Stewart is picked up for shoplifting, no one makes the connection that she is a Traveler woman."

Nearly always, when a Scottish Traveler is arrested for shoplifting, he or she will immediately post bond and skip town. For them, posting bond is merely one of the unfortunate costs of doing business. It's their overhead.

Travelers will, however, do anything they can to avoid jail or prison. To them, serving time is not a disgrace, but it represents clear evidence of their failure to elude authorities. More than that, however, incarceration means a loss of something that is very precious to them: their freedom to travel. According to Detective Wood, "There are a couple of reasons they hate prison so much, but the main reason is the kind of lifestyle they lead. They can just hook up their trailer and leave anywhere they are in fifteen minutes, and that's about as free as you can be in this country today. These people travel, on a day-to-day basis, the way we'd like to when we retire, and they've done it all their lives. When they lose their freedom, they lose something that is integral with them."

He added, "But besides that, when they're in prison, they're put into a position where they have to associate with all those dirt balls who are there -- people they regard as sub-humans, people they can't stand! There are no other Travelers in prison for them to associate with. Then too, the Scotch Travelers literally have a phobia about germs and disease. It's actually an obsession with the Travelers I know. I think that's because they travel so much and are in so many new and different surroundings that they have to be careful about picking up some bug. So the women are unbelievable about keeping their trailers or apartments clean. One of the things apartment managers like about them -- and there are things they don't like as well -- but one of the things they *do* like is when the Travelers move out, the apartment can be rented again that day because when the Travelers were living there, the women were constantly busy cleaning and scrubbing it."

If anyone asks Florida detectives Wood or John McMahan whether Travelers pay tributes to clan leaders or Gypsy "kings," their first reaction is to laugh at such a ridiculous question. Then they'll point out that all Travelers -- Scottish, Irish or English -- are so fiercely independent, the very concept of paying tribute to anyone would be offensive to them.

McMahan admitted that from time to time, he hears claims from Orlando's most influential resident Gypsies that the Travelers will have to pay if they want to operate in central Florida. But he said no Gypsy would actually be brave enough to ask Travelers for money.

"There's good reason for that," Wood said. "The Travelers wouldn't pay. And additionally, Gypsies are scared to death of the Travelers. They know the Travelers would have no qualms about beating the living poop out of them. No qualms at all!"

"The average Traveler would wipe up the floor with the average Gypsy," McMahan added.

"Especially the Scotch," Wood said. "The Scotch really do like to settle disputes with their hands, and some of those guys really work at being accomplished fighters. They work out, they go to the gym, they hit the heavy bag. Gypsies are liars, not fighters. I've had Gypsies tell me, 'Don't you worry about the Travelers. We'll take care of the Traveler problem around here,' and my reaction has always been, 'Yeah, right. Not in *your* lifetime!'"

Wood admits he also has little hope that law enforcement agencies anywhere can ever hope to halt -- or even slow -- the Travelers' criminal activities. "Travelers are intelligent, they're shrewd, and they're more skillful in eluding police than police are in catching them. And make no mistake about it, they've got money, too. Some of them have more money than they'll ever need. My people, the Scotch Travelers, are actually stronger than ever financially. They've already gotten into legitimate enterprises, especially with the investment mobile home parks. We know of a couple parks in Phoenix where they made $500,000 to a million dollars when they turned them over, and they didn't have the parks longer than about eighteen months.

"They're becoming more and more sophisticated as well. Now they're setting up corporations; they're forming limited partnerships. There's a Scotch Traveler who has a condo in Miami on the Inter-coastal Waterway who was at one time one of the largest mobile home park developers on the west coast of Florida. He engineered a ten-million-dollar loan from the Bank of Tokyo to finance one entire development, from buying the land to developing the mobile home park."

Wood grimaced. "I don't know what the solution is, ultimately, to these people. Some of us have been dealing with them for the last six or eight years, and I can't honestly see where we've made a dent in their activities. They're still going strong."


The Scottish Travelers hit south Florida late in 1994 with a new wrinkle on their old termite examiner scam. After the fake examiner discovered termites in the victim's house, he offered to kill them with pesticide at no charge. Then, accidentally, he sprayed the victim's arm. Rushing his victim inside to wash, the Traveler said the pesticide was corrosive to jewelry, and he advised the victim to take off his rings and other jewelry and put them in a glass of milk for an hour. The milk, he explained, neutralized the acidic effect of the pesticide. An hour later, when the victim dumped out the milk, he discovered his jewelry was gone.

In Palm Beach County, that scam went awry for one victim. Unable to remove rings from her fingers, she got into a tussle with the Traveler. She fell and broke her hip and shoulder. She died ten days later in the hospital.

Three weeks later, Scottish Travelers from all over America poured into central Florida. They rented an entire 1,000-room hotel south of Orlando for a weekend Christmas party. The hotel's huge parking lot was not large enough to contain all the vehicles that an estimated 3,000 Scottish Travelers drove there. The vehicles had license plates from California, Arizona, Texas, Washington, Missouri, Kansas, Nebraska, British Columbia and every state east of the Mississippi River.

Parked in the grass, shaded by a small tree near the eastern corner of the hotel, was a new, bright red pickup truck with shining black pressurized tanks in the bed and a rack of aluminum extension ladders attached to the roof. On each door of the truck was a large magnetic sign that said, "Williamson Paving and Sealing. Jack Williamson, Owner."

# 10
# The Scams

It's a long way from Fort Worth to Elkhart, Indiana, but Jimmy Burke's first cousin Paul (not his real first name) relishes making the trip a couple of times each year. Paul and his wife, Sally, regard Elkhart as sort of the jumping-off point for operating their confidence games in the Midwest. For a couple of weeks every summer, they like to camp on the north end of Elkhart in a new travel trailer that they've just bought from a local manufacturer and, while Sally stays in the park with the trailer, Paul scours the small towns of lower Michigan in search of driveway and roof sealing work. Sally always leaves the campground a couple of hours a day, taking her children along, so that she can shoplift from Elkhart's department stores.

In July 1980, Paul recruited a young black man to help him spread sealer on driveways and roofs. The two men were exceptionally fortunate in finding work that summer in the Michigan communities of Sturgis, Constantine, Three Rivers and Benton Harbor, and Paul was able to pay his hired hand quite well. The young fellow wasn't stupid, however, and he quickly realized his employer was a slick crook, not a legitimate businessman. That was okay with him, though; the money was good.

As the two men became more relaxed in each other's presence, Paul told his helper -- called a *guthie* by the Travelers -- details of some of his most successful scams, and the two often joked about how easily people were swindled and how gullible they were. Paul boasted that Sally was an expert at a confidence game called a pigeon drop, but she hadn't been able to work the swindle while in Elkhart because the scam is at its best when it's operated by two people. The *guthie* said his wife, an attractive woman in her early twenties, would be glad to help however she could.

The black couple met with the Burkes at Paul's trailer, and the two wives decided almost immediately that they would be able to work together. For two days, Sally rehearsed her new accomplice in the techniques of running a successful pigeon drop. On July 28, they drove to the Concord Mall south of Elkhart, and Sally told the woman that while they waited for a *pigeon* to appear, they might as well make some money. She led the way to the nearby K-Mart department store and stationed her accomplice in a secluded corner of the parking lot. Then, more to show off than to make money, she walked inside the store and quickly stole a pocket calculator, an expensive bottle of cologne and a few other items. She brought the merchandise outside, doctored the price tags and stuffed the items into a K-Mart bag that she had picked up on her way out of the store. Then she directed the other woman to return the merchandise to the store, claim she had received the items as birthday gifts but wanted cash refunds instead. Five minutes later, the woman walked out of K-Mart with a big grin on her face. She returned to where Sally stood and said, "It was easy! And I got $142!"

The female con artists returned to their car in the Concord Mall parking lot and drove around the mall for an hour while Sally watched shoppers come and go. Finally, she nudged the black woman and said, "There's our pigeon." She pointed to an elderly woman sitting alone in a parked car. Sally parked her own car out of the old woman's line of vision, got out and approached the pigeon from the rear. She walked slowly past the woman, pointedly looking into an envelope she carried. Then she paused, acting as if she'd noticed the old woman for the first time, and walked over to the intended victim, a concerned look on her face.

Sally stopped beside the woman's car and said, "My God, I've just found a lot of money! What should I do with it?" She opened the envelope and showed the old lady a wad of bills.

"Where did you find it?" the woman asked just as a young, well dressed black woman walking past stopped.

Sally pointed behind her. "Right there on the ground. Under that pickup truck."

The black woman approached closer and asked, "How much money is there?"

Sally motioned her nearer, and she in turn walked closer to the woman in the car. Quietly, so that no one else could overhear, she said, "Almost $13,500!"

The old woman's mouth dropped open, and the black woman exclaimed, "Wow! That *is* a lot of money! What are you going to do with it?"

"I don't know. I suppose I'll have to give it back to whoever lost it."

"Don't do *that*!" said the black woman. "Finders keepers, remember."

"I think I'd keep it if I were you," volunteered the elderly woman.

Sally said, "I work at a store inside. I think I'll go in and ask around if anybody lost an envelope full of money. If nobody did, maybe I'll share it with you ladies." She ran quickly inside the building.

The black woman turned to the old woman and said, "I hope she does share it with us. I wouldn't mind having a couple of thousand dollars extra right now."

"Yeah," said the woman in the car. "I'm seventy-two years old, and I can use all the money I can get."

Sally came out of the mall a few minutes later. She was not carrying the envelope. "Oh no," said the black woman. "She must have found the owner." The older woman's spirits sank visibly.

Sally approached and said, "I left the money inside to be counted, and a friend of mine is going to record the serial numbers. I'd split the money with you ladies, but I'd be taking all the risk if the real owner showed up."

The black woman said, "I don't think that'll happen. And to show you how convinced I am, I'll put up six thousand dollars of my own money that I just took out of the bank an hour ago. We'll put my six thousand with the money you found, and if nobody claims the $13,500, we'll split the whole $18,500 down the middle. How does that sound?"

Sally considered the offer for a few seconds and then said, "It sounds okay to me. That way, you're sharing the risk."

The old lady jumped out of her car. "Hey, what about me?" she asked. "Don't I get any of the money? I was here when you found it."

Sally said to the black woman, "She's right. We ought to give her a share if she's willing to put up earnest money the way you're going to."

"I can do it!" exclaimed the old woman. "I've got $6,000 worth of certificates of deposit at my bank."

"Okay, then," said Sally. "You go get your money, and we'll wait for you here."

The old woman drove quickly to her bank, and asked a teller to give her $6,000 from her CDs. Excited about the prospect of making a profit of more than $2,000 in just a few minutes, she told the teller about her good fortune. The teller cautioned her that the chain of events sounded like a confidence game and advised the woman against withdrawing her funds. But the woman brushed aside the advice and returned to the shopping center with $6,000 in her purse. She was relieved to see Sally and the black woman waiting for her; she had been afraid they might decide to split the money without her.

She showed the women her $6,000, and Sally cautioned her not to display it so openly. "Give it here," said the black woman. "I'll put it in an envelope with my money. That way, it's all together, but we can keep it apart from the $13,500." She put the cash in a nearly full envelope and, looking around to make sure no one was watching, stuffed the envelope into a pocket.

Sally said, "Wait a minute. If you don't mind, I'd rather that the money be kept by her." She motioned to the old woman.

The black woman shrugged. "That's okay with me." She took the envelope out of her pocket and gave it to the pigeon. She said, "You'd better put it in your purse, though, before somebody gets curious about it." The old woman opened her purse and dropped the envelope inside.

"Let's go back inside the mall and check on our money," said Sally with a smile.

The black woman hesitated. "I'll be right with you," she said. "I have to go to my car a minute."

"Go on ahead," Sally told the old lady. "I'll wait for her, and we'll meet you inside the mall."

The old woman walked to the mall entrance and stood just inside the door waiting for her new partners. Several minutes passed, and the young women did not follow her. Suddenly worried, the woman opened her purse and took out the envelope. She looked inside it and discovered that it was packed full of sheets of paper. She looked around her, hoping to find someone she could ask to help her. Then she began to cry.

Paul and Sally Burke left Elkhart quickly after the successful pigeon drop, knowing local police officers would issue a bulletin describing Sally. They towed their new travel trailer west on the Indiana Toll Road, bypassed Chicago and stopped at a campground on the outskirts of Madison, Wisconsin. Five families of Irish Travelers --

the Macks, two trailers of Costellos and two trailers of Rileys -- were already camped there, as was a family of Scottish McMillans. Paul's reputation as a first-class con artist was well known among the other Travelers, and they admitted to him that business was very good indeed in the Madison area. All were operating driveway sealing trucks, and they had been so busy with that kind of work that they had not found time to run any other scams except for some shoplifting by the women and children. The Burkes set up camp in the park and prepared for an extended stay they felt sure would be profitable.

The next day, Paul drove his paving/sealing truck through rural neighborhoods, scanning residences that needed either driveway or roof repair. He particularly watched for homes occupied by elderly people -- especially old women. Whenever he spotted an old man or old woman working in the yard, he stopped. If they would not hire him for roof or driveway work, he'd write their names and addresses in a notebook he carried.

Alice Carlson (not her real name) was in her seventies. She had lived alone eight years since her husband died, and although she was in excellent health, she was not physically able to keep her home as well maintained as it had been before her husband passed away. Her sons always promised to make repairs for her, but they were busy with families of their own, and they forgot. A few days earlier, rainwater had leaked through the roof of her home, into her kitchen, and she had called her older son angrily and demanded to know when he would repair her roof. He had promised to hire a workman to fix it in a couple of days.

That was why, when Paul Burke pulled his truck into Alice Carlson's driveway that morning, he received an enthusiastic welcome from her. "I was doin' some roof repair down the street," he said, waving his hand in the general direction of some other houses, "and your neighbors said you'd told them your roof needed sealing. I had some sealer material left in my tank, so I figured I'd offer you a good price if you'd have your roof sealed today. That way, I don't have to waste half a tank of sealer, and I can solve your problem without charging you too much."

Mrs. Carlson was a little puzzled. She did not think she had mentioned her leaky roof to any of her neighbors. She would have been too ashamed to tell them anything like that. But then, she was getting more forgetful the older she lived, and she just might have said something and not remembered it. She thought to herself that it would show her smart aleck sons if she had the roof repaired herself instead of waiting for them to do it for her.

"How much will you charge, young man?" she asked Burke.

"Well, since I have that half a tank left, I'll do the whole roof for you for just ten dollars."

Mrs. Carlson was amazed. She did not know what roof repair work cost, but she was sure it ordinarily cost a whole lot more than ten dollars. "You just get right at it, then," she told the man.

Burke poured fifty gallons of driveway sealer material into his 200-gallon tank and mixed in fifty-five gallons of silver paste. Then he filled the tank with gasoline from a supply he carried in his truck. He unlimbered a set of ladders from atop his pickup truck and carried pails of aluminum-color sealer onto the roof. He worked for two hours, painting the roof with the flammable substance. Then he climbed down and approached Mrs. Carlson, looking sad. He told her, "Mrs. Carlson, your roof's so dry that it's soakin' up my sealer about as fast as I'm puttin' it on. The job's already run into quite a lot of money, and I'm only half finished. But before I did any more, I wanted to check with you to make sure you're willin' to spend so much."

Mrs. Carlson protested: "But I thought you said the job would cost only ten dollars!"

"Yes, ma'am, I did. And that's all I'll charge you for my labor, no matter how long the job takes. But you must understand that I have to be reimbursed for my sealer material. I can't just put it on free."

"Of course not, young man," said the widow. "How much *is* your material, and how much have you used so far?"

"I don't really know how much I've used," Burke said. "But if you'll walk with me to my truck, we'll check the gauge on my tank and find out." They checked the gauge, which Paul had already set at the 100-gallon mark. He said, "I've used 100 gallons, so at fifteen dollars a gallon, your roof job is already costin' $1,510. The other half of the roof could require more sealer than that, though, because it's on the side of the house that gets the most sun."

Mrs. Carlson was shocked. But she could not argue about price; she had no idea what a gallon of roof sealant cost. She could see the side of the roof that Burke had finished, and the silvery shine of the sealant definitely added to the appearance of her house in addition to stopping her roof from leaking. Recalling her resolve to have her roof repaired without help from her sons, she set her jaw and said, "Go ahead and do the rest of it, young man."

Burke was delighted. The stupid old ref woman was a real sucker. She seemed almost anxious to give her money away. Working feverishly, he made a point of refilling his tank, knowing beforehand that the second half of the house would require the full 200 gallons of his *sealant*. He finished the job in two hours and once again led Mrs. Carlson to his truck so that she could see for herself that he had used a whole tank of material. As she walked around the house, examining the job, Burke make out a bill. On it, he wrote, "Unconditional Five-Year Guarantee," knowing that the words were as worthless as the sealant material he had used. When he gave Mrs. Carlson his bill -- for $4,510 -- the widow accepted it with a forced smile and, hands shaking in anger at herself for spending so much money, she wrote a check to the handsome, polite workman.

Paul left the Carlson residence as quickly as possible and drove immediately to the widow's bank to cash her check. Mrs. Carlson tried to return to her yard work, but she had lost interest in it for some reason. Instead, she went into the house, undressed and climbed into bed. She was still there the next morning when her doorbell rang and a businessman from nearby Madison introduced himself and said that her son had sent him to repair her roof. She told him she had already hired the work done and explained to him what had happened the previous day. The man grimaced and asked, "May I use your telephone? I want to call your son. And then I think you ought to consider telephoning the police."

It was not hard for the roof repairman and Mrs. Carlson's son to convince her she'd been conned. She said that deep in her heart, she had known that all along. But she refused to let them call the police. She said she did not want anyone to know how foolish she had been.

But two weeks later, the widow's son read a magazine article about the swindles of the Irish Travelers, and he called the article's author.

The day after Paul Burke pocketed $4,510 of Mrs. Carlson's retirement fund, he rented a motel room near Madison just so he could have easy access to a telephone. Using names and addresses of elderly people that he had recorded in his notebook while scouting rural neighborhoods, he began dialing telephone numbers. Each conversation began like this: "Mrs. Smith, my name is Detective Paul Burke. Do you have a savings account at the branch of the First National Bank that's near your home? You do? I thought so. The president of the bank gave us your name and said you might be willing to help us in an investigation.

"One of the employees at your bank has been embezzling money out of people's accounts. We think we know which one it is, but we have to catch him at it. Here's what we'd like you to do. Go to the bank this morning and withdraw all your money. Take it home with you, and I'll meet you there. We'll record the serial numbers on all the bills. Then you give the money to me, and I'll take it back to the bank and deposit it in your account. That way, when the bank employee tries to steal your money, we'll be able to catch him red-handed with the evidence."

An elderly woman agreed enthusiastically to help the officer with his investigation, and she withdrew $10,000 from her savings account. On the way home, though, she recalled that she had once read about a swindle that involved con men posing as police officers, so she stopped at a telephone booth and called the Dane County police department. She told Officer John Bierd about her conversation with Burke, and he gave her instructions to follow so that the Irish con artist could be caught. But for some unknown reason, Burke did not contact the woman again, and he and his family left the Madison area in the middle of the day.

Paul Burke's Aunt Beatrice -- his mother's sister -- married an Irish Traveler named Tom Riley many years ago, but he died not long after they were married. She gave birth to three illegitimate children -- Thomas, Bridget and Jane. No one among the Travelers knows who fathered the three kids, although there is speculation they were fathered by a married Traveler with whom Bea had an affair and then blackmailed for between $25,000 and $30,000. Beatrice has traveled extensively from Texas and Florida to New York and Ohio, and she has left behind her an impressive list of victims, as well as an extensive arrest record. She's regarded as something of a character by the Irish clan, although she's likable and reportedly has a fine sense of humor. Law enforcement authorities in a few states have warrants out for her arrest, and a police officer in Ohio once said that if she's ever caught in that state, she'll never see the outside of a prison wall again.

Her son Tom is even better known among law enforcement agents than she is -- although he's known by names other than his real one. Like all Traveler children, Tom learned swindles by watching his mother in action, and Bea -- an expert swindler -- taught him well. Tom apparently graduated from his apprenticeship and began running cons on his own during the mid-1970s while he was still a teenager. By the age of fifteen, he had earned a reputation as a "granny man" -- meaning that he would do almost anything for money.

Among the Travelers, rumor is that while still in his teens, he developed a new, high-class swindle. He allegedly scored nearly one hundred thousand dollars by taking out a mortgage on an expensive condominium in the Colorado ski resort area and then "selling" the condo at bargain prices to several people. He is reputed to have collected $10,000 deposits and down payments from his buyers within a few days and then left the state before the new owners could claim occupancy.

According to Tom's nearly legendary reputation among the Travelers, he teamed up with an older non-Traveler woman named Susan Averitt in the late 1970s. Law enforcement authorities have never been able to identify Tom positively as Averitt's partner in the scams that followed that alleged union, but whether he was or not, the unique chain of events provided Tom with a reputation among the Travelers that is virtually unequalled by any other member of the Irish clan.

The documented facts are that a couple using the names of Murphy John Averitt and Susan Averitt were chased out of Ohio in 1977. They operated numerous scams in the Southwest for several months before hitting San Antonio, Texas, early in 1978. There, they bought several automobiles by answering individuals' newspaper ads on weekends and then writing bogus checks. One of the cars they purchased was a two-door red sedan owned by Mrs. Andrea Millican, 21, of San Antonio. As San Antonio and Bexar County authorities searched for the pair, Mrs. Millican and her 25-year-old sister, Mary Venus, spotted Susan Averitt driving the red sedan, and they gave chase in another car. Riding in the sedan with Susan were her five-year-old daughter and a 32-year-old Traveler woman named Susan Walker, who had assisted the Averitts in their used car scam. The sisters caught the women in the stolen car in the northeast section of

Bexar County, but Susan Averitt pulled a gun and killed them. Susan's daughter witnessed the slayings.

In the car with the two dead sisters was Mrs. Millican's six-month-old son. Susan Walker insisted that the boy be taken to the home of a woman who was baby sitting with Averitt's two other children, ages 2 and 1. The two Averitt children were picked up, and the baby was left there. Then the two Susans and Murphy John left Texas with the three Averitt children and headed for New York. They were arrested by FBI agents several days later after checking into an Indianapolis motel. The Averitts were charged with murder, but those charges were dropped against Murphy John when Susan Walker testified he was not at the scene.

In exchange for her testimony against Susan Averitt, Walker was allowed to plead guilty to theft-fraud, and Murphy John was charged with theft. Following a spectacular trial, Susan Averitt was convicted of the murders and was sentenced to two life terms in prison. Susan Walker was ordered to prison for three years, and Murphy John was sentenced to one. According to sources within the Irish Traveler clan, at no time did anyone connect Murphy John Averitt to master con artist and "granny man" Tom Riley.

Murphy John served his sentence and was released from prison, and Susan Walker was paroled after serving one year. They immediately began touring the country with their various confidence games. After one scam in Georgia -- the details of which are not available -- their identities as Averitt and Walker became known to police officers, and a warrant was issued for their arrest for theft and a parole violation. They continued to travel freely, however, living in motels and occasionally with Traveler relatives.

Using a variation of the condominium sales scam, they rented houses in Nashville, Tennessee, and Schaumburg, Illinois, and then re-rented the buildings to several different families, taking security deposits and a month's rent from each one before skipping out. They used the names Marcello in Tennessee and Sheldon in Illinois, and no one connected them with either the scams or the murders in Texas. Law enforcement officers later traced some of their movements under various aliases. Susan Walker, for example, used the names Susan Ramsey Walker, Susan Carol Ramsey, Susan Carol Walker, Sue Weir Averitt, Sue Avery, Sue Connelly, Sue Nell Averitt, Sue Carol Averitt and Susan Corrales.

In June 1981, at the age of 23, Murphy John returned to Texas with Susan in order to take advantage of the economic boom that was occurring there. They avoided San Antonio and went to Houston, which Murphy John realized would be a perfect place for his rent scam because of the housing shortage that existed there. In the city of Spring, a suburb of Houston, they rented a three-bedroom house in a 600-home subdivision. They told Robert Ley, a representative of the development company, Postwood, Incorporated, that their names were John and Linda Marcello. They claimed they were in the business of customizing vans and had just moved to Houston from New Orleans. They paid Ley $500 for one month's rent and $175 as a damage deposit and were scheduled to move into the house June 11, 1981.

The house was left empty, but telephone service was ordered in the name of Linda Belt. Seven days worth of classified advertising space offering the home for rent was purchased in the *Houston Post* by Linda Baye, and rentals of the home began immediately. Murphy John and Susan charged the families first and last months' rent, plus a security deposit. When 28-year-old Don Cook, a Cincinnati mechanic, arrived with his wife Sheri and their three children, Murphy John provided them with several details about the neighborhood, gave them a neighborhood newsletter and told them how to obtain passes to a nearby swimming pool. "He even told us a church was going to be built here soon, and we found out later that was true," Cook said to reporters the following week.

James Reese, 31, and his pregnant wife Linda rented the house before they left their home in Denver with their three children. The plumber later said, "I knew the moment I showed up that I'd been had because I couldn't find the key that was supposed to be left at the house for me."

In a matter of a few days, eight families arrived in Spring to claim the house. John and Marge LaTourneau came from Nisswa, Minnesota. Mr. and Mrs. John Ellis, from Missouri. Mr. and Mrs. Jack Martin, from Tulsa. Mr. and Mrs. Glen Zapalaco, from Houston. Lonnie and Carolyn Well of Houston were among the last to arrive, and when they saw the other families gathered there and heard their stories, they returned immediately to their old residence. So did 35-year-old Odis Patterson of Houston. The scam, which netted a total of $5,900 for Murphy John and Susan, received nation-wide attention when three of the homeless families -- fourteen individuals -- moved into the house temporarily, and sympathetic Texans began collecting groceries and money for them.

As the story of their plight spread, it was fueled by the appearance of a gray-haired mystery lady driving a white Cadillac and refusing to identify herself. She gave each of the families $1,000 in $100 bills and told them God had sent her to help them. Speculation among the Irish Travelers months later was that the woman was none other than Beatrice Riley herself, Tom Riley's famous con artist mother!

Warrants were issued for John and Linda Marcello, and the local sheriff's department assigned an officer full time to the case. Police investigative work could only be described as rotten, however. More was uncovered about the con artists by a private citizen, a Texas newspaper reporter and outside law enforcement officials. A Spring resident, Mike Willis, discovered in only five minutes of telephone work that a white Cadillac driven by the con artists had been leased in New Orleans by a man calling himself John Walker. And *San Antonio Light* newspaper reporter Don Heath connected the con artists to two of the people involved in the 1978 murder case, which he had covered for his paper. He told Bexar County Sheriff's Captain Alfred Carreon his suspicions, and Carreon sent photographs of Murphy

John Averitt and Susan Walker to Houston. The rental scam victims identified the pair as the man and woman who had cheated them. A nation-wide alert for the couple was issued but Murphy John and Susan were never caught.

The man sought as Murphy John Averitt since 1981 appeared to vanish off the face of the earth. The "granny man" Irish Traveler named Tom Riley, on the other hand, has traveled widely throughout America and is an active participant in the social events and lifestyle of the Irish Travelers, along with his wife Elizabeth and their four small children, Betty, Bridget, Thomas and John.

Most Irish, Scottish and English Travelers are relatively easy to track because of their custom of living in the travel trailers that they sell from campgrounds and vacant lots. Any law enforcement official who makes himself familiar with the brand names of trailers that the Travelers peddle can determine quite easily whether members of the clans are in his locale simply by looking for the trailers. It should be evident by now that while the Travelers are selling their trailers, they also are shoplifting at department stores, blacktopping driveways, sealing roofs and running any number of other confidence games, frauds and swindles, but police officers tend to ignore that fact and conclude that, at the worst, the Travelers are in town just to misrepresent the trailers they sell. As a matter of fact, money from trailer sales totals less than one-seventh of any Traveler family's annual income.

The Travelers are aptly named; they love to travel, and they do it extensively. Jimmy Burke once said, "I've been all over. I spend the winters in Florida, usually between Orlando, Tampa and St. Petersburg, and there I mainly sell trailers and relax. After I leave Florida, I'll go up to Elkhart and pick up a trailer, then go over to New York and settle into a campground while I work the truck. When I'm not workin' the truck, I'm travelin' from Elkhart to West Virginia --

Charleston or Huntington primarily, because they're both good towns for sellin' trailers -- then down through Virginia to Alexandria or Richmond. I might hit Michigan, mainly to work driveways and roofs. A lot of Travelers work rods (lightning rods) in Michigan. If I go into a town and there are already some (Traveler) families there, I might pull into a park and work the area anyway because that don't make no difference to anyone. If I know the exact area they're workin', though, I wouldn't go right to that area; I'd find my own area of town to work. In Florida, there are not even any general rules like that. Workin' the truck in Florida is so hard, though, that the Travelers usually only hit the black people."

Like Jimmy, most Travelers follow a pattern when they move from place to place during the spring, summer and fall. But the pattern varies from family to family, and even a family's pattern can change if an area stops producing money or another locale seems to be more promising. The Northern Travelers keep in constant touch with a few old women they call *advisors* who spend most of their time in one community. Information about where the various clan members are, and how successful they are in operating their swindles, is telephoned to the *advisors*, who pass on messages to other Travelers when they call her. Jimmy's favorite advisor was Lizzie O'Roarke, mother-in-law of his older sister Wanda Jessee.

No area of the country is immune to visits from the Travelers. For example, early one spring a team of writers arrived in Fort Worth to research activities of the Irish clan. While they were there, reports of Traveler scams poured into their office from Connecticut, Chicago, New York, Kansas City, New Jersey, Pennsylvania, California, Denver, Louisiana, Minnesota, Indiana, Ohio and even Saskatchewan, Canada. During the period the writers were in Forth Worth, dozens of Traveler families also were selling travel trailers and operating various scams farther south in the Rio Grande Valley; in one day's issue of the *McAllen Monitor*, fifteen Traveler families advertised trailers for sale.

From Connecticut, Fairfield Police Lieutenant Robert Comers told John Jordan, staff writer for the *Norwalk Fairpress*, that local banks had lost several hundred dollars to flimflam artists. The bank flimflam was and is a popular swindle used by Irish and Scottish Travelers -- especially by elderly clan members, who can get away with it easiest. Here's the account Comers related to Jordan: "A person went into a bank with nine $100 bills and spoke in broken English and asked for change in twenties. After the teller counted it and gave it to him, the person lowered the money just below the counter and skimmed off some bills. He then showed the teller a piece of paper (saying) he wanted the change in tens, not twenties. The teller, not knowing the man skimmed money, gave the man change in tens without counting (the $20 bills) before doing so."

The flim-flam artist skimmed some of that money and then showed the teller another piece of paper saying he wanted the change in fives and tens. After receiving those funds, the man said he just decided he wanted the money in traveler's checks, so he began to bargain for a good price on those. Failing to get what he believed was a good price for traveler's checks, he asked for his original $100 bills instead of the fives and tens, which meanwhile he had skimmed. The flustered teller exchanged the original $900 for the smaller bills, glad the series of transactions was about to be concluded. Comers reported the flimflam resulted in profits of $500 from two Fairfield banks.

A few weeks later, a man and woman represented themselves as business people to a Wilton, Connecticut, real estate firm and said they wanted to purchase a property. They looked at several that were for sale and agreed to buy on condition that the real estate agent cash a check for working capital that they needed. They promised to refund the money in a few days when they received cash they were expecting to be sent from another state. The agent gave them $350 for a check he later discovered was no good, and the couple left, never to be seen by the agent again. The routine was one that has been used by members of the Scottish Travelers for at least half a century!

Variations of the pigeon drop swindle were used quite successfully that summer at shopping centers in the New York City metropolitan area. The victims, as usual, were frequently elderly people, and some of them lost their life savings to Traveler con artists. Lieutenant Arthur Buchanan of the Bridgeport, Connecticut, police department told Norwalk reporter Jordan many of the victims of such swindles realized there might have been something shady about the transactions, but they believed they would make money anyway. "If the person isn't willing to make money, then the swindles won't work," he said. "They (the con artists) usually approach twenty-five or thirty people before they get their mark. We used to stake out local banks on Saturdays looking for these guys, and we used to make arrests. But now with all the other crimes we've got to worry about, we can't do it anymore."

Jack Sherlock, a member of the Southern Irish Travelers based in North Augusta, South Carolina, arrived in the Northeast in May that year. Jack had worked his way from South Carolina by selling cheap carpeting and painting barns, but it had not been a very profitable spring, and he needed some big scores before he could justify asking his wife and two sons to join him on his travels.

He rented a motel room in Bridgeport, Connecticut, and scanned the business sections of local newspapers that he'd bought, looking for names of potential marks. In one newspaper, he read that Joe Morris (not his real name) had just been honored by his real estate company for selling more than a million dollars worth of houses and property the year before. Jack Sherlock smiled to himself and looked up the telephone number of the realty company where Morris worked.

When Joe Morris answered his telephone, a voice on the other end said, "Joe, this is Bill Altgeld. I'm the appliance department manager at Sears. Your name was given to me by a friend of yours named Dave. I'm sorry, but I can't remember his last name."

"You probably mean Dave Fairchild," Morris responded.

"Yeah, I think that's it," said Sherlock. "Anyway, Dave suggested I call you because I was tellin' him about a problem we've got here at the store. We're overstocked with color TV sets, and we've got to get rid of 'em. Now, they're last year's floor display models, but they're brand new, and they carry a full guarantee. They retail for $650 a piece, but I'm sellin' 'em for only $200 each just to get 'em out of our store. Dave, he bought six of 'em. Said he was gonna give a couple to his kids and sell the others to some people who work with him. He said you might want a couple of 'em before they're gone, so that's why I'm callin'."

Morris did some quick mental calculations. He knew several people who would be willing to buy bargain TV sets, and he could sell the sets to them for $300 each, making a fast $100 per set. He asked, "How many do you have left?"

"Well," Sherlock said apologetically, "I've got seven of 'em left, but I'm gonna buy one of 'em myself, so I can let you have up to six. I'm gonna call some other people that Dave recommended to see if they want some too."

"Don't call anybody else! I'll buy all six!"

"Okay, if you insist," said Sherlock. "But I have to get rid of 'em today. Can you pick 'em up this afternoon?"

Morris knew where he could borrow a van, so he said, "Yes, about two o'clock."

"Good," answered Sherlock. "I'll meet you at the loading dock at 2. Now, there's one problem. We can't put those sets on your Sears charge account because of the discounts, and I don't have authority to accept checks as large as $1,200, so you'll have to pay for 'em by cash."

"That's no problem," Morris said eagerly. "I'd prefer to do that anyway. I'll bring the money with me."

Four hours later, Morris and Sherlock met outside the loading dock of the Bridgeport Sears department store. Morris gave twelve $100 bills to the man who introduced himself as Bill Altgeld. Morris noticed that the man had a strange accent -- not quiet Southern, but not quite Midwestern -- and that he was dressed in a flashy style of clothes that went out of fashion several years earlier, but he did not dwell on those observations until an hour later.

Once he had the money, Sherlock told Morris, "Back your van to the loadin' platform, and I'll have a couple of fellows load the TV sets in it for you. I'll give you your receipt at that time." Morris followed the man's directions while "Altgeld" walked into the building. Once inside, Sherlock continued on through the store and out the front to his truck. As he drove away, he ventured a quick glance toward the rear of the department store and saw Morris standing at the loading dock, leaning against his borrowed van.

About the same time, Scottish Traveler Henry Cooper proved that even people who knew about some of the scams aren't immune to being swindled. He convinced Gene Mazzotta, owner of Gene's Trailer Sales in New Kensington, Pennsylvania, that the driveway of the dealership needed to be patched and sealed. Gene was aware of the travel trailer sales scam, but he did not know that the same people cheated people with their driveway work. He hired Cooper to seal and patch the driveway for $450. He paid Cooper $350 in advance and withheld $100 until the work was completed. Cooper did a terrible job and, when Mazzotta demanded that the work be done right and completed, the short, stocky middle-aged Scottish Traveler packed up his tools and drove away in his shiny black pickup truck, leaving the work unfinished.

On a beautiful spring Saturday morning in June, a Scottish Traveler named Lawrence Williamson drove his pickup truck through an affluent suburb of Indianapolis. In the truck were his teenage son and his nephew, and the bed of the truck was filled with buckets of dirt from which two-foot-tall saplings were growing. On the doors of his truck were magnetic signs saying, "Williamson Landscaping." When Williamson noticed Paul and Anna Bell (not their real names) mowing grass and pruning shrubbery in their front yard, he stopped his truck and called to them. Paul Bell walked over to the truck, and Williamson smiled and introduced himself: "Hi! I'm Larry Williamson of Williamson Landscaping, and these are my two sons."

Bell nodded a greeting, and Williamson continued, "We've just finished planting some baby oak trees for your neighbors, the Clevelands, and we've got a bunch of saplings left. I'm afraid they're going to die if we don't plant them pretty quick, so if you're interested, I'll give you a bargain price on them and plant them for you free."

Bell looked at the saplings, which were beautiful and obviously fresh, and said, "How much do you want for them?"

Williamson offered, "We'll sell 'em to you for fifteen dollars apiece. That's a real bargain, too, 'cause them are fifty-dollar saplings."

Bell turned to his wife. "How many should we take?"

She replied, "At that price, let's buy twenty."

The agreement made, Bell and his wife returned to their yard work while Williamson and the two boys planted the saplings, spacing them evenly in the area where Mrs. Bell said she wanted them. When the job was completed, Williamson cautioned the Bells: "Now, you have to remember to water them saplings every day for a couple of weeks. And to make sure they take hold properly, you ought to put a little fertilizer around them once or twice." Bell, pleased with the purchase, wrote Williamson a check for $300, and the landscaper left with his truck almost empty of oak saplings.

For two weeks, the Bells watered and fertilized and babied the saplings, but no matter what they did, the little limbs withered and turned black. Bell tried to call Williamson Landscaping but could find no telephone listing for either the company or Lawrence Williamson. Finally, Mrs. Bell contacted an Indianapolis tree surgeon and asked for help. The man asked, "Did you buy those saplings from a fellow named Williamson who was driving a pickup truck?"

"Why yes, we did," she answered.

"Ma'am, I don't know how to tell you this, but you've been swindled. If you dig up one of those saplings, you'll find that it doesn't have any roots. In fact, it's not a sapling at all. It's either just a limb or a sucker that's been cut off an oak tree and stuck in your yard. But if it'll make you feel any better, I'll tell you this: You aren't the only person to be cheated by Mr. Williamson. I've gotten four calls about his dying saplings in the last three days. And I'm sure there are a lot of other victims out there I haven't heard about."

Lawrence Sherlock, police officers later learned, had pulled his baby oak tree swindle on at least ten Indianapolis area families during a five-day period. His average score: $200 per family.

In Winterhaven, Florida, a couple of fast-talking Travelers convinced a blind man that his trees needed trimmed badly. They said they'd do it for fifty dollars. When it came time to pay the con artists, the blind man was far too trusting. He had cashed his Social Security check that morning but had failed to sort his bills in order to know exactly how his $1, $5, $10 and $20 bills were placed in his wallet. So, asking the con artists to help him, he opened his wallet to them and told them to take out the fifty dollars in five and ten-dollar denominations. What happened next was easy to predict, according to former Orange County Detective Bill Morris. The swindlers sorted the blind man's money for him and helped themselves to seven of his twenty-dollar bills!

Both the Irish and the Scottish Travelers hit the Denver area especially hard with their swindles that summer. Ed Donahue was trying to sell travel trailers there for the second straight summer. Donahue, who later would make appearances in Kansas City and Texas, priced his Kentucky Traveler trailer at $7,500; he said it cost him $13,500, but he needed the money because his mother was dying. Oddly enough, he told the same story in Denver the summer before!

Scottish Traveler John Parks, who sometimes uses the last name of Young, was competing with Donahue by trying to sell a new Marauder-built coach at the same motel. Four Scottish Travelers had "For Sale" signs on trailers that were parked in a campground near Golden, Colorado. One of them attracted the attention of trailerist G.L. Filkin of nearby Northglen. He reported, "We had a Layton trailer, but we were looking around for a larger one that we could tow to California. We were interested in a new park model that a woman named McMillan was selling. The other trailers were owned by her father, uncle and brother-in-law. I talked with her, and she told me she had to sell it because she was pregnant and because her husband had to quit his construction job and return to Florida. I took my wife back to look at the trailer, and she gave my wife the same song and dance; she sounded like a recording and never missed one word from the line she gave me. When we left, my wife said, 'She's not pregnant! That was a pillow stuffed under her dress!'"

Outraged, Filkin contacted the local police department but was told no crime had been committed.


Later, a trio of English Travelers -- Jack Harris, Rick Harris and Mike Hanrahan -- were believed to be camped in a park on the outskirts of Lafayette, Louisiana. They were dodging warrants for their arrest from Kansas, where they operated a fraudulent termite inspection scam. They were under indictment of three counts of felony theft and three counts of attempted felony theft. The three men followed this routine: They offered residents of southern Kansas City,

Kansas, free termite inspections and told the homeowners that termites were, indeed, present in the homes. They offered to exterminate the termites for prices ranging from $280 and $550, and they provided five-year guarantees with their work. A suspicious homeowner complained to the Kansas Consumer Protection Agency, which in turn enlisted the help of the Kansas State Board of Agriculture's Division of Entomology. State inspectors examined the homeowner's house and determined that no termites were present. Publicity about the scam caused the Harrises and Hanrahan to leave the state, but not before they collected at least $1,180 in extermination fees. They received another $950 in checks on which payments were stopped. No one knew how many Kansans were victimized but were too embarrassed to complain.

Even the Travelers' suppliers were embarrassed -- and ripped off -- that year by scam artists who grew up in the con artist clans not knowing the meaning of loyalty. They charged several thousand dollars worth of long-distance calls to the companies that supplied them with travel trailers, lightning rods, pickup truck caps and even the plastic material that they used to cover cushions and carpeting in the trailers that they peddled. Brief investigative work revealed that tens of thousands of dollars -- and perhaps more than that -- in phone calls were charged to business phones by the Travelers that year. Technically, the charges were supposed to be paid by those businesses, but when the businessmen claimed they never authorized the calls, the losses were absorbed by the telephone companies.

General Telephone Company of Indiana -- a very small utility in comparison with what was then the Bell System -- was hit hard by calls that were charged to the Travelers' suppliers in Elkhart, Indiana. During the last few months of that year, those suppliers refused to pay for at least $5,000 worth of third-party calls by the Travelers. Third-party calls are those made from one telephone to another, long distance, with charges billed to a third telephone. Calls were made from places such as Denver, Colorado; St. Paul, Minnesota; North Hollywood, California; Orlando, Florida; San Antonio, Texas, and the Rio Grande Valley. A General Telephone investigator said, "During the winter, most of our calls came from the Orlando area of Florida and the Rio Grande Valley of Texas. Between May and August, they were from Tennessee, Kentucky and Colorado. The calls went all over -- to campgrounds, hotels, motels and the callers' relatives. They even called a couple of palm readers."

The largest proportion of calls charged by the Travelers was levied against the telephone number of now-defunct Marauder Travelers in Wakarusa, Indiana. Marauder vice president Joe Mawhorter said the Travelers tried to nick his company for $3,500 worth of long-distance charges; he refused to pay the phone company. Jim Rheinheimer, then president of Eagle Enterprises, also refused to pay for calls charged to his company's telephone. Rheinheimer said he never supplied the Travelers with products they could sell, but he sold caps to them for their pickup trucks. Third-person calls were charged to the Indiana phone numbers of Rush Industries and Kentucky Traveler. Roberts Lightning Protection Company of Missouri, also had calls charged against its telephone, as did Fabulous Fabrics, a company in Elkhart that made plastic coverings for furniture.

Several of the calls were made by women named Martha Hayward, Mary Jane Black and Mary Ann Brooks. All those names were known aliases of the notorious Scottish Traveler named Martha Parks, who was wanted for fraud in several states. Mrs. Parks also used the names of Mary Turner, Joanne Parks, Mary Jane Williamson and Rachel Parks. A telephone company representative said calls were made *to* Martha Hayward in Sullivan, Colorado, from St. Paul. Meanwhile, Mary Jane Black made calls to Kentucky Traveler from Sullivan, and calls to various places were made from St. Paul by Joan Williamson and Angus Keith -- both members of the Scottish Traveler clan.

General Telephone did not know what to do about trying to collect the charges on all those calls and dozens more. Then investigators learned that telephone companies all around the country were losing thousands of dollars each to the Travelers due to third-party calls.

Another favorite scam of the Travelers that year involved posing as utility company workers in order to gain entrance to the homes of old people. The Travelers usually worked in teams of two. One posed either as an inspector for the local power company or as a repairman for the telephone company and, while he kept the old person in the house busy, his accomplice sneaked into the house and quickly checked out hiding places for cash and jewelry. The year before, Irish Travelers stole several thousand dollars from homes in Indiana by posing as representatives of the Northern Indiana Public Service Company and claiming they were conducting energy conservation audits of homes in the area. The Travelers developed that ploy a few days after reading in an Indiana newspaper that the state's power companies were seeking Department of Commerce permission to conduct home energy conservation audits in an attempt to help Hoosiers know whether their homes should be better insulated. Travelers carried clippings of that news article with them as they went through neighborhoods door to door.

In Dayton, Ohio, a 76-year-old woman received a telephone call from a man who identified himself as an employee of the Dayton Power and Light Company. He informed her she had paid her last utility bill with counterfeit money. Of course, she was shocked and asked what she could do about it. He replied, "Gather up all your ten and twenty-dollar bills, and I'll send a man out to check them for you. That way you won't run the risk of being arrested for counterfeiting."

The woman did as he asked, and when the DP&L representative

arrived, she gave him the cash. "I'll have to check these bills with my boss," he said, asking her if he could use her telephone. After dialing a number, he read off the bills' serial numbers and then handed the phone to the woman. She spoke into the phone and waited for a response. When none came, she turned to the man who was holding her money and discovered that he was gone, taking with him about $500 in ten and twenty-dollar bills.

The month of July was especially profitable that year for the Travelers who practiced their scams in Dayton. Besides taking the old woman's $500, the Travelers filled their pockets by posing as police officers, bank agents, Social Security workers and water meter readers in order to swindle gullible Daytonians -- primarily elderly people. In addition, four complaints of driveway sealing swindles were telephoned into the consumer frauds and crimes section of the Montgomery County Prosecutor's office in two days. The three-man Dayton Police Department fraud squad was "swamped" with complaints, according to its chief, Lieutenant Bob Stevenson. In spite of warnings that were published in local newspapers, a 19-year-old woman was the victim of a type of pigeon drop known as *the Jamaican con* in which a swindler posed as a foreigner who didn't trust banks. He convinced the woman to hold his money in a handkerchief and put some of her own with it as a gesture of good faith. When the man left, promising to meet her later, she opened the handkerchief and discovered that it contained rolled up newspaper.

Referring to the outbreak of confidence games in Dayton, Lieutenant Stevenson emphasized, "Greed plays a big part in it sometimes." He told about the Daytonian who realized he was being conned by some professional swindlers, and he decided to turn the tables on them, figuring he could swindle them out of their own money. Instead, he lost several hundred dollars.

Years afterward, Florida investigator John Wood would comment on that strange, but increasingly familiar, phenomenon. No matter how often people are warned about the scams, they continue to be conned, partly because they believe they are too smart to be swindled, he said. "I've made presentations to groups in which, I swear to God, I could see one person looking at the person next to him, obviously thinking, 'Maybe he's stupid enough to be taken, but I'm not.'

"The first step toward being taken is to think you're so smart you can't be. Because these people, the Travelers, are extremely persuasive. And once they start talking to you, you're halfway along the path toward being taken. I tell people, 'If someone comes to your door, just don't talk with them at all. If they engage you in conversation, they're probably going to persuade you to have some work done.' That's what they do. That's what they do for a living, and if they're not good at it, they'll starve."

Many years ago, *Better Homes and Gardens* magazine asked its readers the question, "Can You Be Conned?" Then it answered that question in an article about swindles by stating: "...Knowledgeable, seemingly sophisticated people are defrauded every day by con artists. All it takes is the right scheme, at the right time by the right operator. Older people, especially women, tend to be most vulnerable. Loneliness, concern about retirement costs, a basic trustfulness all contribute to older people's vulnerability. So does the fact that their life savings are accessible in bank accounts."

Senator Warren G. Magnuson warned about the effectiveness of con artists such as the Travelers in his book, *The Dark Side of the Marketplace*. Although badly out of date and generally peppered with inaccuracies about traveling con artists, the 1968 book offered an overview that applies as much today as it did then. The senator, who later was to co-author the important Magnuson-Moss Act dealing with product warranties, wrote: "Unlike the con men of yesterday who were often so heavy-handed that they offended the law, today's modern bandits of the marketplace are the masters of the light touch. With their insidious misrepresentations, silver-tongued lies, half-truths and exaggerated promises, these men can reach even deeper into our pockets without producing a rustle to disturb the law, or even the victim himself...."

Citing a nation-wide study of consumer fraud two years earlier, Magnuson added, "...Nine out of every ten victims of consumer fraud do not even bother to report it to the police. Fifty per cent of the victimized felt they had no right or duty to complain; forty per cent believed the authorities could not be effective or would not want to be bothered; ten per cent were confused about where to report. It is startling to consider that the vast majority of Americans victimized by consumer fraud feel that the law can or will do nothing to help them; but it is even more startling to realize that in many instances, those victims are absolutely correct."

# 11
# Odyssey

Following his final encounter in Ohio with the "Gypsy Hunter," Jimmy Burke returned to Jamestown, New York, briefly before beginning his annual trek to Florida with his brother Paul and sister Peggy. On their way through Pennsylvania at night, they spotted a 22-foot Prowler travel trailer at an RV dealership near Warren, on Route 62, and they stole it. They towed it to Richmond, Kentucky, and put it in storage at the Clay's Ferry campground until they could get a title for it in Alabama. Meanwhile, the trio decided that they ought to try stealing a few other trailers, and that way they could acquire multiple titles at the same time.

Jimmy recalled, "In 1977 I had bought a 32-foot Rogue travel trailer -- a 1978 model -- from Marauder Travelers. I paid $4,500 for it and lived in it through the summer before sellin' it to some people in Owensboro, Kentucky, for $5,500. The man who bought it intended to resell it for a profit. Either he or a friend of his owned a trailer sales lot in Owensboro, and about six months before, when I had been through Owensboro, the trailer had been still sitting there on the lot, not sold.

"Peggy mentioned that if it was still there, it would be a good one to steal. We drove over to Owensboro the next night, and it was still there. I backed the truck to it, and while Paul dropped it on the hitch, Peggy put the steps up. We took the trailer to a little town about twenty miles north of Chattanooga and left it in storage at a tiny motel and campground there. Then we headed for Alabama. It was Sunday evenin', and we had just gotten back on Interstate 75 when Peggy spotted a trailer parked just off the highway. I got off the interstate, turned around and went back, and there it was -- a 1974 model 23-foot Nomad trailer -- parked at a finance company. I figured it had been repossessed. So we hooked onto the Nomad and took it to Kennesaw, Georgia, and put it in storage at the KOA campground there. And once again, we started for Alabama."

Before going much farther, Jimmy decided to earn some money, so the trio stopped at a Woolco department store in Atlanta and shoplifted several items. They returned the merchandise for cash, and as they were leaving the store, Peggy noticed an elderly woman she thought looked familiar. She pointed at her and asked, "Isn't that the Traveler woman who has a trailer lot across the street?"

"Yeah," Jimmy responded. "That's old Bridget from the Village. She's got a new Monte Carlo sittin' out front. Let's go take a look at it."

They drove Jimmy's truck to the dealership, A-1 Trailer Sales, where Mrs. Bridget Williams had about a dozen RVs displayed for sale, and Jimmy opened the Monte Carlo with the master key he always carried. The 25-foot trailer had obviously never been used. It had plastic covers on the carpet and couch -- an extra touch routinely provided by Travelers in order to keep the units from getting dirty.

Peggy said, "It'd be a real blast to steal Old Bridget's trailer!" She laughed and Jimmy laughed, and then they both laughed together. They loved the idea of stealing a trailer from another traveler.

"Let's go outside and look around," Jimmy said.

No one was within sight of the dealership, so Jimmy told Peggy, "Keep watch while I back my truck up to it, and if anybody comes, tell them we're from the factory and we're takin' the trailer back for warranty work." Paul hooked the trailer to Jimmy's truck and they towed it away. They took it to Florence, South Carolina, and put it in storage at the KOA campground, then went to Alabama. There, in various towns, they forged papers and acquired license plates and registrations for each of the trailers. The names of all four stolen trailers were changed to *Regency*.

Jimmy explained later how that was done. "When I was in California, I stopped at an RV dealership to look at a trailer, and I noticed that the parts store had a bunch of big decals -- some sort of coat of arms -- that said *Regency* across them. I thought to myself that Regen-

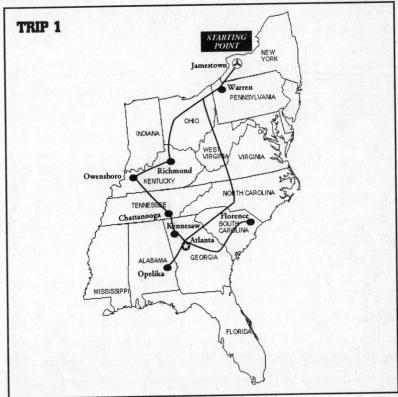

cy would be great for a trailer name if I needed to change the name of one, so I bought ten of the decals."

Using paint remover, the real names of the four trailers were removed from the front and rear awnings and were replaced by Regency decals. "We started our own brand!" Jimmy boasted. "I even made little stickers for on the sides of the trailers. I cut index cards the right size and used the portable typewriter I always carry with me to type 'Regency Trailers, Inc.' on each card, along with an address in Ontario, Canada, that sounded good. Then I typed on the model number, the length, the serial number and the date of manufacture. I bought thin strips of plastic from K-Mart to put over the card and stick it on the side of the trailer. If anybody looked at it, it would seem normal and state that the trailer was manufactured in Ontario. It wasn't likely anybody would try to track down a company in Canada, and if the cops or anybody else asked me about it, I'd say, 'The company just went out of business.'"

Since several detours had already delayed the Burkes' trip to Florida, the trio returned to New York for a brief visit before picking up the trailers and trying to sell them.


The first night back in Jamestown, the Burkes joined Diane and some of Jimmy's local friends for a night on the town. Their initial stop was Big Mike's Bar for drinks. Liquor and laughter flowed freely at first, but the bar suddenly quieted, and when Jimmy looked toward the door, he saw the reason: Buck, Kathy and a friend of theirs named Tom had just entered.

Peggy said later, "Jimmy was obviously surprised because he hadn't seen them since before he left for California. He walked over to Buck, and Buck said he was livin' with the other guy but wanted to be friends with Jimmy. Jimmy agreed, but said he expected Buck to pay for the bad checks he wrote. Buck said they'd get it straightened out, and he asked us to have a drink with him. Paul, Jimmy and I did, but then the other guy, Tom, started sayin' things, personal things, just to agitate Jimmy."

Hot-tempered Peggy finally said, "Tom, why don't you shut up?"

Kathy responded, "Peggy, I think you should mind your own business."

"And I think you should do the same," Peggy retorted.

"Well, this *is* my business. Danny is a good friend of mine and so is Buck. I'm glad they're talking again, so let it go."

"You don't tell me what the hell to do!"

Kathy said, "Peggy, you're just sponging off your brother, and you should go somewhere to make your own life."

Peggy moved closer to Kathy and answered, "I don't take advice from a nigger lover, and I hear that's what you are."

Kathy tried to slap Peggy, but Peggy dodged the blow and hit Kathy in the face with a fist. Kathy screamed and grabbed Peggy's hair with both hands. Big Mike pulled them apart and ordered them to leave, but once outside, Peggy tripped Kathy and shoved her into a snowbank, then began punching and kicking Kathy.

Buck and his friend left the bar and pulled Peggy away from Kathy; then the trio drove away in Buck's car. Relieved the fight was over, Diane suggested that the party be moved to a diner on Third Street.

"When we got to the diner," Peggy said, "a woman that we all knew named Donna was there. She and I had become acquainted sometime earlier, and I knew she'd do about anything for fun. She was about six-foot-four and weighed over 250 pounds, and she was all muscle from liftin' weights. She usually rode a Harley and ran with a tough crowd, and she didn't take no shit from nobody."

While her brothers and friends found a table and looked over dinner menus, Peggy talked with Donna. "How'd you like to go someplace with me and have a little fun?" Peggy asked the other woman.

"Is it legal?" asked Donna.

"Do you care?"

"Hell no. Let's go."

Later, Peggy reported, "Jimmy was drivin' a new Grand Prix that he had just bought, and I asked him if I could borrow it because Donna and I needed to go somewhere. He gave me the keys. I had a pretty good idea where Kathy and that Goddamned wimp Buck were; Buck was so scared of his shadow that he never varied his routine, and I figured he'd be at the Holiday Inn. So Donna and I drove there, and sure enough, Buck's Cadillac was in the parkin' lot. I told Donna what I had in mind, and we looked in the trunk of Jimmy's car and found what we needed -- a big hammer, a crowbar and a huntin' knife. We used the knife to slit the tires on Buck's car, and while Donna busted out all the windows with the crowbar, I used the hammer on the outside metal. We were gonna rip apart the upholstery too, but a couple of guys must have heard the noise because they came runnin' out of the motel shoutin' for us to stop. We got in Jimmy's car and drove back to the diner. We weren't gone more than fifteen minutes."

Just as the group was finishing dinner, two police officers arrived and asked who was driving the Grand Prix with the temporary Ohio tag. Jimmy said it was his.

"What's your name?" one of the officers asked.

"James Burke."

"Do you have some I.D.?"

Jimmy showed the officer his driver's license.

"Did you ever go by the name James Murphy?" the policeman asked.

"What?"

"Do you know anybody named James Christopher Murphy?"

Jimmy answered, "The name don't sound familiar."

"Where have you been for the last hour?"

"Right here," Jimmy said.

The officers asked for confirmation from the diner's manager, who said, "Yeah, he's been here for at least half an hour, probably more like an hour."

A policeman turned back to Jimmy. "Who had your car during the last hour?"

"Some friends had it."

"How long ago?"

"Until just a few minutes ago."

"Where are they now?"

"They left."

"Where did they go?"

Jimmy answered, "Somewhere in Pennsylvania. They live in Erie."

"What are their names?"

"Susan Rafferty and Martha McMillan."

"What's their address?"

"I don't know."

The officer said, "You don't know, but you let them use your car?"

Jimmy answered, "I met them at a bar, and they seemed nice enough."

"Well, your car was involved in an incident up at the Holiday Inn. Do you know a man named Buck?"

Jimmy said, "The name sounds familiar, but I can't place him."

"Well, he knows you. He said someone in your car went to the Holiday Inn parking lot and flattened all the tires on his brand new Cadillac. They busted out all the windows and used a hammer to beat on the car up one side and down the other. He said he thinks you did it, and he also said you're wanted for writing bad checks under the name of James C. Murphy."

Jimmy said, "I don't know what you're talkin' about."

The policeman said, "We'll just see about that in a few minutes. We're waiting for a detective to come in with some pictures."

A few minutes later, a Jamestown detective arrived with a photo from a driver's license in the name of James C. Murphy. The policemen showed the picture to Jimmy and asked, "Are you honestly going to tell me this isn't you?"

Jimmy answered, "It's me. You got me. But if you take me in, you better take Buck in too because it wasn't my signature on all those checks."

The police officers handcuffed Jimmy and took him to the county jail in Mayville. He was there three weeks until bond was set at $2,600, and because he was short of funds, Jimmy borrowed several hundred dollars from his parents so he could post bond and hire an attorney. The businesses where Buck had written the bad checks agreed to drop their complaint if Jimmy repaid $1,300. Those funds were taken out of his bond money, and the rest was returned to Jimmy after charges were dismissed.


After he was released from jail, Jimmy told four of his friends about the trailers he, Peggy and Paul had stolen, and they were intrigued by the story he related. The four young men -- named Mike, Bobby, David and Allen -- regarded Jimmy's life as one big adventure after another, and they asked if they could go along on the next trip. Jimmy agreed to take them, and since Paul and Peggy had an International Travelall they had borrowed from their parents, he said they would all go to Florida in that and his Grand Prix. Peggy wanted to drive her own car, a 1975 Monte Carlo sedan that Jimmy had bought for her a few months earlier.

Later, Diane would have this to say about the man she knew as Daniel Burke and his friends: "Those guys who are supposed to be friends of Danny's are just a bunch of bums. None of them works that I know of. They are really close to him when he has money; they're around him all the time, then, and they spend his money for him really good. But as soon as he's broke or doesn't spend as much money on them, they cause trouble for him. He told them about his aunts and mothers shoplifting, and they talked him into showing them how to do it. I was afraid. I just knew that one time they'd all get caught and Danny would end up in jail."

She said the young men -- who were all older than Burke -- nagged "Danny" about taking them on an adventure, and although they were somewhat frightened knowing the Burke family was part of a nation-wide crime network, they were excited about the prospect of earning large amounts of cash by stealing trailers and operating confidence games.

"Paul and Peggy weren't any better," Diane said. "When Danny first moved here, he decided he was going to settle down. Paul and Peggy found out he was here -- well, he let them *know* he was here -- and they moved in. They called him and told him how broke they were and what they needed, so he sent Peggy money to come up here, and he went to Florida after his brother. While he was here without them, he was doing very well, but when they got here, all the old family troubles started all over again."

Diane added, "Peggy's rough! She's very different from anyone else I've ever met, and she parties a lot. In fact she parties all the time! And I don't think she has any real friends. She makes friends, but then they won't agree with her on something or won't go along with her on something, and she gets angry. I think she's capable of almost anything. I don't think there is any limit to what she would do. Paul is a lot like Danny -- and would look just like him if he gained some weight -- but when Paul's with Peggy, he's completely different; he starts acting wild like Peggy."

Two days after his release from jail, Jimmy left for Florida with Peggy, Paul, Bobby and Mike. Their first stop was Chattanooga, where they picked up the stolen Rogue travel trailer. Jimmy's plan was for the gang to sleep overnight in the trailer in order to keep expenses to a minimum because, after paying his fines and his lawyer, he was nearly broke. The trailer, however, had apparently not been properly winterized, and its water pipes had burst. Jimmy said,

"When we tried stayin' in it the first night, water leaked all over the floor, and we had to move out of it and dry out the carpet before we could sell it."

They towed the renamed "Regency" to Columbia, South Carolina, and put "For Sale" signs on it in front of motel rooms they rented with the balance of their funds. A newspaper ad offering the trailer for sale was published the next morning, and at 10 o'clock, a prospective buyer arrived to look at it. Peggy told the man she and her husband had bought the trailer but were getting a divorce, so she wanted to sell it quickly at a low price so her husband would not try to take all the money away from her. Peggy was offered $5,000 for the Regency. Jimmy recalled, "The guy who wanted to buy it was gonna put it out as a rental, but he didn't know the pipes were bust-

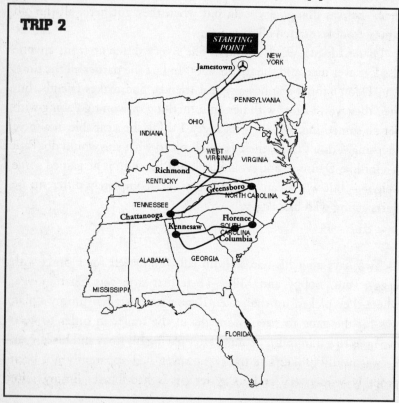

ed. We went to the title office, and the manager gave me a big hassle about the Alabama title. I tried to explain that Alabama didn't have no title for travel trailers, and Peggy was sittin' there not knowin' what to say because the trailer was in her name. The title office had to call Columbia to make sure everything was acceptable before we could get our money, and that took time. Meanwhile, our buyer invited us to go to lunch with him at a local steakhouse, and since we didn't have any money, we went. Well, he walked through the line, ordered a meal and paid for it, and that was when we realized he wasn't gonna pay for our meals. We scraped together enough change to buy two glasses of iced tea, and we shared those among the four of us. The guy said, 'I thought y'all were hungry,' and I said, 'No, we decided to wait until later.' I couldn't say, 'We're broke.' But after we got our money for the trailer, we went out to a nearby cafeteria, and everybody went wild!"

The next stop was the KOA in Kennesaw, Georgia, to pick up the Nomad, which also had been renamed "Regency." That trailer was towed to Greenville, South Carolina, where it was sold from the Kings Court Motel for $3,300. The gang then relaxed for a couple of weeks and spent most of the money on partying, nightclubs, clothes and music tapes. "They loved to see us comin' at the music stores because we spent $150 or $200 each," Jimmy said. "Or, we'd go into a clothing store and buy five or six sets of clothes. Once durin' the trip, me and Bobby and David, who joined us later, flew to Vegas for a few days. We lost several thousand dollars, but we had a good time!"

The gang spent so much money, in fact, that they had to replenish their cash supply by shoplifting from department stores.

From Greenville, the gang drove to Florence, South Carolina, and picked up the Monte Carlo trailer that was in storage at the KOA there. After changing its name to Regency, they towed it to Greensboro and stayed at the Smith's Ranch Motel while they advertised the coach for sale in a local newspaper. Two days later, Jimmy sold the trailer for $5,500. Next, the Prowler/Regency was picked up from Richmond, Kentucky, and towed to Florence, South Carolina. The plan was to sell that trailer before continuing to travel, but Jimmy learned that a relative had died in Florida and his parents wanted him to attend the funeral. Peggy and her parents were not on speaking terms at that point, so she, Mike and Bobby returned to New York in the Travelall and Peggy's car while Jimmy, Paul and David flew to Orlando after storing the Prowler/Regency with Jimmy's car in the Florence airport parking lot. After the funeral, the three men returned to Florence, picked up the Grand Prix and Prowler/Regency and drove to Jamestown, New York.

Two weeks later, Jimmy tried to kill himself.


A week before Jimmy's attempted suicide, he, Peggy, Paul, Bobby, David and Mike left for Florida again. They drove Jimmy's Grand Prix, Peggy's Monte Carlo and the International Travelall and towed the Prowler/Regency trailer. Mike remained in New York. The Travelall stopped running near Washington, D.C., so it was dropped off at a garage in Alexandria, Virginia, for repairs. At Orlando, Jimmy offered the Prowler/Regency for sale from a Gulf service station on the Orange Blossom Trail. A tourist paid him $600 and gave him a 1972 Nomad trailer in exchange. Jimmy then sold the Nomad to his parents for $1,600, and they in turn sold it for $3,000.

The rest of the gang was unhappy with Jimmy for not supplying them with more money, and they wanted to leave Florida so they could steal more trailers and shoplift at department stores while they traveled. Jimmy, who was barely 20 years old, became depressed.

"I started lookin' at where I was goin' and what I was doin', and I couldn't see that I was accomplishin' anything," he said a year later. "It was just the same kinds of things over and over, day after day, non-stop. All the stealin' and runnin' from here to there and tryin' to hide from the cops but needin' to make money. I wanted something different, but I didn't know what to do or how to go about it. Everything just kind of got to me. To Peggy and Paul and the others, everything was a party. They wanted to make money, but they didn't really take nothin' seriously. I was the only one who had enough sense to do things in such a way that we weren't goin' to be locked up. They were so harem-scarem that if things had been in their hands, they would have already been in prison. It all came down on me. I was disgusted with everything in my life. It was all never-endin'.

"One night I had a bottle of 100 diet pills I'd gotten from a doctor in North Augusta. I was supposed to take one a day. I took the whole bottle and then drove from Winterhaven to my Uncle Doug's house in Orlando and passed out. Doug called an ambulance and then discovered the empty pill box in my car. At the hospital, they

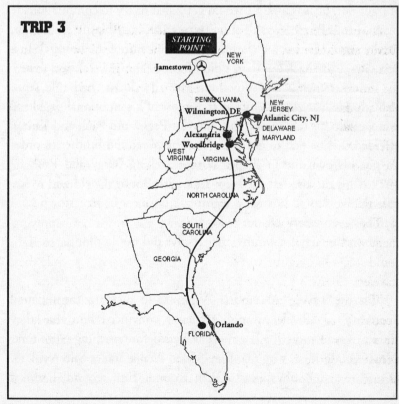

pumped my stomach, but a lot of the medicine had already gotten into my system. They put me on a heart machine and I almost died. The doctor said the pills caused my heart to work so fast that if I had gotten to the hospital thirty minutes later, my heart would have exploded. Once I came off the effect of my pills and got off the heart machine and the I.V.'s, I was still a nervous wreck. I couldn't think right, and I was in a depressive state. I'd just cry uncontrollably, and nothing fit together in my mind."

After Jimmy was in the hospital about a week, his doctor insisted that he enroll himself in a thirty-day psychiatric evaluation program. Predicting that Jimmy was facing a complete nervous breakdown otherwise, the doctor told him he was considering seeking a court order to prevent Jimmy from leaving for at least thirty days. "He said if I got out, he was afraid I would get killed or try to commit suicide again. I told Peggy I wasn't goin' through any psychiatric evaluation, so she brought me some clothes and I snuck out of the hospital. In a few days, I was back out there doin' the same things I'd always done."

Jimmy remembered something else the doctor had told him, though. He had warned Jimmy that most of his emotional problems were due to his taking responsibility for Peggy and Paul, and Jimmy decided that he had to get away from his sister and brother in order to put his own life in shape. Without telling Peggy and Paul, he packed his car and left for New York with Bobby, David and Mike. His resolve was to operate a legitimate business in Jamestown, and perhaps even marry Diane.

Unfortunately for Jimmy, that resolve did not last long.


On the way to Alexandria, Virginia, to pick up the repaired International Travelall, Jimmy's friends convinced him that they ought to steal and sell a few more trailers before reaching New York. Near Woodbridge, Virginia, they passed Azalia Trailer Sales on U.S. Route 1, and Bobby yelled, "Turn around! Turn around! I seen a bunch of trailers back there." The dealership sales lot was packed with Prowler and Nomad travel trailers, but Jimmy was especially attracted to a 28-foot Prowler that sat by itself at the rear of the lot -- obviously in storage. Jimmy pointed it out to the others and told them, "We'll come back tonight, and if no one is around, we'll take that one."

It was still morning, but the gang stopped at the Statesman Motel on the Richmond Highway and told the desk clerk they wanted a room for the day. Jimmy recalled, "I had a Canada identification card under the name of Carl Gunnerson which I showed him, and I said we had just got in from Canada and had been drivin' all night, that we wanted to rent a room but we didn't want to stay all night. We just wanted to take showers and get cleaned up and a little bit of sleep. So he said he would rent the room to the four of us for fifteen dollars if we were out by ten o'clock that night. We slept until about six and left. We went back to Woodbridge and got something to eat, then went to the trailer lot about eight o'clock. It was closed. I backed the Grand Prix in front of the trailer. Bobby helped me back up and hook on to it, and Michael put on a license plate on that I had from another trailer. David made sure the steps were up and the doors were closed, and in a matter of five minutes, we were rollin' away from the dealership with the trailer. We got about a mile down the road, and the trailer was draggin' the ground because we hadn't hooked up the weight equalizing bars. So we pulled into a shopping center and unhooked the trailer. I stole a pair of pliers from the Revco Drugs in the shopping center and used them to hook up the equalizing bars."

They towed the Prowler to a Ramada Inn at Wilmington, Delaware, and camped overnight in the parking lot. The next morning, they stored the trailer at a campground near Atlantic City after telling the manager they had to return to Virginia because of a death in the family. They drove back to Alexandria, Virginia, that day.

Jimmy's bill for repair of his parents' International Travelall was

$300, but he had only fifty dollars. Jimmy telephoned his parents in Florida, and his mother sent $300 via Western Union. While he waited for the money to arrive, Jimmy and his friends added $250 more to their monetary fund by shoplifting at Alexandria department stores. Then they picked up the Travelall and returned to New Jersey, where they took the stolen trailer out of storage during the middle of the night without paying its storage fees. Following a brief casino stop in Atlantic City, the gang went on to Jamestown, New York, where they left Mike, who said he was homesick, and visited with Diane before heading out again to Crittendon, Kentucky, where they put the stolen Prowler in storage at a KOA campground.

Meanwhile, Jimmy telephoned his uncle in Florida and learned that the Monte Carlo sedan he had bought Peggy had been stolen from her, and she wanted Jimmy to call her at the Florida motel where she was living. Although Jimmy figured there was more involved than a stolen automobile if Peggy wanted him to call her, he made the call anyway. His expectations were correct. Before her car was stolen -- with all her money locked in its trunk -- she had used it to steal a Mallard travel trailer from a campground in Winter Garden. She had towed the trailer to the Parliament House motel on the Orange Blossom Trail where a security guard Peggy knew allowed her to park it on the property in a grove of orange trees.

Jimmy reported, "She asked me if I would come down and get the trailer for her and pull it somewhere so that she could sell it and get money to buy another car. I told her I wanted to think about it."

Jimmy considered his options. "I had already decided that once we got rid of that stolen Prowler, I was goin' back to Jamestown and settle down. I was through with it all, with the stealin' and the scammin' and the runnin'. If Peggy hadn't asked Doug to have me call her, I probably could have done all right because I would have money from sale of the trailer to go into a business. All I wanted was to operate a legitimate driveway pavin' business in Jamestown. I know I could have made it work. I know the town and the people; I know

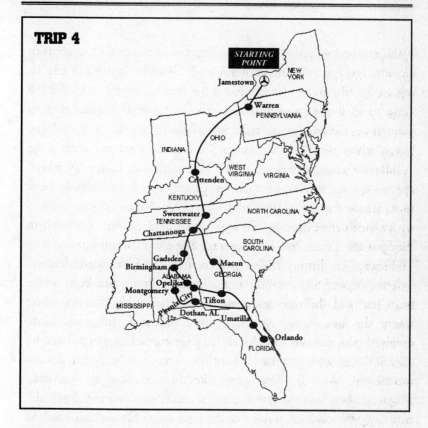

what they've got there and what they haven't got and what people want."

He decided to ask his sister Wanda for advice. "Wanda warned me not to go to Florida for Peggy. She said, 'Every time Peggy and Paul call, you're there.' She said, 'Let them make it on their own this time. Don't go to them. They'll just get you in trouble.'

"I said, 'But what can I do? They need my help.'

"She said, 'If it was you askin' for help, they wouldn't go. They're not as worried about things as they're pretendin' to be.'

"I said, 'Well they're down there by themselves. Their car is gone, their money is gone, and they have no clothes. They're stuck in a motel with a hot trailer. If the cops find it, they'll know who it belongs to, and Peggy and Paul will get locked up.'"

Later, Jimmy recalled, "I really didn't have the money to go back down there, but I ended up goin' anyhow with Bobby and David, and we got there the next morning. I picked up Peggy at my uncle's house, and she showed me where the trailer was. We pulled it to Umatilla to the Chisholm Trail Campground about 40 miles north of Orlando. By then it was about three or four days before Easter, so we decided we would stay in the trailer there until after Easter. We stayed about a week, then left the trailer in storage there so we could go back to Kentucky for the stolen Prowler I had left there."

As they drove through Georgia, Peggy and Bobby shoplifted in Tifton at the Rose's and K-Mart department stores, and on their way back to the expressway, they passed the Jim Duke Pontiac dealership. "There were a bunch of Trans Ams lined up across the front of the lot," Jimmy said. "Peggy asked me to stop and let her look at a white Trans Am that was out front. I pulled in and as she was lookin' around at the cars, I started lookin' at a Grand Prix. A salesman came over and was talkin' with me, and then I seen that Peggy and Bobby were in the salesroom. They came back out and asked if I was ready to go. We got into the truck and left, and when we got down the street, Peggy pulled several sets of keys out of her bra and said she had the keys to the Trans Am and that she wanted to go back and take it that night. I told her I wasn't goin' to be any part of stealin' a car, that I was scared we would get caught."

Peggy replied, "Well, somebody stole my car and the police have never found it, and I don't think they ever will. So I want you to bring me back here tonight, and I'll take the Trans Am myself."

That night, Peggy stole a Florida license plate from an automobile in the parking lot of the Davis Brothers Motel, and Jimmy drove her to the Pontiac dealership. Peggy recalled later, "The car was under a spotlight right in front of the dealership. I gave the keys to David, and he drove the car off the showmat and back to the rear of the lot. He put the license plates on it for me, and then we got in and I just drove away. Jimmy was waitin' for us at the ramp of the interstate."

They drove quickly to Phenix City, Alabama, where they created a fake bill of sale on a form they had acquired from the Kentucky Department of Motor Vehicles several months earlier. They also used a notary seal that Peggy had stolen from Lloyd's Used Cars dealership in Lexington, Kentucky. Peggy said, "Bobby filled out the bill of sale, and David signed the notary seal as 'Fred Hughes.' Paul took the papers to the courthouse at Opelika and got a registration tag for the car, then we drove to Montgomery, Alabama, and put the Trans Am in the airport parking lot."

From there, it was on to Chattanooga, where the gang shoplifted at Zayre's department stores. Jimmy recalled, "On the north edge of Chattanooga, called Northridge or something like that, Peggy and Bobby went into a Zayre's while me and David and Paul waited in the International. After a few minutes, they came walkin' out, and a heavy-set stocky guy came out behind them. He pulled out a badge and grabbed them by the arms. Bobby had a ballglove in the back of his pants with his shirt pulled out over it, and the security guard told them they were under arrest for shopliftin'. Peggy broke away from him and ran and hopped into the front seat of the International and locked the door. He had Bobby by the arm and was walkin' him back in, when the ballglove fell out of Bobby's pocket onto the ground. The guy reached down to grab it, and when he did, Bobby pushed him against the building and started runnin'. Just as Bobby grabbed the door handle of the truck, the security guard grabbed him again, but Bobby managed to get loose again and hopped into the truck and we took off. The guy was left standin' in the parking lot with Bobby's shirt in his hand."

Undaunted by the close call, the gang went immediately to nearby Rose's and K-Mart stores and shoplifted nearly $300 worth of merchandise. Then they stopped at another Lincoln-Mercury dealership near Sweetwater, Tennessee and, while Peggy and Bobby diverted the attention of two salesmen, Paul lifted several sets of keys off a hook inside the salesroom and stuffed them into his pants pockets.

They had decided earlier that since Peggy had stolen the Trans Am so easily, they probably would be able to swipe a couple more new cars. From a nearby Quality Courts motel, they took a Georgia license plate from a parked automobile. Returning to the Lincoln-Mercury lot that night, Paul put the Georgia tag on a green-and-white Mercury Cougar and Jimmy put the Florida tags used earlier for the Trans Am theft on a red-and-silver Cougar. Bobby placed baby toys in the back window of the red-and-silver car to make it look less suspicious, and he put bumper stickers on the rear. David followed his example with the green-and-white Cougar. Bobby tried to steal a third Cougar, but it would not start.

Jimmy said, "We stayed in a Holiday Inn at Gadsden, Alabama, that night, and the next morning Bobby wrote out a bill of sale for my car -- the red-and-silver Cougar -- and we got a license plate and registration to it under the name of Jo Ella Pate. David signed the notary, and Peggy took the papers into Gadsden and got my registration."

He explained, "In Alabama, you don't have to have a title, registration or certificate of origin on a '74 or older car. You just need a bill of sale. So when Bobby filled out the bill of sale, he made it for a '74 car. Then after Peggy got the registration, he changed the 4 to a 9 so it would match the model year of the car more closely." (Later, Jimmy's knowledge of how to circumvent title and registration laws would shock and amaze law enforcement officials.)

For registration of the green-and-white Cougar, David took its bill of sale to the courthouse in another Alabama town and registered it under the name of Gary Compton. Then both automobiles were stored in the parking lot at the Birmingham airport while the gang returned to Crittendon, Kentucky, to pick up the stolen Prowler trailer they had stored there. Once again, they took the trailer out of storage during the middle of the night so they would not have to pay storage fees. They returned to Birmingham, picked up the two Cougars, then went on to Montgomery and recovered the stolen

Trans Am. As a joke that would later prove to be valuable, Jimmy put an "I Love New York" bumper sticker on the rear of the Trans Am. Jimmy was several months behind in finance payments on his Grand Prix, so he abandoned it in the airport parking lot.

As they headed toward Florida, they must have been an impressive sight. Jimmy Burke led the convoy in an International Travelall towing the Prowler trailer. Bobby followed in the red-and-silver Cougar, followed by Paul Burke driving the green-and-white Cougar and Peggy Burke in her new Trans Am.

They stopped for a meal at a Stuckey's restaurant, and Jimmy telephoned his mother in Florida. "I told her I had a trailer that I had taken in on trade for another trailer I had bought, and I didn't have much money invested in it. Since I owed Mom and Dad about $3,000 from the bad check case, I told her if they wanted the trailer, they could just give me $4,500 and consider the $3,000 I owed them paid." With that phone call, Jimmy Burke was, in effect, scamming his own parents by offering to sell them a stolen RV!

The gang stopped overnight at Dothan, Alabama, and Bobby wrote a bill of sale for the Prowler which David signed as Michael Sullivan. Another was created for the stolen Mallard trailer to Cathy Burke, Jimmy's sister. Peggy had Cathy's birth certificate and was using Cathy's name at the time because she had skipped bond under her own name. Jimmy and Bobby applied for title to the Prowler at the nearby town of Enterprise and then went to a lawyer's office there to get another bill of sale for the same trailer made out from Bobby to Jimmy. Jimmy explained that ploy later: "I wanted a legal bill of sale on the Prowler to take into the state of Florida so I could be sure and get a Florida title for it. In other states -- and especially in Florida -- they question Alabama's registrations because titles are not issued on travel trailers." Jimmy also did not want his parents to know positively that the trailer he was going to sell them was stolen.

At Orlando that night, the gang parked -- without registering -- at the Yogi Bear campground near Disney World and then left before the campground office opened the next morning. They took the Prowler to the Day's Park on West 33rd Street where Jimmy's parents were camped. Edward and Wanda Burke bought the stolen trailer. Jimmy gave Bobby and David each $500, and Jimmy kept the rest of the $4,500, hiding $3,000 under the floormat of his Cougar. He intended to use that money to settle in New York, but he told his friends he would use it to rent and furnish an apartment for the whole gang. Bobby and David rented a room at the Parliament House motel and stayed drunk for most of the week they were there. They called Mike in New York, and he insisted upon being given a share of the proceeds from the stolen trailer; Jimmy gave another $500 to Bobby so it could be sent to Mike, who immediately flew to Orlando and joined his two friends on their drinking spree.

After Jimmy picked up Peggy's stolen Mallard trailer from the orange grove where it was parked and towed it to the Chisholm Trail Campground near Umatilla, he returned the borrowed International Travelall to his parents and put a trailer hitch on the red-and-silver Cougar.

Meanwhile, Peggy rented a room at the Southern Sun Inn and Jimmy registered at the Day's Lodge. Peggy said later, "I went back to the same bar I was in when my Monte Carlo was stolen, hoping to see it in the parkin' lot or spot someone who might have taken it. I loved that car, although I really did like my new Trans Am better. I had a few drinks and went outside to check the parkin' lot again, and damned if the Trans Am wasn't gone! Somebody had stolen it too!"

Jimmy said, "She hammered on my door in the middle of the night, and when I let her in, she started cryin' and sayin' that her car had been stolen. But there was nothin' I could do about it, you know. We sure couldn't call the police!"

The next day, as Jimmy and Peggy drove along Orange Avenue in Orlando, he saw a white Trans Am similar to Peggy's going the other direction. "I looked back, and sure enough, it had an Alabama tag on it and a sticker on the back bumper saying 'I Love New York,' so I knew it was Peggy's car. I told Peggy, 'There can't be two of them like that!'"

Jimmy turned around and followed the Trans Am until he could pull up beside it. Then Peggy rolled down the passenger side window, and Jimmy said to the other driver, "Nice car you've got."

"Thanks," answered the man.

"Where'd you get it?" Jimmy asked.

The driver looked at Jimmy suspiciously and did not answer. Jimmy asked, "Would you like to pull it over there and park it and get out and walk off?"

"What d'you mean?"

Jimmy said, "That car belongs to my sister."

The other driver gassed the Trans Am and ran a red light, but Jimmy followed behind him. "Now, I know Orlando as good as anybody else," Jimmy reported later, "but some kid came out of nowhere on a bicycle, and I had to slam on my brakes to keep from hittin' him, so I lost the Trans Am. I cruised through the neighborhood but couldn't find it. My uncle Doug lived near there, so I went to his house and told him what happened, and Doug said, 'Come on. I'll follow you, and we'll see if we can spot him again.'" Peggy agreed to stay at Doug's house in case either of them called with news about the car.

"Just as we were comin' off a side street from Doug's house onto the main highway, Michigan Avenue, here came that Trans Am, right past me. I took off after it and Doug followed behind. The guy looked back and saw us and kicked down on the gas again. Now, I'm driving a hot Cougar, and I'm stayin' right behind him, so finally, he sees he can't lose me, and he goes up over a sidewalk and into an orange grove. I stayed right behind him, and we rolled in and out and around those orange trees until he hit one and the Trans Am stalled. He jumped out and took off on foot. My uncle chased him, but he jumped a fence and got away."

Doug, who didn't know Peggy had stolen the car herself, said, "Let's call the cops and tell them we got the car."

Jimmy replied, "No, that's okay, we've got it. Let's not bother with the cops and their paperwork."

Later, Jimmy laughed when telling about the chase. "I picked up Peggy and took her out to get the car, and she started cryin' that the guy who had stolen it had burned a couple of holes in the seat and wrecked the front fender when he hit the orange tree. It was funny in a way, because she was cryin' about it as if she'd bought it and paid for it!"

The next morning, Peggy took the Trans Am to a body shop on Old Winter Garden Road so it could be repaired, and she told Jimmy she wanted to tow the Mallard trailer to St. Petersburg and sell it so she would have money to pay for her car repairs. Meanwhile, Jimmy went to the airport to pick up another of his New York friends -- Allen -- who had flown to Orlando to join the gang. When Jimmy returned to his uncle's house, Doug reported that Peggy and Paul had gone across town in the green-and-white Cougar to pick up some marijuana, but she wanted to meet Jimmy at the campground where the Mallard was stored. He, Bobby, David and Allen left immediately for Umatilla; Mike stayed behind at Jimmy's uncle's house.

Unknown to Jimmy, Florida police had been checking campgrounds routinely in an effort to keep tabs on Travelers, and two Lake County deputies had learned that the Mallard trailer stored near Umatilla was stolen. According to their information, the trailer had been stolen by a young Irish Traveler woman named Peggy McNally -- one of Peggy Burke's favorite aliases -- who was wanted in at least three states on charges ranging from fraud and theft to armed robbery. Correctly figuring that Peggy would soon return for the trailer, the deputies staked out the campground from an orange grove and used binoculars to scan the vicinity for a young, short, plump blonde woman. For thirty-six hours, the deputies watched the trailer, and by noon, they were tired of eating cold sandwiches and drinking luke-warm coffee from a Thermos. They decided to take a lunch break and eat a hot meal. At precisely that time, Jimmy and his friends arrived at the campground in Jimmy's stolen red-and-silver Cougar.

When Jimmy went into the campground office to pay storage charges on the Mallard, the manager said, "The cops were here yesterday looking at that trailer. They thought it was one that was stolen from the KOA campground at Winter Garden a week or two ago. They brought a tow truck out here and were fixing to tow it off, but for some reason, they left it."

Jimmy paid the storage charges and went outside. He told his friends what he had learned. "I don't know what to do about the trailer," he said. "If we just drive off and leave it, the man in the office is going to get suspicious because I told him I was here to pick it up, and he might call the cops and give them a description of us and what we're drivin'. Then they'll pick us up down the road, and we're drivin' a hot car. But if we try to tow away the trailer, we might get arrested because it's possible someone is sittin' here waitin' for us to pick it up."

After a few minutes of contemplation, Jimmy made a decision. "Either way we go," he told his friends, "we could be through, so we might as well get the trailer and see what happens." Figuring that the campground manager might call police and alert them the trailer was being taken, Jimmy hooked up the trailer quickly and drove north on secondary highways as fast as possible until he crossed the state line into Georgia. He stopped for the night at the large Florida/Georgia KOA campground just off Interstate 75.

When the Lake County deputies returned from lunch to their stakeout site, they were shocked to discover that the Mallard trailer was gone. They questioned the campground manager about its absence and asked their department's dispatcher to put out a statewide bulletin about the trailer and a tall young man the manager said had towed it away. The manager had not noticed Jimmy's friends as they waited outside in the Cougar and, in fact, could not even identify the type or color of vehicle that was used to tow away the trailer.

From Georgia, Jimmy telephoned his uncle, and Doug said Peggy and Paul had not left Orlando yet, but Jimmy's friend Mike was there waiting for them to return so he could leave with them. Not wanting his uncle to know about the stolen trailer, Jimmy asked to speak to Mike. "I told Mike what happened, that we had to pull the trailer out of the state, and I said he should tell Peggy if she didn't come up and get her trailer, we were just goin' to leave it because we weren't goin' to get in trouble for pullin' that thing around with us wherever we went. I was just doin' her a favor, but she didn't seem to care enough. It was the middle of the night, and she was still out partyin'."

The next morning, April 24, the gang drove to Macon, Georgia, and after renting rooms at the Day's Inn, they called Orlando and informed Peggy where they were. Peggy told him, "I'll be there tomorrow. The weekend is comin' up, and we can probably sell the trailer there in Macon, so will you put an ad in the newspaper for me and park the trailer where it can be seen? When I get there, you and the others can leave, and Paul and I will stay there until we sell it."

As Peggy had requested, Jimmy parked the trailer at the Day's Inn and placed a classified ad in the *Macon Telegraph*. Then that evening, he took his stolen Cougar to the nearby Penney's automotive shop. The car was not designed to tow a heavy trailer, so the transmission was slipping. Jimmy also wanted to buy heavy-duty shocks and set of stereo speakers for it. He ordered the work done and then walked to a nearby bar where, over the next two hours, he got seriously drunk. On his way back to Penney's, Jimmy stumbled and fell into a ditch. Lying there, he vomited all over himself. Finally regaining his feet, he returned to the Penney's garage and asked a mechanic if he could use the shop's shower room. There, he undressed, showered, and then, because his clothes had vomit on them, he put on a mechanic's uniform that he found hanging in a locker.

Meanwhile, the auto center manager had called security guard Neil Godbee and reported that a young man who was having mechanical work done on his car appeared to be very badly drunk. The manager was afraid the young man might cause trouble. Godbee was actually a Bibb County sheriff's deputy who worked at Penney's during his off-duty hours, and he was accustomed to dealing with drunks. He had no intention of arresting the man, but he also did not want him to drive while under the influence of alcohol.

Godbee recalled later, "I went over to the shop, and the boy came walkin' out dryin' his hair. He was still pretty drunk. I asked him for his I.D., and he showed me a West Virginia driver's license under the name of Carl Gunnerson. I glanced over at the car. It had Alabama tags on it. It was a beautiful car. A Mercury Cougar. Brand new. And a big trailer hitch on the back end of it."

Godbee told Jimmy, "Look, you have to go back in there, take off that uniform and put your own clothes on."

Jimmy replied, "Well, I can't do that because I got sick and my clothes are messed up."

"Do you have any more clothes in your car?"

"Yeah."

"Okay, get some out of there and change."

Jimmy said, "No, I don't want those clothes. I want to put on clothes I have back at my motel."

"Well you can't do that. You're not leavin' here with that uniform. And you'd better do what I say because I can write you up right now for bein' drunk."

Jimmy opened his trunk and quickly removed some clothing before Godbee could see inside it. While he changed clothes, Godbee called his headquarters and asked that the license plate number and the Carl Gunnerson name be checked out on the department's computer. Later, Godbee said, "The tag came back as not being on file. That may not have meant anything, though, because some small counties didn't have computers for recording license plate numbers. There also was nothing listed about Carl Gunnerson. But then, for some reason I can't explain, I took the vehicle identification number off the car and ran it through the computer. It came back 'Stolen from Sweetwater, Tennessee.'"

# 12

# Trailer Scam

On the same day that Jimmy Burke and his gang sold their stolen Nomad/Regency travel trailer in Greenville, South Carolina, a freelance magazine writer walked into the office of Newton Kindlund, owner of central Florida's Holiday of Orlando RV dealership. The writer was an editor of the popular *Trailer Life* family of recreational vehicle magazines, and Kindlund was one of the most successful RV dealers in the country. The two men had known each other several years.

Expecting a warm greeting from Kindlund, the writer was stunned by the intensity of the dealer's first words: "When in the hell are you and your magazine going to do something about the gypsies?"

The writer laughed, thinking his friend was joking. Within the RV industry, so-called "gypsy" RV dealers had been considered a bothersome nuisance for several years because they sold cheap travel trailers at cut-rate prices from campgrounds and vacant lots. The writer knew almost nothing about gypsy dealers; he figured they jerry-built trailers in their back yards and sold a few now and then to tourists. He had considered writing a magazine article warning about gypsy trailer sales, however, because nothing had been published on the subject for many years.

"Don't laugh," Kindlund said. "Those people are selling five trailers for every one I sell. Last year, the gypsies probably sold in excess of 1,000 units just in central Florida! A lot of this state's legitimate dealers went out of business in the last year, but the gypsies just keep on selling trailers, one after another. And every one of those trailers is misrepresented as being something it isn't."

As he talked, Kindlund became more animated, and he began pacing his office. "If you go to a campground down on 33rd Street to look at a trailer, you'll probably see three generations of gypsies living in it and probably two or three trailers parked next to it that are owned by the same person. You'll also see either an asphalt dump truck or a pickup truck, probably with some kind of ladder rack on the side of it and a compressor in the bed. There might be a sign on the door of the truck that says, 'B & B Roofing' or 'X-Y-Z Asphalt Paving.'"

The writer asked, "How do they misrepresent the trailers, just by telling people they're worth more than they are?"

Kindlund responded, "If it were that simple, that would be okay. But when you talk with the people who are selling a trailer, they'll give you a sad story about why they're being forced to get rid of it right now. You've got them over a barrel, and they'll say, 'My wife just died' or 'My wife needs an operation' or 'My wife just ran away with another man' or 'We bought this trailer as a wedding present for my son, but he broke his engagement.'

"Then they'll tell you that because of a friend or a relative, they were able to buy the trailer directly from the factory in Indiana. Of course, it has a full warranty, and they'll produce warranty papers that, if you look at carefully, do not obligate the manufacturer to very much. They also have the appliance warranty papers which, for some reason, they forgot to sign and mail in, so you can take advantage of their forgetfulness and do it yourself and therefore get the full warranty. Then they'll produce what looks like a bill of sale that shows they paid between $9,000 and $11,000 for the trailer. But because of their hardship, they'll let you have it for $7,000."

Two hours later, convinced that at least a preliminary investigation of gypsy trailer sales was warranted, the writer telephoned the local newspaper, the *Orlando Sentinel Star*, and asked an editor if the newspaper had ever done articles about trailer sales by gypsies. The editor said he was familiar with several gypsy scams, but not one involving trailer sales. He said he wanted to assign a reporter to assist in an investigation if the writer agreed. The writer consented and made arrangements to meet reporter Denise Braziel.

Like many other young reporters who had been inspired to start their journalism careers by the investigative teamwork which exposed the Watergate scandal, Braziel was excited by the prospect of going undercover to investigate gypsy con artists in her community. She smiled happily when the writer told her they were going to pose as a husband and wife vacationing in Florida while they "shopped" for travel trailers at the Day's Park campground. Denise had already prepared for her assignment by scanning the classified section of her newspaper. Among the ads, she found one that said: "Kentucky Traveler -- 1980, 32 ft. park model with tip-out room, patio door, roll out awning, twin beds, deluxe interior, many extras."

Denise and the writer found it difficult to determine, once they were inside the park, which of the trailers was the one advertised. A couple of dozen coaches -- all obviously new, and all with "For Sale" signs on them -- were parked together in one section of the campground. Several were Kentucky Travelers; many were Rogues, Marauders and Lariats. Denise was impressed by the attractive exterior appearance of all the trailers; the units were clean and seemed well maintained. The coaches were surrounded by new, colorful vans, pickup trucks, Cadillacs, Lincoln Continentals and Corvettes. Inside the beds of the pickup trucks were air compressors and tanks of the kind used to mix and spray paint or asphalt sealer.

Selecting a Lariat trailer at random, the writer knocked on the front curbside sliding patio door and was immediately greeted by an attractive, well dressed woman who was beautifully groomed and decorated with expensive gold jewelry. She identified herself as Mary Daugherty when Denise asked if the couple could look at her trailer, and she invited them inside.

Denise and the writer exchanged puzzled glances. This was obviously no *gypsy* woman. The writer wondered if he had made a mistake. The light-skinned and apparently affluent Mrs. Daugherty did not look like any gypsy he had ever seen!

As the woman showed them through the sparkling clean trailer, she told them why the nearly new coach was being offered for sale. She and her husband, Sam, purchased it directly from the factory through a relative who worked there, she said. It was intended as a wedding present for her daughter, but the girl had broken her engagement and did not want the trailer any longer. Sam and Mary already had a trailer -- it was parked on the next site and was for sale too -- so they were being forced to sacrifice the daughter's coach. In addition, the family had decided to return to their home in West Virginia because they were disenchanted with Florida and because Sam had not been able to find enough work in the construction field to keep him busy. Also, she added, her smaller children did not like the Florida schools in which they were enrolled, and the Day's Park manager had implemented several unreasonable policies which made them decide to leave the area more quickly than they had intended. Other campers in the park also felt the rules were intolerable and had decided to leave, and that was the reason so many trailers had "For Sale" signs on them, she reported.

"The park has just changed hands, and the new manager is very disagreeable," she explained.

Her husband, Sam, arrived just then and said he had "put almost

$11,000 into" the trailer, but because he needed to sell it quickly, he would let it go for only $7,500. He emphasized that the trailer was new -- only a few weeks old. "It was custom-built," Sam said. "I even watched while it was being put together. It's probably worth $13,000 or $14,000. I got it for less than that because I have a relative who works at the Marauder factory."

The writer admitted the price sounded good, but he expressed concern that if the couple bought the trailer, they would have to pay approximately $300 in state sales tax. "Don't worry about that," Sam said reassuringly. "I'll work with you on that."

Acting confused, the writer asked how he could control the amount of sales tax to be paid.

Sam smiled patiently and answered, "As far as the state's concerned, you'll pay me only $2,000 because you're giving me an old trailer in trade. That way you have to pay sales tax on only $2,000."

Denise asked, "What about warranty work? Are there any dealers here in Orlando who handle this brand?"

"I don't really know," Daugherty answered, "but it doesn't matter because any RV dealer will be happy to do the warranty work on this coach, free. All that's necessary is for him to call the manufacturer in Indiana and get approval for the work to be done." His wife interrupted and said she had forgotten to fill out the warranty cards for the trailer's appliances, so the couple could fill them out themselves and mail them in, and the appliance manufacturers wouldn't know the difference.

Denise said the couple was very interested in the trailer but had only just begun shopping for one to buy, and they wanted to check out a few others before deciding on which one to purchase. Daugherty smiled and said, "I don't blame you. But before you make a decision, come back and see me. We might be able to shave a little off that price I gave you." He admitted he was anxious to sell the trailer as quickly as possible. He said the family was preparing to go to a wake for a relative that afternoon, and he wanted to leave the state immediately afterward if possible.

Years later, the writer would learn that hundreds of other Irish Travelers would be attending that wake, including a young man named Jimmy Burke who had interrupted a travel trailer theft expedition in order to take part in it.

Before Denise and the writer left the campground, they looked at a couple more trailers, including a new Kentucky Traveler offered for sale by an attractive and well-dressed middle age woman who identified herself as Mrs. Edward Burke. She was Jimmy Burke's mother. The writer had no way of knowing it then, but Mrs. Burke -- Wanda -- and her family would play an extremely important role in his life during the next fifteen years.

That afternoon, the writer parked his camping van outside the same campground and unpacked the only camera he had with him -- a 35 mm Nikon with a wide-angle lens. It was definitely not the camera he needed to photograph the gypsy encampment, but it would have to do. Alice Robison, editorial director of *Trailer Life* magazine, had told him an hour earlier that she wanted him to prepare a series of articles about the gypsy trailer sales scam, and she wanted photos to illustrate it. Using the wide-angle meant the writer would have to get as close to the trailers as he could to shoot pictures, and he was certain someone would spot him.

He was right.

As he focused his camera on the encampment, two children walked around the side of a trailer. They spotted the writer immediately and ran quickly to the door of another coach. Two tall, husky men stepped outside, saw the writer and sprinted for a brown pickup truck parked nearby. The writer ran to his van, started it and tried to pull onto the roadway of Orlando's 33rd Street, but traffic was heavy, and by the time he had merged into the northbound flow, the two men were only a few hundred feet behind him in their truck. As he reached Orange Blossom Trail, the truck crowded out an automobile and cut in behind the writer's van. One of the men was waving a fist out the window and shouting for the writer to stop. The writer sped south on the four-lane Orange Blossom Trail until he was stopped in the curb lane by a red traffic light. His heart felt as if it had dropped to the pit of his stomach when he realized he was blocked by heavy, cross-flowing traffic and the two men had gotten out of their truck and were walking toward him menacingly.

Suddenly, the cross traffic thinned slightly, and the light started to change colors. Not waiting for the green signal to appear, the writer floored his accelerator, leaned on the horn and jerked the van to the left in front of the car sitting beside him. He crossed seven lanes of traffic with his horn blaring, figuring the worst that could happen would be a traffic accident or a citation for reckless driving, and at that moment, he welcomed the opportunity to be arrested. The gypsies' truck was effectively blocked from following by the flow of vehicles, and the writer turned down a series of back streets just to make certain he had eluded pursuit. When he was sure he was not being followed, he parked the van behind a K-Mart store and shut off the engine.

For ten minutes, he sat there trembling. All he could think of was a firm resolve that he would not tell his wife what he had just done.

During the next two days, the writer counted sixty-seven *gypsy* trailers for sale in six Orlando area campgrounds, and he spotted 126 more of them in three parks near Tampa. Telephone calls to RV dealers around the state revealed similar trailers were for sale in campgrounds and at motels in Fort Lauderdale, Miami, Fort Myers and Daytona Beach. But at that time, the writer did not realize the so-called "gypsies" were everywhere along the Gulf Coast that winter, from Mobile, Alabama, and New Orleans to Houston, Corpus Christi and the Rio Grande Valley.

After gaining access to files at the *Orlando Sentinel Star*, the writer started compiling sketchy and conflicting information about Florida's *gypsies*. Central Florida had a significant permanent population of true Romany Gypsies and, over the years, several members of that community had been arrested and prosecuted for various swindles as well as for home intrusion thefts and burglary. A primary activity of those traditional Eastern European Gypsies was operating quasi-legitimate fortune telling and palm reading businesses. They also were responsible for some of the driveway/roof sealing scams reported throughout the state.

However, there appeared to be a great deal of confusion about the identities of the transient families who moved into Florida each fall in travel trailers. They did not seem to be part of the Gypsy community, but police and newspaper reports linked them together as if they were. There were occasional references to the infamous Williamson, but those people appeared to be Irish or Scottish, not Romany Gypsies. Frequent references to *gypsies* called up images of dark-skinned women in long gowns with bandannas on their heads, but those images did not match, in any way, the well dressed women the writer had encountered at the Orlando campground.

Because the writer already knew some details about the Williamson family, he theorized -- incorrectly -- that for some reason, the Williamson bloodlines were being blended with those of the Romany Gypsies and that the two diverse ethnic groups were becoming one. If that theory were correct, he decided, it would explain the seasonal appearance in Florida of light-skinned families everyone called *gypsies*.

He would soon learn differently.


On the western edge of Orlando, Dick Charron paced the floor of his office angrily, stopping frequently in front of a window in order to glare at two *gypsy* trailers that were being offered for sale across the street from his Coachmen RV dealership. The offending trailers were parked on the front edge of a KOA campground, and Charron fumed as he watched a pair of tourists walk to the coaches and look inside. He turned, and the writer could read an expression of frustration on his face.

"The owner of the campground said when those two trailers are gone, he won't allow any more of them to be sold on his property," Charron told the writer. "But I had to do a lot of talking in order to convince him his customers were being ripped off by gypsies who were selling trailers out of his park."

Charron took a seat behind his desk, sat there a few seconds, then bounced up and walked to the window again. He turned his head toward the writer and said, "A fellow who was camped across the street came in here one day and said he was interested in buying a used, late-model travel trailer. I told him what we had available, and we discussed prices. Then he informed me he could buy a new Marauder from across the street for less that I would charge him for a used Coachmen. He started to tell me about the people who were selling the Marauder, but I interrupted him and said, 'Don't go any farther. Let *me* tell *you* about them.'

"I said, 'The man who owns it just bought the trailer, and he's had it only a couple of weeks. He and his wife came down here from up north, but they had a death or a sickness or an accident in the family, so they've got to leave here and go back home. They're willing to sell their trailer at a sacrifice, even though they'll lose money on it. The plastic is still on the cushions and the floor, and they haven't even remembered to fill out the warranty cards. But they don't care; they need the money to get back home. They have the title in their hands, and it was titled out of state.'"

Charron said to the writer, "The customer looked at me and smiled. He said, 'You know the guy!' I then proceeded to tell him that no, I didn't know the guy, but it was an old, familiar story to me. I went through the whole bit with him. I said, 'Look under the sink to make sure it has complete plumbing. Check out the workmanship. Look closely at the cabinets and appliances.' I finally thought I convinced him about those people and their trailer, and he left. Do you know, he bought that trailer anyway!"

The writer asked, "If this is so clearly a scam, why do campground and motel managers allow the gypsies to sell trailers on their properties?"

Charron answered, "Sometimes, they get kickbacks. Maybe the phone number listed in the newspaper ad is the motel's or the campground office's. If someone who calls in response to that ad buys a trailer, the gypsy who sells it will pay the manager a one-hundred or two-hundred-dollar referral fee. The typical campground or motel manager in Orlando is not paid very well; he probably doesn't earn much more than a couple hundred dollars a week. If he can help move four or five of those gypsy trailers each week, he can increase his take-home pay by $500 or $700, and he doesn't have to pay taxes on any of that money."

The writer remembered all the trailers that were offered for sale at the Day's Park campground, and later, he telephoned the manager, a young man named Bob Meyer, and asked bluntly if Meyer were receiving kickbacks. Meyer expressed outrage at the suggestion. "If somebody said I'm getting kickbacks, he's a damned liar!" he stated emphatically. "I wish I could stop them from selling their trailers here. You tell me how to do it, and I'll do it. We're not running a business here for those people; this is *our* business. I would be so happy to be able to ask every one of those people to move out of here, but I don't know how to do it without risking a lawsuit."

Meyer asked the writer, "Are you aware that they're into a lot more businesses than just selling trailers? They're in the painting business, the blacktopping business, the roofing business. Several of them have little utility trailers packed full of purses and other items they sell to people. You name a con game, and they're into it."

He paused and then added, "They're not really gypsies, you know. They call themselves *the Irish clan* or *Irish Travelers*. They all have Irish names. In this park, we have several Donahues, lots of Burkes, several Raffertys, some Rileys, Daleys, Carrolls and Sherlocks."

Remembering one of the women who tried to sell a trailer when he and Denise had posed as shoppers, the writer asked, "Do you have a Mrs. Edward Burke registered?"

"Yeah. Her first name is Wanda. The reason I remember that is because she has two daughters named Wanda -- a little girl and a woman in her twenties that's married to an Irish guy named O'Roarke."

The writer had never before heard the term *Irish Traveler*, but during the next fifteen years, he was destined to hear a great deal about them. And he also was destined to learn a great deal more about Wanda Burke and her entire family of con artists.

Back in his office after leaving Florida, the writer discovered that his magazine series about the gypsy trailer scam had a life of its own, even before it could be written. Its progress was almost like a rollercoaster ride over which he had no control. One telephone call led to five others, and those led to an additional fifty; an investigative field trip revealed several more that needed to be scheduled. Within a few weeks, the writer had interviewed nearly one hundred individuals and traveled more than 8,000 miles gathering data. The flood of information that poured into his office each day threatened to overwhelm him.

He needed time to sort out the facts, but there was no time left.

He was facing an immediate magazine publication deadline, and there could be no delays. From its sparkling new office building in Agoura, California, *Trailer Life* magazine had already committed the largest block of editorial space it had ever devoted to a single subject. The *gypsy* trailer scam report was scheduled to lead the June 1980 edition with an eight-page section of three articles. Those would be followed a month later by a five-page section of two more articles. Several of *Trailer Life's* regular features had already been bumped from the magazine in order to make room for the special series.

From Ohio came a report that two years earlier, the Bureau of Motor Vehicles arrested twenty-five *gypsies* at various times for violation of state laws. Most of the arrests were made by the bureau's "Gypsy Hunter," Wayne Johnson. Among the arrest records the writer acquired from Ohio were those involving Edward and Elizabeth Burke, and the writer wondered at the time if they were related to the Wanda Burke who had tried to sell a trailer to him in Orlando. Vehicle registration records revealed that the Burkes had titled twenty-seven travel trailers in Ohio during 1978; so their state tax assessments would be low, the Burkes told BMV registrars they paid very small amounts for the trailers. Among the coaches they titled were three new Rogue trailers that Ed said cost him between $925 and $1,595 each; he claimed they were damaged. Included in the other Burke registrations were a new Rogue that Daniel A. Burke claimed was a gift -- and on which he paid no taxes -- and another for which he said he paid just $500 because it was damaged. Wanda Burke registered a Rogue she said cost her $925; it was also reported as being damaged.

Frank Tiebout, chief investigator with the Ohio BMV, told the writer that until the year before, hundreds of *Irish gypsies* routinely towed their travel trailers into Ohio and sold them. But the bureau, led by Wayne Johnson's field work, had arrested so many of them and forced so many others to leave the state that in 1979, only one family had tried to sell a trailer in the state. "And before that family even got settled up near Cleveland, Johnson was there with the sheriff's department, and they were told to move on."

Tiebout explained, "We get them for showing trailers and offering them for sale without a dealer's license."

The writer asked, "Can't they get around that by saying they're selling the trailers as private individuals?"

"No, not in this state. Our law says a trailer is not a used unit until the ultimate purchaser in the chain has it. These trailers are coming here directly from the factories; they carry Indiana manufacturer certificates of origin with assignments from either Marauder Travelers in Indiana or Jeffery Trailer Sales in Louisville, Kentucky, but that's a joke. Authorities in Kentucky have told us there is no Jeffery Trailer Sales at Louisville; there was at one time, but not any longer."

Pursuing the *Irish gypsies* aggressively, Ohio enforcement officers also arrested family members for making false statements on vehicle registration forms, Tiebout said. Most of the *gypsies*, he explained, stated on the registrations that they had residences in Ohio, but they did not. The addresses they listed always turned out to be vacant lots, motels or businesses.

Some of the family names of *gypsies* arrested in Ohio were the same as names the campground manager in Florida had given the writer: Burke, Donahue, Rafferty, Daley, Carroll, Gorman, O'Roarke, Sherlock. To those names, Tiebout added four more -- Linzy, Riley, O'Neil and Williamson. The last name struck a chord with the writer, and he asked Tiebout if it were possible all the *gypsies* were part of the infamous Williamson family.

"No, I don't think so," the investigator said. "Everyone in Ohio law enforcement is familiar with the Williamsons, and although these gypsies run the same kinds of scams, it's my understanding that the Williamsons are Scottish, and most of these people claim they're Irish."

Tiebout added, "Now, there are a few exceptions to that. Apparently the Linzys are not Irish, but we aren't sure what they are. And there's a guy named Joe Smith that we hit five times last year. He apparently builds Custom Delux trailers in Elkhart, Indiana, and sells them any way he can. We don't know how he fits in, either. We've also got several warrants out for a woman named Martha Parks, and I understand she's part of the Williamson group. We don't expect to see her again in this state."

A woman named Beatrice Riley, he said, appeared to be some sort of matriarch in the Irish clan. "She's wanted for questioning in several states, but she apparently operates out of a mobile home park near North Augusta, South Carolina."

Reaching into a file cabinet, Tiebout pulled out a huge folder with arrest records and warrants. "If you're going to do research about these people, you ought to start with a list of individual names," he suggested. "That way, you can track them all over the country."

Later, the writer used copies of public records to try contacting Ohio residents who were listed as either having bought trailers from the *gypsies* or sold trailers to the con artists. In several cases, the buyers or sellers were not listed in any directories. Years later, he learned virtually all those trailers had been stolen; the buyers and sellers listed on public records simply did not exist.

The writer did, however, contact several individuals who had bought gypsy trailers in Ohio. A resident of Amelia told the writer he paid $5,000 for a 32-foot Kentucky Traveler he purchased from Steve Linzy. When the writer noted the man had told the bureau of motor vehicles he paid only $2,500 for it, he admitted, "Yeah, I was just gettin' out of payin' taxes."

Marion Myles of Liberty Center had just paid James J. Gorman a $300 deposit on a Marauder trailer when Mercer County Chief Deputy Bertkey arrived and arrested Gorman for selling a trailer without a license, giving a fictitious address on his driver's license and a fictitious address on the registration of the trailer. His driver's license had been suspended in Ohio earlier for speeding and driving while intoxicated. The address he used on both documents was actually for a popular Holiday Rambler RV dealership. "When the police showed up, I didn't know what to think," Myles told the writer. "It took a couple of months before I got my deposit back, but I've still got the keys Gorman gave me for the trailer; he never asked for them back."

Following a lead from Ohio, the writer tried to learn more about the woman named Beatrice Riley, who allegedly was an Irish clan matriarch operating out of South Carolina. That information later proved to be incorrect, but it did steer the writer to an Irish Traveler enclave known as Murphy Village. The writer telephoned Samuel L. Woodring, editor and publisher of the *North Augusta Star*. Woodring, who several years earlier had been awarded one of the most coveted honors in the newspaper industry -- the Elijah Parish Lovejoy Award for Courage in Journalism -- was familiar with the Irish Travelers.

"They reside not in North Augusta," Woodring reported, "but on the outskirts in an unincorporated area named Belvedere. Just inside the Aiken County line is an area which we know as Murphy Village where, for years, these people have lived in mobile homes. It's a society outside the normal society and the cultural heritage of this part of the country." He said many of the Murphy Village residents were known to travel widely and operate a variety of home improvement scams.

Within a few months, the writer would journey to Murphy Village and learn first-hand about the unusual Irish inhabitants of that community.


Meanwhile, the writer made repeated telephone calls to Kentucky Traveler, Rush Industries, Marauder Travelers and a couple of other RV manufacturers in hopes of convincing someone at those factories to consent to an interview. At Kentucky Traveler, the president declined to be interviewed and referred him to Tom Jeffery in Louisville. Jeffery said he had had no contact with Travelers for several years and referred him back to Indiana. Each time the owner of Rush Industries was contacted, he said simply, "No comment." A spokesman of a trailer company in Nappanee, Indiana, admitted his company had fallen on hard times and was selling trailers to Travelers, but he declined to be interviewed. Finally, in March the writer convinced Lloyd Moore, secretary/treasurer of Marauder Travelers, to participate in a tape-recorded interview.

Moore candidly admitted selling trailers to the Travelers, but he contended those individuals were a legitimate outlet for the company's products. He emphasized Marauder had a bonafide dealer network and that its dealers did not object if the company sold Marauder, Rogue and Lariat trailers to the Travelers. He also said Marauder had "fifty or sixty" service centers throughout the country, but he declined to identify them. Pressed to name his dealers, Moore said he regarded the Travelers as dealers, not as retail customers, and said they bought coaches at wholesale prices, not at retail prices. He claimed no one at Marauder had ever heard reports of Travelers who misrepresented trailers by telling people the coaches were higher priced than they were and then selling them as distressed merchandise for considerably less.

"Let's face it," Moore told the writer. "The American public is after only one thing -- getting as much as they can for the amount of money they have."

In the June issue of *Trailer Life* magazine, the "gypsy trailer scam" series was published. It was followed in the July issue by the interview with Marauder executives and an outline of how extensive the scam was, nation-wide. Reaction to the articles was immediate -- and extensive. Telephone calls and letters from law enforcement agencies, RV dealerships, consumer groups and victims poured in from around the country.

One call to the writer came from Neil Godbee, a Georgia deputy sheriff. Godbee said he had just arrested a young Irish Traveler man named James Burke, and Burke had told Godbee he wanted to meet and talk with the writer.

# 13

# Busted

In Macon, Georgia, Jimmy Burke did as the cop told him and changed into his own clothes, replacing the J.C. Penney mechanic's uniform that he had borrowed. Then he paid cash -- in $100 bills -- for work he had ordered on his stolen Cougar sedan. He was preparing to leave Penney's garage when he heard the police officer's voice behind him: "I want you to put your hands on the desk, and don't move. You're under arrest."

Jimmy asked, "What's this about?"

Bibb County Deputy Neil Godbee told him, "That car you've got there is stolen." The deputy handcuffed Jimmy.

Godbee was dumfounded by the young man's response. He said later, "He starts cryin'! He's about six-foot-two and weighs 210 pounds, but he's cryin' like a baby. I drove the patrol car I had with me into the auto center and put him in the back seat, and he commenced tellin' me how he had bought the car from his girlfriend in Florida and that there must be some mistake. He told me her name and address and everything. I looked in the glove box of the car, and there it was, a registration to Jo Ella Pate, who he told me was his sister-in-law. He said he was pickin' up the payments for her."

Aware that computer errors sometimes occurred, especially if just one digit of a vehicle identification number were entered incorrectly, Godbee told Jimmy, "Look, buddy, I don't try to railroad anybody, and if this is a mistake, it'll get cleared up. I'll go out of my way to make *sure* it gets cleared up."

He said later, "That boy had me convinced! I stayed there at Penney's for an hour and a half tryin' to get the mistake cleared up. I even called the city in Alabama where the car was registered to see if they had a phone number for the previous owner. But I finally had to tell him I had reached a dead end and there was nothin' else I could do. Then I had the office call Sweetwater, Tennessee, and ask for a description of the stolen car. It came back fitting the one the boy had perfectly!"

Knowing he would have to make out an inventory of the arrested man's possessions, Godbee opened the trunk of Jimmy's car. "Besides a big wad of clothes, he had a Sears portable electric typewriter and a little plastic case with it. I opened the case, and inside was a bunch of paperwork. And I mean a *bunch* of paperwork! There were blank bills of sale from Kentucky and a blank certificate of origin. Those things are supposed to stay with the dealer, and you don't get them when you buy a car. That's when I started wonderin' about the guy. Then I found a $10,000 bill of sale that matched the blank ones; it was for a 1980 twenty seven-foot Prowler travel trailer, with him -- Carl Gunnerson -- as the purchaser. It was notarized from Fayette County, Kentucky, and stamped with a notary seal. In the same box was the notary seal machine. Then I knew I was onto something. This case was startin' to get deeper and deeper."

In the car trunk, Godbee next found an estimate for body work on a 1979 Trans Am in Orlando, a birth certificate for Carl Gunnerson and birth certificates for James William Burke, Bobby and David. The young man carried a wad of $700 in his pocket. Astounded that the young man had so much money and clothes as well as clear ownership to a $10,000 trailer, he asked Jimmy, "Buddy, what do you do for a livin'?"

Jimmy answered, "I drive a taxicab."

Godbee said later that he thought to himself, "Boy, I'd better quit sheriffin' and start drivin' a cab!" Several days later, Jimmy would inform Godbee that he had hidden $3,000 in cash under the floor-mat of his Cougar. Godbee looked for that money in the impound-ed car, but it was gone.

As Godbee took Jimmy to jail, the young man became quite agi-tated. "He was gettin' real upset, and the way he was actin', I thought maybe he was on dope or somethin' and was afraid he wasn't goin' to get dope when he needed it. He was shakin' like a leaf. He asked about bond, and I said, 'You ain't goin' noplace, especially since I don't know for sure who you are.'"

Godbee asked the young man, "Now, are you James William Burke, or are you Bobby or David, or are you Carl Gunnerson?" Jimmy admitted his real identity and told Godbee his place of birth and his parents' names.

After placing Jimmy in a jail cell, Godbee drove to the Day's Inn where Jimmy had admitted he had a room. There, he learned Burke had left a message that he would be in a room at the Ramada Inn if anyone asked for him. Godbee and his partner, Jim Reid, then drove to the Ramada, and as they turned into the parking lot, they saw Jimmy's New York friends, David and Bobby, standing nearby, but they did not pay much attention to the young men. Godbee asked clerks at both motels to call him if anyone asked for James Burke or Carl Gunnerson. The next night, an employee at the sheriff's office called Godbee at home and said, "There's a boy down here asking about the fellow you arrested yesterday."

Godbee replied, "Good. Put him under arrest for possession of stolen goods, and I'll be right down to talk with him."

That young man was the third member of Jimmy's New York gang, Allen. At the jail, Godbee read Allen his rights and asked him what he knew about James Burke. "I knew Jimmy was into something, but I never knew what the business was," Allen answered. "Jimmy was very hush-hush about everything. I met him at a bar in New York, and he sent me money so I could fly down to Orlando and spend some time with him. I don't know much about what's going on, but there are two more fellows over at the bus stop right now who know about everything. They're waiting for me to come back with some money from Jimmy so we can leave town."

Godbee said, "Buddy, you ain't goin' noplace. We're gonna use you as a material witness."

The deputy then called for help, and he went with other officers to the bus stop where Allen said his friends waited. They were not there. The officers drove around Macon, checking every bus and every bus stop in an effort to find the men Allen had described to Godbee. Then, on the way back to the county offices, a deputy asked Godbee, "What was the description of those boys?"

Godbee answered, "One was short and husky, wearing bluejeans and a blue shirt, and the other one was blond, had on a Navy shirt with jeans and looked like a sissy."

The deputy pointed toward the YMCA, and Godbee said later, "It was like the Lord had sent them down to us."

Godbee stopped the car and said to the two men, "I'm Officer Godbee with the sheriff's office. I need to see some I.D."

One of them said, "We don't have any with us."

Godbee asked that one, "What's your name?"

"Bobby."

Godbee said, "You're under arrest. Put your hands on the car."

He turned to the other man and asked, "What's you name?"

"David."

"You're under arrest too."

After those two were locked in cells, Godbee's supervisor informed him that he and Jim Reid were relieved from patrol duties so they could concentrate upon investigating the stolen car case. The next day, Reid called police officers in Tennessee to check on the stolen Cougar, and just as he did, the Day's Inn desk clerk called Godbee. The deputy said later, "At the very instant the police in Tennessee were tellin' Reid there was another Mercury Cougar stolen the same night, except it was green and white, the woman at the motel was tellin' me there were two boys and a blonde girl who spent the night in Gunnerson's room, and they were drivin' a green-and-white Mercury Cougar!"

Immediately, Godbee and Reid drove to the motel. They stopped the Cougar just as it was leaving the parking lot, and they arrested Peggy and Paul Burke and Jimmy's friend David. Godbee recalled, "I told the girl we had her brother in jail, and right away she said, 'He's got a stolen Mallard travel trailer parked behind the Day's Inn, and I'll tell you anything about him you want to know.'

"Sure enough, there was a Mallard trailer there with a for sale sign on it. There was an Alabama tag on the trailer and a West Virginia tag inside it along with some other license plates, so we had trouble trackin' down where the trailer was stolen. Trackin' everything down took us three or four days. Meanwhile, because of what Theresa (Peggy) said when we picked her up, we started questioning her right away. She said her brother had stolen ten travel trailers since January."

Questioned about the Trans Am she was driving, Peggy told police, "Yeah, it's stolen too. Jimmy said he would give me some money if I would drive it from Orlando. He stole it somewhere in south Georgia."

Using the body shop estimate sheet from Orlando on the Trans Am, Godbee telephoned the body shop and asked for information about the car. An employee there replied, "You know, those people who brought that car in were funny acting. There were five or six of them in a big four-wheel drive truck. They just didn't look right, and the girl who was driving the car was real nasty-acting."

Godbee asked for a description of that girl, and the body shop employee said, "She was short, heavy and blonde." Peggy.

A computer check of the Trans Am revealed it had been stolen from Tifton, Georgia. Police there provided full descriptions of individuals who were looking at cars, and the descriptions matched Jimmy, Peggy, Bobby, David and Paul. "That let us know right away that, although Theresa was trying to hang her brother James, she was involved," Godbee said. The deputy then recalled that, among Jimmy's possessions in the trunk of his car was a photograph of Peggy and David standing in front of a white Trans Am with a Prowler travel trailer in the background.

Godbee asked Peggy about the bill of sale he found on the Prowler trailer, and she said, "He stole that trailer up around Washington, D.C., and sold it Mommy and Daddy for $5,000." A few days later, after spending hours on the telephone, Godbee discovered where the Prowler trailer had been stolen, and he asked the Alexandria, Virginia, police department for theft reports and a vehicle identification number. With that data, he contacted a detective in Orlando and suggested that the campsite be checked where Peggy said her parents were camped. The trailer was there, but Peggy's parents were not, so police officers impounded the trailer. Inside, they found bank wrappers from what had once been stacks of hundred-dollar bills.

Godbee recalled, "Theresa put everything off on Jimmy. She tried to remember places where he stole travel trailers, and she said, 'He jumped bond from New York where he was hanging bad checks.' We called New York, Virginia, Pennsylvania, Florida, Ohio and several other states tryin' to find out where all Jimmy had been."

In the process, Bibb County officers learned that Peggy had been arrested earlier in Augusta for aggravated assault and armed robbery, but charges were dropped because the victim left town before he could testify in court. Although Jimmy admitted stealing about a dozen travel trailers during the preceding eighteen months, no charges could be filed in Macon for those thefts because neither the owners nor the trailers could not be found. (Months later, using only the information Jimmy gave to Bibb County police, the writer found owners and buyers of some of the trailers.)

Jimmy, Peggy and Paul Burke were charged with vehicular auto theft. Bobby, Allen, James and David were, at first, held as material witnesses. Then they were released into their parents' custody before officers realized they were actually involved in the car and trailer thefts.

Godbee said whenever Jimmy and Peggy were together, "they made statements to each other in a language none of us had ever heard before." And, he said, at their arraignments, Jimmy and Peggy "were cussing each other in the Irish Traveler language, and the judge finally had to tell the girl he'd slap her with contempt of court if she didn't shut her mouth."

In actual fact, just after they were arrested, Jimmy told Peggy in Cant, "Nijash tharry sajicks," which meant "Don't say nothing to the cops."

During the arraignment, Peggy was particularly unhappy about statements made by Bobby. She told Jimmy, "I'm thorieing on the radget sobvine he's carbing my'jell." Translated from Cant, that meant, "I'm telling on this idiot because he's crucified me."


A week after the arrests, Godbee traveled to Orlando to attend a police seminar on vehicle theft. During the seminar, an investigator with Florida's Orange County sheriff's office made an announcement: "The *gypsies* are on the move with their trailer scam." The officer tossed two magazines onto the middle of the table -- the June and July editions of *Trailer Life*.

Godbee picked up one of the magazines and read the articles. As he did, he told those sitting at the table, "My God, I just arrested some of these people!"

When he returned to Macon, Godbee related to Jimmy Burke details about the Travelers that he had learned from the magazine articles. "How come you know all this?" Jimmy asked him.

Godbee replied, "I just read an article about gypsies and Travelers in *Trailer Life* magazine."

Jimmy's face brightened. "I've heard about them articles. All the Travelers are talkin' about 'em. The guy who wrote 'em found out a lot about The People, but some of the the the stuff he had was not exactly right."

Godbee suggested, "Maybe you ought to straighten him out."

"I'd like that. If you can let him know about me, I'd be willin' to talk to him."

That afternoon, Godbee called the writer and made arrangements for Jimmy Burke and the writer to meet for the first time in what would ultimately become a series of meetings stretching over nearly fifteen years.


It would be six months before Jimmy Burke and the writer could meet for their first interview. During the interim, police learned that Peggy had police records and there were warrants for her arrest in several states under the aliases of Eleanor Hernandez, Evelyn Hernandez, Patti LaFertz, Nancy Sweet, Peggy McNally, Larry Burke and Kathy Burke.

Realizing he, Peggy and Paul might be facing heavy sentences if they were convicted of all the crimes they had committed, Jimmy sent word to a well known Romanian Gypsy in Orlando named Johnny Johnson that he needed help.

Johnson, a permanent resident of Orlando, was one of four Gypsy brothers who gained a great deal of influence in central Florida by acting as intermediaries between law enforcement authorities and other Romanian Gypsies. Gradually, Irish and Scottish Travelers who were facing prosecution also used the brothers' negotiating skills -- for a price. After two of the brothers died and the third, Archie, moved to Tampa and became somewhat inactive, Johnny Johnson became regarded as the *baro* -- the big man -- by the Gypsy and Traveler societies. The base of his power rested largely with his daughters and sister-in-law, who became established in central Florida as three of the best fortune tellers in America. However, Johnson himself became quite adept at finding -- again, for a price -- talented legal counsel for Gypsies and Travelers alike.

Months later, Jimmy would tell the writer, "Any time any of our people got into trouble, Johnny Johnson usually was able to get them out of it. There was always a price, but usually he could do it. Before Bobby White died last year, his nephews, Mike and Pat, were arrested in New Jersey for runnin' drugs. It looked pretty bad for them. They had somethin' like $50,000 worth of drugs on them when they were caught. Johnny went up there and made some payoffs or somethin' and got them out within thirty days."

Jimmy said, "Another time, Mickey McDonald convinced an old man in Texas to leave Mickey everything in his will. Finally the old guy died. I never heard the full story, but Mickey was supposed to have killed him. The police locked him up and charged him with murder, but Johnny Johnson went to Texas and got Mickey out of it for $25,000 or $30,000. Mickey got the old man's property and now is supposed to be one of the wealthiest men in the Travelers."

Jimmy added, "Me and Peggy figured Johnny could get us off if anybody could. He came up here to see us about three weeks after we were arrested and said he could get all three of us off with six months of supervised probation if we'd give him $25,000. That meant we still could have traveled all over, and all we'd had to do was fill out a probationary report and mail it in once a month for six months.

"We didn't have that kind of money, but ordinarily $25,000 is never a problem for a Traveler. Whenever someone gets in trouble, all The People are supposed to pitch in together and get them out, no matter what it takes. But for us, no one wanted to pitch in any money. I think that was because we're half Traveler and half ref. If it had been anybody else, The People would have gotten the money together."

Finally, the Burke family hired a Macon law firm to represent Jimmy, Peggy and Paul. Jimmy was sentenced to eight years in prison while Peggy and Paul received prison terms of up to six years.

Deputy Godbee said, "When it came down to the end, Peggy was the meanest and toughest of the bunch. She cussed me out pretty good."

He added, "The whole thing was something like you'd read in a book. I didn't realize that people really lived that way."

After the sentencing, Peggy decided she would do anything she could to keep from going to prison. She convinced the woman who shared her cell to help her escape. She told the woman, "All we have to do is set fire to a mattress and yell loud enough that the guard in the control booth hears us. When she sees the smoke, she'll come runnin'. Then we'll knock her out, take her keys and escape."

Using a cigarette lighter she had stolen from another inmate, Peggy set the mattress ablaze, then she and her cellmate began screaming. As Peggy predicted, the female guard in the control booth ran to the cellblock, but before she did, she called for help. Peggy and her cellmate attacked the guard and took the keys, as planned, but before they could escape, several other guards arrived and subdued Peggy and the other woman. The attempted escape added six years to Peggy's sentence for first degree arson and aggravated assault.

# 14

# At Murphy Village

On Easter weekend of 1980, just before Jimmy Burke and his gang stole the white Trans Am in Tifton, Georgia, the writer drove to Georgia himself, crossed the state line at Augusta and searched out the South Carolina mobile home park known as Murphy Village. He went there because he believed Murphy Village was the national base of operations for the Irish Travelers and their travel trailer sales scam.

He was wrong in both respects.

Instead, what he found in South Carolina was an Irish sub-culture that existed -- and even seemed to be thriving -- outside the normal realm of American society. It was a culture based in part upon the ancient framework of Ireland's Tinker community and, in part, upon an uncertain blend of pioneer family life and modern technology. Murphy Village existed as if time had passed it by and left it and its citizens still struggling through the 1940s and 1950s. The 350-family Village was trying, desperately, to keep its identity a secret from the rest of the world, but it was failing in that attempt.

North Augusta newspaper editor Sam Woodring had told the writer earlier, "Everyone in this area is familiar with their existence. There are four or five major family names, including the Rileys, the

Sherlocks, the McNallys and the Carrolls. They are very strongly Catholic. But they in-breed, and by doing that, they create problems for themselves and the community in that many of the children are retarded or intellectually slow. The tribe resents being known as *gypsies*; they want to be called *Irish Travelers*."

The writer had been surprised when Woodring told him he did not think the Murphy Village Travelers sold travel trailers. "I know they are involved in painting houses, fences and barns and a few other things, but this RV thing is news to me," Woodring had said. "The men in the Village load up their painting and spraying equipment and leave there in caravans every spring. They're gone three or four months at a time, traveling throughout the country."

Emphasizing that Murphy Village Travelers dealt only in cash, he said, "They don't trust each other, so the paper money each fellow earns is kept at night in a pillow under his head, and they throw their coins in the gasoline tanks of their trucks. Then when they return, they take the gas tanks off and empty out the coins. The coins, in the meantime, have turned black. We see those coins in circulation throughout the community all the time, and we know where they came from."

Murphy Village consisted of several dozen mobile homes -- both old and new -- crammed on small lots in a patchwork grid on both sides of half a dozen narrow streets, but just off U.S. 25 near the Village was a small subdivision of large homes, also occupied by Travelers. Woodring had explained that this way: "With affluence has come a desire to move out of their mobile homes, so they bought land and built fantastic houses on it. Their houses are a copy of what we have in our culture. I'm told the houses are basically empty, with furniture in only a few rooms. Then they attach their mobile homes to the rears of those tremendous homes and continue to live in the trailers and maybe one room of the houses. They do that because they are culturally deprived, but they want to show people in the community they are as good as the rest of the residents."

During his visit, however, the writer learned not only that the houses were, indeed, fully occupied, but also that there was a simple explanation for the mobile homes that were parked next to the houses. In general, the mobile homes were occupied by elderly parents, in-laws or grandparents who had lived all their lives in mobile homes and did not want to vacate them -- and relinquish their privacy -- in order to live in a "big house." When young adult Travelers built a new home, they either moved the older folks' mobile home to the property or bought a new mobile home as an expression of their devotion.

Almost a year later, the writer would learn that only part of what Woodring said about the black coins was true. Unfortunately, he also would verify that the newspaper editor's comments about the Village's high incidence of mentally retarded children was true. That, the writer would learn was, indeed, the direct result of inbreeding, including the Travelers' practice of encouraging marriages between first cousins as a method of keeping Traveler bloodlines pure.

One of Woodring's comments seemed to the writer almost too farfetched to believe: "When an Irish Traveler from the Village dies, it's traditional for his friends and family to send floral tributes in the shape of what the dead person liked most in life. So if you drive past the cemetery during a funeral, you might see a ten-foot-high television set made of roses. If the dead person was a baseball fan, it might be a twenty-foot-long baseball bat. If he liked Coca-Cola, a ten-foot-tall Coke bottle made of roses." The writer later would be astonished to learn such floral displays were part of the Irish Traveler tradition.

Woodring had also said, "The period during the World Series is their big holiday season. Everything in and around Murphy Village comes to a standstill then. Baseball is their national sport."

Later, an Irish Traveler from Murphy Village would tell the writer with a chuckle, "We observe three primary holidays -- Christmas, Easter and the World Series!"

During his first visit to Murphy Village on Easter weekend of

1980, the writer was anything except inobtrusive. Driving a brightly colored high-top camper van, he was recognized as an outsider within seconds of turning onto the narrow road into the Village. Whole Traveler families left their mobile homes and watched, unsmiling, as he passed. No one made a threatening gesture; no one attempted to block his path or stop him; no one said a word to him. But the writer did not need an interpreter to understand the message the Travelers were communicating to him with their glares: He was not welcome there.

Later, the writer returned and drove along the blacktopped street of the small subdivision near the Village. Immediately, he understood what Woodring meant by saying the typical Traveler home was "a copy" of traditional American residences. The houses were large, and in another more urban setting, they probably would have cost up to half a million dollars each -- an enormous price for a western South Carolina home by 1980 standards. Many of them were, however, a hideous blend of traditional styling and garish poor taste. Their exterior colors were pastel pinks, blues and greens or combinations that clashed outrageously. One house featured a facade of black coal chunks and red brick. Parked alongside several of the houses -- and connected to them by electric umbilical cords -- were mobile homes of various age, sizes and colors.


At the nearby S & S Truck Stop restaurant, the writer identified himself to a small group of Travelers, including a 27-year-old named Jim Penn Sherlock, who lived in one of the houses. All the men were about six feet tall, with black hair and ruddy complexions. They were well dressed, but a few years out of fashion, with bright silk shirts, white shoes, tan trousers, and sports jackets.

Penn Sherlock emphasized to the writer that Murphy Village's Irish Travelers were not in any way associated with the Scottish Williamson family, although Penn admitted he admired the Williamsons a great deal. Penn regarded himself as a professional barn painter and expressed pride that he was able to earn a substantial living for his family with that occupation. He said he charged $75 to paint each section -- he called it a *bin* -- of a barn.

Most Murphy Village Travelers, he claimed, would prefer to live in the large houses, and not in the mobile home park, "if they could afford it." Penn flashed a large ring on his left hand that the writer admired and asked to see. Penn smiled and held out his hand proudly. The ring, in the shape of a western saddle, was encrusted with large diamonds. It would not be the last time the writer would see or hear about the famous saddle rings of the Irish Travelers.

Penn insisted that the Village's residents -- he called them "Southern Travelers" -- seldom engaged in the travel trailer sales scam. "Those are the Northern Travelers who do that," he said disdainfully.

"Where are the Northern Travelers located?" the writer asked. Penn laughed as if everyone knew the answer to that question.

"They don't have homes," he answered. "They're footloose and irresponsible. Our Travelers don't have nothin' to do with them."

Most Murphy Village Travelers, he explained, earned their livings by selling floor covering throughout the country, and the most skillful salesmen eventually graduated to painting barns and fences. He claimed nearly all Southern Travelers were honest businessmen who were unreasonably persecuted by police officers because of the "shenanigans" of the Northern Travelers and Williamsons. Southern Travelers, he insisted, were hard workers who earned enough money each year to buy themselves new cars and trucks as well as fine clothing and jewelry for their families. "We need new trucks," he said, "because we drive between 50,000 and 60,000 miles every year, and we have to have trucks we can depend on."

Penn said that like himself, most Murphy Village children quit school in the seventh or eighth grade because they did not need high school educations in order to succeed in their chosen fields of work.

Besides, he said, high school environments tend to breed disobedi-
ence and drug abuse, and he claimed that not only had the Village
never experienced a drug abuse incidence, but that "ninety per cent
of the people in the Village don't drink, and most of the kids don't
smoke cigarettes."

When the Irish Traveler clan first moved into the South Carolina
area during the 1930s, they set up a tent encampment on the outskirts of North Augusta among a large grove of pine trees. From the
encampment, they traveled the eastern half of the U.S. trading horses and mules. As years passed, splinter groups of Travelers left the
encampment and formed the nucleus of what later became three distinct enclaves -- the itinerant Northern Travelers, the Memphis-based
Mississippi Travelers and the Texas and California-based Western
Travelers. Known at that time as *The Travelers' Rest,* the pine grove
continued to serve as a campground even after the main body of
Southern Travelers bought mobile homes and settled in the park they
named Murphy Village in honor of a beloved local priest.

Coincidentally, the writer parked his van at the site of *The Travelers' Rest,* now called The Pines campground. When questioned about
Murphy Village, the elderly manager said he was quite familiar with
the Travelers. "There are some good 'uns and some bad 'uns; it's just
like it is anywhere else. There are some real skunks, too, but that's
just my opinion. My personal opinion is, they get more criticism
than they deserve. They're professional salesmen."

The writer pointed out law enforcement officers preferred to call
them professional thieves. "I don't believe it!" the park manager said.
"Some of 'em might be, but not all of 'em. Sure, some of 'em have
been caught stealin', but I'll tell you, you'll meet a lot of thieves out
on the street wherever you're goin'. The majority of 'em are good
people....Well, average, anyway. They're thrifty. The women usually
carry the money, and I'll have to admit, some of them women, I

wouldn't trust too far. If you've got somethin' they want, they'll worry you to death 'til they get it."

He added, "If you really want to see somethin', be sure to go over to the Catholic church on Easter Sunday. It's quite a show. All the women try to outdress and outshine all the others."

The manager of North Augusta's Amoco service station told the writer that stories about the Irish Travelers had reached almost legendary proportion. He claimed it was not unusual for a Traveler to walk into a local bank and deposit $100,000 in cash packed in a shoebox. "I've seen them buy money orders for up to $110,000 to pay for the paint they use on barns and fences!" he exclaimed.

But he added, "Nobody in town trusts them. They steal everything they can from stores, and the owner of one supermarket got a restraining order to keep them out of his place."

Months later, it became clear to the writer that an intense rivalry -- almost a hatred -- existed between the Northern Irish Travelers, of which Jimmy Burke was a member, and the Southern Travelers of Murphy Village. During the writer's first interview with Jimmy Burke, the young Traveler referred to the Murphy Village residents as *Sorries*.

Not certain he had understood Jimmy correctly, the writer asked, "What did you call them?"

"Sorries. Our Travelers call them Sorries. We say they're sorry. They are the lowest class of Traveler, the very lowest you can see. None of them over there have nothin'. If you'd drive into the Village right now, you'd see a bunch of mobile homes and brand new cars, but they might have them cars today just because the man from the finance company ain't found them yet. Most of our Travelers pay cash for their cars and trailers and everything, and most of us have some money and are pretty well off. But them people over there, when they go to buy a car, they don't ask how much the car costs;

they ask how much down and how much they can get financed and how much the payments are gonna be. Then they might keep the car a couple or three months or six months, run it all over and then let the finance company take it back and go buy another one somewhere else."

He added, "You might even see a Sorry drivin' around in a brand new Cadillac. But if you look at the gas gauge, you'd see that the tank is empty 'cause they won't have a dollar to put gas in the car."

The writer pointed out, "But they've built several nice homes near the Village."

"Yeah, they've got some pretty nice homes. But how long they're goin' to keep them, you don't know. They'll have them as long as they can keep up the payments on them, but if they stop makin' payments, they'll just go back down and live in the Village."

The writer said, "They told me they're into floor coverings and barn paintings, that they don't sell travel trailers."

Jimmy nodded. "They don't sell trailers ordinarily, but I think the reason for that is most of them can't afford to buy one, since we do have to pay cash for the trailers the minute we pick them up. I don't think you could find one person in the Village who could afford to buy a trailer."

The writer observed, "Some of them certainly appear to be better off than that."

"There are a few of them who have made some pretty good touches where they'd get $15,000 or $20,000," Jimmy said, "but they'd make it one week, and the next week it would be gone; that's just the way them people are over there."

He added, "If I was there, they wouldn't think nothin' of comin' up to me and sayin', 'I'm broke. Will you let me have some money for gas?' With our people, even if you don't have money for gas, you wouldn't do that. You'd still have to put on that front as if you had three thousand dollars in your pocket whether you were broke or not."

Later, Jimmy told the writer his older brother Pat married a girl from Murphy Village -- Rose Mary Sherlock. The writer asked, "What was your family's attitude toward Pat's marriage of a Village girl?"

"They didn't like it at all. Mom and Dad didn't speak to Pat and Rose Mary for about two years after they got married. And then, when they did start speakin', it was only for about a month or so. Only within the last two years have my parents accepted the marriage." At that point, Jimmy's brother and sister-in-law had three children -- Winifred Ann, Sean Patrick and Edward Thomas, known as E.T. A fourth, Kelly Nicole, was born two years later, followed by William.

The writer asked, "For the Northern Travelers, which is worse -- marrying into the Murphy Village group or marrying a ref?"

"Marryin' into Murphy Village! My mother and father have said several times that they'd much rather have a son or daughter marry a ref than someone from the Village."

The writer said, "Earlier, you told me some of the people from Murphy Village have made scores of $15,000 or $20,000. How do they typically do that?"

"The men who make those scores are the ones who go off in old highway patrol cars that have been souped up so they can outrun the police. Sometimes they travel the country for months at a time before they find their mark, but when they do find one, it's usually a good one. Normally, the mark is an old man or woman that they approach as being a doctor and his assistant from the Social Security office. They tell the old person he is goin' to get a raise in his Social Security payments, but before the raise can be approved, the person has to get a checkup by the doctor. So they take the old person into a bedroom and get him stripped down and lyin' on his stomach, and while one Sorry is playin' doctor, the other one is goin' through the old person's clothes for money. Meanwhile, two or three others who were hidin' outside in the car are busy searchin' the rest of the house. If the old man or woman refuses a checkup, he or she is usually tied up and set aside until the Sorries are through with the search."

Asked about whether Murphy Village Travelers keep coins in their fuel tanks, Jimmy laughed and said, "What you have heard about that is not true. First of all, most of them people don't have any money. And if they had it, they sure wouldn't put it in their gas tanks. As stupid as some of them people are, I think they still know better than to do that because, they'd know if they did, one of those monsters they call kids would steal the entire gas tank if necessary in order to get the coins. See, our Travelers have a code: One of us could leave a thousand dollars layin' around, and no one else would touch it. But the Sorries have no code; they will steal and cheat among themselves as much as they'd steal and cheat someone else."

Asked about the floor coverings sold by Village residents, Jimmy said, "They'll put a couple of small rolls of carpet or linoleum in the trunk of a car and go through the country lookin' for their marks. When they find an old woman alone, they'll try to sell her a piece of the carpet and promise to come back and give her another piece free. Then two of them will get out of the car with the carpet and hold it up in front of her so she can't see the others in the car, and the others will go inside the lady's house and search it for cash and jewelry. I've heard of them stealin' up to $200,000 over a short period of time doin' that. There's a certain bunch of them from the village that that's all they do."

A few months later, the writer would have opportunity to interview Irish Travelers from Murphy Village. And from them, he would get a completely different perspective on the people known as *The Sorries*.

# 15

# End of the Trail

The writer met 19-year-old Irish Traveler James Burke for the first time at Georgia's Bibb County Jail during early December 1980. That initial interview could have been quite awkward. But Jimmy, in typical Traveler fashion, approached the session with a grin and an openness that caught the writer off guard. He stood as the writer entered the interview room and offered his right hand so the writer could shake it. He was tall and slim, about six-foot-two and 180 pounds. His thick black hair -- obviously styled by a professional -- was carefully combed backward, not a strand out of place; it had not yet been ravished by a jailhouse barber's electric razor. Burke beamed at the writer as if he were in the presence of a close personal friend. "Hi," he said. "I'm James Burke. I'm really glad to see you 'cause you're the most famous person I've ever met!"

The writer laughed and realized that the interview was probably already out of his control.

Burke's dark eyes flashed, and his smile widened as he waited for the writer to respond. The writer's mind went blank. The well-thought-out, probing questions he had prepared were forgotten, and as he nervously tried to push the correct buttons on his portable tape recorder, the writer stammered, "Can you tell me a little about yourself, where you were raised and that sort of thing?"

"Sure," Burke said agreeably. He sat in a straight-back chair at the conference table and, like any polite host, motioned for the writer to take a chair too. "I was born in Orlando, Florida. My mother was not a member of our people -- I mean the Travelers. She is what is referred to as a ref by the Travelers which is one of their words which just means someone who is not one of them. It was hard for us growing up because we were considered by my mother's people as gypsies and by my father's people as refs. Sometimes when I was a kid, I got into fights with some of my relatives over that. We'd be playing together and one of them would call me a ref, or we'd be staying with my grandmother and she'd get mad and call us gypsies. It was kind of a hard spot for a kid to be in."

For the next three hours, James Burke talked, virtually non-stop, about himself, his family, the Irish and Scottish Travelers and the secret society into which he was born and raised. He halted only long enough for the writer to change tapes on his recorder or ask for clarification on some points. The monologue ended when a jail guard told the writer his visiting time was over. "Already?" Burke asked. "I'm just gettin' started."

As the writer left the jail with Burke's attorney, Russell M. Boston, he felt as mentally drained as if he, and not Burke, had spent the last three hours talking.

Boston laughed. "That was quite an experience, wasn't it? You ought to see the look on your face. You look stunned, as if you can't believe what you've just heard."

"That's just it," said the writer. "I DO believe it! What he said was unbelievable, but I do believe it."

A day later, the writer returned to the jail for another three-hour interview. That time, he insisted on asking specific questions, and Burke responded enthusiastically to each one. The writer and Burke met again at the Georgia Diagnostic and Classification Center in

Jackson, and that meeting was followed by a series of tape-recorded interviews arranged by Boston and then regular telephone conversations that also were recorded. Unexpectedly, a friendship developed between the writer and the young Irish Traveler -- a friendship that was destined to last more than a dozen years, a friendship that would be documented by dozens of tape cassettes and letters. Initially, the writer addressed James Burke by the common nickname, "Jim," but as their relationship developed, Burke said, "I'd sure like it if you'd call me Jimmy."

Almost from the first minutes of his initial meeting with Jimmy Burke, the writer realized he was being given information that probably no other living person outside the Traveler clans had ever heard. Jimmy not only had verified the existence of an Irish Traveler clan that operated separately and distinct from the infamous Scottish Williamsons, but he had also indicated that the various clans consisted of substantially more members -- at least several thousand -- than anyone in law enforcement knew existed. The significance was obvious: Ethnic con artists in enormous numbers were operating a wide variety of scams and swindles throughout America -- and had been for at least 100 years! Jimmy also gave the writer valuable tools for researching the activities and lifestyles of the clans. He told the writer the names of a few other Travelers who might consent to be interviewed, and he provided expert advice on how to find and identify Travelers. The contacts Jimmy provided resulted in further introductions until finally, the writer was being fed regular information from several sources within the Traveler clans, including from Jimmy's wild sister, Peggy.

Gradually, a clear picture began to emerge of the entire Traveler sub-culture.

Within the over-all Traveler ranks are three ethnic groups: English, Irish and Scottish. Of those, the Irish Travelers are the most diverse, with families aligned to one of four divisions -- the Northern Travelers, of which Jimmy Burke was a member; the Southern Travelers of Murphy Village, known derogatorily by the others as *Sorries*; the Mississippi Travelers, who reside in a mobile home park on Shelby Drive near the Memphis International Airport, and the Western Travelers, whom the others refer to as the *Greenhorn Carrolls*.

Scottish Travelers -- those known in law enforcement circles as the Terrible Williamsons -- are dispersed widely throughout the country, but concentrate their activities in the Southwest, California, the western Midwest and the Northeast. Although they are the best known of all Travelers, current evidence indicates they might well be the smallest Traveler clan of all.

English Travelers -- without question the least known of all Traveler groups -- perform most of their scams in the states east of the Mississippi River, although they also range westward from time to time. They have permanent enclaves in Spiro, Oklahoma; Acworth, Georgia; Sunrise, Louisiana, and Arena, Wisconsin.

It was from Jimmy Burke that the writer first confirmed the Irish Travelers spoke their own language. Called Cant, it was a version of Gammon or Shelta, which was formed from Irish Gaelic words and spoken in Ireland by that country's Travelling People, the Tinkers, for at least 250 years. "No one else can understand it," said Jimmy. "We don't have a word for everything, but it pretty well covers most situations. If someone hears me speakin' it, I just tell him, 'It's Irish.' Most people wouldn't know the difference, but it's not the Irish language; it's the Travelers' own language. How it came to be, I don't know, but my people have been using it for as long as any of them can remember, and from the time the Traveler children are old enough to talk, they are taught to use it."

With Jimmy's help, the writer was able to record important parts of the Cant vocabulary:

| ENGLISH WORD | CANT WORD |
| --- | --- |
| Mother | Mauker |
| Father | Arker |
| Killed (or hurt) | Carbed |
| Mad | Narked |
| Jail | Quad |
| Clothes | Athie |
| Pants | Briskies |
| Non-Traveler | Ref or Gajo |
| Leave | Mishlie or Jowl |
| Here | Anosha |
| Dog | Commer |
| Coming | Bugging |
| Morning | Morjin |
| Night | Neiah |
| Stupid | Leerkey |
| No good | Tathey |
| Eat or Food | Lushing |
| A Dress | Griffin |
| Mouth | Thulup |
| Check | Kite |
| Hair | Grooge |
| Stay | Steash |
| Store | Stirah |
| Hard | Gamie |
| A Penny | Nuck |
| $100 | Shade |
| $1,000 | Kade |
| Fat Person | Chew |
| Old Man | Fringe |
| Old Woman | Cabbage |
| Home | Kear |
| Gun | Nuggie |

| | |
|---|---|
| Understand | Konch |
| Embarrassing | Ladgeing |
| Shoes | Brouges |
| Prostitute | Ludney |
| House | Keentha |
| Hands | Malluas |
| Teeth | Fakeleys |
| Eyes | Sooleys |
| Nose | Schmerick |
| Ears | Lugs |
| Talk | Thorie |
| Look | Soonee |
| Crazy | Radged |
| Steal | Chore |
| Car or Truck | Lork |
| Man | Guick |
| Women | Buer |
| Child | Poystoha |
| Sell | Shalk |
| Buy | Eage |
| Thing or object | Inik |
| Trailer | Runga |
| Good | Monuah |
| Luck | Ses |
| Work | Grubber |
| Love or like | Shan |
| Married | Lospeed |
| Paint | Chat |
| Gas | Gear |
| Motel | Compaul |
| Sleep | Kullah |
| License plates | Chits |
| Driver's license | Slangs |

| | |
|---|---|
| Police | Sajick\Sajo |
| Money | Glonth or Kush |
| Boy | Sobiune |
| Girl | Lockiune |
| Purse | Gothup or Busker |
| No | NeJaySh |
| Yes | StaySh |
| Idiot | Kull |
| Black person | Guthie |
| People | Neagie |
| Campground | Runk |
| Bathroom | Ruthie |
| Water | Ishka |
| Alcoholic beverage | Schkim |
| Dime | Jay Niucks |
| Quarter | Sharker |
| Dollar | Schtammer |
| $5 | Quid |
| To talk | Tharry |
| Do not | Nijash |

After three or four generations in America, the Scottish Travelers stopped speaking with their Scotland brogue and adapted to a style of speech without a distinguishable accent. They considered the brogue too distinctive. Irish Travelers, on the other hand, proudly maintained their brogue, and even by the mid-1990s, it was common to hear an Irish clansman speaking with a lyrical lilt as if he had just immigrated from Dublin.

Several years after the writer's first interview with Jimmy Burke, he met central Florida police investigator John McMahan. McMahan, also of Irish descent, had developed his own lilt and had also taken time to learn some of the Irish Traveler language. It was not unusual for McMahan to use the brogue -- and a few Traveler words -- while holding conversations with Travelers. He admitted to being amused by Travelers who spoke openly with a brogue even though they had never been to Ireland.

"I especially noted that Irish lilt when I covered the Gorman-Carroll wedding earlier this year," he told the writer in 1995. "We surfed the parking lot and took long-range photos and copied down as many tag numbers as we could get -- about forty or fifty vehicles. Later on, we went to the reception at the Heritage Inn. I arranged for us to get some work shirts with name tags, and we mingled.

"While I was in the restroom, I was listening to the young kids talking with each other, and it was like they'd just come over from Ireland. They had a lilt to their voices, and then they'd swing into Cant so any *sajick* nearby wouldn't understand what was being said. They were always checking me out. I was an outsider, and even though I had a uniform that indicated I could have been a maintenance man, I still didn't belong to their group. I heard a couple of weeks later that they had a lovely time and they didn't see a *sajick* one."

McMahan added, "Later, when I popped Matt Carroll and Mike Donahue, I said in my own Irish way, "God, wasn't that a lovely weddin' that Billy and Katherine had? You all looked so grand down there in those tuxedos and the lovely green gowns. And it was a lovely reception. Katherine had such a nice rock on her hand, and I'd never seen the women dressed so well. It was really somethin'. The Heritage Inn sure put on a fine spread for you.' I did that simply to let them know we knew what was going on, that we knew who was there. And I know the word got around instantly. It wasn't long after that many of them packed up their trailers and left Orlando for Tampa."

Central Florida -- and, to a lesser extent, the Rio Grande Valley of Texas -- is regarded as the center of social activity for all Northern Travelers, the easternmost members of the Scottish Travelers and English Travelers and some of the Fort Worth-based Western Travelers. Dances scheduled in either Tampa or Orlando on Christmas Eve and New Year's Eve attract several hundred, and sometimes a few thousand, members of the various clans. Entire country clubs or nightclubs are reserved exclusively for Travelers, and popular bands are hired to provide music. Throughout the winter, smaller parties are held to introduce teenage Traveler girls to eligible young men.

Dating and courtship are highly structured, and although marriage between Travelers and non-Travelers is not strictly forbidden, it is seriously discouraged. Jimmy reported, "The girls are not allowed by custom to even speak to a boy who is not a Traveler. If they're caught even talkin' to one, much less messin' around with one, the word is spread all over among the Travelers before the end of the day. Even if a girl just sits down and talks with a non-Traveler boy, by the next day, it's goin' to be all over that she was caught in bed with him. If that happens, she can just about forget any idea of gettin' married to a Traveler boy."

He continued, "Traveler girls usually meet their husbands by goin' to the dances or the parties. A girl usually won't see the boy all year until they go to one of the dances. There, they'll meet, dance together a few times and then get engaged. If they get engaged, they can start goin' out on dates together, but only if at least three or four couples go out together. After they get engaged, usually the boy's family will travel with the girl's family that summer so they can get to know each other. Then they'll get married the following winter in Florida."

Traditionally, Traveler girls become engaged at the age of twelve or thirteen and are married before they are seventeen, Jimmy said. His older sister, Wanda (Jessee), was married at fourteen and became a mother a year later. Like most other Traveler girls, she married an older Traveler man; her husband Billy was twenty-four when they married.

Another popular tradition is for Traveler brothers to marry sisters. For example, Jimmy's cousin, Pat Rafferty, married a fifteen-year-old Traveler girl when he was twenty-four, and a year later, his twenty-eight-year-old brother married that girl's fourteen-year-old sister.

Marriages between Scottish Travelers and Irish Travelers were relatively rare until the 1950s, then began occurring more frequently. In spite of inter-clan rivalries, occasional feuds and religious differences -- Irish Travelers are Catholic, Scottish Travelers Presbyterian -- the marriages appear successful. Generally speaking, however, Irish Travelers seldom marry Rom Gypsies. Marriage between Scottish Travelers and Gypsies occur slightly more often, but the Rom custom of requiring cash payments for their daughters puts the damper on more than a few of those proposed nuptials.

Although Jimmy Burke was not inclined toward marriage because of his sexual orientation, he said, "Even if I was to get married, I would not marry a Traveler girl because they're all, to put it frankly, a bunch of snobby bitches. They keep their noses in the air and think they're better than everybody else. Their mothers are the same way, especially toward refs. To them, country people are totally beneath them. All Travelers are like that, though -- even the men feel they're better than someone who is not a Traveler. I've always been the type of person -- even when I was a kid in school -- that treats someone by the way he treats me. No matter who they are, whether they're black or white or Traveler or country. And if someone's nice to me and I become good friends with someone, I'm going to treat that person the way I'd want to be treated, and no matter what anybody thinks, I'm going to stick up for that person. That's just the way I am."

Relationships between Traveler men and women are a strange combination of male machismo and female domination. Men make decisions on where the family will travel and which trucks and trailers to buy. They tow the trailers, pave the driveways, seal the roofs and install the lightning rods. Women raise children, sell trailers, perform pigeon drops and other light confidence games, peddle rugs and handbags, and shoplift. Women also handle the family's money and decide, for the most part, how it will be invested or spent.

Among Travelers, divorce is rare. Jimmy explained, "Divorce is really against our beliefs. Couples are supposed to stay together no matter what. If a couple gets divorced, it's more or less the same as the girl who gets caught sleeping with a guy -- they won't get nobody else to marry them."

He added, "My sister Cathy is an exception to that. She got married when she was eighteen to a guy who was not a Traveler. He was a mess -- a wino and everything. They went up to New York and stayed with me, and he jumped on her one night. Me and him got into it, and I threw him out of the house, so they separated and she ended up divorcin' him. Tony Robertson, the guy she's married to now, is a Traveler, but that was kind of a funny situation. His father died about seven years ago, and all Tony had left was his mother -- he had no more immediate relatives. Then two years ago, his mother died. My sister was camped right next to him in a campground all summer, and she was helpin' him out. They ended up gettin' married, and now they have a baby of their own. But it's kind of unusual for something like that to happen." Tony, a "settled" Irish Traveler from New Jersey, was the first cousin of Wanda Burke O'Roarke's husband, Billy.

Although two of the primary social functions in Traveler society are funerals and weddings, male members of the clans historically avoid participation in the actual wedding ceremonies. Weddings are regarded as women's functions, and the men are not even obliged to attend. Men are, however, expected to take part in wedding receptions, and most do since that is where the heavy drinking takes place.

Florida Investigator John Wood took note of that phenomenon in 1995 when he observed a Scottish Traveler wedding. "The women were dressed to the nines, and the men looked like shit. The men never went inside the church. They stayed outside in the parking lot drinking beer and pissing in the bushes."

For Travelers, image is extremely important, the writer learned from Jimmy Burke and other clan members. And enviable images are easily achieved by displaying wealth. It is assumed that a successful Traveler exhibits only a fraction of his personal wealth. Therefore, if a Traveler man owns a couple of new cars, a new truck and a new trailer; if he and his family members dress in expensive new clothes; if he and his wife wear diamond rings and gold jewelry; if his wife collects high-priced imported china and keeps full-length sable and mink coats in her closets; if he flashes wads of $100 bills in restaurants and buys everyone drinks in bars, then it is clear to everyone he is living up to the standard that a successful Traveler is expected to achieve.

Even Jimmy Burke, who claimed accumulating money was not important to him, tried desperately to meet the Traveler standard. From prison at the age of nineteen, he said almost apologetically, "I never really made no big scores like the rest of them have. I'm the type of person that likes to have nice things; I like to drive a nice car and live in a nice house and wear nice clothes, but money to me is just something you have to have, and as I got it, I spent it. It has no real value for me except that it's there to spend, whereas most of the Travelers are always tryin' to get more and more, and they're never happy, no matter how much they've got. So if I could keep myself up to what was considered their standards, whether I had $50, $500 or $5,000 in my pocket was immaterial to me. I more or less lived day by day. I made money daily and spent it daily; but to look at me, you would have thought that, like any of the rest of them, I had $10,000 or $20,000 stashed away somewhere. You play the game. You go out to a bar, and whether you've got fifty or five-hundred bucks in your pocket, you buy everybody a drink. If that leaves you broke, you still buy those drinks. You've got to play the part."

Diamonds and jewelry are important parts of "playing the part." One of the biggest misconceptions about Travelers among law enforcement officers is their idea that the saddle-shaped diamond rings worn by a majority of Traveler men have a special, secret significance. In fact, it has no significance other than the fact that it is flashy, looks expensive -- and quite often is! -- and is a popular, simple method of displaying wealth. The rings are custom-made at the Diamond Mart in New York City where large, recirculated "estate" diamonds can be purchased and set into the rings at a relatively low cost.

Years later, Tampa investigator John Wood would tell the writer, "Their whole culture is based on flash. And a lot of jewelry. A lot of gold. The men wear thick, custom-made gold I.D. bracelets, Rolex watches and gold nugget rings."

Police officers also have a major misconception about the enclosed utility trailers Travelers tow with them in their travels. Police assume the trailers are used for some mysterious reason such as hauling gear the Travelers do not want anyone else to see. In actual fact, the trailers serve three purposes: first, because they are expensive, they are a convenient display of wealth; second, they serve as a storage shed for carrying supplies such as rugs or purses that the women sell; third and most importantly, they are simply safe places where clothing, collectibles and personal belongings can be kept temporarily after sale of the travel trailer in which the family is living.

In late January 1981, almost a year after the writer began his investigation of the Travelers by posing as a trailer buyer at the Day's Park campground in Orlando, Jimmy Burke penned a short note from his prison cell. "There are very few Travelers staying at Day's Park in Orlando this year," he wrote. "Probably not more than three or four families, one being my mom and dad, who are staying there right now.

"One reason for this is that Day's Park has a new manager who is not very fond of the Travelers, and my mom tells me that he will not allow them to put trailers up for sale there anymore. Another reason is that most of them are in Tampa this year, staying at the Happy Traveler Campground or Marty's Trailer Park, or any other countless number of trailer parks, campgrounds or motels in and around the Tampa area. By now, as always after the holidays are over with, most of the Travelers have drifted off into small bunches and scattered across the entire state of Florida and southern Georgia and Alabama in hopes of selling their trailers before time to start heading up north for the summer."

Although most Travelers settle temporarily in campgrounds, motels and apartments in the Orlando and Tampa areas while they spend their winters in Florida, many also move throughout the state during the periods when no major parties, funerals, weddings or other social gatherings are held. Considering the huge number of Travelers wintering in Florida, only a relatively small number of scams are performed while they are there. The Travelers as a whole frown upon activities that might increase law enforcement's attention to them. Most winter scams, therefore, are of two types: driveway and roof work in black neighborhoods and low-key travel trailer sales, targeted at tourists, from campgrounds.

Wood said, "While they probably don't work Florida in winter to the magnitude that they do the rest of the country during the summer, that's not to say they won't keep their hand in. Florida is a good training ground for their kids. Contrary to popular belief, when those guys come to Florida, they're here for months; unlike when they're on their road trips, they do not hit a place and leave. Here, they're either in travel trailer parks or they lease apartments, usually in a bloc."

Wood's associate, McMahan of Orange County, added, "Pat Riley and Donald and Joseph Burke are even staying in some of the best hotels. They've got enough money to stay where they want. Usually, though, they do what they call *'chuckie'* -- they arrange to stay there free or for low cost. This year (1995), they got one of Heritage Inn's best suites for rock-bottom prices. We started shooting pictures and copying down license tags, and they left, trashing one of the rooms as they did."

Because Travelers who are actively working scams in Florida are vulnerable to prosecution while they are there, they take extreme measures to prevent victims from complaining to authorities until after they leave. Posing as representatives of legitimate home repair businesses, they provide full guarantees with their work and supply their victims with telephone numbers where they can be reached in the event problems with their workmanship develop. The phone numbers, however, are simply answering services.

Wood explained, "The reason they do that is that the answering service will hold off complainers for months. It's amazing how patient people are. When the victim calls the telephone number of a business card that the Traveler had printed for him the day before, the answering service will answer, 'Stewart Painting. May I help you?' Well, the victim doesn't know he's speaking to an answering service; he thinks he's speaking with someone at the Stewart Painting office. He says, 'Can I talk with Mr. Stewart?' and the answering service says, 'He's not in right now, but I'll take a message.' Stewart will call him back three days later and say, 'I can't get out there this week, but I'll be out for sure next week.' Of course, he doesn't show up next week. And that goes on and on, buying Stewart time until he leaves Florida."

Beginning in early spring, Travelers leave Florida and spread throughout the country in groups of between three and thirty families. One of the first stops for many Travelers is Elkhart, Indiana, where they buy new travel trailers. While in Elkhart, they camp at the Poplar Mobile Home Court on Cassopolis Main Street and the Elkhart Campground north of town on County Road 4. On almost any day between March and November, dozens of Travelers' trailers can be seen at those campgrounds while family members spread out into lower Michigan and northern Indiana to perform their scams. Throughout the country, law enforcement officers regard Elkhart's lack of attention to the Travelers as shameful and lazy. Several police officers have even questioned whether Elkhart County lawmen are taking payoffs in exchange for not bothering the clans, but there is no indication of that. In actual fact, Indiana's laws on consumer fraud and home repair swindles are so poorly structured that enforcement efforts are largely a waste of time. As a result police officers in Elkhart County, as well as elsewhere in the state, give consumer fraud complaints very low priority.

Although many law enforcement officers believe Scottish Travelers -- and particularly the Williamson family -- still use Cincinnati as a home base, they do not. A few retired clan members apparently make the Cincinnati area their home, and Scottish Travelers do continue to bury family members occasionally in Spring Grove cemetery, but most of the clan roams through Oklahoma, Texas, California, Nebraska, Iowa and the Dakotas during the spring and summer. Both the Scottish Travelers and the Western Irish Travelers specialize in installing lightning rods as well as operating roof and driveway sealer scams.

Jimmy Burke admitted he did not know most of the Travelers who were active primarily in the West. "But," he added, "one thing about it is, no matter where I am, if there's a Traveler there, I have a friend, even if I never met him and don't know him. There's still something that's almost like a family bond between us."

One popular activity among Travelers that police officers have never tied to them is travel trailer theft. And Travelers steal enormous numbers of travel trailers every year from campgrounds, RV dealerships and even from owners' driveways! Jimmy admitted he usually stole trailers from the storage areas of campgrounds. He explained,

"A lot of campgrounds, especially up north in the wintertime, have storage lots for them, and nine out of ten times, they won't even have fences around them."

Because many Travelers carry master keys that open most popular RV door locks, they can choose from a wide variety of brands and models when they decide to steal a trailer from a campground or dealership. "It don't take but a matter of five or ten minutes to hook one on and be gone with it, and I've never heard of anyone being caught trying to take one," Jimmy said. "The only time police are likely to charge you with trailer theft is if they catch you actually hooking onto the trailer and towing it off the lot. Once you're gone with it, if they catch you with it, the most they could do is charge you with being in possession of stolen property; they couldn't prove that you're the one who took it. Then all you have to say is, 'I was haulin' it for someone. I didn't know it was stolen.'"

Once a trailer is stolen, it is given different serial numbers and brand name, and a new title and license plate are acquired for it. Jimmy boasted, "The Travelers know everything about a trailer. I know everything about a trailer; I've been brought up with them all my life. All you have to do is grind down the serial numbers on the tongue and make new ones with a set of taps, then peel the sticker off the side and type up a new sticker on a card. Usually, with most trailers, the name of the manufacturer is on the front awning, and sometimes they'll have an initial on the wheelbox. In that case, all you have to do is take the name off the front and back awnings with paint remover, peel any decals off with the name on them and, if you have to, take the covers off the wheelbox and put some back on that don't have initials on them. Then you get some new decals -- any kind of decals -- and put any kind of name on it and change the name, the serial numbers and everything; then it's a different trailer, and there is no way anyone can track it down. Even if the person who owned it found it, it would be almost impossible for him to prove it was his."

The writer asked Jimmy, "Did you ever consider that with your intelligence, imagination and salesmanship, you could open a legitimate business and make a lot of money?"

"Yeah."

"And that doesn't appeal to you?"

"Yes, it does appeal to me. That's what I would like to do when I get out of jail. I'm really sick of this mess I'm in now. I've tried to settle down before, but I'm hoping that the next time, I can make it work. This experience has really taught me something: No matter how much money you earn the other way, it's just not worth it if you have to spend time in jail."

The writer asked, "If you had not been arrested, were you planning to settle in one place or continue traveling?"

Jimmy answered, "I had planned to settle. For the last two or three years, I wanted just to go somewhere and stay there. What I really was intendin' to do was ask Diane to marry me. I wanted to settle in New York with her and stop the travelin'. I know that I'll never be as much a Traveler as the rest of The People. Sure, I've traveled all over the country and have been everywhere -- two or three times, probably -- but since I've been on my own, I don't do half the travelin' that the rest of them do."

Jimmy was silent a few minutes, thinking. Then he said, "But whether I'll just be able to settle somewhere and not move again, I don't know. The travelin' kind of draws me; it pulls at me. I've been sittin' in jail for eight months, and I miss the road so much! I'm not used to stayin' in one town, let alone sittin' in one building. I guess I'm afraid I've just got travelin' in my blood and that even if I would be settled down and have a house and everything, I'd probably leave it all anyway. All through my life, it was nothin' for me to just to pick up and go. I could be in a place today and have everything I owned in a house and look like I'm there for life, and the next day there might be no trace of nothin'. That's just the way I've always lived. It's nothin' for me just leave a place, all of a sudden. It's so easy to do it if you want to, especially when you're used to doing it."

"How has your relationship with Diane been since you were arrested?" the writer asked. "Have you talked with her?"

"Yeah. When I first got locked up, I called her. She wouldn't believe at first that I was in jail because she always thought I was just loaded with money, and she never thought I did anything illegal. She thought I owned my own pavin' business, and at the time, I don't think she had much knowledge about gypsies or Travelers. I guess she just thought I was a rich kid. So when she found out I got locked up here, and I tried to explain things to her and tell her a little bit about my life, I stopped gettin' letters from her. And now, I just don't hear from her at all. A lot of people, when they can't understand something, just don't try to. They just put it off to the side. Other peoples' lives are so completely different from what ours (the Travelers) are that they just can't understand it."

He added, "See, I was going under the name of Danny Burke, and that's what everybody up there called me. Then after I was arrested, she found out my name was James Burke. I think she really felt kind of betrayed because I wasn't more open with her in the beginnin'. But it was just something I couldn't be open about with everybody. So she wrote me a letter."

Jimmy took the letter out of his pocket and read it aloud. As he did, a tear rolled down his left cheek. "It was like she was tellin' me off, but I guess she was just sayin' what was on her mind. She said, 'Danny, I love you as a very close friend and I always will. You're a beautiful person, but I'm not sure I know you. The Danny I thought I knew, I love. James Burke, I don't know at all. You're so eager to reach out to somebody; it's like you're constantly reaching and wanting somebody to love you. You give so much of yourself to another person almost immediately, and then when you don't get that in return, it hurts you. You try so hard to be somebody's friend that you end up getting hurt.'"

Jimmy refolded the letter carefully and put it back into his shirt pocket. "I've pretty well gotten over her now," he said, "but she made me take a good look at myself because of what she wrote."


One of the questions the writer asked Jimmy was, "Do the Travelers know about me?"

"Yes, they do," the young man answered. "They don't know that I'm talking to you, but there's been a lot of talk about you since the articles came out in the magazine."

"What kind of talk?"

"Talk about how you were causin' a lot of trouble for them with their tryin' to sell the trailers and so forth. A few of them are scared to go here or there with the trailers after those articles. Once every few years, some writer will pick up a little something on the Travelers, but they never really make nothin' out of it. A few years later, it's all over and forgotten. Those articles in *Trailer Life* magazine were the biggest splash for quite a while, anyhow."

Later, as the writer expanded his network of sources within the clans, a broader awareness of him and his research began to spread throughout the Traveler community, and occasionally, he would receive unsolicited telephone calls from unfamiliar Travelers. Nearly always, the calls were by Travelers who just wanted to talk with him, but a few of the callers indicated the writer would be smart if he stopped investigating the clans. On more than a few occasions, friendly Travelers would greet him by name at restaurants, highway rest areas and campgrounds; how they recognized him on sight, he never learned.

Neither the writer nor his family felt threatened, however, until one day early in 1982 when several Travelers called him with alarming news: The owner of a company that supplied equipment to the clans had announced he would pay $10,000 to anyone who could make the writer "disappear." The Travelers emphasized that most clan members regarded the man as "crazy," and it was unlikely anyone would try to cash in on the "contract." As a precaution, however-er, the writer took several measures to ensure his family's safety.

# 16

# Reaction

Response to the trailer scam articles in *Trailer Life* magazine was phenomenal. Telephone calls and letters poured into the writer's office nearly every day for several months.

A woman in Lincoln Park, Michigan, reported she bought a Rogue trailer from a Traveler named Charles Halliday the year before. A caller said two Travelers were offering new Kentucky Traveler and Lariat trailers for sale near Minneapolis. Irish Travelers hit Albany, New York, in force, selling Rogue, Lariat, Safari, Regal and Kentucky Traveler trailers. One of the states hit the hardest was Illinois, where ten families of Travelers sold dozens of travel trailers from the Great Falls campground in Springfield at the same time they blanketed neighborhoods with their driveway and roof sealing scams. Fifty miles from the Illinois state capitol, the area around Decatur was flooded by Irish Travelers who moved in and out of campgrounds constantly as they dispersed throughout the upper Midwest.

Scottish Travelers descended upon Rapid City, South Dakota, in force that summer. Several elderly residents paid thousands of dollars each for lightning protection equipment to be installed on their homes, only to discover later that either the work was not done at all or only partial lightning rod systems were used. Complaints about driveway and roof sealing scams poured into the offices of the Pennington County Sheriff's Department. Rapid City department stores experienced a sudden surge in shoplifting. And at the same time, the classified section of the *Rapid City Journal* contained several "must sell" advertisements for Kentucky Traveler, Rogue, Lariat, Marauder and Regal travel trailers. Vehicle registrations from Texas and Iowa revealed that the individuals were named Ferguson, Donahue, McMillan and Williamson.

Apparently, no one associated with law enforcement in the Rapid City area considered the possibility that the same people were involved in all those crimes.

Bob Trupe, owner of Mid-State Camper Sales, complained to police about the trailer sales, however, and immediate action resulted. Assisted by the State Division of Criminal Investigation and the state attorney general's office, Pennington Deputy Duane Pluckert planned a sting early one morning before the men could leave camp in their pickup trucks. However, the day before the sting, a police officer leaked details to a local television station, which broadcast a report on the ten o'clock news. The next morning all but two families of Travelers were gone. Pluckert and highway patrol officers escorted those families to the Nebraska state line.

Sixty-year-old Irish Traveler John Rafferty towed his travel trailer into the largest campground in Maine that summer and set up a base of operation while he scoured the residential neighborhoods in nearby Biddeford. Small, thin and fragile looking, Rafferty sold five trailers from the campground after telling prospective buyers he needed to raise money quickly because he was dying of cancer. A year later, he returned and brought a large contingent of Rileys with him.

FBI Special Agent Ron Dox telephoned the writer and asked for information about Rafferty. The writer told the agent he had never heard of John Rafferty before. But six months later, the writer would be introduced to Rafferty near Orlando, Florida, and the two men would discuss the Traveler lifestyle while they ate doughnuts in adjoining booths at a coffee shop on the Orange Blossom Trail. Rafferty laughed heartily when the writer told him he had heard the old man was seriously ill. "Never been sick a day in my life," Rafferty boasted.

By December 1980, the RV industry was in the middle of the most serious economic downturn it had experienced since the 1974 Arab oil embargo. Lou and Betty Pusch, who operated Auburn RV Sales and Service in central Illinois, were attending what they feared would be their last RV industry show in Louisville, Kentucky. "The Travelers have about wiped us out," Betty said. "We haven't sold anything since August 17th, but the Travelers have sold trailers to at least five of our customers -- and probably to more we don't know about. I figure we lost fifteen or twenty sales to Travelers in the last three months. If something's not done about them, they'll put us out of business."

The Pusches hoped to see some relief after the *Trailer Life* articles appeared that summer, but although state law enforcement agents pledged to halt the trailer scams, they did not. A nearby RV dealer told Betty one of his neighbors bought a trailer in order to help a Traveler family who needed money quite badly. The dealer reported that the neighbor said, "It was such a sad case. The woman had four little kids in that trailer, and her husband had died, so she couldn't keep the trailer."

Betty said that while the *Trailer Life* articles were effective in communicating the trailer scam to its readers, they did not reach the people who were most often victimized -- the first-time buyers. "Most of those people have never owned an RV, so they don't buy *Trailer Life*. And nine out of ten of them are old people."

Tears welled in Betty's eyes and rolled down her cheeks. "We've worked so hard," she said. "I just hate to see these people come in and put us out of business."

A few years later, the writer tried telephoning Pusch's dealership to talk with Betty and Lou, but there was no longer a phone listing for Auburn RV Sales.

Among daily mail to the writer's office were almost always several clippings from newspaper classified sections. All the ads offered trailers for sale by the Traveler clans. Initially, the writer created a log of the clippings so that he could identify where the trailers were being sold, but within a few weeks it became clear to him that the Travelers were active in virtually every section of the country.

The writer also received numerous inquiries from law enforcement agencies asking if either the police or the newspaper in Elkhart, Indiana, had ever investigated the Travelers.

A telephone call to Steve Bibler, business writer for the *Elkhart Truth*, revealed that the newspaper had never reported anything about the Travelers and their connections to the community, even though numerous area residents had been victimized over the years. Bibler asked the writer to meet with him and provide details about the Travelers' activities in Elkhart. The writer did, and the two men toured the community by automobile, checking out RV plants, campgrounds and other favorite haunts of clan members.

More than a year passed, and no article about the Travelers was published by the *Truth*. Law enforcement officers continued to ask why the newspaper was silent on the subject, so the writer telephoned Bibler and advised him he was tape-recording the conversation. He asked Bibler if an article were planned.

"We are interested, but we're very lazy, and it's kind of hard to tackle something like this," the reporter answered.

The writer asked, "So it wasn't a matter of someone at the paper killing the story?"

"No. After we talked last year and you took me around, I retraced those steps with some other people, and we actually went to one factory north of Elkhart and took pictures of units coming off the lot. I went through the motions and tried to buy a unit from a young lady there. I went out west of Elkhart and talked with people who were there offering a unit for sale, and I got the same story you said I'd get: 'We have to sell this right away because we're moving to Goshen and need the money for down payment on a house.'

"I tracked some blacktoppers, following them around town anticipating reports that they were in town. I even found out one of our employees had an uncle who hired one of those fellows to put a new roof on his barn, and the barn was now leaking. So everything fell into place exactly as you said it would. It was just that the magnitude of the story made it something that was hard to tackle..."

Bibler added, "We've done some other investigative work that has been killed. I'm a little disappointed in myself as well as the paper, but after you've spent $100 or so trying to develop a story and it doesn't see the light of day, you kind of lose your fervor for doing other things."

The reporter concluded, "I guess I was just waiting for next spring to arrive."

A couple of years later, Bibler was promoted to the newspaper's managing editor job -- a position which gave him the power to assign articles to any reporter. Even so, not once during the next fourteen years did the *Truth* publish a report of any kind about the Travelers or their scams.


On the south end of Atlanta, Cleveland Avenue bisected Interstate 75, and just off eastbound Cleveland, the writer found a Woolco department store, exactly as Jimmy Burke had described it in his statement to police officers following his arrest in Macon. It was the same Woolco from which Jimmy, Peggy and Paul had shoplifted during the long trailer-stealing expedition in 1980. Police officers had said they were unable to locate most of the individuals and businesses from whom Jimmy and his gang had stolen trailers. But as the writer approached the Woolco store in his car, he looked across the street, and there was the A-1 Trailer Sales from where Jimmy had stolen the Monte Carlo trailer from an Irish Traveler woman named Bridget Williams.

The writer parked at the dealership and was greeted by a stocky young man in his late twenties with a broad smile and the indescribable but unmistakable appearance of an Irish Traveler. "Can I help you?" the young man asked.

The writer answered, "I'd like to speak to the manager or owner, please."

"I'm the manager," the man said. "My name's Tom Carroll. What can I do for you?"

"I've got some information for you about a Monte Carlo trailer that was stolen from you last year."

"Are you a cop?" Carroll asked, his Southern Traveler accent and his inherent suspicion obvious.

"No, I'm a book author trying to retrace the route of the people who stole your trailer. They're Irish Travelers."

Carroll laughed. "Well then, you need to talk with my grandma. She'll want to hear what you've got to say."

Carroll led the way to a nearby residence and introduced the writer to an attractive elderly woman he identified only as Mrs. Williams. The writer told them how the theft of their trailer occurred and that it had been renamed, registered in Alabama and sold to a woman in Greensboro, North Carolina. The writer said he could not tell them the identity of the Travelers who stole the trailer.

"It had to have been Travelers, Grandma," Carroll said. "They're the only ones that would know about registering trailers in Alabama."

Mrs. Williams nodded and told the writer, "We've had six trailers stolen from here."

"Things have changed," Carroll said. "Years ago, one Traveler wouldn't steal from another. The whole world's changed."

"These people who took that trailer are not really mixed with the Irish Travelers at all," Mrs. Williams insisted. "They're a different breed."

"Are you saying they might be Scottish?" the writer asked.

"No, that's not what she means," said Carroll. "See, the only Irish Travelers we recognize are from Georgia or Memphis."

"Why is that?"

"Because them are our people," Carroll answered.

Mrs. Williams interrupted. "Wait a minute, Johnny. He's talkin' about the Northern Travelers or the Greenhorns."

The writer responded, "The people who took your trailer are Northern Travelers."

"Okay," said Carroll, "what kind of work do they do, blacktopping and sealing?"

"Yes."

"None of our people would do that," Carroll insisted.

The writer asked, "You consider yourselves part of the Murphy Village group, don't you?"

"Oh, yes. My mother lives in Murphy Village."

The writer asked Carroll if he lived full time in Atlanta instead of traveling on business. "Yeah, I live here, but I travel in the summer."

It was then February, and the writer noted, "A lot of the Travelers are in Florida right now."

"Them is the Northern Travelers," Mrs. Williams said and then asked, "Do you know the names of them that stole our trailer?"

"Yes," the writer answered, "but I can't tell you their names?"

"Are they in jail?" she asked.

"Yes?"

"Where?"

"I can't tell you that. I have to protect my sources. You recognize that. You do the same thing."

She said, "As far as I'm concerned, I wouldn't bother them; it's all water under the bridge."

Carroll said, "They were sorry and no good to come steal that travel trailer, and we'd be sorry to have something done to another Traveler."

The writer noted Carroll's use of the word "sorry," and he asked if Carroll knew the Northern Travelers refer to Murphy Village Travelers as *Sorries*.

"Yes," Carroll answered, "but you see, that's just a word we use a lot. Them Northern Travelers visit the Village a lot, and they pick up the word. We'll say something like, 'That's a sorry car' or 'That's a sorry place to go' or 'That's a sorry person.' It means 'no good.'"

The writer pointed out, "The Northern Travelers look down on the Murphy Village people."

"Well, we look down on them!" Carroll exclaimed. "Everybody thinks they're higher class than the other ones. We look down on them for travelin' around in trailers because we settled years ago and got homes. So naturally, we're goin' to look down on them. But if we met, we'd know one another as Travelers. Sometimes we talk, and sometimes we don't."

Mrs. Williams added, "There are about 350 families of Southern Travelers in the Village, and more all the time. But there are a lot more Northern Travelers and Western Travelers. It was the Western Travelers that first started callin' our people Sorries, and when they did that, we started callin' them the Greenhorn Carrolls. Now everybody calls them Greenhorns. They don't like to be called that, and we don't like to be called Sorries, but them labels have been used since World War II."

The writer asked Mrs. Williams what she knew of the Traveler history, and she said, "They came from Ireland and landed in New York, and they worked and sent back for their people at different times. I've heard the first one over was old Tommy Carroll. He was the father of Old Foozie and Old Bessie and Old Nannie. He's buried out here in Westview Cemetery. My father was born on a boat comin' from the old country. His name was O'Hara. There were the McNamaras, the Carrolls, the Sherlocks, the Rileys, the Gormans. You know how the wagon trains went west? Well the old timers, 75 or 100 years ago, drifted down here to the Southern states where it was warmer. I was born here and christened here at Immaculate Conception Church. I've been here all my life -- sixty-eight years."

She continued, "The young generation is not like the old generation at all; they hardly associate with one another. They'll look you in the face and won't speak to you. They're more like American people. Now, them Northern Travelers, they're the real thing."

Traditionally horse traders and painters, the Southern Travelers began selling floor coverings during the Depression, Carroll said. "You see, the farmers were in bad shape and couldn't buy horses, and our Travelers could buy and sell floor covering cheaply."

The writer asked, "Why do the Southern Travelers still concentrate primarily on floor covering and painting instead of paving, roof sealing and lightning rods?"

Mrs. Williams answered, "Our people have never done that. Just the Northern Travelers, the English Travelers and the Gypsies do those things."

"Floor covering and painting are all our people know," Carroll said.

"What do you think is going to happen to the Travelers?" the writer asked.

"It's gonna end," Carroll said.

"Why?"

"Because they're just not like they used to be. They're goin' their different ways and mixin' in with everybody."

Mrs. Williams responded, "Nahhh!"

Carroll said, "The old woman don't believe that."

"No, I don't," she said. "There's too much trash outside The People. Never in a million years will the Travelers end because we don't mix with rubbish and trash."

Carroll added, "Well, it's true that the Travelers have a whole lot better qualities than these people out here have got." He waved his hand toward Atlanta. "A lot better qualities!"

The writer said, "I've never heard of widespread alcoholism and drug abuse in the Travelers."

"We don't believe in that!" Carroll insisted. "We don't believe in drugs whatsoever. Not any of our people down here!"

Mrs. Williams responded, "Some of the boys, I heard, smoke them cigarettes."

"No, they don't," Carroll insisted. "If just one of them as far away as Texas smoked marijuana, we'd hear about it here. That's the kind of gossip it would cause. You might hear rumors, but in the Village, nobody's smokin' no marijuana."

Mrs. Williams said, "They might drive fast and tear up a good truck..."

Carroll interrupted, "Or tear up a car. Or something like that. But it's a big thing with them that ladies is ladies and gentlemen is gentlemen..."

"And they work hard for what they get," Mrs. Williams added.

Carroll said, "That's all the boys and men know is work. They don't drink; they don't run around. They travel to different towns, but they go to bed early, get up early and go to work, come back to the motel room and go to bed after supper and watchin' some television. They have their good times when they come home where their people's at. At the Village, they've got their own dances, their own church, their own school. They've got it all."

Mrs. William changed the subject: "Look here," she asked the writer, "are you goin' to tell me the names of them people who stole our trailer?"

"No, I can't," the writer replied.

"Then you ain't gonna finish the book you're workin' on. You'll lose it. Somebody will steal it from you."

Carroll told the writer, "You know more about the Travelers than anybody -- any country person -- I've ever met."

Mrs. Williams asked, "What was your mother's name before she was married?" The writer told her. "Uh huh. Uh huh. You've got Traveler blood in you. I knew it."

Carroll said, "If you've got Traveler blood in you, you've got some fine blood."

Mrs. Williams added, "Maybe you're kin to us."

Carroll said sadly, "Our people are called gypsies, but we're not gypsies. It's hard to know what to tell your children when they're in school and they're called gypsies by the other kids. So we just tell our children, 'Don't worry about it. Let them call you gypsies if you want.'"

# 17

# Horse Traders and House Painters

Nearly fifteen years passed between the first time and the last time the writer visited the Irish Traveler enclave called Murphy Village. In 1980, the Village consisted of some 350 old mobile homes -- many of them dilapidated -- jammed together in a small complex on US 25 northeast of North Augusta, South Carolina. At that point, the mobile home court also contained three gambling dens, a floor covering salvage outlet, a dance hall, a small Catholic church and a convenience store. In a small subdivision nearby, about a dozen luxurious homes provided testimony that a few Traveler families had discovered the American Dream.

By 1995, all the mobile homes except about fifty relatively new ones were gone from the central Village. The salvage operation had moved to larger quarters, the convenience store had burned down, and a fund-raising effort was underway so that a new church could be built. In place of the three gambling dens was a four-room mobile home that was occupied occasionally by card players but sat empty most of the year.

During the intervening fifteen years, residents of Murphy Village became affluent. The vague boundaries of the Village now included about 150 homes valued at between $200,000 and $500,000 each; an equal number of new factory-built modular homes and double-wide manufactured homes occupied adjoining properties -- sometimes literally in the back yards of the opulent houses.

There were other changes, too. Murphy Village's Travelers now drove flashy new trucks, sparkling new Cadillacs and Lincolns and a wide range of expensive foreign-built cars bearing brand names such as Lexus, Acura and Infinity. Two enterprising brothers had started their own paint manufacturing company; several Travelers had opened legalized video poker parlors; the Village business enterprises had been expanded to include sale of tools and equipment to automobile repair shops, and numerous residents of the Village were earning enormous profits from investments in the stock market, real estate and bank certificates of deposit.

With their new wealth, however, the Travelers became more visible -- and, more famous. Network television crews, newspaper reporters and magazine writers competed with each other to inform other Americans about the clannish, secret society of Murphy Village's nearly 3,000 citizens. Gradually, the Village became somewhat of a tourist attraction, drawing curious motorists from nearby Interstate 20 and serving as a Sunday afternoon destination for South Carolina and Georgia residents who wanted to show visiting relatives *the gypsy camp.*


When the writer visited Murphy Village for the first time in 1981, the very existence of a nation-wide Irish Traveler sub-culture was virtually unknown. And, except for the residents of Edgefield and Aiken Counties in South Carolina, few Americans had ever heard of Murphy Village. The Village's anonymity and its isolation from the rest of society contributed in large measure to the willingness of some Travelers to talk with the writer, however; the invasion of curious tourists and reporters had not yet begun, and the Travelers felt free to express themselves about their culture. Those early conversations proved to be quite valuable in clearing up the writer's misconceptions about the Murphy Village Travelers and the way they lived.

For their part, twenty-eight-year-old John Carroll and his wife's sixty-eight-year-old grandmother, Bridget Williams, were interested in hearing stories their *country* neighbors told about the Village and its residents. The writer said, "Here's one: 'You can always tell when the Irish Travelers are back in town because black coins start showing up.'"

"That's true!" Carroll nodded. "Black coins from the gas tanks. But that was years ago."

Mrs. Williams said, "Let me tell you how it was. When they (the Travelers) filled their gas tanks, if they had a quarter or fifty cents or a dime, they'd drop it in their gas tank to save it for a new trailer home or car. But I ain't heard of that bein' done in twenty or thirty years."

Carroll replied, "I remember when they done it. I was only that high, but I used to like to see the cars turn corners because you could hear the change shifting around in the gas tanks."

The writer said, "Country people who know about the Village also are curious about the nice houses with mobile homes plugged into them."

Carroll laughed. "They can't figure out why somebody would back a trailer up against one of those beautiful homes."

"That's right," the writer admitted, "and I can't figure that out either."

"Well, I'll tell you why: because them that own the houses don't care what the people up and down the street say about them. All they care about is themselves. You see, all them nice houses belong to one family. Penn (Sherlock) is one of them with a trailer sittin' beside it. The house beside Penn's is his brother-in-law's, and across the street is his other brother-in-law. The trailers are usually for the mothers-in-law to live in, and they're next to the big houses so the daughters can take care of them."

He added, "My sister built a house down there sixteen or seventeen years ago. As you pull into the Village, it's the first one on the right. My grandfather built one across the street. No other Travelers had houses then. The reason they built houses was that they discovered they could build a house about as cheaply as they could buy a trailer home, and the house was better and more valuable than a trailer. But when they started building houses, they built small, regular houses, not like they are now. It's like everything else, though; the houses got bigger so the people could keep up with the Joneses."


Not long after the first Irish Traveler immigrant -- Old Tom Carroll -- arrived in America around 1850, he and his relatives migrated southwest from New York through Pennsylvania until they reached central Georgia. There, they supported the Confederacy during the Civil War and, gradually, came to regard Georgia as their home. Most of the Georgia Travelers, as they came to be known within their own close-knit society, traded horses and mules in the state and elsewhere in the South. Meanwhile, a more itinerant segment of the clan -- the nucleus of what was to become the Northern Travelers -- ventured farther afield, trading livestock and peddling fake Irish lace and linens throughout America.

In 1927, Georgia lawmakers enacted legislation aimed at controlling itinerant livestock traders. It required individuals such as the Georgia Travelers to pay an annual $250 tax in each county where they did business. Reacting to enforcement of that law, the Georgia-based clan packed their tents and moved just across the state line into South Carolina. And, hampered in their livestock trading by more and more restrictive state laws as well as a steady replacement of mules and horses with tractors, trucks and automobiles, the Travelers began diversifying by selling floor coverings, painting barns and fences and engaging in a wide range of home improvement endeavors. Although most still called themselves *Georgia Travelers*, gradually they came to be regarded as *Southern Travelers*, as opposed to the more widely traveled *Northern* group.

Meanwhile, the Irish Tinker traditions and social structure that Old Tom Carroll brought with him to America were maintained by his daughters, Foozie, Bessie and Nannie, and their offspring. The Northern and Western Travelers modified many aspects of those traditions to fit their own needs, but the foundation of Old Tom's social structure was still intact when John Carroll was a youngster growing up in Murphy Village. Then, as now, the societal focal points were the extended family, the Catholic Church and seasonal business travels.

In the Village, education was important only to the extent that children could be taught to read, write and use simple mathematics. Compulsory education was regarded as a threat to the highly restrictive Irish Traveler society because it exposed children to unwanted outside influences. Traditionally, boys were schooled only through the eighth grade; girls, through elementary grades. The primary role of girls was to prepare themselves for marriage to appropriate Georgia Traveler boys selected for them by their parents. Each boy's commitment was to learn the businesses in which his family specialized so that he could support a wife and children of his own. High school attendance was considered undesirable because that environment fostered close relationships with non-Travelers, and those relationships were discouraged.

Like most young men in the Village, John Carroll quit school after the eighth grade even though his father had completed twelve years of education. At that time, most boys and some girls attended classes at Our Lady of Peace School in nearby North Augusta, although St. Edward Catholic Church in the Village also provided elementary schooling for girls. By 1990, a few dozen boys and girls also were enrolled at nearby Belvedere Elementary School in Aiken

County and Merriwether School in Edgefield County, and more value was beginning to be given to to the education of all Village children.

"When I was a teenager," John Carroll told the writer in 1981, "we didn't date outside the Travelers. And the dates we had were strictly clean dates -- no sex involved. We had our own dances at the Village, so we'd go to those. They were held every year at the same time, for every occasion -- on Easter, Christmas and Valentine's Day. If there were certain girls you liked, you'd dance with them and tell them you wanted to date them and then go from there."

The writer asked, "You didn't have to get the girls' parents' permission to date them?"

"No, because everybody knew everybody else, you see. So the girl could judge you right then, whether you were okay."

"Are Georgia Travelers' dates heavily chaperoned?"

"Definitely. A girl can't get into a car with a boy if there aren't others along. That would be a disgrace!"

The writer said, "That doesn't allow a Traveler boy much chance to raise hell. What does he have to do, go to Augusta and try to find a girl there?"

Carroll smiled. "Yeah. The boys work out of town a lot, you know. And they'll go to places where young people hang out. They'll meet some girls and won't tell them who they are. They'll hand them a line of bull and try to get 'em in the sack. But the Traveler girl's lifestyle goes this way: She gets up of a mornin', cleans her mother's house, goes with her mother to town, comes back, goes to church, says her novina. Generally, she'll have a boyfriend that she'll wait on to come home, and when the boys come back the next weekend, she's like a little flower. She can date any Irish Traveler -- any Georgia Traveler, who you call Southern Travelers or Sorries -- or any of the rest of the Travelers except Northern Travelers."

"There are occasional marriages, though, between Northern and Southern Travelers," the writer pointed out.

"No! Not with the Georgia Travelers! The Georgia Travelers are not goin' to marry Northern Travelers!"

The writer responded, "But I know of a few cases..."

Carroll interrupted. "Them are Georgia Travelers that are considered trash and Northern Travelers that are considered trash."

Asked about brides' dowries or so-called *bride-price* arrangements in which the girl's parents are expected to pay the boy's parents prior to marriage, Carroll said, "If I have a daughter and I see this boy that I want for her, I have to pay for him. But I wouldn't give the money to the boy's father; I'd give it to my daughter. Then I'd say, 'Listen, my daughter's got X amount of dollars if you marry her.' The more money your girl's got, the better chance you stand of gettin' that boy for her. And often, you don't really tell what she's got. It's like this: In the Village, everybody pretty well knows how the other one's sittin' and how smart they are and how many girls they've got and what they're in a position to do. And if I've got a million dollars -- although no Traveler's got money like that -- and I get out there an holler and scream and make a fool out of myself, it don't matter how much money I've got; I'll keep my daughter. We want good, quiet people that work hard, have money and stay home and mind their own business; that's the kind of people you want to put your boys with. Being like that'll move your girl a lot quicker than money."

According to Georgia Traveler tradition, one father is paid an agreed-upon bride-price for his son, and the son becomes the property of his father-in-law. He works for the father-in-law as an indentured servant until the father-in-law declares the dowry free and clear. If the father-in-law dies, the debt is canceled.

Although most marriages in the Village are arranged by parents, John said he would not necessarily arrange his children's. "I've got a son. I wouldn't tell him he had to marry a certain girl. Ain't no way I'd do that. But there are people I wouldn't let him marry. I'd want him to marry a Traveler, but I wouldn't let him marry some of 'em."

"What if he falls in love with a ref girl?"

"A country girl?"

"Yes."

"If she's in a nice family...I wouldn't want him to do it, but I'm hopin' my son will go to college, so I'm sure I'll probably face that. I'm lookin' to face it. I'd say he'll marry outside the Travelers. I would prefer he didn't. I would love for everything to go perfectly, for him to go to college and be a doctor or lawyer and come back and say, 'Hey, Daddy. I want to marry a Traveler.' But I don't believe it's goin' to be that way. I figure he's goin' to college and bring a girl home to me some day and say, 'Here, Daddy, is the girl I want to marry.' If he does, I'll just have her checked out, and if her family's okay, I'll welcome her."

The writer asked, "What do you want your son to be when he grows up. Are you serious about his becoming a doctor or lawyer?"

"I want him to be something more than a painter," Carroll responded. "I want him to be in position to go to college and do what he wants to do. I just want him always close to me!" He said he observes families separated, with a son living in one town and parents living many miles away, visiting each other only occasionally. "I couldn't take that. If he didn't want to be around me, I'd hate it, but I'd accept it and say, 'Well, he's goin' to have to live with that decision.'"

He added, "The first thing to a Traveler -- the number one thing to a Traveler -- is his child. Everything else steps to the side. That child comes in front of everything, and everything the Traveler does is for the benefit of that child. Ninety per cent of the Travelers would die for their children. Just to show you a for-instance, Traveler children are not allowed to cross the street by themselves. They're the particularist people you'll ever see about their children. Now I'm talkin' about *my* Travelers; I don't know what the Northerns do. You won't see a Travelin' child with a dirty face, and if there's only three dollars in all the family for food, it's the child that eats. That's just our nature."

Asked about wedding traditions at Murphy Village, Carroll said, "All of our girls are virgins when they get married. And they -- the young people, that is -- make a big joke about sex after the weddin'. They'll all get around the girl and try to scare her. It happened with my wife. I couldn't have five minutes with her after we were married before they came and got her, and she came back scared to death. And I couldn't talk to her about it because boys didn't talk to girls about things like that, no matter whether they were married or not. After you live together, then you can talk about it. And the boys came to me the next mornin' and asked, 'Hey, what went on last night?' So you tell your best friend because he won't tell on you."

Although many marriages were performed at the tiny St. Edwards Church in the Village, large ceremonies were scheduled at churches in North Augusta or across the state line in Augusta, Georgia. "They'll also elope, too," Carroll said. "Our Travelers kind of got away from the big weddin's. They like to just get married and get it over with; they don't have long engagements like the Northern Travelers do. My oldest sister got married about seventeen years ago. She got engaged on the first day of April and was married April second. She had a big weddin', a dance and the works, and my mother had to go to town that day and buy the weddin' dress."

Carroll left Murphy Village when he married his wife, who had grown up in the Atlanta area. "My brother married my wife's sister," he said.

The writer said, "I wanted to ask you about that. I understand it's traditional that, if you marry a girl, her brother or sister would be expected to marry your brother or sister."

"Yes," he answered, "if the deal was made that way. Like if a boy twenty years old wants to marry a girl fourteen or fifteen, but he hasn't decided which one, his parents would look around for a family with a girl that age and also a boy about twenty years old that could marry their fourteen or fifteen-year-old daughter. And the boy's parents would say to the father of that other boy and girl, 'You've got a nice looking girl, and I've got a nice, smart young fella. I'd also like to have your son be *my* son. What do you say we make a deal: My boy can marry your girl, and your son can marry my daughter?'

"The two fathers talk about it and agree on how it should be handled, and then they tell their children what has been worked out. But the marriage is left strictly to the children. The sons check out the girls and then come back and give their fathers their word that they'll marry the girls."

"What if one boy says, 'Dad, I don't want anything to do with that girl'?"

Carroll responded, "Then that'd be it. He wouldn't have to marry her. But ninety per cent of the brothers are less concerned about themselves than they are about the boys their sisters will get. They know that everything pretty well depends upon the man. They know that they can make things work for themselves, no matter what, but they want a good husband for their sister."

The writer asked, "What *is* the role of a typical Murphy Village woman?"

"Well, it's like this," Carroll said. "Everybody knows which woman is the business woman -- one who knows when to spend money and when not to, one who knows how to take care of business for her husband. I'll give you an example: My mother. My father never knew when we had a payment due; my mother took care of everything. If there was a business proposition and my father was out of town, she could handle it. Like shares to be bought in a bank, or stocks or an investment in something else. She'd consult him, but he knew she was smart enough to handle it, and he'd let her go ahead and do what she wanted to do. Some Traveler women, you know, can't do that; all they know is to go to town, go to a cafeteria or buy themselves dresses. You know, Don, it's like everywhere else, except that none of the Traveler women take jobs. It's almost a disgrace for them to work...well, not exactly a disgrace, but the husbands don't want them to work. The husbands can provide what the family needs."

The writer visited Murphy Village twice during the 1980s, and both times he was regarded as a trespasser and watched carefully by residents. However, when he toured the Village in mid-1995, there was little of that watchfulness; he was virtually ignored. By then, of course, Murphy Village's Irish Travelers had become accustomed to seeing curious *country* people driving slowly through their community, pointing, staring and shooting photographs.

The differences between Murphy Village of the 1980s and the Village of 1995 astounded the writer. Not only did the mobile home park contain only a fraction of the families it once held, but the houses built around the park in the intervening ten years were larger, more expensive and more tastefully designed. Whereas once the houses shared their space with old, dilapidated mobile homes that looked as if they had been dragged to their sites and dumped, now the properties were shared with new, rather expensive manufactured housing.

To most local *country* people, the Irish Travelers continued to be regarded as *gypsies*, even though nearly all evidence of a gypsy-like lifestyle had been discarded. Sightseers touring the Village for the first time during the 1990s were puzzled by what they saw there, according to Joe Livingston, an investigator with the South Carolina State Law Enforcement Division (SLED). "People don't comprehend who the Travelers are," he said as he guided the writer on his 1995 tour. "When they go to *the gypsy camp*, they start looking around for covered wagons and dark-complexioned people. It really blows their minds when they see the blond-haired, blue-eyed people and the enormous houses they live in."

Stories about the Travelers' unusual lifestyle and habits have been told throughout western South Carolina and eastern Georgia for many years, although most of those stories -- such as the one about keeping coins in automobile gasoline tanks -- refer to events of the distant past and not to the more modern activities of today's Travelers. For example, although the Georgia Travelers once iced or froze the bodies of dead family members until mass funerals could be held in Nashville or Atlanta, that practice was discarded nearly thirty years ago, and funerals are now held in the Village without fanfare or announcements a few days following a death. But even today, stories are told by non-Travelers about frozen bodies and mass funerals.

The facts are quite different from many of the stories. One fact is, like all other Travelers, the Murphy Village residents are fiercely independent and have no king, queen or chieftain. The most influential community members are those such as Jim Penn Sherlock and his brothers Ned and Michael "Mikey Boy" who have achieved significant financial success. The Travelers do not sell fake Irish lace, although they did sixty years ago; they devote their energies to much more lucrative endeavors. Although many are avid recreational gamblers, the men of the Village do not earn their livelihood gambling. Village residents are not the skilled shoplifters that the Northern Travelers are, and even those who do shoplift for money do not typically steal their family's clothing and food from stores; store diversion theft is a primary activity of many dark-skinned Gypsies -- the people Travelers call *Turks*.

And although reporters frequently repeat the assumption that there are only eleven surnames among the Murphy Village Travelers, there are several more than that -- the residents include Carrolls, Sherlocks, Rileys, O'Haras, O'Roarkes, Gormans, Raffertys, McNallys, Williamses, McNamaras, Daleys, Macks, Costellos, McGuires and Mulhollands as well as a few families of English Travelers.

The truth about Murphy Village Travelers makes them seem somewhat less eccentric, but no less colorful, than most of the stories tourists are told. Although it is true that the Travelers usually prefer cash transactions and frequently have large sums of cash on them or in their homes, the most successful residents of Murphy Village now invest their earnings in legitimate or quasi-legitimate businesses, certificates of deposit, stocks and bonds. In recent years, two Traveler brothers even made a substantial investment in a Kentucky bank along with the former governor of that state. A few years ago, Internal Revenue Service agents, hoping to convict one well known Traveler for failure to report taxes, visited the individual's home armed with a search warrant. The agents found more than $400,000 in cash at the home, but they were forced to return the money when the Traveler's lawyer claimed the cash was from inheritances and marriage dowries.

Sometimes, events surrounding those dowries are much more colorful than even the stories about the Travelers' legendary swindles. First-time visitors to the Village, for example, are usually surprised to see several partially completed homes where construction work clearly has been stopped. Non-Traveler residents of South Carolina and Georgia enjoy telling tourists a wide variety of stories about why the houses are not finished -- ranging from a belief the buildings are inhabited by evil spirits to legal disputes with contractors over funds. In actual fact, most of those homes are being built as bridal dowries, and work often is begun a few years before a young girl is old enough to marry.

One particular dowry became very well known throughout the Village -- and even outside it, to some extent -- because events resulting from the dowry affected nearly everyone living in and around the community. In 1993, Tommy Girard "Wink" Riley paid Traveler George Carroll (not his real name) $50,000 for Carroll's son to marry Riley's daughter. The Carrolls had achieved much higher stature in the Village than Wink's family, so the proposed marriage was a social achievement for the Rileys. The Carroll youth traveled with Riley that spring and summer while the wedding was being planned by Riley and Carroll's wives. But that fall, when all the men returned to the Village in time for the World Series, George Carroll told Riley, "I'm not gonna let my son marry your daughter."

Riley, visibly upset, demanded that his $50,000 *bride-price* be returned. Carroll refused, saying, "That was your fee for using my son all summer."

The two men argued for several minutes, and Riley suggested, "Let's duke it out."

Carroll agreed. "I'll meet you out near Route 25."

Instead of going to the designated fight area, though, Wink Riley sent for a tough young non-Traveler -- called a *guthie* -- who worked for him during the summer. State police officer Joe Livingston reported later, "The guthie beat the hell out of the other father, and it was turmoil in the Village from that point. People from all around that part of the state started calling my office, saying, 'There are men fighting out in the middle of the road.' Edgefield and Aiken Counties sent officers, and the state even sent down a couple of agents. And everyone in the Village turned out either to watch or take part in the fighting. Imagine 1,500 adult Travelers, each one driving a car or pickup truck, converging on an already-congested area to see the fighting. And everyone there was offering odds and taking bets on the outcome!"

After being soundly beaten by Riley's guthie, George Carroll asked one of his sons-in-law, Eddie Tommy Smith -- an English Traveler from Acworth, Georgia -- to intimidate Wink Riley and his friends. Carroll expected his son-in-law to use his fists, or maybe a baseball bat, but the English Traveler took a shotgun with him to the fight scene, and he fired it -- whether in the air or at someone was never clear. Livingston said, "Well, that really scared hell out of the Village's Travelers because they won't have anything to do with weapons. They immediately scattered and went home. I called Edgefield and told them who had fired the shotgun, but the word quickly spread throughout the Village that deputies were looking for Eddie Smith, and he hightailed it back to Acworth."

More recently, "Raid" Riley promised his son to another Traveler's daughter for $100,000 in cash. The boy was not happy with the deal, however, because he was in love with a Memphis Traveler girl from Mississippi. He left the Village and joined his sweetheart and her family. Raid, faced with demands that the $100,000 *bride-price* be refunded, decided to drag his son back home. He recruited a relative, Pete Patrick O'Hara, and Pete's *guthie,* and the three men went to Mississippi and grabbed the boy off the street.

Unfortunately for them, the abduction was witnessed by a Mississippi state senator's wife, who immediately notified police she had just seen a kidnapping. She had written down the license plate number of Raid's truck, and because it was a South Carolina tag, the FBI was called. The woman's story was reinforced by the boy's sweetheart and her parents, who also filed a kidnapping complaint.

In South Carolina, Aiken County authorities were informed by the FBI that a vehicle registered to a local resident was involved in a Mississippi kidnapping, but local police quickly realized what had really transpired was not a criminal abduction, but simply an Irish Traveler *bride-price* dispute. Kidnapping charges against Raid and his accomplices were dropped when Raid's son told investigators he had returned home willingly and had not been abducted by his father.


Among non-Travelers who are most intrigued by the Murphy Village lifestyle, Easter Day is regarded as the best time to visit the Village. On that day, not only are all the Travelers present and plaster icons of Jesus and the Virgin Mary displayed prominently in every yard -- offering tourists plenty of photo opportunities -- but Easter is also the traditional time for the unique activity the Travelers call *looping.*

If you can imagine a huge 1890s-circa Easter parade combined with the mobility of teenage *cruising* from the 1960s, you have a rather good picture of Easter Day *looping* at Murphy Village. Virtually everyone gathers at The Front, which is simply a parking lot just off U.S. 25 at St. Edward's Catholic Church. From The Front, women and girls of all ages, dressed in their finest new clothes, parade into the old mobile home park and then circle (or loop) through it on the grid of streets that once provided access to mobile homes where all the Travelers lived. As they walk past the now-vacant lots and the scattered mobile homes that still remain, they are watched by an audience of men and boys who line the roadways on lawnchairs or cruise the streets in their cars.

*Looping* serves several functions: It exhibits the Village's young girls to prospective husbands and their families; it allows adult women to display their wealth and fashions to other Travelers, and it serves as a Village-wide social gathering that leads to spring parties, dances, *bride-price* negotiations and engagements.

The following fall -- during World Series week -- Traveler men with daughters of marriageable age (generally twelve to twenty years old) make their *announcements*, in effect verifying publicly that their daughters are committed to marrying specific young men.

Generally speaking, adult men leave the Village each year after the Christmas and New Year's holidays; they travel throughout the South, the Midwest and the Northeast, occasionally driving as far west as Texas and Colorado in search of customers for their painting and home improvement services or their floor covering products. Their summer excursions begin after the Easter celebrations, and on those trips they are usually accompanied by their sons and their prospective sons-in-law. Following the fall *announcements*, they hit the road again, most often without their school-age sons, but nearly always taking along their future sons-in-law. Back at the Village once more for Christmas, the men relax, socialize with other Traveler males and take part in their children's weddings.


Jim Penn Sherlock -- the first Murphy Village Traveler the writer met in 1980 -- was "one of the wheels" of the Village in 1995, SLED

Detective Joe Livingston reported as he pointed out Sherlock's residence to the writer during a tour through the community. Penn, who was among the first to build a house near the mobile home park in the late 1970s, had moved into more luxurious quarters for the '90s. His new home, just a short distance off U.S. 25 on Penn Street, was easily identified by the mailbox out front which said, simply, "Penns" on it. The house, obviously worth nearly half a million dollars, was clear evidence that Jim Penn Sherlock was doing quite well with a paint manufacturing company he had started earlier with another well known Village resident, Jim Suedle Carroll.

Livingston insisted that nearly all Georgia Travelers, including the Sherlocks, were obsessed with becoming rich and then exhibiting their wealth to other members of the community. That obsession, he said, was underscored in a video tape acquired from Franklin, Virginia, after a couple of Murphy Village scam artists were arrested. "They interviewed one of the *guthies* they also arrested, and the *guthie* told an investigator on tape, 'These people (Travelers) are money-struck. I've seen them wake up in the morning when it was so cloudy and raining that they couldn't go out and make money. They'd get physically sick! They'd all get diarrhea because they couldn't go out!'"

An article in the February 17, 1991, edition of the Augusta (Georgia) *Chronicle* also made special note of the Travelers' focus on wealth. Authors Dan Adkins and Cheryl Hardy wrote, "While they cling to cultural and religious traditions centuries old, their lifestyle is ostentatious, often to the point of seeming gaudy. They display a near-obsessive compulsion to accumulate material goods: luxury automobiles and shiny new pickup trucks, expansive and ornately appointed homes, and elegant clothing and jewelry."

The ways in which they earn their wealth have brought them to the attention of law enforcement officers around the country. While Livingston and other police officers who regularly track clan activities are hesitant to say all Murphy Village residents are scam artists (the Travelers themselves insist only a few "bad apples" engage in illegal activities), law enforcement records clearly indicate that a high proportion of the Georgia Travelers have been investigated for cheating, swindling or robbing non-Travelers from the Carolinas to the Rockies.

Individual members of the Murphy Village community are famous for five types of scams:

•They spray-paint barns, houses and fences with a mixture consisting of up to eighty per cent gasoline and twenty per cent paint.

•They cover roofs with a silvery concoction that has no value as a weather sealant.

•They pose as government or utility company employees in order to convince victims to buy worthless products and services they offer.

•They invade homes of elderly people and steal cash from obvious hiding places, usually in bedrooms.

•They peddle cheap but overpriced tools and equipment to automotive repair shops.

Typically, when they are arrested following a scam, they escape serving jail time either by making voluntary restitution to their victims or by jumping bond. In 1982, while Northern Traveler Jimmy Burke was behind prison bars in Georgia, two Murphy Village men were arrested in Cullman County, Alabama, for stealing $600 from an elderly woman after gaining entry to her home by posing as Social Security workers. Charged with second-degree theft, they simply put up $25,000 bonds and then left the state.


Murphy Village residents began selling shop machinery during the late 1980s when they discovered they could acquire low-priced tools, lifts, jacks, heavy-duty presses and motor hoists from a manufacturer in South Carolina. Regarded as the company's distributors, Travelers purchased the equipment at a small fraction of its retail price and, misrepresenting it, peddled it to automotive service stations and repair shops. Milwaukee police detective Dennis Marlock wrote about that enterprise in his 1994 book, *License to Steal*: "A $3,690 hydraulic hoist is sold to the distributor for $150, a horizontal-vertical band saw that lists for $4,980 costs him $400, and he pays $150 for a 30-ton press retailing for $3,180. A Traveler can sell $15,000 worth of equipment for $5,000 and still make a $3,000 profit."

Marlock added, "Travelers seldom ask anywhere near the list price...To rationalize selling equipment well below list price, they use a variety of plausible excuses...They often say that the man to whom the consignment was shipped died while his merchandise was in transit. More frequently, the items are reported to be left over from a machinery producers convention where the paint was scratched and the driver was told to sell them 'at cost' rather than ship them back to the factory where they would have to be repainted. The Traveler may also state that the equipment is from a resale outlet that is closing down and the company doesn't want to ship the machinery back to the warehouse and then have to ship it out again to another retailer."

Joe Livingston, who alerted Marlock to the scam, emphasized, "There is no law against overpricing equipment that you sell, and that is basically what's involved -- an overpriced product." The scam aspect enters in because the product is misrepresented, and sometimes Travelers even hint that it's stolen. "It's such a good deal that the repair shop manager can't resist it."

Aiken County Chief Deputy Jody P. Rowland agreed. "That's the key to any scam: greed. Or, when you think you're getting something for nothing or for a fraction of what it's worth."

Rowland said a motor hoist sold by Travelers is represented as costing $10,500 even though the same type of equipment can be purchased from most automotive supply stores for $250 or $300. Typically, he added, Travelers sell shop managers 50-ton presses that are actually 5,000-pound models.

Marlock wrote that although the manufacturer guarantees its

equipment for 90-180 days, "all guaranteed servicing must be done at the company's factory in South Carolina, and the customer is responsible for freight charges both to and from the factory. Since most of the items are heavy, crating and shipment charges normally exceed the original cost of the equipment. When most items break down -- and most items do break down -- they are usually sold as scrap metal."

The Traveler practice of arranged marriages involving brides of fourteen or fifteen years old sparked opposition from Catholic Church authorities in South Carolina. In 1988, Bishop Ernest Unterkoefler instructed Father Sam Miglarese to speak out against it. Miglarese, who was then pastor of Our Lady of Peace Church in North Augusta, did so. The *Augusta Chronicle* quoted the priest as saying, "I told them the church is not going to accommodate it. I also told them I believe in them and I believe they can change."

The newspaper reported, "Father Miglarese's message sparked an unexpected response: Several Traveler families withdrew children from the church's school in North Augusta."

About a year later, following a huge Irish Traveler wedding in North Augusta, a video tape of the event was turned over to a police officer. Since then, the tape has been widely copied and circulated among law enforcement agencies because it provides a unique insight into the social culture of Murphy Village.

On the tape, five young couples are presented to the community following a mass wedding ceremony. The brides, who appear to be between fourteen and eighteen years old, are shown in bridal gowns and evening dresses as each one walks the length and width of a large reception hall several times while hundreds of Travelers watch from the sidelines. The girls are heavily made up and adorned with diamonds, gold jewelry and sable or mink accessories. Following the reception, the tape shows young girls of eight to twelve years old --

all wearing full makeup, high heels, expensive prom-type evening dresses and a wide array of jewelry -- dancing enthusiastically while dozens of women watch them perform. Clearly, the children are being exhibited to prospective mothers-in-law. Scenes also show even younger girls wearing lipstick, eye shadow, facial makeup and adult jewelry -- a public parody of little-girl dress-up that is far too realistic for comfort.

To date, the most extensive media coverage of Murphy Village was the 1991 special report in the *Augusta Chronicle*. The article noted that although Village residents were increasingly famous for their scams and swindles, individual members of the community also had their supporters. "Among them is Eddie Knight of Millville, Kentucky, a farmer who regularly hires Michael 'Mikey Boy' Sherlock to paint his barns," the article said.

"Mr. Knight said Mr. Sherlock's crews have painted his barns for the last ten years. He praised Mr. Sherlock's work, saying that on two occasions when he was dissatisfied, Mr. Sherlock returned and repainted the barns."

The article added, "Joyce Traylor, a florist at Kroger's Martintown Road store, has dealt with the Travelers for more than a dozen years. She describes them as kind, generous, deeply religious people who look after their own. 'They are the best Catholics you'll find. In prayers every day, they ask for their needs,' Mrs. Traylor said.

"Clyde Rains has done business with the Travelers for more than forty years, first with a convenience store and later with a dry-cleaning business that served Murphy Village. 'They will do anything in the world for you if they know and like you,' he said."

The newspaper also quoted Father Bill Blier, former pastor of St. Edwards Church, as saying, "I think God for the opportunity to have been at St. Edwards Church. The Travelers have a rare beauty about them in the religious love they have for their God. And they nurture that love in their children. There is a beautiful simplicity that comes from them...There's very little drug and alcohol use and almost no divorce. They take care of their own."

Elsewhere in the *Chronicle* report, however, were details about civil and criminal suits that had been filed against four Murphy Village residents by the Indiana Attorney General's office. The four were arrested after swindling six Indiana residents out of $5,445 in home improvement scams. Pat Anthony Carroll and Bridgett Carroll were fined a total of $6,825; Barney J. Riley and Jimmy J. Carroll faced default judgments totaling $29,957, but they could not be found so the judgments could be served.

Unlike most other Travelers, the Murphy Village residents do not depend heavily upon shoplifting for their day-to-day cash. In fact, the Georgia Travelers insist that they do not shoplift at all. SLED's Livingston, however, said a Jim Carroll from the Village was once caught shoplifting at a Belks department store in Augusta, and the officer added, "I guarantee you, if one of them does it, hundreds of them have done it."

Some of the Georgia Travelers are engaged in other illegal activities that apparently are unknown to other Irish clans. Loansharking and extortion, for example, are among the crimes a few of the Travelers commit within the Village itself. Frequently, both activities are tied to gambling, and it is not unusual for a Traveler to lose several thousand dollars at Atlantic City gaming tables and then borrow replacement funds from a Village loanshark at a 40% interest rate. Those who are slow about repaying their loans risk Mafia-style collections.

During the 1980s and early 1990s, Travelers learned how to bypass older motels' main telephone switchboards and access outside lines for free long-distance calls. There is evidence they made several thousand dollars worth of calls to friends and relatives all over the world before the motels they victimized updated their telephone systems.

Of all their illegal activities, though, their barn-painting and roof-sealing scams are the most successful and lucrative. A few years ago, Livingston was asked to help police officers near Rochester, New York, locate some Irish Travelers so that an NBC documentary could be filmed. The New York cops knew some of Murphy Village's Travelers were working painting and sealing scams in the area, but searches for the Travelers had proven to be fruitless.

Livingston could not find the Travelers at first, either, but he spotted numerous silver roofs and newly painted red barns, indicating the Travelers were active in the Rochester area. At last, by staking out economy-price motels along the interstate highways near farm areas, Livingston spotted two Traveler families. Local police officers and the TV crew wanted to film the Travelers at work, so Joe recommended, "You need to split your team in half and follow both families at the same time." Because the officers were in unmarked automobiles, he figured they had a good chance of following the Travelers to their work sites.

Livingston reported later, "One member of the team did break off and follow a Traveler to another motel where his guthies were staying, so the guthies were arrested. But the rest of the team -- in five unmarked police cars -- followed the other Traveler. At one point, the fellow made a wrong turn on a four-lane highway, so he made a U-turn and headed back the other direction. All five police cars behind him made the same turn!" A few minutes later, the Traveler reversed directions again with another U-turn, and as he passed the five police cars that were going the opposite direction, he smiled and gave them an obscene gesture.

Finally, unable to film a Traveler at work, the police and newsmen stopped at a farm where a red barn, a white garage and an outbuilding with a silver-painted roof provided testimony that the Travelers had been there. From an elderly woman living there, they learned that the Travelers had stopped at the farmhouse two weeks earlier and offered to paint all the buildings at a bargain price. When the woman asked how much the work would cost, she was told, "We won't charge you for the labor, just for the paint."

The Travelers then showed their victim a twenty-five-gallon bucket of paint which said $24.95 on it. Livingston said, "She thought that was the cost of a bucket of paint. It wasn't. It was the cost of a *gallon* of that paint! It said 'per gallon' in small letters, so the cost was $125 per bucket. The Travelers bought that paint for $18 per bucket from their paint plant in South Carolina, so they made $107 per bucket profit for every bucket they used. And they used *lots* of buckets to paint all the buildings on that farm!"

Johnny Frances "Hook" Mack is one of the Village's most notorious characters. For several years, he specialized in home invasions, posing as a Social Security employee or a utility company inspector in order to gain access to elderly couples' homes. Then he or his companions would search the homes for cash. Early in 1992, Johnny Mack and two half-Traveler cousins of Jimmy Burke -- John and Lloyd Compton -- were identified as the perpetrators of a series of home invasions throughout the Northeast. Investigators familiar with the Irish Travelers speculated that Jimmy Burke's older brother Pat -- The Viking -- also was involved because a few of the victims had been tied up with duct tape -- Pat Burke's favorite method of incapacitating people he intended to rob. Maine state police issued a warrant for Mack's arrest but were unable to find either him or the Comptons.

Almost two years later, Mack's son, Patrick "Jude" Mack, was arrested in Charlotte, North Carolina, for buying clothing at several department stores using counterfeit $100 bills. He was going from store to store in a large mall, but an employee at one of the shops became suspicious and called police after following the young man from one store to another. Jude Mack was arrested and jailed, but an accomplice who was working the same mall escaped. That accomplice was believed to be one of Mack's brothers-in-law.

In 1995, Johnny Mack also was arrested for counterfeiting -- that time, in Greenvile, South Carolina -- and a check of his FBI file revealed that he was wanted in Maine on the home invasion charges. Before serving time for counterfeiting, Mack was escorted to Maine by U.S. marshals to stand trial there. State trooper Mike McCaslin, following new leads on the 1992 home invasion incidents, verified that Mack's accomplices were the Comptons and Pat "The Viking" Burke.

Murphy Village Traveler Michael "Twin Mike" Sherlock was a well-known car buff. He seemed to have access to an endless variety of flashy automobiles, but his favorite was a gray Ford Thunderbird with a red, white and blue license plate holder. Late in February 1995, Twin Mike and two other Village residents -- Tommy O'Hara and Peter "Pete Skeet" Sherlock -- hatched a complicated plan to steal the life savings from an 87-year-old Jasper County man living near Tillman, South Carolina. The plan involved using two-way radios; police scanners tuned to local frequencies, and five different getaway vehicles, including a lookout truck and three cars that would be swapped within a twenty-five mile stretch of backcountry road.

The victim would be a man named Boyles that Twin Mike had scammed in a home improvement swindle several months earlier. During that scam, Twin Mike had learned where the old man had hidden his savings, but when he returned later to take it, the cache was empty. Since Boyles lived in a small double-wide mobile home, Twin Mike was certain he could find the money if he had time to search for it.

On March 1, 1995, the three men knocked on Boyles's door and introduced themselves as representatives of the Social Security Administration. They said he was scheduled to receive an $80 increase in his monthly check, but they needed to verify the condition of his living quarters before they could approve the increase. After the men inspected the mobile home and left, Boyles discovered that his entire life savings -- $70,000 -- was gone.

"This looked like it was going to be a real tragic case," said Jasper County Sheriff Randy M. Blackmon. "I've been knowing Mr. Boyles for years, and I just couldn't believe something like this happened."

Fortunately, police had one important lead: The old man's nephew remembered seeing a gray Ford Thunderbird with a side-mounted antenna and a red, white and blue license plate holder speed away from his uncle's driveway. That lead was conveyed to Aiken County's chief deputy, Major Jody Rowland, a few days later. Rowland, who began his career with the adjoining Edgefield County sheriff's office, knew most of the Irish Travelers in Murphy Village, and he said, "When I heard about the gray Ford Thunderbird and the red, white and blue license tag holder, I almost knew right then who they were talking about."

Rowland created a photograph lineup using driver's license photos of Twin Mike and several other Murphy Village residents, and from that selection of photographs, Boyles identified Twin Mike and Pete Skeet as two of the Social Security Administration employees. Then Rowland, armed with warrants issued by Jasper County, paid a visit to Twin Mike's home in Murphy Village.

"I drove up to the house, saw the gray Thunderbird and knew I had who I was looking for," the chief deputy said. "I knew the minute I saw the car that somebody had made a big score. They (the Travelers) aren't usually at home this time of year unless they've come into some money."

Rowland informed Sherlock he was under arrest and then checked the man for possession of weapons. He was due for a surprise. "While I was doing an officer safety pat-down, I felt something in Mike's sock. It was $14,060 in cash!"

During the interrogations that followed, Twin Mike and Pete Skeet named Tommy O'Hara as their accomplice, and Pete Skeet told officers how the cars were swapped and where the men went after the theft. Then, following a period of legal negotiating, the men agreed to return all of Boyles's money in exchange for lighter sentences.

Later, Sheriff Blackmon said, "Handing that check to Mr. Boyles was probably the most gratifying thing I have done since I became sheriff of Jasper County. You don't have many moments like this as a police officer. I will savor this one for the rest of my life."

Boyles responded by asking the sheriff how much he owed police officers for their trouble. "I told him all I wanted him to do was put that money in a bank, and he did it."

Following his last tour of Murphy Village in 1995, the writer pointed out to South Carolina police officers Joe Livingston and Jody Rowland that the residents of Murphy Village had obviously prospered during the last fifteen years, but law enforcement efforts to halt residents' criminal activities appeared to be largely unsuccessful. He asked if local law enforcement had any hope of stopping -- or even slowing -- Irish Traveler crime.

Livingston smiled and said, "Our motto here in South Carolina is, 'While I breathe, I hope.' What we hope is that somewhere down the line, we educate other police officers and the public about the Travelers. My ideal, though, is to legitimize these people. I don't have anything against them if they do their work legitimately. And they should! They could make lots of money performing their skills legitimately."

In fact, the Murphy Village Travelers are already learning how to enrich themselves through more legitimate enterprises. Not long after the South Carolina Supreme Court ruled that video poker was not a game of chance because skill was involved in playing it, and therefore video poker machines were legal in the state, enterprising Travelers opened video machine parlors along both sides of U.S. 25 near I-20 in Edgefield County. Today, that section of highway looks like a small Las Vegas strip.

Another interesting piece of evidence about Irish Traveler investments came not long ago from an unlikely source: a New York-based automobile recovery company that was hired by Nations Bank to repossess two cars in the Village. After picking up those vehicles, a recovery specialist contacted a corporate executive at the bank and said, "There are still six vehicles here that are in arrears of their payments. Should we pick them up for you?"

The banker replied, "Probably, but I'll check on it and get back to you."

A short while later, the banker telephoned the recovery specialist and said, "Don't touch those cars! Those people and their relatives have forty-three million dollars worth of certificates of deposit with our bank."

# 18

# Texas Scams

About the time Jimmy Burke began operating his automobile insurance frauds in New York and Pennsylvania, thirty-two Fort Worth businesses involved in RV sales, supplies and service asked the regional office of the Texas Division of Motor Vehicles for help in stopping Travelers from selling trailers there. The appeal was made on behalf of the Tarrant County Chapter of the Texas Recreational Vehicle Association. Informing the DMV that Travelers did not comply with state laws on the sale of vehicles, the chapter said, "These (Travelers) advertise as individuals, yet they are selling trailers with a manufacturer's statement of origin. At many locations advertised as 'individual must sell,' one can find four or five units parked on the property. More importantly, we are not discussing a mere handful of trailer sales....We find that the two major brands sold by the (Travelers) place fourth and fifth in Tarrant County."

The DMV replied it was not interested in becoming involved with enforcement action against the Travelers.

Another regulatory agency, the LP-Gas Division of the Texas Railway Commission, said it did not have enough law enforcement officers to pursue motor vehicle regulation action. The Texas Comptroller General's office said it was interested in possible tax code violations, but it also did not have enough personnel to conduct investigations. The Texas Motor Vehicle Commission replied it could not become involved because it did not regulate sales of non-motorized vehicles such as travel trailers. The Texas Highway Department referred inquiries back to its Division of Motor Vehicles.

Eight months later, Texas RV dealers finally found a sympathetic ear when they sent copies of the *Trailer Life* trailer scam articles to Attorney General Mark White. White was planning to enter the upcoming political race for governor, and his advisors told him he needed an important law enforcement issue that could help him gain more positive exposure to voters. When the advisors learned from *Trailer Life* that the Travelers misrepresenting and selling cheap trailers were the same people who were scamming elderly Texas citizens with home improvement schemes, they recommended that the attorney general's office become involved. White immediately assigned his consumer protection and antitrust division to investigate.

In Austin, a team of enforcers prepared to do battle under provisions of a seldom-used civil statute, the Deceptive Trade Practices Consumer Protection Act. That statute allowed the attorney general's office, as a public enforcement agency, to sue individuals -- without requiring a victim's complaint -- if the agency had reason to believe the act was being violated. Under criminal deceptive trade statutes, enforcement by county attorneys and local police forces was required, along with victims willing to file complaints and testify in court.

The investigative team of Assistant Attorneys General Zoleta Courtney and Michael Thornton and Consumer Analyst Nora Dominguez learned that the Texas Department of Public Safety had begun preparing files on numerous Travelers several years earlier. By the winter of 1980-81, the trio concluded they should devote their attention to the Rio Grande Valley of South Texas because DPS officers said the Travelers tended to gravitate that direction during cold-weather months.

At the very time the investigators prepared to do battle, a young Irish Traveler named Wayne Gallagher was offering a new Lariat trailer for sale along Highway 83 in the Rio Grande Valley. Questioned by a magazine writer about the coach, Gallagher said he paid $10,500 for it but was being forced to sell it for $6,900 because he broke his arm and needed to go to the hospital so it could be reset. Not far away, Scottish Traveler Nora McDonald offered a new Safari trailer for sale that she said cost $10,500 when she bought it directly from the Indiana factory, but she was being forced by financial difficulties to sell it for $7,200. English Traveler Pat Jennings displayed a Marauder for sale in front of a motel near McAllen; he wanted $6,500 for the trailer and said he had paid $10,700 for it. Within the space of a week, Traveler Lucille Croughin sold at least three new Lariat trailers to tourists wintering in south Texas.

In January, English Traveler Tommy Young stopped at the residence of an 85-year-old McAllen woman who was living on a blind disability pension. Young offered to clear her home's sewer pipes for $100. After he did the work and was paid, he looked at her house and said, "Lady, you need some roof work done."

She said, "Well, I can't afford that right now."

Young answered, "You can't afford not to do it. Your roof could collapse the next time it rains."

"Oh, my, I had no idea," the elderly woman said. "What should I do?"

"I don't do that kind of work, but I'm associated with someone who does. I'll bring him over tomorrow to talk to you."

The next morning, Young returned with Traveler Lester Callahan, who told the woman, "I've got some material left over from a previous job, and I can give you a good price on it." He sprayed diluted paint on her roof for twenty minutes and collected $500 from his victim. Later, relatives told the women she had been cheated and recommended she call police. McAllen's Department of Public Safety notified the attorney general's office, and Courtney and Thornton rushed to the Rio Grande Valley to investigate.

"She was the cutest little old lady you ever saw," Courtney said about the victim. "It just made me sick that they took her money. Those were two guys we really wanted to get."

The victim filed a criminal complaint, and Young and Callahan became the first Travelers cited under the Texas Consumer Protection Act for engaging in "false, misleading and deceptive acts or practices." Both criminal and civil charges were filed, and a temporary restraining order was issued prohibiting the two men from doing home repair work in the state. Charges included:

•Making home solicitations without informing consumers of rights under federal and state laws.

•Failing to provide prospective customers with required three-day cancellation notices.

•Representing that their work or material was guaranteed for a specific period of time even though Young and Callahan intended to leave the area without providing a means to have the guaranty work performed.

•Representing that the work was guaranteed even though they did not have the resources or personnel required to satisfy the guarantees.

•Failing to provide addresses or telephone numbers where complaints and claims for warranty work could be made.

•Representing that the roofing work would seal, protect and coat the roof sufficiently to cure leaks when, in fact, the material was purely cosmetic in nature and of no value structurally.

•Representing that the roofing work was of a particular quality when it was not.

•Failing to inform the customer about the itinerant nature of Young and Callahan's business practices.

Civil penalties for those charges were set at $2,000 to $10,000.

However, Young and Callahan apparently left the state and could not be found in spite of a state-wide police alert. A few days later, Thornton filed a similar civil suit in Austin against Traveler Paul Edward Smith for swindling an elderly Travis County couple in a roof sealing scam. Like Young and Callahan, he left Texas before he could be fined.

Next, the attorney general's office focused its attention on what was then the best known Irish Traveler trailer sales operation in Texas.

For several years, an Irish Traveler named Jim Carroll operated JR Trailer Sales in Fort Worth. The business's sign was displayed on a storage shed at a residence on Circle Park Boulevard, and a listing in the Yellow Pages offered "discount prices on Kentucky Traveler, Lariat, Marauder." Actual sales were handled either from the residence's kitchen or from the nearby home of Carroll's daughter, Mary Donahue, also known as Mary Burden. Carroll also operated an asphalt sealing business from the Circle Park location.

After receiving numerous complaints from RV dealers that alleged Mary Donahue was misrepresenting the trailers she sold, Courtney sent investigators to Donahue's and Carroll's homes posing as potential buyers. Based on the investigators' reports, Courtney filed a civil suit against Mary Donahue and her sister, Sue. The suit made several charges:

•That the women represented themselves as casual, one-time sellers of RVs when in truth, they customarily offered RVs for sale to the public.

•That the women made false or misleading statements of fact about the reasons why trailer prices were reduced.

•That they represented that the trailers carried warranties they did not.

•That they claimed the RVs would be serviced and maintained by RV dealers in Hidalgo and Cameron Counties when, in fact, the local dealers refused to service those vehicles.

•That they claimed they had paid more for the trailers they sold than they did.

Mary Donahue immediately visited Courtney's office objecting to the action. Later, Courtney recalled, "I got a kick out of Mary because there she was, telling me I was terrible for accusing her of all that stuff, and her husband said it was the first time she'd ever sold an RV and that she was just selling it because he was away at work. I knew that was not true, and she knew I knew it! She was very irate with me. She told me that she knew the women we sent out to 'shop' her were investigators."

The sisters were fined $200, and a permanent injunction was issued prohibiting them from engaging in deceptive or misleading practices as well as the types of claims alleged in the attorney general's law suit. Courtney reported, "It was not a matter of our trying to chase them out of Fort Worth; it's where they live. And the money is not as important to us as getting them under an injunction so that they have to stop misleading people."

A few years later, Mary Donahue Burden moved her trailer sale operation to Mission, Texas, in the Rio Grande Valley. There, she opened two legitimate, permanent RV dealerships on Highway 83. She now hires repair work done by another nearby, well known RV dealership and has responded satisfactorily to all complaints about her business that have been filed with the local Better Business Bureau. Among many Irish Travelers who aspire to more settled lifestyles, Mary is regarded as somewhat of a role model.

Mary's success in operating dealerships in the Valley encouraged three other Traveler families to establish RV businesses there. An English Traveler couple now has a sales lot on Highway 83 near Alamo; two Irish Travelers operate a dealership near McAllen on the same highway, and a well-known Irish Traveler couple sell travel trailers and operate a sealing and paving business west of Mission. All complaints filed about those operations with the Better Business Bureau have been resolved satisfactorily.

On the day Mary Donahue was cited for deception, a similar civil suit also was filed against Richard and Anita George, who claimed they were not associated with any Traveler clans, but lived permanently in the Rio Grande Valley. Permanent injunctions were issued prohibiting them from deceptive trade practices and misrepresenting RVs that they sold, and the attorney general's office agreed to an out-of-court settlement that did not include monetary fines. Courtney reported, "The key to a permanent injunction, of course, is that if they violate it, they go to jail."

The same day, a restraining order was issued to Irish Traveler Pete C. Carroll ordering him to stop misrepresenting both the travel trailers he sold in Texas and the quality of the materials he used in roof sealing scams. He also was ordered not to move his RV from the campground where it was parked, but he breached that order by leaving Texas in the middle of the night. Since the attorney general's citation was a civil action, not a criminal charge, no arrest warrants were issued when Carroll did not show up in court. Several days later, fines of up to $10,000 were issued against Carroll, but Courtney said, "We'll have to find him in order to collect that money."

Almost a year later, Carroll was arrested near Lafayette, Louisiana, for attempting to sell RVs without a license.

In mid-February, two Scottish Travelers named William West and George Bishop swindled a 75-year-old Austin woman out of $700 in a roof sealing scam. Police officers in Austin were outraged and began searching for the two men. Even hard-core narcotics officers insisted upon joining the search. West and Bishop were arrested and taken to the attorney general's office to be interviewed. Courtney reported, "The police made West stand up and clean out his pockets, and I remember thinking to myself, 'My God, you can't do that!' I just knew my boss would have a fit if he walked in. Later, West hired a lawyer who called me on the phone and screamed at me for thirty minutes for unlawfully detaining her client and breaching his constitutional rights. I thought, 'Oh, my golly, I can just see them suing the attorney general over this.'"

Thornton and Courtney filed suit against the two men, but because the woman victim's health was poor and her son wanted her to avoid stress, no criminal charges were filed, and no action taken beyond issuance of restraining orders.

At the same time, Scottish Travelers Lulu B. and Alfred Collins Sr. were arrested in Nacogdoches on both civil deception and criminal fraud charges after operating driveway sealing scams there. Permanent injunctions were issued against them, and they paid a $2,000 criminal fine.

Two months later, Scottish Traveler Robert Lee Stewart attempted to swindle a suburban Austin woman with roof sealing work, but she had already read about the sealing scam, and after she made arrangements for Stewart to return the next day, she telephoned Bastrock city police. Officers were waiting for Stewart when he returned to the woman's house, and he was arrested. A computer check revealed he had swindled an Austin resident out of $500 with the same scam earlier, so he was jailed. A civil restraining order was issued and a criminal hearing date set, but Stewart jumped bond and left the state.

The attorney general's office continued to file civil suits against Travelers for consumer fraud, and resulting publicity increased the voting public's awareness of Attorney General Mark White dramatically. When he entered the governor's race soon after that, a significant portion of his election campaign focused on his office's successful efforts to prosecute con artists who swindled elderly Texans out of their savings.

To no one's surprise, White was elected governor of Texas.

Although enforcement efforts included suits against Travelers who operated both RV and home improvement scams, the attorney general's office focused most of its attention on the paving and sealing schemes. Courtney candidly admitted, "The RV dealers are screaming at us because the trailer scams are hurting their business, but as a practical matter, we're more concerned with the paving and sealing because that's how all the little old ladies are getting ripped off."

She added, "The sad thing about our trailer cases was that we did not have one single consumer complaint. Not one person contacted our office and told us he had been duped. We filed suits anyway because of what we knew about the scams through RV dealers and from the *Trailer Life* magazine articles. But it takes some of the blood and guts out of a case when you can't go before a judge and say, 'This person was duped.'"

Without a complaining victim, Courtney explained, criminal arrests could not be made. "If we don't get any consumer complaints (about trailer scams), we cannot justify putting all our energy into investigating trailer sales when we have a series of real complaints that need our attention. Twice, we tried to gather criminal evidence in the field by following Travelers when they left their campgrounds, but both times, they spotted us. I think they could smell us a mile away!"

Even so, Courtney pledged to continue issuing restraining orders against Travelers for all their scams. "And, with assistance from the Texas Rangers, the Texas Department of Public Safety and local police agencies, the Travelers can be hassled until they realize they have very little freedom to operate scams in our state."

Key assistance to Courtney's enforcement action came from Texas DPS officer Joel Young, who was headquartered at McAllen in the Rio Grande Valley. "The problem we've always had here," he told the writer while chasing Travelers, "is that when the scammers come in here, they stay for a month or two or three, and they don't pull a whole lot of scams until just before they leave. Then, most of the scams they do pull are on people eighty or ninety years old, and by the time we get complaints, the bad guys are gone. We've also had difficulty because often, the old people don't recall what the scammers looked like."

Young said, "We get the same crew in here every year. They always show an address in Fort Worth that is nothing but a campground (Sanna Dean Trailer Park at 6036 East Belknap). They used to come in here with Illinois, Ohio and Florida license plates, but we started hassling them about operating in Texas on out-of-state tags, so now when they arrive, the first thing they do is register their vehicles and get Texas plates. They represent themselves to be locals, and they hire answering services so they'll have local phone numbers. Then they put magnetic signs with those phone numbers on their pickup trucks. The signs impress old people, and the local phone numbers give the impression they are established local business people."

Asked about the lack of complaints from trailer scam victims, Young said, "We've told tourists in the Valley about those trailers, but they say, 'I don't care. It still sounds like a good deal to me.'"

He added, "The Carrolls, Raffertys, Croughins, Gallaghers, McDonalds and Meskers always show up here in January and leave in March. While they're selling their trailers, they're also sealing roofs and paving driveways. I guess they're also shoplifting at stores, but there's so much of that here anyway, it would be difficult for us to tell who's doing it. We've had almost no luck in arresting any of the Travelers, although we have cited a few of them for traffic violations. There are a bunch of warrants out from last year for John and Mary Mesker, and the attorney general has an injunction on John that prohibits him from working in Texas.

"About three years ago, an old man who owned a grocery store in Mission was scammed out of $360 by the Meskers. They seal-coated his roof with that silver paint they use, and he was upset because they sprayed some of it on his old Cadillac. He went home and washed his Cadillac, and the silver stuff came right off. That night, it rained, and every place the Meskers had stepped on his roof, the water came through. It just poured into that store and about ruined everything."

A year before that, Young recalled, an elderly woman in Edinburg responded to a local newspaper ad that offered free termite inspections. The con artist who arrived for the inspection crawled out from under her house and told her, "The termites have plumb eaten up the beams in your floor, and the whole house is ready to collapse."

Young said, "That about scared her to death. She was old and used a walker and was unable to crawl under the house to look at the damage. The inspector said, 'I don't do this kind of work, but I've got a friend who does.' The next day, the inspector's friend came out and carried a bunch of two-by-fours under the house. The lady heard him hammering and banging, and she assumed he was working under there. When he got through, the exterminator went back in and sprayed everything. It all cost her $5,500. She told a neighbor about it and said, 'My whole house was fixin' to cave in, and they changed the floor braces.' The neighbor said, 'I can't believe that!' and he crawled under the house and saw that all the con artist had done was nail some two-by-fours on the sides of the beams. But the beams were in perfect shape."

When Edinburg resident Robert McDowell answered his doorbell one Saturday morning in May, he was greeted by an short, stocky man of about forty who introduced himself as George Stewart. "I have a roofing business in McAllen," the affable Stewart said, "and I just finished putting an acrylic roof coating on a house down the street. I noticed that your roof looks like it needs to be recoated, and since I have some materials left over, I thought I'd see if you'd like us to do the job while we're here."

McDowell answered that he might be interested, depending upon the price, and Stewart said, "I normally charge $375 if someone calls me to come out, but since I have my crew with me and the extra material, I'll sealcoat your roof for only $200." The man showed McDowell a brochure for Perma Rock brand acrylic roof coating and said the treatment would reflect the sun's rays and reduce the house's interior temperature by up to 20 per cent. He said he had sealcoated numerous homes in the area, including Dr. Arnulfo Martinez, who -- like McDowell -- was employed at nearby Pan American University.

Later, McDowell recalled, "My wife and I were a little suspicious, partly because of his smooth sales pitch and partly because he waved that brochure at us but pulled it back immediately when we started reading it in detail. But I talked it over with my wife, and it appeared to be quite a bargain, especially since it was very hot that day. I told him I would like to have the job done, but since I had only a little money in my checkbook, I couldn't pay him until Monday."

Stewart agreed to those terms and immediately began work with his crew, which consisted of a blond, fair-skinned man, a tall dark-haired man and a blond-haired teenager. Noting that one of the trucks had a telephone number on it, McDowell telephoned the number and discovered it was an answering service. "I then called Dr. Martinez. He told me that someone had done a roofing job for him about four years ago which hadn't done anything to improve his roof." McDowell could find no listings in the local telephone directory for either George Stewart or the names listed on the work crew's pickup trucks -- W. Reid and H. Keith.

Thirty minutes after they started, Stewart and his crew completed their work. McDowell said, "The roof looked very white and quite pretty except that they had got the white material all over the gray trim on the roof and also on the swimming pool deck, the patio furniture and the shrubbery around the house."

Stewart told McDowell, "I'll have someone come here about 5:30 Monday night to collect our $200. I'd appreciate it if you'd have the money ready in cash because I have to pay off some Mexican boys who are workin' for me."

McDowell asked, "Is there a guarantee for this work?"

"I can't give you a written guarantee," Stewart replied, "but if you're not satisfied with the job, you can call me anytime, and I will come out and make sure you're satisfied."

"Would you mind telling me what's in the material you sprayed on my roof?"

"It's a mixture of acrylic, lime and cement," Stewart said.

After Stewart and his crew left, McDowell contacted a neighbor who was in the construction business and asked him to examine the roofcoating job. The neighbor told McDowell the material was either whitewash or a mixture of latex paint and water. He wiped his hand on the roof and then rinsed it off easily with water. Next, he sprayed a hose on the corner of the roof, and the white coating material washed away immediately. McDowell then called police.

"On Monday morning," McDowell recalled, "I noticed several other houses which had rather bright white roofs and looked like they had been recently painted. I stopped at one of those houses and spoke to the owner, who told me had hired the same people who had done my roof on Saturday. They had charged him $250."

Monday evening, when Stewart, Reid and Keith returned to McDowell's house to collect their money, they were arrested by police on orders of the state attorney general's office. The three men immediately posted bond and left the state. Subsequent investigations revealed they had coated between 400 and 500 roofs in the Rio Grande Valley during a two-week period, earning between $200 and $300 per job -- enabling them to pocket nearly $150,000!

Fifteen years later, some of the same Travelers were still sealing roofs and driveways and selling travel trailers in Texas. In spite of the injunctions against them, John and Mary Mesker worked their scams throughout the Valley during 1995. Their well known kinsmen, Matt and John Clay Mesker, also were quite active. John and Mary's son, Danny, married another Traveler named Dorothy Ann Daugherty and, for a few years, was quite successful in Florida with his roof-sealing work. George, Matt, Tom and W.M. Mesker also built reputations throughout the western half of America with lightning rod scams. A spokesman for the Better Business Bureau of South Texas reported, "We've always warned people about the Meskers, but usually, when we're called about them, it's after they've done their work and left the area."

Pat Jennings, the English Traveler who sold trailers throughout the Valley in 1980 and 1981, already was being sought in connection with installing fake lightning rod systems. He was kicked out of an Orlando, Florida, campground in 1982 along with a few dozen other Travelers, including Jimmy Burke's sister Wanda and her husband Billy O'Roarke. For the next dozen years, he continued traveling around the country, leaving victims in his path. During the summer of 1995, he sold trailers and sealed roofs and driveways in Missoula, Montana, until the campground manager asked him to leave and notified police. He was last seen towing his fifth-wheel trailer in the direction of Lolo, Montana.

# 19

# Missouri

Sharon and Leon Jacobs, residents of Independence, Missouri, wanted to buy a recreational vehicle so they could travel and see America. They had friends who were campers, and they enjoyed hearing stories about the trips their friends took and the sights they saw. Sharon Jacobs was a meticulous shopper, and she spent several days looking at RVs at dealerships, comparing prices and features. She also checked newspaper ads for trailers and, when she saw an ad for one that seemed promising, she examined the coach and made notes about its strong and weak points.

Sharon did not know about the so-called *gypsy* trailer sales scam, and she had never heard of the Irish Travelers. So she was totally unprepared for the outgoing personality and salesmanship of Rose Carroll.

For more than a dozen years, Rose Ann Carroll and her husband Edward spent the spring and summer in the Kansas City area. Rose sold travel trailers from campgrounds, motels, mobile home lots and vacant lots. Edward, after acquiring an occupational permit from the city of Independence, paved driveways and sealcoated roofs. The Carrolls used a post office box in Sugar Creek, Missouri, but listed their home addresses as either 3800 Summit or 242 West Highway 24 in Kansas City; neither address existed. While in the area, they hired a telephone answering service to handle inquiries about trailer sales and paving/sealing jobs, but they also had a telephone in their trailer.

On May 5, 1981, the Carrolls advertised a new Indiana Traveler trailer for sale through the *Kansas City Star* for $7,300. Sharon and Leon Jacobs answered the ad and were attracted by the appearance and price of the coach. When they asked the Carrolls why the price was so low, Rose replied that they had paid $9,600 for the trailer but had to sell it for less because of a family emergency. Rose said the trailer was worth much more than $9,600, but they had bought it for less because Edward had done some asphalt work for the manufacturer. Convinced they were buying a bargain, Jacobs gave Rose a cashier's check for $7,300.

A few weeks later, friends told Sharon they thought she had been swindled. They gave her copies of the 1980 *Trailer Life* magazine articles about the *gypsy* trailer scam, and Sharon immediately telephoned the Indiana Manufactured Housing Association and asked for details about the swindle. Then, armed with that information and the magazine articles, she called Missouri Attorney General Mary Ernest's office. Assistant Attorney General Angela M. Bennett was assigned to handle the investigation.

Bennett, who also was not familiar with either the trailer scam or the Irish Travelers, arrived at the Jacobses home to interview them, and Sharon showed Bennett the IMHA material, the magazine articles and a copy of cashier's check made out to the Carrolls at a fictitious address. When Bennett saw the material, her face illustrated her alarm. "Oh, my God," she said, "I think I goofed. I sent them a letter notifying them of the complaint against them. If they skip out, the department of revenue is going to have my head."

Two days later, Sharon received an unexpected visit -- from Rose and Edward Carroll. The Carrolls demanded an explanation for the letter they received from Bennett which stated they had been paid $9,600 for their trailer. Sharon agreed with them that the wrong sales price had been included in the letter, and Rose insisted that Sharon sign a note on the back of the letter admitting contents of the letter were false.

"No, ma'am, I won't do that," Sharon replied. "But I will call the attorney general's office in the morning and get that point straightened out."

"Are you tryin' to ruin our good name?" Rose asked. "My husband has a reputable business, and something like that letter could hurt it. If you were unhappy with the trailer, why didn't you call us?"

Sharon responded, "Imagine how upset we were when we were told it was a gypsy trailer."

"Who told you that?" Rose asked.

"Several people."

"I suppose you read that *Trailer Life* article where our name was used. Everyone in our group was sittin' around laughin' about the article and callin' each other gypsies."

"Well, that was part of it," Sharon admitted. "Plus, I've talked to a few more people, and I've got a lot more information and some literature on it."

"Do you mind if I see it?" Edward asked.

"Sir, I can't show it to you because the attorney general's office has it," Sharon replied.

Rose pointed out, "Indiana Traveler was not even listed in the *Trailer Life* articles. Don't you think if we were gypsies, we would be gone from here by now? We have lived in this area off and on for five years. The trailer we're living in is just like yours. Do you think we would have one and live in it if it was a gypsy trailer? *Trailer Life* published that article for the benefit of the RV dealers, so they can get three or four thousand dollars more out of the trailers they sell. An ordinary person can go to the factories in Elkhart, Indiana, and purchase trailers cheaper than they can get trailers from RV dealers.

*Trailer Life* and the author of them articles are both gonna get sued."

After minutes of additional conversation, the Carrolls convinced Leon Jacobs -- but not Sharon -- that they were not part of the con artist clans and did not earn profits from selling travel trailers.

"If you want your money back, we'll give it to you," Rose said. "If you don't like the trailer, we'd rather sell it to someone who will be happy with it."

Leon answered that he wanted to keep the trailer. Later, Sharon reported, "I went along with him at that time for one reason: I wanted to talk to the attorney general's office to see if taking our money back would stop the investigation." Sharon hoped to stop the Carrolls from selling trailers, and she was willing to lose her $7,300 in order to see the state attorney's investigation completed.

The next day, Sharon asked Angela Bennett whether the investigation would be halted if she and her husband accepted a refund of their money. "Heavens no," Bennett told her. "That won't have anything to do with our investigation. Our main objective is for you to get your money back."

Sharon then telephoned the Carrolls and said, "Rose, we've changed our minds. We want our money back."

Rose asked, "Did you talk to your husband about this?"

"Yes, Rose. He agrees with me."

The other end of the telephone was silent for several seconds, and then Rose asked, "Don't you think we ought to talk about a usage fee?"

"What do you mean, a usage fee?" Sharon responded.

"Well, you've had that trailer several weeks. Don't you think you ought to pay something like you would if you rented it?"

"I don't know, Rose. We'll talk about that later." Sharon hung up the phone.

The following day, Rose called Sharon about arranging the refund. Sharon asked, "Is there going to be any squabble over a usage fee?"

Rose replied, "Well, I don't know. I've turned it all over to an attorney."

Sharon Jacobs had not exactly sat at home waiting for the telephone to ring with news of whether or not she would get her refund. First, she telephoned her attorney and told him about the trailer sales scams. He said he had never heard of such a scam, and he told her, "To put your mind at ease, this could be just gossip. Call the trailer factory. If the factory tells you there's nothing wrong with that trailer, forget it."

So she phoned Indiana Traveler Enterprises near Middlebury, Indiana, where her trailer was built, and asked president Daryl Zeck (not his real name) if the coach she had bought was a *gypsy* trailer. Zeck answered, "No ma'am, there's not a thing wrong with that trailer." Their coach had a suggested retail price of $9,600, he said.

(A few months later, Zeck would recant and admit to the writer that he had sold two brands of trailers to Irish, Scottish and English Travelers, but he had decided not to continue that practice. He offered to sign an affidavit pledging he would never again sell products to Travelers. He even provided the names of all Travelers who had bought RVs from him; Rose and Ed Carroll and their son Edward Jr. were on that list. He admitted he knew the Travelers were misrepresenting his products and earning thousands of dollars in profits from them. Zeck said Rose and Ed paid him $5,190 for the trailer they sold to Sharon and Leon Jacobs. Zeck also said Rose's claim that Edward had done asphalt work for his company was false. "I've never even met her husband," he insisted.)

Meanwhile, Sharon ran a license plate check on the truck Rose and Edward were driving and discovered the plate was registered to Roger Dale Smith of Brookline, Missouri. Ed Carroll said later Smith was his nephew. Sharon also discovered two of the addresses the Carrolls used were fictitious, and she learned the Carrolls were related to a woman named Sarah Donahue who apparently was living in Liberty, Missouri.

She also started collecting names, addresses and telephone numbers of individuals she thought might be operating trailer sales scams, and she tracked down people who had been swindled by some of those con artists. She gave that information to Angela Bennett.

On July 18, she wrote to Tim Weiner, a *Kansas City Star* reporter who had earlier written an article about a home furnace scam. "I would like to advise you that I, too, am the victim of a similar scam on a gypsy trailer," she wrote. "I hope you will see the need also to expose these ripoff artists as you did the furnace company owner. My experience has been costly and sad, but I would be very glad to provide you with any help I can to stop these ripoffs."

At the request of the attorney general's office, Sharon began keeping a diary of every conversation and event associated with her purchase of the Carrolls' trailer, and she connected a tape recorder to her telephone. She also contacted the writer who had authored the sales scam articles in *Trailer Life* magazine.

A meeting of the Jacobses and Rose Carroll was scheduled July 23 so that Leon and Sharon could accept their $7,300 refund and Rose could retrieve the trailer. Rose insisted that a local RV dealer be permitted to inspect the coach beforehand to look for possible damages, but when she arrived at the Jacobs home, she said the dealer had scheduling conflicts but she would check the trailer herself and then tow it to the dealership to be checked later. Sharon wrote in her diary, "She inspected it and left. On the way to the bank (to sign legal papers transferring title back to the Carrolls), I told my husband there was no way she was going to take the trailer off our property until the papers were signed. 'She can take it to the dealer and later claim none of the appliances worked.' He agreed with me."

At the bank, Leon and Sharon signed an unusual "release and

agreement" in which they promised not to "sue or in any way harass, gossip about or publicly or privately criticize one another" about events prior to the date of the agreement. As Sharon would learn later, that agreement did not prohibit those types of activities about events *after* that date. Sharon, Leon and Rose returned to the Jacobs home so Rose could inspect the trailer; then Rose and Sharon drove back to the bank to complete the necessary paperwork, in the form of a notarized gift affidavit, and refund.

On the way home, Sharon began perspiring heavily -- a reaction to stress and the medication prescribed for her following a nervous breakdown several months earlier. Sharon wrote in her diary, "She (Rose) asked many questions about it. She also told me many times...that her children had been harassed, threatened, and notes had been left. I asked her if she had turned the notes over to her attorney and was told no, because the notes weren't handwritten so it wouldn't do any good. I assured her it wasn't coming from us, and she said, 'What about your friends?' I told her very few people knew anything about it, and if they did, my friends wouldn't do anything like that."

The following afternoon, while Sharon was shopping, Leon Jacobs answered a ringing telephone at home and realized he was listening to a recording. Immediately, he turned on the recorder connected to the phone. A woman's voice said, "Everything I told you was ninety per cent untrue. I said it to confuse and mislead you. I know my phone is monitored and our conversations are being recorded. We just want you to leave us alone. I take the Fifth Amendment."

Sharon wrote in her diary, "My husband recognized the voice as Rose Carroll's."

According to Sharon's diary, "Two minutes later, the telephone rang again, and it was Rose Carroll in person." Rose said the department of revenue would not accept paperwork for the trailer title transfer, and new papers would have to be signed. She wanted Leon to go with her to a bank and sign new papers. "She came with an affidavit and a note which said, 'Please fill this out and return.' It was signed R. Hill above a Department of Revenue stamp." At the bank, new papers were signed, and Rose took the note out of Leon's hand, claiming she needed it.

Later, Sharon wrote, "I called every (department of revenue) branch in the K.C. area, and none had an R. Hill in their offices. I also read the (original) gift affidavit to a person with the department of revenue and was told it should have been acceptable. I asked if there was any way Mrs. Carroll could have used the (department's) stamp when they weren't watching. I was told this was highly unlikely, but it wasn't impossible to have a rubber stamp made."

She continued, "My husband thinks the recording was for my benefit. Since she pumped me...so much about my nervous breakdown, he thinks she meant for me to hear it either to work on my nerves or she may have thought I would be angry and call to chew her out, which would break the release agreement. Or I might call some agency and tell them about it, and they would contact her about it, and she would tell them, 'That lady is crazy. She's hearing things.'

"My husband never mentioned the recording (to Rose). I think she meant for me to hear the recording and just used the gift affidavit as an excuse to come over and see if I was home. I still feel she is up to something because of the way the release was worded. As far as we are concerned, we don't ever want to talk to or see them again unless it is in court."


Over the next few months, sparked by her anger at the Carrolls, Sharon began a one-woman investigation of trailer sales scams in the Kansas City area, and she tried -- but failed -- to enlist support from a wide range of public agencies, including the state department of revenue, the highway patrol, the local F.B.I. office, the Kansas City

Better Business Bureau, the county prosecutor's office, the city prosecutor's office, her state representative and the state's Consumer Affairs Regulations and Licensing office.

Sharon tried to recruit help from the local RV dealer organization. A meeting was scheduled to discuss trailer sales scams, but only four dealers from the metropolitan area attended. The organization's secretary told her, "Sharon, I called six others, but they all said, 'This has been going on for years,' and they're not even interested in hearing about it."

The city editor of the *Kansas City Star* told Sharon he would ask a reporter from the newspaper's Independence office to interview her; it was almost a month later before a writer from that office talked with her. Kansas City TV stations were interested in reporting on the scams, but Angela Bennett asked Sharon not to talk with reporters for a couple of weeks until investigations could be completed. Meanwhile, Jim Summers, executive director of the Recreation Vehicle Dealers Association -- a national lobbying organization for RV dealers -- asked Kansas City RV dealer Truman Knox to assist Sharon in any way he could.

Knox, a semi-retired business owner who had extra personal time to help Sharon, immediately contacted the attorney general's office and then called *Trailer Life* magazine. As might be expected, he said, most of the Travelers were using their RVs as bases from which they operated various scams, especially driveway and roof sealing, throughout the Kansas City area and westward into Kansas. Supported by Angela Bennett, Knox and Sharon began recording vehicle license plate numbers so registrations and titles could be checked.

Well known Traveler names began finding their way onto a list being compiled by the attorney general's office: Bob Gorman, who operated an asphalt truck in Sugar Creek; Otis Young, asphalt truck; E. Daley, asphalt truck; Bill Pierce, selling a Kentucky Traveler trailer with Iowa license plates and driving a Ford truck with Wisconsin tags; John Gorman, asphalt truck; Sally Harrison, offering a Kentucky Traveler trailer for sale behind the Best Western Motel at Platte City, said it was owned by an in-law, Jerry George; Robert (also known as Ronald) Jeffrey offered a Lariat trailer for sale at the Broadmoor Gardens Mobile Park in Belton.

Word spread quickly among the Travelers that some type of law enforcement agency had initiated an investigation. Those selling trailers and working home improvement schemes were advised to be careful about misrepresenting their services and their products.

Knox said, "I volunteered to get into the act and help them (the attorney general's office) a bit, so I went out and caught the pitch on a couple of Travelers. At a campground at Bates City, even the people in the office seemed to be Travelers. And I never saw such a collection of them in one place as I saw in that campground. There must have been a reunion or a convention or something. There were license plates from all over the country. And they were really spooked. I went in posing as a buyer, but they wouldn't misrepresent anything to me except they all made up stories about why they were selling their trailers. Insofar as telling me about warranties or holding tanks or other equipment, they were very cagey."

An Irish Traveler named Edward Donahue was a particular target of the attorney general's office. Investigators had solid evidence that Donahue operated an unlicensed asphalt business and misrepresented trailers on numerous occasions, but to solidify their position, they asked Knox to pose as a prospective buyer and contact Donahue. At the Independence mobile home court where Donahue offered a Safari trailer for sale, Knox was not told anything that he considered to be a gross misrepresentation. Clearly, Donahue was suspicious of him. Finally, figuring Donahue was not going to tell him lies about the price, quality or equipment of the trailer, Knox asked, "Are you in the business of selling trailers?"

Obviously surprised by the question, Donahue answered, "Oh, no. No."

"When you sell this trailer, are you gonna replace it?" Knox asked.

"No," Donahue replied.

Within a few days, Donahue did sell that trailer, and he immediately replaced it with two more, providing the attorney general's office with evidence it needed that Donahue was operating as an unlicensed RV dealer.

Donahue's name was brought to the attorney general's attention because his son had sold a Marauder travel trailer to a Kansas City couple named Edwards in 1977. Young Donahue told the couple the trailer was the first home for him and his bride, and they were traveling with his father, who was living on the adjoining campsite in an identical trailer. Edward Donahue Jr. said he specialized in water-powered house and barn painting, and he needed to sell both trailers so he could find a cherry-picker to make his work easier. Donahue offered to sell the trailer for a fraction of what he said he paid for it. The couple was interested in the trailer but emphasized they needed a coach that was completely self-contained. Donahue assured them the Marauder met that need in every way.

After the couple bought the trailer, they learned it had no sewage holding tank, and for the next eighteen months, they tried to sell it. They were dumbfounded when every RV dealer in the Kansas City area refused to accept the Marauder as a trade-in on another coach, and no dealer would even give them an estimate of the trailer's wholesale or retail value. Finally, a sympathetic employee at one dealership told them they owned what she described as "a gypsy trailer." It was at that point they filed a complaint with the consumer fraud section of the state attorney general's office.

Research by the attorney general's office revealed that both Edward Donahue and his son had sold numerous travel trailers throughout the Kansas City area during the intervening months. Supported by statements from victims and Truman Knox, legal action was prepared against the older Donahue by Angela Bennett; the whereabouts of Edward Donahue Jr. was unknown. Subsequent investigations also revealed interesting family relationships among some of the Travelers: Edward Donahue's wife, Sarah, was Rose Carroll's sister. Another of Rose's sisters, Jane, was married to Rose's husband Ed's brother, Nick.

One of the trailers the Donahues had offered for sale disappeared from its spot in Independence, so Leon Jacobs telephoned Edward Donahue to ask if it had been sold. The woman who answered the phone sounded like Rose Carroll, so Leon hung up. Later, Sharon asked a friend to call the number and record the conversation. A woman answered the phone and said, "The people who have this trailer are out of town. I'm just their calls forwarding service." There was a pause, then the woman added, "Well, I don't even know who has that trailer for sale. In fact, I didn't even know there was one for sale."

Sharon recognized the voice as Rose Carroll's, and when she played the tape for Angela Bennett a few days later, the assistant state attorney agreed it was Rose.


During Sharon Jacobs' personal investigation of the Travelers, she drove to nearly every campground and mobile home park within a fifty-mile radius of her home, looking for trailers with "For Sale" signs on them that she thought might be owned either by Travelers or their victims.

Together, Sharon and Knox recorded the brands and prices of trailers that they confirmed were being sold by Travelers. By mid-August, they had identified nearly sixty different Traveler families selling trailers and working other scams in eastern Jackson County alone.

The first victims of a trailer sales scam that Sharon identified were a family in Blue Springs named Roese. The Roeses had advertised their Lariat trailer for sale through local newspapers. Sharon telephoned the family and asked Mrs. Roese if she had bought the trailer from *gypsies*.

"I really don't know," the woman responded, "but my husband sure is mad about something regarding that trailer."

Later, Sharon reported, "About that time, Mr. Roese came home, and his wife gave him the phone. Sure enough, he'd been swindled, and he was trying to sell the trailer just to get rid of it." Roese volunteered to show the trailer to Sharon, so she drove to Blue Springs. "He'd just retired and was planning to take the trailer to Alaska for the summer," Sharon reported. "The guy who sold it to him assured him it had everything that he would need, even if he never had access to sewer or water hookups. But there was no water tank or sewer holding tank on it!"

Alerted by Sharon, the attorney general's office began an immediate investigation of the individuals -- named Sawyer -- who had sold the trailers to the Roeses. The Sawyers owned residential properties in the Kansas City area and lived in permanent homes, and it was unclear whether they were settled Travelers or just local, opportunistic con artists. But investigators did learn family members had been involved in several travel trailer sale transactions and that at least one member of the family was using multiple I.D.'s and operating an unlicensed home improvement business.

The next victims Sharon found were a North Kansas City family named Sharp. She spotted their Kentucky Traveler trailer parked near an apartment project and asked the project's maintenance supervisor if he knew who owned the coach. Not only did he know the owners, but he also was familiar with the trailer scam, and he said he believed the Sharps were victims. Sharon gave the man her telephone number, and a short time later, the Sharps called her. They told Sharon the couple they bought their trailer from said they needed money badly because they had serious health problems, including heart attacks, and were totally disabled and unable to find jobs. The Sharps reported the couple said they were living on food stamps.

Several other families who said they were victims of trailer sales scams provided Sharon with details of their purchases.

Armed with data gathered by Sharon, Knox and its own team of investigators, the Missouri attorney general's office began issuing restraining orders to various Travelers -- and the Sawyers -- prohibiting them from misrepresenting the trailers they offered for sale. That action prompted WDAF-TV in Kansas City to broadcast its own investigation of the Traveler scams, and the *Kansas City Star* finally published an article about the sales scam.

Ironically, during the investigations, Knox's son accepted one of the best known Traveler trailers as a trade-in on a new RV. The coach was damaged, so Truman Knox volunteered to drive to Elkhart, Indiana, and purchase replacement parts for the unit. He figured that while he was there, he would learn as much as he could about the manufacturer and its operation. Since Knox knew every RV company in America was in desperate need of dealers due to the current nation-wide recession that had forced hundreds of dealerships to close their doors, he told a representative at the trailer plant that he was interested in stocking the company's brands in Kansas City. The factory rep informed Knox that the owner of the company was not available, and he would not be able to provide Knox with a dealership informational packet without the owner's permission.

"He wanted to ship it to me," Knox reported later, "but I told him I'd be back in a couple of weeks, and I'd pick it up. When I went back, everyone was busy because several Travelers were there picking up trailers. The owner said he was going to be tied up two or three hours, so he couldn't talk with me. I said I would wait. I sat there for a few minutes, and the owner sent word to me that he just couldn't handle any more dealers at that time."

In September, Knox and the writer toured the Elkhart, Indiana, area together, comparing Travelers' license plate numbers with a list of those recorded in Kansas City and taking note of the Travelers who were at their three primarily trailer suppliers' plants and at area campgrounds. They also stopped at the factory of a new company -- Stateside Homes, which was building Vagabond and Stateside travel trailers for sale to Travelers. At the plant, the two men noticed a seal-coating truck with Michigan plates driven by a tall man about forty with salt-and-pepper hair. A sign on the truck advertised "Ted Lovell, Professional Seal-Coating." The writer would learn later that Lovell was the brother of Traveler Eddie Lovell, a friend of Jimmy Burke's who had married a Canadian Traveler named Suzy Hart but had left her and was then living with his parents in Wilmington, Delaware. Ted Lovell was, at that time, sought by police in Michigan for swindling a woman out of several hundred dollars in a roof sealing scam.

Knox and the writer went inside the Stateside plant, and Knox asked the owner, Bob Wilson, if he were interested in placing his brands with Knox's Missouri RV dealership. Flashing a big smile, Wilson answered, "Absolutely!" He told Knox the dealer's price for a 35-foot park model trailer with double tipout extensions, air conditioning, sofa and chair was $8,000. Dealer price for a 32-foot travel trailer with TV antenna, air conditioning, sofa and chair was $6,200.

Knox said, "The problem is, I hear you are supplying trailers to the Irish and Scottish Travelers."

Wilson frowned and shook his head regretfully. "What can I say? Yeah, I won't lie about it. We sell to Travelers once in a while."

Stateside Homes built one or two trailers daily for several months before closing its doors. Members of the Irish Traveler clan told the writer the company's prices were too high.


By fall, partly due to the coming of cool weather and partly because of the Missouri attorney general's stepped-up enforcement efforts, most Travelers had packed up their sealing/paving equipment and trailers and left the Kansas City area for friendlier climates. Irish Travelers moved south into the Rio Grande Valley of Texas and to central Florida. Some Scottish Travelers also traveled to Florida, but many headed west to Arizona and southern California. The majority of English Travelers pointed their rigs either toward south Texas, stopping along the way in Spiro, Oklahoma, to visit relatives, or to southern Louisiana, where they would discover police officers waiting for them.

Truman Knox said, "What we've done here is generate a lot of heat for those people. Maybe we can keep something going so that we can really make things hot for them when they come back next spring."

In spite of the injunction issued to them, the Sawyers continued to sell travel trailers in Kansas City, using aliases. But Sharon's persistent efforts exposed them and, for the rest of that year, the family did not offer any RVs for sale.

Early in October, Sharon told the writer that since mid-May, she had found seventy-two travel trailers being sold in the Kansas City area by Travelers; by the end of that month, the figure would total eighty-seven. The writer said to her, "I know why I'm involved in this. Why are *you* involved?"

Sharon laughed. "Everybody asks me that. I'll tell you why. It's like I said earlier, I never dreamed we'd get our money back from Rose and Ed Carroll, and I'm grateful we did, but I just don't think it's right for the Travelers to cheat people and for people not to know they're doing it, and I'd like to see the cheating stopped."

"That's a good motive," the writer said.

Sharon responded, "I've been praised by every legal agency I've called, but except for the attorney general's office, the dummies won't do anything themselves!"

She paused and added, "I've really gotten depressed a few times this summer when I couldn't get people to listen to me, and I thought, 'To heck with all this!' Then I'd talk to somebody who would boost my spirits again, and so I just kept going."

The writer asked Sharon if she knew he was planning to write a book about the Travelers. "No, but I could sure add some information to it!" she answered.

"You already have. I've got a tape recorder going on you."

She laughed. "Oh, that's nothing. I've got one going on you, too!" They both laughed.

In mid-October, the writer was asked to meet with Angela Bennett at the attorney general's office in Kansas City. The writer had addressed a consumer fraud seminar in Austin, Texas, for the state's intelligence division of the Department of Public Safety, and he was on his way to northern Missouri to visit the plant where Travelers bought their lightning rod equipment. While in Kansas City, he dialed Edward and Rose Carroll's telephone number and, when Rose answered the phone, he told her his name.

"Do you know who I am?"

There was a long pause, and finally Rose answered, "Yeah."

"I'm in Kansas City doing some research for a book I'm writing about the Irish Travelers, and I was hoping that you and Ed..."

"I don't have nothin' to do with 'em," Rose insisted. "Don't *want* nothin' to do with 'em. Not involved in any way. Just want to try and live. Don't want any problems with 'em; honest to God, I don't." She started to sob. Then, crying more loudly, she asked, "Would you just leave me and my family alone, please? Would you?"

"I don't understand," the writer said.

Crying harder, she said, "Would you please leave us alone? We haven't done anything...(sobbing)...to anybody. *Please* leave us alone!"

"You aren't willing to talk with me, then?"

"No! I haven't done nothin'. I don't want to be destroyed and have my children destroyed. Please!"

The writer answered, "I don't want to do that. I don't think you *have* done anything except...."

"Talk to anybody else if you want. I haven't done nothin'. Please?

We just try to live every day. We don't even...We don't even belong to nobody. Nothin'. We ain't doin' nothin'."

"You don't take part in what the Travelers do anymore, then?"

"No, sir. No way. Don't want nothin' to do with 'em. Don't want my family to have nothin' to do with 'em. Absolutely not. Have nothin' to do with 'em."

"Would you be willing to..."

"No, no, I don't want nothin'." She stopped crying.

"Please, let me ask you this: Would you be willing to talk with me on an off-the-record basis?"

"I don't want to talk to nobody. (Sobbing again.) Honest to God, I don't. I don't want nothin', please."

"Okay, I understand," the writer said. She stopped crying again.

"Are you gonna cause us any problem?" she asked.

"No. Absolutely not."

"You give me your word?"

"Absolutely."

"Honest to God? I don't want to have nothin' to do with them people. You don't know what we went through." She started sobbing again.

"How long has it been since you've been involved with them?"

"I *know* them. They come and go. I say hello. I don't get involved, though. I mean, you can't say you don't know people, sir. I'm not gonna lie. I know them. I ain't gonna say to them, 'I hate you. Go away,' but we just don't get involved with 'em."

Rose stopped sobbing again and became calm. "They come and stay here. They leave. We say hello. We try to be in the middle with everybody, just not involved, though. Honest to God, we are. (Resumes sobbing.) I don't know what to do or where to go to hide. It's like we're lookin' for a concentration camp someplace. (Crying now.) I don't know what to do. I'm gonna take a nervous breakdown with it. I can't believe it! (Crying more loudly.) I can't talk to you."

"Is Ed there?"

"No."

"Well, I'm sorry if I've disturbed you. I didn't mean to do that. I just wanted to try to get with you to sit down and..."

"No, sir. I don't have nothin' that could help you. I don't want nothin' to do with them people. I ain't sayin' one word for 'em or against 'em. I don't want nothin' to do with 'em. Please understand that."

"I do. I understand." She stopped crying once more.

"We try to live here like everyday people. We go south in the winter, yes. But we don't go with The People. We don't go around 'em. Once in a while we go down because we can't work, but we aren't tryin' to do nothin'. Honest to God, we aren't."

"You haven't been associated with them for some time, then?"

"That's right. That's right. Only when they come and stay here and I see them. But I don't have nothin' to do with 'em. For four-teen years, we've been here."

The writer said, "I certainly don't want to cause you any prob-lem."

"Well, I hope you won't," she responded. "You *can*! I know you can and you know you can."

The writer had begun to believe what Rose said. Perhaps, he thought to himself, the Carrolls were trying to settle in Kansas City and operate legitimate businesses. Then Rose began lying.

"We sold a trailer this spring. You know that. We gave the people their money back if they didn't want it (the trailer). The woman signed a statement that she lied about everything. I *have* the state-ment. She signed it in front of my lawyer. I asked her just to leave us alone, but all summer long, it's just been goin' on. Threats to my family, to us."

"I wasn't aware of that."

She started crying again. "Well, nobody is. What difference does it make? Who would care about us anyway? What leg would we have to stand on? I have no rights."

"I care," the writer said.

"Well, I'll see if you care later on because you're in the position to destroy me, my children, my family, everything we've ever cared about."

A few years later, Rose Carroll joined Fort Worth-based Irish Traveler Mary Donahue in establishing an RV dealership near Mission, Texas, and not long after that, she opened Rose's RV Sales three miles west of Mission on Highway 83. Edward operates Mister C's Asphalt Sealing from the same location and not only joined the South Texas Better Business Bureau in 1989, but also participated in its special customer assistance program. From 1993, when the BBB opened a file on Rose's dealership, through most of 1995, no consumer complaints were made to the bureau about her business practices. Only one complaint was filed against Mister C's, and that was resolved satisfactorily, according to the bureau.

Although Rose's RV sells primarily the trailer brands ordinarily associated with Traveler sales scams, the dealership apparently is a legitimate operation providing repair service to its customers. Rose and Edward operate their businesses during fall and winter months and travel in cooler climates most of the rest of the year. In September 1995, Rose and Ed were parked in a campground east of Elkhart, Indiana, with another Irish Traveler family. The trailer in which they lived had a "For Sale" sign on it, and they were towing it with a Mister C's asphalt sealing truck.

# 20

# All That Glitters

A second series of articles about travel trailer sales scams was published in the July 1981 edition of *Trailer Life* magazine. That series not only revealed, for the first time, the structure of the Irish Traveler clan, but it also contained excerpts from interviews with a young Traveler identified as Jim Murphy.

"Jim Murphy learned to steal by watching his mother and favorite aunt shoplift from department stores when he was only seven years old," the magazine series stated. "By the time he was ten, his father had taught him how to swindle people out of their savings by working a series of sophisticated confidence games. When he was eleven, he earned between $600 and $800 a week selling 75-cent handbags in bars for twenty or thirty dollars each after telling his customers the purses were handmade by his poor, widowed mother who was trying desperately to raise eight small children by herself. By the age of fifteen, he was traveling the country on his own, paving driveways and sealing roofs with worthless materials and selling cheap travel trailers for thousands of dollars more than their market value.

The series continued, "Jim is twenty-one years old now. He is part of a clan of itinerant con artists and thieves whose members call themselves Irish Travelers. Like most of the clan, he grew up believing that anyone who was not a member of the Travelers was simply a ripe, potential victim. Jim specializes in selling misrepresented travel trailers to unsuspecting buyers and, at the same time, swindles homeowners with his driveway and roof-sealer scams. But like most other Irish Travelers, he also delves occasionally into other illegal activities: RV theft, shoplifting, insurance fraud, tax fraud and welfare fraud."

The young man in the articles was, obviously, Jimmy Burke.

Once again, reaction to the magazine series was immediate, and widespread. A letter from Robert J. Ryan, president of the Suffolk County Police Emerald Society, praised the articles and said, "Hopefully, the public will become more knowledgeable and will be more willing to complain and testify because of your articles."

But he added, "I did note, however, one area on which I feel you missed the boat. Nowhere in any article did you ever state that the activities of the Irish Travelers were not representative of Irishmen in general...I feel it is your responsibility to see that there is no confusion or generalization made in reference to any group."

Kevin Mischler, an agent with the Indiana Department of Revenue, revealed the articles were quite interesting to him because they provided a good foundation for his suspicions that tax fraud was being perpetrated as part of the trailer sales scam. He said he had already begun to build a file of potential tax code violators, and he intended to begin his own investigations immediately. "In order to be exempt from paying Indiana sales tax," he reported, "you have to be a bonafide dealer. If you are an individual coming to Indiana to pick up a trailer, you are subject to Indiana sales tax." Also, he said, by failing to report their correct states of residence on Indiana vehicle registration forms, Travelers unlawfully prevented the collection of state sales taxes from them.

From his prison cell, Jimmy Burke penned a brief note to the writer: "The response to your magazine article has already started among the Travelers. I called my uncle Doug last week, and my mom just happened to be there. Me and her talked until my five minutes were up, but we didn't really talk -- it was mostly her yelling at me. Yes, she knew who Jim Murphy was.

"Her and Dad were in Georgia last weekend. They went to see my brother and sister (Paul and Peggy in prison), but they didn't even bother to come see me. That really hurt me, but I'll get over it. I also received no letters or money from any of the Travelers in the past two or three weeks, whereas I was receiving two or three letters a day along with occasional money. Oh well, what can I say? I also quit writing to any of my family or relatives since then."

The writer's wife sent Jimmy a small check and shipped him a carton of cigarettes for trading to other inmates, a new pair of shoes and batteries for his watch and portable radio.

From Illinois, Des Plaines Detective Norman Klopp reported that Travelers had just hit his area hard with driveway sealing scams, trailer sales misrepresentations and other swindles. "We have a public relations officer who is constantly putting something in the local newspapers about all these scams, and yet people still fall for their sales pitches," Klopp said. "Now we've got a male and two female Travelers going around doing daylight burglaries of homes while people are working in their back yards. We know they're connected to the same people who are selling travel trailers from every empty lot along River Road, but so far, we haven't been able to find them so we can arrest them."

From Louisiana, a production supervisor for Gulf Oil Company said a small RV dealership near Baton Rouge was selling most of the trailer brands mentioned in the *Trailer Life* article. "I was supposed to go back tomorrow and negotiate with that fellow on a Kentucky Traveler trailer, but after reading those articles, I got kind of skeptical. He's got those travel trailers right next door to his residence, but I don't believe he's what you'd call a fly-by-night operation other than the fact that he's selling all those brands at ridiculously low prices." That business, the writer had already learned, was one of the few dealerships claimed by Marauder Travelers; it had no service facilities. Several years later, the wife of the owner and his daughter would scream at the writer over the telephone following publication of another magazine article about trailer scams. They informed him he was going to be sued "for everything you own." The women refused to identify themselves, but the writer was able to learn their identities anyway.

Meanwhile, reports poured in that Scottish Travelers George, Mary and Edith Watson were offering trailers for sale in New Orleans. Louisiana authorities were alerted, and the Watsons left the state.

Mike Gleason, an investigator with the New York attorney general's office, reported cautiously: "I have some experience with -- how should I say this -- with your traveling families." Numerous elderly New York individuals were swindled regularly by them, Gleason said. "In the area of home improvement and blacktop scams, we try every spring to saturate the newspapers with articles warning people to beware. Sometimes, we get county districts of attorney involved, but in this state, the attorney general's office enforces only civil cases in the area of consumer fraud, and with civil suits, by the time we can serve papers on the Travelers, they're gone." Convinced the Travelers were violating federal interstate commerce laws, he tried, without success, to convince the Federal Trade Commission to open its own investigation.

He added, "Public education is a help. Maybe, that way, we can reach fifty per cent of the potential victims. Quite frankly, a lot of people don't complain. There are two reasons for that. First, they're elderly and easily intimidated or he's too embarrassed, and second, some of the swindlers appear to do a good job, so the victims don't know they've been swindled for several months."

Asked why he was so cautious in talking about the Travelers, Gleason said, "There is an indication that certain members of the families have settled down and are doing good work in blacktopping and home repair. One has to be careful not to indict an entire group of people."

From Saskatchewan, Canada, came reports that Travelers had crossed the border and were operating both home repair and travel trailer sales scams.

Frank Tiebout, chief investigator with the Ohio Bureau of Motor Vehicles received an interesting call from an investigator in Alaska. Tiebout reported, "The Travelers are now sending to Alaska for vehicle registrations that are mailed back to them. Then, they move into a locality and tell people they were following construction crews around the country, that they were in Alaska but now that they've returned to the lower forty-eight, they don't want the trailer anymore. They're using fictitious addresses when they try to get registrations out of Alaska, and Alaska wants to put a stop to it."

He added, "Boy, they're something else! They think of all the angles."

During that summer, renegade Irish Traveler Joe Dougherty teamed up with bank robber Terry Lee Conner after Conner was mistakenly allowed to walk away from Maricopa County jail in Phoenix. The two began robbing banks in the Midwest, frequently taking bank managers hostage and forcing them to open vaults as the banks opened. They were arrested in March 1983 in Chicago and sent to prison in Oklahoma. They escaped and were subsequently featured on one of the first episodes of *America's Most Wanted* TV show. They robbed banks for eighteen months before Dougherty was caught in a laundromat in Antioch, California, in late 1986. Conner was sentenced to 249 years plus two life sentences, consecutively. Apparently, both Dougherty and Conner are still in federal prisons.

The publishers of *Trailer Life* magazine were notified by an attorney representing Marauder Travelers that civil action was being contemplated due to publication of recent articles naming the company and its products. Response from the magazine's attorney, Corinne S. Shulman, was immediate. In a letter to Indiana attorney Thomas P. Loughlin, Shulman said, "As you may be aware, the articles published recently in our client's magazines (*Trailer Life* and *RV Dealer*) were follow-ups on articles which appeared in *Trailer Life* in June and July 1980. I assume that your client did not turn over to you a copy of those articles...

"It has always been our client's policy to fairly cover all sides of an issue, and we feel that has been done in this case, as the published interview (with Marauder executives) appears to cover all of the points you wanted featured. However, in line with our client's policy, if you feel more is required, we are certainly willing to consider printing either your letter or a letter directly from your client in the Mailbox section of the two magazines together with our client's explanation. Alternatively, we are open to any other suggestion you have...

"Two things should be made clear at the outset: My client will not have its future course of editorial content dictated by your client, and if in light of that firm policy, you intend to apply for an injunction, I would suggest you do so somewhere where the First Amendment does not apply. I find it difficult to believe that Indiana fits that description. I am more than willing to amicably resolve this matter, but would appreciate a cessation of meaningless threats."

Two months later, owners of Marauder Travelers consented to be interviewed again in spite of advice from their attorney that they not do so.

From Maryland, county detective sergeant Wayne Marshall reported that the entire area around Washington, D.C. had been hit hard by a wide range of Irish and Scottish Traveler scams, including vehicle insurance fraud, TV sales swindles, home improvement scams, pigeon drops, trailer sales, quick-change currency flimflams, home rental swindles, welfare fraud and bank examiner schemes. Travelers had even been caught linking their RV electrical systems to outdoor lights at shopping centers -- in effect, stealing electricity while they parked overnight!

"We've had problems with Gypsies -- primarily Mitchells -- and the Travelers for the last ten years," Marshall said. "They usually stop here in the late fall and early spring while they're traveling between the northern states and Florida. During those periods, we're flooded with calls about blacktopping, roof sealing and money exchange flimflams, but by the time we're called, the culprits are gone."

He added, "Every spring, we get reports on four or five pigeon drops. That means there are probably fifteen or twenty others that weren't reported. Those and the phony repairs to elderly peoples' houses. Two years ago, the Travelers sold a woman a squirrel deflector, if you can believe that! She paid them $3,000, and they nailed a four-inch piece of tin across the top of her roof to keep squirrels from getting into her attic. Another Traveler went around with a walkie-talkie and false I.D. and told women he was from the IRS and that the banks at which the women had cashed their Social Security checks had been hit with counterfeit currency, and he wanted to take their money back to the bank so he could check the serial numbers. One woman gave him $800!"

Alerted to automobile insurance fraud schemes, detectives staked out Travelers they thought were involved. "A few days ago," Marshall reported, "one of them bought a $43,000 Mercedes and also an identical one that had been totaled for $5,000. We're sure they're going to try something like an insurance scam with those cars, so we're just waiting to see what they do."

A variation of the TV sales scam also was being used in the D.C. area, the detective said. "Instead of saying they were selling last year's floor models at department stores, they said they had a truckload of TVs out of Florida and were overstocked. They collected cash payments and sent their victims to a semi-truck parked nearby to pick out their TV sets, and while the victims waited for the truck doors to be opened, the scammers got into a car and drove away."

Another Traveler swindled a D.C. resident out of $25,000 by collecting a security deposit and two months' rent on a large, very expensive suburban home. At the same time, Travelers known to be camped in Maryland in their travel trailers were collecting welfare payments from Philadelphia.

Marshall said, "Last week, personal friends called me about the articles in *Trailer Life* magazine. They had been looking at travel trailers, and they made about forty calls after seeing so many nearly new trailers listed for sale in the newspaper classified section. "Every trailer they went to look at was being sold exactly the way it was described in the magazine -- the family had come on hard times, or someone was having a baby or getting married or there had been a death in the family."

In September, a 33-year-old Irish Traveler woman named Gloria
Williams was arrested in Indianapolis for trying to bilk All-State
Insurance Company out of $18,785. She claimed a fur coat, a rare
bird and an Oriental rug were stolen from her, but investigations
revealed they had been sold.

A few weeks earlier, Irish Traveler Jim Carroll stole a travel trailer
in Tennessee, renamed and retitled it in Alabama and then towed it
to Illinois, where he bought an insurance policy on it before selling
it to a family in Bloomington for $5,000. Carroll, who died a few
years later, was one of the writer's information sources within the
Irish Traveler clan. The day Carroll sold the stolen trailer, he reported to police that it had been stolen from him overnight from in front
of his motel room. He submitted an insurance claim for $7,200 and
was reimbursed for his loss a week later. On his insurance forms, he
had listed the writer's name, address and telephone number in a
block reserved for personal references.

When the family who bought the trailer from Carroll tried to buy
license plates for it, the coach's vehicle identification number showed
up on the department of motor vehicles' computer as stolen from
Tennessee. Police confiscated the trailer.

Meanwhile, Carroll's insurance claim was among dozens being
reviewed by investigators with the National Insurance Crime Prevention Institute. When they ran the VIN through their computers, they
learned for the first time that the coach had been reported stolen
twice -- once in Tennessee and later in Illinois. Two different clients
of the institute paid theft claims totaling more than $15,000. Inves-
tigators were unable to find Carroll to question him, partly because
the address he had listed on the insurance application form had
turned out to be a motel room; his telephone number was an answering service. The only other lead to his whereabouts was the name,
address and telephone number of the writer, so investigators imme-

diately began probing into the writer's background.

On October 19, the writer received a call from a representative of the insurance crime prevention agency who identified himself simply as Mister Samuelson. Samuelson asked if the writer were familiar with an individual named Jim Carroll.

"Yes, I am," admitted the writer. "Why are you asking?"

"He listed your name as a personal reference on an insurance application form," Samuelson said. "Am I correct in understanding that you are a book author and an editor with *Trailer Life* magazine and that you have written several articles -- and maybe even a book -- about scam artists?"

The writer laughed. "It sounds as if you've done your homework. That's correct, except the book you mentioned has not been written. Why are you asking about Jim Carroll?"

"Do you know where I can find Mr. Carroll?"

The writer laughed again. "Apparently Jim has pulled off some sort of insurance scam. Is that right?"

The investigator was silent a few moments and then answered, "We're investigating several cases in which individuals apparently sold items and then filed insurance claims, saying those items were stolen."

The writer said, "And you think Jim Carroll put in an insurance claim for something that he sold and later said was stolen?"

"Something like that," admitted Samuelson.

The writer said, "Well, right now, Jim Carroll could be anywhere in the United States or Canada. So far as I know, he doesn't have a home. He's a professional con artist. What else can I tell you?"

Samuelson replied, "That's all for now. Someone else from the institute probably will be in touch with you later, though."

A few days later, a Midwest-based investigator with the insurance crime institute named Joe Kemper called. After brief introductory conversation, he told the writer, "We recently ran a sting operation in Marion County, Indiana, and over a space of several weeks, we recovered about one million dollars in stolen merchandise. My job starts now, trying to find out how much of that was from insurance ripoffs where people sold the stuff and then reported it to police as stolen before turning in insurance claims."

The writer said he could not verify that the con artists he was researching were involved in those specific scams. "These people call themselves Travelers," he told Kemper. "Have you ever heard of the Irish Travelers or the Scottish Travelers?"

"Are they like gypsies?"

"Yes."

Kemper said, "I was over in one of the adjoining (Indiana) counties with a state police detective, and I told him about a slip-and-fall insurance case that I had going in Indianapolis, and he said, 'Well, we've got some gypsy families that came through here, and they were pulling that kind of thing.' He said he thought they were just clumsy and were falling down all over town."

The writer pledged that although he knew nothing about specific individuals who were engaged in those types of insurance fraud schemes, he would make inquiries the next time he talked with one of his contacts within the clans. "But please understand," the writer emphasized, "I can't tell you who my contacts are or where you can find them, and I won't do anything else that will put them in jeopardy."

"I understand," Kemper replied, "but can you tell me this: Are any of those people ever involved in insurance fraud?"

"Yes," said the writer. He told Kemper about the Travelers' automobile insurance fraud scheme and added, "I've heard some of them do pull slip-and-fall scams, but I don't know anyone who actually has done it."

Kemper said, "I realize a lot of the insurance companies are pretty flaky when it comes to settling claims. They'll settle them as quickly as they can if they think the claim is a nuisance. But those individuals have to be someplace they can be contacted by an insurance adjuster, either by telephone or by mail. How do they handle that?" The writer told him and then asked how suspected insurance frauds were investigated.

Kemper said he and other investigators filed names and claims details with a national indexing bureau so that records could be searched for similarities. "Any time a fraud suspect has an insurance claim, it's recorded there. So I get a copy of the incidents that list the dates, the names of other persons involved, the insurance company and how much was paid. Then we establish a chart of incidents in chronological order and make comparisons with insurance claims. I have access to the claim files of just about every insurance company in the country."

He added, "The thing we noticed on the slip-and-fall incidents was that the same people were filing maybe four claims each in the same day at four different locations. They even duplicated hospital reports and used each other as witnesses, following each other from place to place posing as victims and witnesses. It literally grows from one person to a bunch of them."

The writer told Kemper how he could acquire copies of the *Trailer Life* articles, and a few days later, Kemper called again. "These articles have really stirred my interest," he said. "My God, I can see the possibilities on something like this. Tracking those people (Travelers) down is going to be a trip for someone, though."

In November, Jim Carroll telephoned the writer's office. "I hear you want to talk to me," he said, referring vaguely to the Irish Traveler communication network.

"I sure do," the writer said. "You used my name as a personal reference on an insurance application form, and an insurance investigator called me with a bunch of questions. What's it all about? Did you pull an insurance scam?"

Carroll chuckled. "Yeah. Collected some big bucks on it, too. Are the cops lookin' for me?"

"I don't really know," the writer answered, "but I think so. I wish you hadn't used my name as a reference."

"Sorry about that," said Carroll, "but the agent wouldn't sell me a policy without it, and you were the only country person I could think of on the spur of the moment. I didn't think they'd contact you. I won't do it anymore."

"Okay," the writer said. "I've agreed to keep your identity confidential, and I expect you to respect my reputation."

"Yeah, I get the message," Carroll answered. "Is that all you wanted?"

"I'd like to know the details of that scam, Jim."

Carroll laughed. "I'll bet you do. I think it would be better for both of us if I told you about it another time. What you don't know can't hurt me, if you know what I mean."

Two years later, following two near-fatal heart attacks and less than a year before another attack killed him, Carroll told the writer details on how he collected from an insurance company for the trailer that he had stolen and then sold. The two men did not speak again, and it was five years before the writer learned about Carroll's death.

Illinois state crime analyst Terry Getsay was beginning to build a nation-wide reputation for his research on scam artists such as Gypsies and Travelers. Although tending to classify all itinerant swindlers as *gypsies,* Getsay's detailed file on individuals, their arrest records and their activities became an invaluable resource for law enforcement agencies all over the country. Before he retired and founded his own intelligence consulting business in Evans City, Pennsylvania, Getsay provided American law enforcement agencies with thick three-ring binders filled with information. During the 1980s, most books and magazine articles about gypsies or scam artists referred to Getsay's expertise. In 1983, he was asked to testify before the U.S. Senate's Special Committee on Aging; his testimony was titled

"Combatting Frauds Against the Elderly." Following his retirement, the key role he played in tracking swindlers of all kind was assumed by a woman analyst named Lex Bittner, who continues to provide the same informational services to police officers.

On October 27, two separate newswire articles from Washington, D.C., were published by newspapers around the country. One was a United Press International article that stated, "Big-city law enforcement officials say career criminals cause most of the crime in the United States, even though there are relatively few of those offenders." Testifying before a subcommittee of the Senate Judiciary Committee, the lawmen said "If the few career criminals were locked up for long periods, crime rates would decline drastically."

The second article, filed by the Associated Press, quoted the new Federal Trade Commission chairman, James C. Miller, as saying at a news conference that the FTC should stop protecting consumers from defective products. "Consumers are not as gullible as many people and many regulators tend to think they are," he explained.

Miller was quoted as saying the "imperfect products" should be available because consumers "have different preferences for defect avoidance" and that "those who have a low aversion to risk, relative to money, will be most likely to purchase cheap, unreliable products."

Early in December, two English Travelers using fake identities approached a prospective pigeon they had studied for several days. Their mark, Roy Carney (not his real name), was a salesman for a New Orleans boat company, and the Travelers had learned about him from a brief newspaper item in the business section of the *New Orleans Times-Picayune* which noted that 66-year-old Carney had won honors as his employer's top salesman.

The Travelers told Carney his name had been given to them by mutual friends who said Carney might be interested in a business venture of theirs. One of the men said, "We have recently acquired several bars of almost pure gold that we'd like to sell. Our friends indicated you might be interested in buying them."

Carney frowned thoughtfully. "Where did you get them?"

"We'd rather not say," one of the man answered. "Let's just say we have an uncle who works aboard a ship that just sailed for Mexico."

Carney smiled. "In other words, they're stolen."

The man held up both hands in a cautionary manner. "I didn't say that."

"Where's the gold?" Carney asked.

One man opened a briefcase, and the other lifted out a bar that was inscribed "South African Gold, 32 oz., troy weight." He handed the bar to Carney along with a small hand drill and said, "Go ahead. Drill into the bar anyplace. Then take the shavings to a jeweler and ask him to examine it."

Carney drilled into the bar just as the English Traveler suggested, and later that day he took the shavings to a jeweler he knew and trusted. The jeweler told him the shavings was gold of a high purity and estimated the value of the bar Carney described at nearly $10,000. The following day, Carney received a telephone call at his office from one of the two Travelers.

"Did you have the shavings examined?" Carney was asked.

"Yes."

"Are you interested in buying the gold from us?"

"Yes. How much do you want for it?"

"Two thousand dollars for each bar," he was told.

"How many bars do you have?"

"Seven."

Carney took a small calculator from his shirt pocket and entered some numbers. "I'll give you $12,000 for all seven," he offered.

"I don't know," answered the other man. "Hold on a second. I'll have to ask my partner." Carney could hear voices at the other end arguing quietly. Then the conversation ceased, and the other man told Carney, "Sorry, we can't let them go for that."

"Then it's no deal," said Carney.

"Okay, hold on again." Carney could hear more arguing, and he smiled to himself. All seven gold bars, he knew, would be worth about $70,000, and he knew just how to market them for their full value.

The voice returned. "Okay, $12,000, but we've gotta have it in cash. You understand that, don't you?"

"Yeah," said Carney, his face split by a wide grin. "I understand."

The men made arrangements to meet that afternoon at a drive-in restaurant on the outskirts of New Orleans, and there, Carney paid the Travelers $12,000 in $100 bills and took possession of the gold bars, which the other men stacked in the trunk of his car for him. Atop the stack was the bar Carney had drilled, the small hole in its facing clearly identifying it.

"Give me your drill so I can check out the other bars," Carney said.

The other two men looked surprised. One of them moved close to Carney and said in a quiet but angry voice, "Listen, shithead, you already ripped us off for a couple of thousand on this deal. Now ya got the nerve to ask us for our drill? I oughta kill you right here. C'mon, Tom, give this clown back his money, and let's take our bars somewhere else."

The other Traveler gripped his partner's arms and said, "Easy, Ed. Don't cause no trouble. You know what happened the last time you got mad." He turned to Carney and explained, "My friend lets his temper get away from him sometimes. It's okay. But we left our drill at home. It didn't occur to us you'd want it. If you want to drill holes in all the bars, that's okay. I understand. But we'll have to give your money back and postpone this deal to another time."

Ed said, "Yeah, and in the meantime, we'll look for another "buyer.""

Carney, clearly frightened, but more afraid of losing his bargain gold bars, answered, "No, I trust you. A deal's a deal." He closed the lid of his trunk, got into the car and drove away.

The two Travelers looked at each other and grinned.

At his home, Carney drilled holes in six of the bars and discovered that they were some kind of hard metal overlaid with a thin veneer of gold plating. He examined the seventh bar -- the one with the drill hole already in it -- and realized it was not the same bar he had tested the day before.

Then he called the New Orleans police department.

# 21

# Spare the Rod

Sitting at a beat-up table on the edge of a work area in the lightning rod manufacturing plant, the writer knew he would not get very much useful information from the president of the company. The man, Norman Roberts (not his real name), was affable enough, but he was almost incoherent, and three times during the interview, he stood up abruptly, walked to a nearby cabinet and poured liquid from a bottle into the coffee cup that he held constantly in one hand.

The writer had driven to Maryville, a small town in the northwestern section of Missouri, to learn more about Roberts Lightning Protection Company, a manufacturing firm that its president readily admitted sold its products to members of the Scottish and Irish Travelers. Both ethnic clans had started installing fake and partial lightning protection systems on farm houses and barns during the late 1940s. They misrepresented the systems as providing complete protection against the ravages of lightning storms when, in fact, most of their work was so shoddy and incomplete that the lightning rods they installed were actually more likely to attract lightning than protect a building from it.

During the 1950s and 1960s, numerous newspaper articles were published around the country warning residents not to fall victim to the lightning rod swindles. Those articles, as much as anything else, focused a great deal of unwelcome attention on the clans, although at that time, the swindlers were thought to be part of a relatively small network of Williamson family con artists. Gradually, Travelers switched most of their attention from *rods*, as they called that work, to driveways, roofs, travel trailers and their broad array of home repair frauds. Throughout the upper Midwest and West, however, lightning rod scams continued to flourish from time to time.

Lightning rod manufacturers, engineers, contractors and vendors formed their own industry association, called the Lightning Protection Institute, in an effort to set equipment standards and expose disreputable business practices. By the 1980s, the institute consisted of about 150 members representing virtually every major producer and wholesaler of lightning rods in America. But Roberts Protection Company, which had begun selling equipment to Travelers in 1945, refused either to join the association or adhere to its standards. At one point, the Missouri company's general manager, Harold Van Sickle, resigned following a dispute with Norman Roberts over sales practices and opened a competing manufacturing operation elsewhere in Maryville.

When the writer arrived at the Roberts plant late in 1981, he told Norman Roberts he was researching a book about the Irish and Scottish Travelers. Roberts invited the writer into the plant, promising him a tour of the facilities and offering to share whatever information he could.

The writer took a small tape recorder out of his pocket and asked, "Is it all right if I record our conversation."

"No, not just yet," answered Roberts. "Maybe later. Let's see how it goes."

Roberts told the writer that he was proud of his business relationship with the Travelers, and he said, "They do a wonderful job of installing our rods." He added that the Williamsons were particularly interesting people and that he thought a book should be written about them. Between sips from his ever-present coffee cup, Roberts related stories about individual travelers: how Robert Sherlock had beat a rap in Illinois on income tax evasion; how some Williamsons swindled Zza Zza Gabor by treating her Beverly Hills driveway with pink sealer that was so diluted it washed off and ran into the gutter before they could drive out of the neighborhood; that the western Williamsons were headed by two brothers, Ralph and Alfred Williamson, who headquartered in Oklahoma, and by an individual named "California Tom" Williamson; how Cowboy John Sherlock of Chicago was one of America's best lightning rod and driveway sealer scam artists.

Asked by the writer why the company was not a member of the lightning rod trade association, Roberts at first said he had never been invited to join. Then he claimed a federal investigation was underway because institute members were trying to force him to join. He said the institute wanted to charge him $3,600 per month, plus ten per cent of his gross sales if he did join, and the Federal Trade Commission was prepared to cite the institute's members for restraint of trade.

Suddenly, without explanation, Roberts left and walked quickly toward the plant's office area. He returned about fifteen minutes later, slouched into a chair and stared intently at the writer. When the writer asked him additional questions about his company and his sales to Travelers, Roberts remained silent. Then he said, "Would you like to tell me who you really are?"

"What do you mean?" the writer asked.

"You're a private investigator, aren't you?"

The writer laughed. "No, I'm exactly who I said I was. I'm researching a book about the Travelers."

"No you're not. I've had someone checking you out. You're a private detective from Indiana."

The writer insisted he was not a private detective, and he offered to provide names of law enforcement officers in Missouri who would verify that. Roberts rejected the writer's offer, claiming police officers would say anything to safeguard another investigator's undercover work. His face was red and flushed. "I have my own sources within law enforcement," he insisted, "and they're at work for me right now."

The writer stood. He decided Roberts was in an unstable emotional state. "I think it's time for me to leave."

"I think you're right," said Roberts. "But before you do, let me tell you one more thing. The Williamsons will do anything I ask. And if I asked them to take out a contract on you, they'd do it. I'm not saying I'd ask them for that, but I just might."

Outside, the writer walked to the van he was driving. The vehicle had been provided to him by Coachmen Van Conversions and Chevrolet for a series of trailer-towing tests that would later be made part of several magazine articles. Inside the van, the writer's wife was waiting. "What's going on?" she asked.

"What do you mean?" the writer asked.

"While you were inside, two people came out and went behind the van. They copied down the license plate number and left. Then a police car drove past twice."

The writer started the vehicle and looked in his rearview mirror. "The police car is back," he said as he pulled away from the curb. A Nodaway County sheriff's cruiser followed close behind as the writer drove out of Maryville; it followed until the county line was crossed, and then it stopped.

The writer and his wife breathed sighs and relaxed. Their expressions of relief would later prove to be premature.


The presidents of four other companies that supplied products to Travelers were much more willing to talk than Norman Robbins. Daryl Zeck, co-owner of Indiana Traveler, Incorporated, reported he had stopped selling his coaches to Travelers due to bad publicity and the objections of his dealers. Originally pressed into doing business with Travelers by the nation's poor economy, Zeck said he sold units first to the Raffertys and Carrolls in Texas -- including JR Trailer Sales of Fort Worth. Then, as word spread, more and more Travelers began ordering trailers from him.

"When you get started on some of this, it's hard to shut them off because it gets so you feel like you know them," Zeck said.

He added that when he told Rose Carroll he would no longer sell trailers to her or the other Travelers, she responded, "You owe it to us to sell us trailers because of all the business we gave you last winter."

"One way I shut them off was to raise prices. I had been selling them a 32-footer for $5,190, but they claimed that was higher than the other trailers they were buying. Even then, I was selling them (Travelers) trailers below dealer cost. I almost had to do that in order to deal with them, and that always griped me because I don't like to have two different prices; I don't think it's fair. But...I mean, when you've got a payroll to meet...And I hate to lay people off. Last winter, those people were calling for trailers every day! I just didn't have to worry about selling a trailer. In fact, I had a hard time building my dealers' trailers. And the Travelers always paid in cash, so I didn't have to worry about collecting my money."

Terry Trulli, president of American Traveler of Elkhart, Indiana, admitted he designed a trailer -- named the Ambassador -- especially for sale to Travelers because he needed the cash the Travelers paid him in order to remain in business. George Bemis, an owner of the company that built Skylark trailers, said he also sold products to Travelers so that he could keep his plant operating. "I don't like the way they do business and misrepresent our coaches, but there's nothing I can do about that," he said.

Officers at Marauder Travelers asked the writer to interview them a second time, and during that session, the officers said they regarded Travelers as their dealers and intended to continue using clan members to market their trailers even though the company was attempting to build a bonafide dealer network.

During the next several years, American Traveler and Marauder Travelers would cease operating and Skylark would close periodically and then reopen under new management. Indiana Traveler, Incorporated, however, would build a highly successful dealership system throughout the country and, by 1996, would be regarded as one of the fastest growing RV manufacturers in America.

On October 25, nine days after the trip to Maryville, the public relations director of Coachmen Industries telephoned the writer. She said the company had been notified by Troop H of the Missouri Highway Patrol that Coachmen's van -- the one the writer had driven to Missouri -- was "involved in an incident" at Maryville. The highway patrol demanded that Coachmen release the name of the driver to a police officer in Missouri or face prosecution for the "incident" by the state attorney general. That police officer was Sergeant Russ Johnson of the Nodaway County sheriff's office.

The writer telephoned Johnson and asked about the alleged incident. Johnson replied that a citizen alerted him about a "suspicious" van that was in Maryville. The citizen complained that the van's driver had a tape recorder in his pocket and that although the van was clean, the license plate was so dirty the number could not be seen, Johnson said. The sergeant reported he asked Maryville police to check out the van, but by the time an officer arrived, the van was gone. At that point, he said, he asked the highway patrol to determine who owned the van, and the patrol informed him later it was owned by *Trailer Life* magazine. Johnson said he was not certain what the reported incident in Maryville had been, but he intended to talk with Norman Roberts about it because it was reported by "an associate" of the lightning rod company president.

The highway patrol revealed it had no details about any incidents in Maryville and had only responded to a request from Johnson for information about the driver of the vehicle.

At that point, angry that a deputy sheriff apparently was pursuing an investigation of him sparked by Norman Roberts, the writer telephoned Johnson again and tape-recorded the conversation.

"When we were talking earlier," the writer said, "you asked me about the tape recorder I had in my pocket. Why was that important?"

"I don't suppose it would be," Johnson admitted. "It wouldn't make me any difference, but it would to the people. Personally, it wouldn't make a damn bit of difference to me if you had two or three of them hanging out of your pocket."

"Did they indicate to you why it was important to them?" the writer asked.

"Well, no. Just that it was a little odd. That was the only thing. And the license part."

The writer responded, "Now, that's another thing. We pretty much came directly home from there and were not involved in any bad weather. I checked the license plate, and it's as clear as it can be. If it had been dirty in Maryville, it would have gotten dirtier, not cleaner. And yet someone told you it was dirty. Who told you it was dirty?"

"I won't divulge that to you," the deputy said. "But that's what brought it to my attention."

"Was it a law enforcement agent who told you it was dirty?"

"Huh?" Johnson asked, clearly surprised by the question. The writer repeated his question.

"No. That's why I called the P.D. (Maryville police department). The van was spotless and the license plate was dirty."

The writer said, "In our earlier conversation, you asked me about my association with *Trailer Life* magazine. How did you know I was associated with *Trailer Life* magazine?"

"That's what the Troop H told me on the phone."

"How did they know that?"

"I suppose from the license plate. I don't know."

"Did Troop H get back to you and tell you my name and say I was driving the van?"

"I don't know...It came through their officers there, and that's when I asked them to have you call this office...Did they tell you to call this office?"

The writer answered, "Yes, they did. But it was they who said I was associated with *Trailer Life*?"

"Well, they just said *Trailer Life* or whatever it is. They didn't say you were associated with them. That's who the license came back to."

The writer said, "The license had nothing to do with *Trailer Life*."

"Well, whatever."

The writer pressed on: "But it was them that told you that, correct? My point is, in my conversation with the people in your area, I did not once mention to anyone that I was with *Trailer Life*. I made a point of not doing that. And when you mentioned *Trailer Life* out of the clear blue sky, it kind of worried me."

"Well, that's where I got it. I tried to run the thing (the plate number), and it came back as an invalid plate. Evidently I was transposing figures."

The writer said, "When the highway patrol called Coachmen, they told Coachmen that the van was involved in an incident in Maryville on Friday and they wanted the name of the driver immediately, and if the company wouldn't give them the name of the driver, they would inform the attorney general of that. Is that standard operating procedure?"

"I don't know how the highway patrol runs its business. All I can do is tell you how we run ours. It's not uncommon for us to run license plates."

The writer said, "You should know that tomorrow, I intend to call the attorney general's office myself."

Johnson became angry. "Now, why don't you come and talk to

the sheriff. I'm gettin' tired of jackin' with you! Listen, if you want to come up and discuss this with the sheriff, or if you want to take my word for it, fine. If you don't, then you just go ahead and talk to the attorney general or do whatever you want to do! I'm tired of it!"

The writer pressed again, "You're tired of it?"

"You bet I am! I explained to you why we done it and that's all I have to tell you. Now is that clear enough for you?"

The writer responded, "Mister Johnson, I am simply trying to get information so that..."

"Well, I believe you've got all the information you need. And as far as your dealer tag, I'm not sure you're even within the law by runnin' it in the state of Missouri. I'll have to do a little checkin' on that."

The writer told him, "Please do. And I am definitely going to talk with Sheriff Estes and the attorney general about this."

"Fine. You do that very thing. You talk with the attorney general if you want to." Johnson slammed down the phone.

Over the next two days, the writer conducted his own investigation. He learned that Johnson had not asked the Maryville police to check out the van. Sources in Maryville described the sergeant as "a good ol' boy" and said he was not expected to be employed by the sheriff's department much longer. Missouri Assistant Attorney General Angela Bennett reported she had already received complaints from citizens about specific sheriff's deputies in the Maryville area, and she vowed to halt any action against the writer that might be considered by police officers there.

From prison in Columbus, Georgia, Jimmy Burke was finding it harder than ever to cope with a life that was dramatically different from the one he had always led. Early in November, he wrote, "I am having a lot of problems right now. I am very down and depressed. Frankly, I wish I were dead. It seems like I am so very alone. I am in the hole as I write you this letter. I sit alone in a small four by eight room with nothing in it except a steel bed and a toilet and sink. It is so quiet in here, it almost feels like I'm the only person on earth. I am dying for a cigarette and the loneliness I am feeling is almost unbearable.

"Let me explain what's been going on. All the guards and staff here know who and what I am, and I'm not well liked by them. They curse me and call me a 'damn gypsy.' They seem to think that I'm from Murphy Village in Augusta, so I am constantly being harassed and agitated by the guards and staff here. When we're out working during the day, I'm always given what is commonly referred to as the 'shit details.' If someone is needed to go down into the sewer to fix something, or chop the grass down a very steep slope, or chop down a large pine tree, you can believe I am the one they call on. And no matter what I do, according to them, it's never done right. The other white inmates here laugh and seem to see some type of sick humor in all of this, and the blacks don't like it at all.

"I have found that I fit in better with the blacks here than I do the whites. So I have a large number of black friends who have helped me out a lot and stick by me, while I only have one or two white friends, and I wouldn't exactly call them friends because they only associate with me in private because they are scared of what their other white friends would say or think if they were seen with me and my black friends. People down here are very prejudiced, but the whites don't say anything to me 'cause they know that the blacks will stick up for me, and it would only end in a racial riot. These guards seem to try their best to make me blow on them so as they can give me a court sheet, take my good time and put me in the hole, but I have somehow managed to be cool because I am so close to getting out now.

"But the end of October, I was cleaning up around the outside of the kitchen when this white guy came by and threw a rock at me. The rock hit a window and cracked it. A guard came out of the kitchen and said that he had seen me throw the rock and crack the window. I couldn't believe it. The white guy just walked by and smiled at me, and the guard wrote me up for damaging state property. I went before the warden in a kangaroo court and was given seven days in the hole.

"After I got out of the hole, a moving slip came around to move me into an all-white dorm. I knew I was being set up by the white guy who worked in the I.S. room. I refused to move, and the guard wrote me up for failure to follow instructions. I did another seven days in the hole. When I came out of the hole, they put me in the all-white dorm anyway. I went to my counselor and explained the situation to him and asked for a transfer to Macon, but he told me that I could not get a transfer because I was attending college. Meanwhile, life in my dorm was impossible. I was scared to come out of my room. I couldn't take a shower in peace, and I heard talk of several white guys planning on raping me and then killing me the next time I took a shower, so I went to the captain and asked to be moved back to my old dorm. I told him what was going on, but he only laughed and put me out of his office. The next day, I went to see the warden. I explained the situation to him and asked him to transfer me. He said that he couldn't because of my being in college, so I asked him to move me to my old dorm, and he said that was up to the captain. So I asked him to put me on segregation until I could be transferred, but he said all of the segregation cells were full. I was stuck. I went back to the dorm feeling defeated. I wrote three letters to the State Board of Offender Rehabilitation in Atlanta, explaining my situation and requesting an immediate transfer, but I got no reply or help from them.

"One night I was taking a shower when three guys came in with a knife and tried to force me to do things with them. I don't know how, but I got away from them and ran out to the guard. I told him what had happened. I told him about the knife, but he insisted that there is no way that an inmate could have a knife in here. He took me back in the dorm and hung around until I was in my room. He didn't even search the guys for a knife. That was Friday night. Saturday morning I seen a black guy, a friend of mine, at breakfast. I told him what had happened. He said for me to meet him in the yard that afternoon. When I did, he brought me a long ice pick with a handle on it and told me to keep it for protection. Even though I never hurt nobody in my life, I realized that I would have to protect myself 'cause no one else was gonna help me. I had tried to do things the right way and had gotten nowhere, so I figured if push came to shove and it was a my-life-or-theirs situation, I would have to try and make it theirs, so I carried the pick with me.

"Sunday morning on my way to breakfast, the lieutenant pulled me out of the line and took me to his office and searched me. He felt the pick in the sock and told me to give it to him. When I leaned over to get it, he hit me in the face with his knee and knocked me against the wall. Him and another guard stripped me down and put me in the hole. They later came back and read me my rights. I told the lieutenant I was gonna put a suit against him. He then said he was charging me with 'carrying a concealed weapon' and 'attempted aggravated assault.' He said I tried to stick him with the pick and that's why he had to hit me, but he's lying. I know that no one will ever believe an inmate over a lieutenant.

"The sergeant also came around today and gave me an inmate disciplinary court sheet, so I have to go before the warden to a kangaroo court in the morning at 8:30 where I will probably receive fourteen days in the hole with one meal every three days, 180 days time out, and a disciplinary transfer to Georgia State Prison at Reidsville, Georgia. They are also talking about taking me to free world court and giving me some more time. But I don't think they can legally do that. I believe it's called double jeopardy.

"I wrote to Russell Boston (my attorney in Macon) about the matter. I know this seems like a soap opera, but it's true. You wouldn't believe some of the things that still go on in prisons down here.

The buildings themselves may be new, but inside it's still run like the old time chain gangs.

"I don't know exactly what will happen, but I'll let you know as soon as I find out. I only know that I can't live like a caged animal too much longer. We are treated worse than animals. I would rather be dead."

More than a year later, the writer learned one reason why Jimmy was the focus of so much persecution while in prison. Because of his gentle nature and his bisexuality, he was raped repeatedly until he finally became the personal property of a convicted black murderer named Anthony Turner. Turner, who was serving three life sentences, was regarded by other inmates as someone with nothing to lose. He was big, tough and mean, but he protected Jimmy and supported the young Irish Traveler both financially and materially.

"If it hadn't been for him," Jimmy said later, "I would have given up several times, and I sure wouldn't have made it. He helped me through those times, and I'll always be grateful for that. I grew real close to the guy. This ring that I'm wearin': He gave me that ring and a watch, and he sent for this necklace. He was always buyin' me things."

Jimmy became regarded as a *she*. He began dressing, as much as possible, like a woman, and he assumed the name Jamie Turner.

Before Jimmy was transferred to his final prison, at Alto, Georgia, Turner was moved to the state prison at Reidsville, and without Turner's protection, Jimmy became fair game for the other inmates. He was traded from one inmate to another and was sometimes the object of gang rapes. Following his punishment for the rock-throwing incident, Jimmy telephoned the writer and announced he intended to kill himself.

Both the writer and his wife responded to that announcement with letters, and the writer telephoned Jimmy's uncle Doug in Florida. The writer suggested that Doug ask members of Jimmy's family to visit him and write to him.

Doug told the writer, "You've gotten yourself close to him by talking with him and corresponding with him. Now, I have been through that myself. I do not believe he will go through with that (suicide threat). He needs to have enough strength to deal with the things that are happening to him. I love Jimmy, but Jimmy did put himself where he is. This should be the biggest waking-up period of his life -- the best thing that's ever happened to him if he uses it constructively."

Doug added, "As far as his family goes, I am most emphatic: I consider him not to have a family. They're con artists. They wake up in the morning and they think of nothing except bucks. I don't. I think of a home-cooked meal, Christmas and holidays and that sort of thing. And good family relationships. Jimmy has not had that. And even if he were here today, he would leap right back into the kind of life he knows and loves."

The writer asked, "So you think it would be best for him to sever his relationship with his family?"

"He's not going to sever it, but you're damned right, I believe that."

Doug said although he would write to Jimmy, and perhaps even drive to Georgia to visit him, he would not ask any of the Burkes to write or visit. He added, "I love Jimmy, but he's not the most important thing in my life at all. In fact, he gets very little of my thoughts at this moment. Basically, what he needs, on an intellectual and psychological level, is to be around the proper company, and he's not going to find that in prison. His family is not at all good for him in those regards. They would start in on him because of who he hangs around with or his habits, and that's why they don't want to see him. That has nothing to do with love and feelings. It's hideous!"

Before Jimmy could become the type of person he was capable of being, Doug said, he had to escape his family's influence. "Which he cannot do!"

He added, "I have, myself, severed myself from his mother -- my sister. She is a very common -- and I emphasize that word, common -- person. She would get along very well where Jimmy is. His mother and father say they love him, but they don't. They express undying, unfailing love for all their children. Bullshit! All you have to do is talk with any of those children for a short while, and you realize that none of them knows where their lives are going. They only know their lives are centered on the kinds of things they're doing and that they've always done. I don't want anything to do with those sleazy people. And if Jimmy travels with them when he gets out, he can forget about me."

The writer told Doug that Jimmy had been raped several times, and the Traveler's uncle responded, "You have to look at it this way. What about the men who are straight, who are married, who can't stand the thought of physical contact with another man? Now, think about that. But as far as Jimmy's concerned, I'm sure it's just fantastic. Even if it's not the preferred person that's raping him, you have to remember, his sexual preference is a man. Tell Jimmy that, because he's not thinking about the straight fellow who's had his ass tore open. That would be a whole lot different. It would affect the straight guy in such a way that he may never get over it. But with Jimmy, the worst of it is, it's just the wrong man doing it."


Several days later, the writer's mail contained another letter from Jimmy. He had been transferred to the prison at Alto, Georgia. "I received your letter last week and was glad to hear from you," he wrote. "Say, don't worry about my family's reaction to those articles. Sooner or later, they will get over it. Maybe some day they'll learn to accept me for the individual person that I am and stop trying to make me into what they want me to be. I can just imagine the stories that you have to tell me about your experiences with the Travelers, and I can't wait to hear them."

Within two weeks, another letter revealed Jimmy was in a better frame of mind: "Just a few lines to say hello. I received your most welcome letter a few days ago and was glad to hear from you. I deeply appreciate both your and Pam's support and concern for me and my present situation. It means a great deal to me to know that I have two friends out there such as you who are concerned and pulling for me. Thanks for everything. Most of all, thanks for being a friend when I have needed one the most.

"Other than you and Pam, the only other people who have stood by me are my uncle Doug and my friend Diane in New York. As for my parents or the rest of my family, they have let me down, and it hurt me and bothered me for a long time. It still hurts a bit to realize that they care so little, if any at all, but after so much for so long, it doesn't really bother me anymore. It was only a matter of taking a good look and really seeing, realizing and accepting the facts.

"I plan to make a new and better, honest life for myself once I am released from prison. A life that doesn't include the Travelers or their lifestyle.

"I have put you and Pam on my visiting list as my aunt and uncle. That is the only way that I can get you on it, and I do hope that you can stop and visit."

Jimmy did not know it at that time, but he was already scheduled to receive an early release from prison. And when he left Alto, he would take something with him besides a prison record and a memory of the abuse he had experienced. During his incarceration, probably during the period he was traded back and forth among the other inmates, his body was the receptacle for a newly discovered, deadly bacteria that would ultimately kill him. Jimmy Burke was almost certainly the first Irish Traveler to be infected with the HIV virus.

Posing as utility company inspectors and generally following the path of Interstate 10, Irish and English Travelers rolled through Alabama, Mississippi, Louisiana and east Texas during the first three months of 1982. Along the way, they informed elderly residents that the utility companies required their homes to be grounded and protected against lightning damage immediately. The Travelers offered to do the work for $200 as a favor to their victims after outlining a less acceptable option: that the utility companies would charge $300.

A typical lightning rod installation consisted of nailing two feet of lightning rod to the ridge of a roof, then wrapping ten or twelve feet of aluminum cable around it; one end of another cable was stuck into the ground, and the rest of that cable was nailed to the side of the house, with the second end stuck under a roof shingle so that, from the ground, it appeared that the two cables were connected under the roof. The entire device was worthless.

On January 20, the Travelers hit Lake Charles, Louisiana; two days later, they scammed an elderly couple in New Orleans; on February 16, they struck Herford, Texas; they swindled two elderly women in Ouachita Parish, Louisiana on February 18 and 19; hit Decatur, Alabama, February 24 and Mobile Alabama on March 2, and the next day, they scammed an elderly couple in Gulf Port, Mississippi.

Louisiana state police issued an alert for Irish Travelers Harry Gorman, also known as John Gorman and J. Stanley; Bryan Gorman, also known as B.J. and Bartley Gorman; John Donahue, and Matt Donahue. Also sought were English Traveler John Jennings (John Donahue's brother-in-law) and an individual named Bill Rosser. They were driving pickup trucks with magnetic signs that said "Roberts Lightning Company." Subsequent investigations revealed that thirty units of lightning protection equipment had been shipped to John Donahue by Roberts Lightning Protection Company, but a representative of the company insisted none of the men was a Roberts employee.

Meanwhile, Louisiana state police issued warrants for several English Travelers who were selling travel trailers and operating roof, driveway and septic tank cleaning services in the Lafayette area without appropriate state licenses. Those sought included Jack Harrison, Andy Young, Ronald L. Claybern, Stanley Joles, Bonnie Coffy Sullivan, Billi Guss Young and Shirley Young. Investigations also were launched on individuals named Sherri McKinnon, Earl Young, Willie McCool, Richard D. Walker, Gary Bates, Clark Rawls, Nathan D. Young, Evert Young, James L. Janis, William Sullivan, Harry A. Young, Jeffrey Morris, Carla A. Staib, Clark Wells, George E. Stephens and Elzie Boswell.

Early in March, Louisiana officers issued a warrant for Irishman Tom McNally -- a member of the Mississippi Travelers -- for operating a home improvement scam in Lafayette. While searching for McNally, police discovered that six other Mississippi Travelers who were traveling with McNally had defrauded a local motel, and warrants were issued for their arrest too. The seven men were traced to another motel, and six Travelers were arrested: Thomas J. Carroll, Jimmy Joe Gorman, James Gorman, John Anthony Gorman, Thomas Costello and Pete G. Carroll. McNally escaped. Within hours after the arrests, the six were released without being charged with crimes. A police report stated, "It was...verified that the persons arrested were related to the subjects sought on the warrants but were not, in fact, the same (people)." Only their names were, coincidentally, the same.

In April, two Travelers claiming they represented Roberts Lightning Protection Company told a farmer in Marshall County, Indiana, that they had been hired to examine his lightning rod system. While the farmer talked with one Traveler, the other one examined the farmer's system and then showed the victim wires that appeared to have been cut. "Lightning has already struck your system, and it has been destroyed," the farmer was informed. "To prevent your house from burning down in the next electrical storm, you'd better get it repaired."

The Travelers agreed to repair the system for $32.36, but when the job was completed, the farmer was presented with a bill for $323.60. He agreed to pay a smaller amount, but later, realizing he had been swindled, he called the Marshall County sheriff's office.

# 22
# Monitored

While Jimmy Burke struggled to cope with his new life behind prison walls, other members of his family were having their own problems with the law. His brother Pat was spending the winter in a mobile home near Murphy Village, and one night he and his wife Rose Mary got into a loud dispute over a dog. The Edgefield County sheriff's office was called, and rookie deputy Jody Rowland was sent to the scene along with another officer. Pat was not there when the deputies arrived, but he returned before they left and charged at the deputies, shouting threats and obscenities.

At six-foot-two and nearly 200 pounds, 27-year-old Burke was an imposing figure. He demanded to know why the police had been called, and Rowland replied, "Mr. Burke, you're under arrest."

Rowland, who was only 21 years old and as tall but much slimmer than Burke, attempted to put handcuffs on Pat, but The Viking had no intention of being arrested. He jerked loose and slugged each of the officers. The deputies wrestled Pat to the ground, but Pat was strong enough to trade blows with Rowland for about fifteen minutes before he could be subdued. The deputies pulled Pat to his feet and attempted to put the second handcuff on him, but Pat broke loose again and tackled Rowland. Rowland sat up and "swapped licks" with Pat several more times before Pat sunk his teeth through Rowland's trousers and into the deputy's shin. Gnawing on Rowland's leg like an animal, he chewed off a bloody chunk of flesh from Rowland's shin and spit it out on the ground.

Once more, the deputies dragged Pat to his feet and tried to force him into their police car, but Pat nearly broke free again, and the three men fell across the hood of the car, denting it and knocking off a radio antenna. Pat's father, Edward, picked up the antenna and, using it like a whip, slashed Rowland's partner with it until he shredded the deputy's shirt, then he leaped on Rowland's back. Using his legs and his left hand to cling to Rowland's back, Edward gripped Rowland's throat with his right hand and tried to rip out the deputy's adam's apple. Rowland paused in his attempt to subdue Pat long enough to break the little finger on Edward's right hand, whereupon Edward ran across the yard screaming and disappeared among the mobile homes. Finally, the deputies were able to put the second handcuff on Pat and drag him into the police car. Later, convicted of public disorderly conduct and resisting arrest, Burke was fined $100 and sentenced to fourteen months in the county jail. For almost a year after the fight, Rowland visited his doctor's office twice a week to have his damaged leg treated. The wound became infected and had to be opened, disinfected and bandaged each time Rowland saw the doctor. And for the next fourteen years, the young police officer watched Pat Burke's criminal career with a great deal of personal interest.

Peggy Burke, Jimmy's wild sister, was sent to Georgia's Hardwood prison not long after she set fire to her cell in Macon. With six years added to her sentence, it looked as if Peggy would spend a great deal more time behind bars than her brothers. As part of Georgia's rehabilitation program, Peggy was assigned to one of Hardwood's trade schools, and while attending co-educational brick masonry classes at the prison, she became pregnant by another inmate.

Several months earlier, her youngest brother, Paul, who had been arrested in Macon with Jimmy and Peggy, was paroled to Florida in the custody of his non-Traveler uncle, Doug. Jailed when he was just 17, Paul spent his eighteenth birthday behind bars in Bibb County before being transferred to Hardwood. Like his brother Jimmy, young Paul was repeatedly raped by other inmates until, in a desperate attempt at self-preservation, he agreed to serve as the sexual property of a prison gang leader.

In Orlando at his uncle's house, he complained constantly about being raped in prison and said he would kill himself before he would return there, but he refused to find a job, and his parole officer threatened to revoke the parole.

A few months after Paul was released from Hardwood, his parents, Wanda and Edward, arrived in Florida to be with Wanda and Doug's mother, who was dying in a hospital. Several days later, Doug reported, "My sister had been drinking heavily -- something she and Edward and many of the other Travelers do every day. She was drunk, in fact, and she verbally assaulted not only me, but other members of the family in the lobby of the hospital. Paul was protective of his mother, and he left the hospital with her. He is with his mother at this moment, and I would rather he not be with her because I know how she is. She thinks of Wanda and only Wanda. She's an emotionally distraught person."

Doug said, "When Wanda's father died, she called me crying and said she had taken an overdose of pills. Bullshit! All she wanted was pity. I could hardly recognize her voice. She didn't take an overdose; she was drunk. She was lying on the floor of a motel room. She was not able, she said, to call a doctor or any other kind of help, but she could call me! I just gave the phone to one of her children who was here."

He added, "I don't know where any of them are now. You see, I don't really want any of them in my house. They don't live the way I do. They're loud, they drink and they're night people. The women don't do any kind of work; they rob, they steal, they con. Paul lied to me. He didn't tell me he was going with his mother; he told me he was going with his sister. And if anything comes up because of it, I'm going to tell him to get his ass out of my house."

Doug said he had already promised Peggy she could live with him upon her release from prison, and he said he wanted to take care of his niece until she could straighten out her life. "I've kept her before when she had nowhere else to go," he explained. "When those children are here, I make sure they've got their own rooms, transportation and cigarette money. They have three meals a day without TV dinners, and they have a good family atmosphere. And still, they can't help associating with other Travelers. I know there will always be something of a Traveler in Peggy, but she has promised me that when she gets out of prison, she will not travel with her mother. She can't travel by herself, either; she's too insecure by herself -- all of them are insecure by themselves. They have to be with somebody."

Unable to cope with periodic arguments between his uncle and his mother, Paul asked for his parole custody to be assigned to another of his mother's brothers in Charleston, South Carolina. A week later, he returned to Florida but then had his parole assigned to Macon, Georgia, where he moved into an apartment with a drag queen. Paul found a job as a clerk in a shoe store, and within a few weeks, he was promoted to assistant manager. Unfortunately, his Traveler training reared its ugly head, and Paul was caught stealing money from the cash register. His parole was revoked, and he was returned to Hardwood where, once again, he became a sexual plaything for other inmates. Since no additional time was applied to his sentence, he was released on parole a year later; almost immediately, he violated that parole by shoplifting in a Georgia department store.

Paul spent the next four years in and out of jail because, while he was out, he constantly violated his parole. Finally, in 1987, he was arrested in Erie, Pennsylvania, following a high-speed police chase after an anonymous caller -- who, according to official police documents, was Paul's sister, Wanda Jessee -- informed officers where Paul could be found. From his cell, Paul penned a note to his mother, telling her that he could not bear the thought of being returned to prison, where he knew he would be raped repeatedly. From shredded pillowcases, he fashioned a crude hangman's noose and then quietly, alone in his cell, 24-year-old Paul killed himself.

In September 1982, the writer received a surprise telephone call from Peggy Burke. "I'm out!" Peggy announced.

"How did you get out?" the writer asked. "Were you paroled?"

"Well, not exactly," she answered. "They let me out to have my baby. It's due early next month. I'm supposed to go back to Hardwood after the baby's born, and my sister Cathy is supposed to keep the baby. But I'm not goin' back."

"What are you going to do?"

"I'm not sure, but I'm never gonna go back to jail again. I'm gettin' out of Georgia for good."

Peggy lived with her sister Cathy and her brother-in-law, Tony Robertson, until her baby was born October 13. She named the boy Douglas in honor of her uncle, then left Georgia for Florida, where she later married a black man named Martin. The writer never talked with her again. Over the next several years, Peggy had seven more children -- three of whom died -- and, by 1992, while using more than thirty different aliases, she had been arrested forty-six times on charges ranging from prostitution and theft to possession of cocaine.

A few months after her Peggy's first baby was born, Jimmy would tell the writer sadly, "I thought being in Hardwood might change her, but it didn't. She's as wild as she ever was, or moreso. She loves to party and use drugs. I've tried to convince her to settle down and give up the drugs, but she won't. She's got a different name and a different I.D., and she says she ain't goin' back to prison. I guess they'll get her eventually, but until they do, she'll roam around. It's inevitable that they get her because of the way she's livin' and the people she's runnin' with. She's still shopliftin' and swindlin' and stealin' whatever she can get her hands on."

Pat Lynch, a New York-based producer of CBS-TV's highly regarded *20/20* television show, learned that members of the Scottish Travelers -- the Williamsons -- had begun to invest funds in legitimate business ventures, and she wanted to prepare a *20/20* segment about those activities. She asked the writer for help with her research. Noting that individuals within the Scottish clan had made significant profits from buying and selling mobile home parks in Scottsdale, Arizona, she asked the writer if he would point her toward similar investments by other "Williamsons."

The writer replied that he was reluctant to become involved in her research effort because he did not have much confidence in the accuracy of reports prepared by the broadcast media.

Lynch said, "I've been told you know a lot about the RV industry and the Williamsons' involvement with the Indiana companies that build trailers for them. Would you be willing to meet me in Elkhart and show me around?"

The writer responded, "Sure, I could do that."

"And maybe we could get you on tape for a couple of minutes talking about the trailer sales scam," she suggested.

"Maybe."

She pressed on. "How about that young Traveler you wrote about in the magazine -- James Murphy? Do you think he'd be willing to talk with us on camera if we disguised his voice and showed him in shadows?"

"I doubt it, but I'll ask him. He's in prison now, but he's scheduled to be paroled soon."

A few days later, the writer posed the question to Jimmy Burke, and the young Traveler consented to be interviewed after his release from prison.

Jimmy Burke was released from prison on Thanksgiving Day, 1982 -- a week earlier than scheduled. He telephoned the writer that evening with the news. "Mom and Dad picked me up at the prison, along with my little sisters, Winnie and Wanda Mary. I got paroled to Augusta (actually, to Murphy Village, South Carolina) in the custody of my sister Cathy and her husband, Tony. They're livin' over there in a rented mobile home. But I talked to her last night, and they're not goin' to be there, so now I've got to go over there and find me a place to live and a job and get my life goin' on my own. My brother Edward is in Texas, and he took up a collection from a bunch of the Travelers for me. I was kind of surprised; I didn't expect it."

Reporting that he received his high school equivalency degree and attended some college classes while in prison, Jimmy said he intended to enroll in college at Augusta and find a job. "I'm not going back to the same thing, you know. I'll be on parole for almost two years, and I'm not goin' to do anything to get me in trouble."

"Do you have to stay in South Carolina or Georgia all that time?"

"No, I don't have to. To tell you the truth, I don't want to even be here. But about a month ago, the parole office told me, 'The parole board in Atlanta has decided to give you a pre-release. Where do you want to go?' My cousin Robert Daugherty in Baltimore was the only name I knew to give them. They put it through for out-of-state assignment, and after about three weeks they told me, 'You can't go there. He's in jail.' I didn't know where nobody else was, you know. I thought about you, and for a minute I was goin' to give them your address, but then I decided I'd better not because I didn't know how you'd react. So then I found out my sister was in Augusta."

During his three years in prison, Jimmy's weight had dropped from 225 pounds to 155, and his waist size had shrunk from 34 inches to 28. At six-foot-two, he was quite thin. His parole was for eighteen months and carried conditions: Although he could leave the state so long as he acquired a travel permit, he had to observe a midnight-to-six curfew, not associate with convicted felons and not carry firearms. "But I never carried a gun anyway," he said.

Asked if his parents would support his resolve to settle down, attend college and get a job, he replied, "Well, that's not really something we talk about."

He added, "I went through hell while I was locked up, and I'm not ever goin' to do something to land me back in there. It's something I don't ever want to go through again. A lot of times I felt like givin' up. I just kept hangin' on for the day I'd get out. The only thing that kept me goin' was knowin' that eventually, I would leave there. I think the time I spent in there (prison) taught me a lot. I was always used to havin' whatever I wanted, and there, I learned to do without. I learned how to be more patient, too."

A week later, he revised those comments: "I don't think prison really teaches anyone anything," he said. "The only thing it really taught me is I don't want to go back."


Jimmy used most of the money his brother had collected for him to buy an automobile, and he stopped at the motel room his parents had rented near Murphy Village in order to show it to them. "My sister Winnie told me they had went down to get something to eat, and about that time, Winnie Ann McNally's son Johnny from the Village pulled up and spoke to me. Me and Johnny used to travel together and work together. I told him I was goin' to find Mom and Dad, so he got in the car with me, and we went down Washington Road to the Red Lobster, where I saw Dad's van, and we went in. Dad was pretty well lit by then. Johnny sat down with my Mom at a table because she knows him so well; he's like a son to her. And I sat in a booth with my dad. Johnny and Mom was laughin' and carryin' on. We all had dinner and a couple of drinks, and by the end of dinner, Dad was pretty well out of it. When we left the restaurant, Dad said he'd pay the bill, which was about sixty dollars. So me and Johnny went out and got in my car. When we got back to the motel, Dad pulled the restaurant tab out of his pocket and showed us. Mom said, 'Didn't you pay that?'

"He said, 'No. I just walked out.'

"She said, 'That's nice. Our son's on parole, and if he's caught for this, he'll be in bad trouble over a sixty-dollar bill. That was stupid.'

"He said, 'Oh, you were in there laughin' and carryin' on with your friend Johnny, sittin over there huggin' on him and kissin' on him. And you call *me* stupid.'

"One thing led to another, and they started swingin' at each other. I had to stand between them and break them up. I pulled them apart, and Mom ran to the door. Dad was tryin' to get at her, and I was holdin' onto him. He said, 'Move out of the way!' I said, 'Sit down. I'm not gonna let you go out there with her so you can kill each other.' So I held him there while Mom took Winnie and the baby outside. Dad said, 'Move out of my way, or I'll send your ass back to prison.'

"I said, 'You can't send me back to prison.'

"As Mom pulled out, she called to me, and I left too and met her down the road. She sat with me cryin' and then went back to the motel, and Dad was gone. We found out he had took a bus to Florida. She gave me fifty dollars that Dad didn't know she had, and she left the next day in the van. They probably got back together when she arrived in Florida. They go through that kind of fightin' about two or three times a month. It's nothin' new. It's been goin' on since I was a kid. At least I know I'm home again!"

As Jimmy drove back to the Village, he passed the site of the original Irish Traveler encampment, *Traveler's Rest*, which had been developed into a combination mobile home park and campground called

The Pines. Spotting Safari and Marauder trailers parked there with a new Corvette, a Cadillac and two flashy one-ton pickup trucks, he stopped and knocked on the door of one trailer. "It was Johnny Sherlock, the one they call Mare's Face. He's supposed to be a big wheel among the Northern Travelers. He had just drove through the Village to show off his outfit. His daughter Katherine had the new Corvette; his son had one of the trucks towin' the Safari; his wife was drivin' the new Cadillac, and he was towin' the Marauder with a new flatbed Chevrolet truck. It must have looked like a wagon train goin' through the Village!"

Jimmy said, "We talked awhile, and I started gettin' antsy just hearin' what he had done and where he was goin'. He kept tellin' me how much money he made last summer, and he said he was gonna try sellin' one of his trailers and then go on down to Florida. There's really gonna be a big crowd in Tampa over the holidays this year. There's already a crowd there because Sam Rafferty is gettin' married sometime this month, and all the Travelers are pourin' in for the weddin'. They're goin' to video tape everything and have chauffeurs with Cadillacs comin' out to the campground to pick people up and take them to the weddin'. It's supposed to be a really big deal."

Jimmy paused, then added, "I sure wish I could go."

Early in December, TV producer Pat Lynch informed the writer that she had resigned from CBS and had joined NBC News as a producer of a new television "news magazine" show named *Monitor*. The first episode of the new program -- scheduled in February opposite *60 Minutes* -- would focus on scams of the Irish and Scottish Travelers, she said. To prepare for that episode, she wanted to film the RV plants in Indiana where trailers were built for the clans, and from there, she would drive to Cincinnati and examine Spring Grove Cemetery, historic final resting site of the famous Williamsons.

Lynch and the writer met in Elkhart a few days later. While they toured Elkhart, the producer said she had interviewed famous Texas attorney Percy Foreman the day before. Foreman had represented various members of the Scottish Traveler clan for many years, she said, "and he's been very helpful on the story I'm working."

The TV producer and her film crew tried, without success, to interview presidents of the companies that produced RVs for the Travelers, but they did train their cameras on individual Travelers who were in the process of hooking new coaches to their tow trucks. Then, from Indiana, Lynch telephoned Norman Roberts in Missouri and asked the lightning rod manufacturer if he would consent to be interviewed about the Williamsons.

"I'd be glad to!" Roberts responded. "I've known them for forty-some years. I could tell you stories -- true stories -- that would curl your hair."

"I'd love to hear them," Lynch said.

Roberts continued, "For example, Zsa, Zsa Gabor? She had that fancy house in Beverly Hills or wherever. They asked her if they could pave her driveway. She said that since her house was pink, she'd like to have her driveway pink."

"Pink?"

"Pink! They said, 'Well, that's no problem, Ma'am. We'll make it pink.' So they put a dye in with the fuel oil and blacktop, and she paid them. She was tickled to death. And as they drove down Sunset Boulevard, a rainstorm came up, and the pink driveway washed off and followed them."

Roberts paused, then added, "You know something funny? In all the forty years we've done business with them, our complaint file has had very few complaints against them. They're mostly mismaligned."

Lynch said, "That's exactly what Mr. Foreman said. He said they're victims of a lot of prejudice."

"They sure are," Roberts said, "and they do a good job of installing our lightning rods. Lightning rods are a lot more complex than most people realize."

Later that day, Jimmy Burke telephoned the writer from Murphy Village, discouraged because local government bureaucracy was hampering his efforts to lead a non-criminal life. Pointing out that three years earlier, he could have acquired a forged driver's license, birth certificate and other documents quite easily, he said trying to acquire those papers honestly was considerably more difficult. A department of motor vehicles clerk, for example, refused to issue a driver's license unless he submitted his birth certificate.

"I lost it," he told the DMV clerk.

She said, "Well, you have to send for a duplicate."

Jimmy responded, "It'll take me weeks to send for a birth certificate and get one back, and I need a license now because I've got to drive."

She said, "Well, I can't do nothing for you without a birth certificate."

Jimmy decided that while he waited for a duplicate birth certificate to be sent to him from Florida, he would buy insurance for the car. Jimmy told the writer, "But the insurance company wouldn't sell me insurance without seein' my driver's license! I left there and went to get my tags, but to get my tags, they wanted to see my insurance papers."

Frustrated and nearly out of money, Jimmy applied for food stamps. "I sat there in the food stamp office for three hours before I could see anybody, and they made me fill out a hundred forms. They told me I could get the stamps Wednesday -- sixty-two dollars for the rest of the month. They expect sixty-two dollars to last me twenty days!"

He continued, "Then I want lookin' for a place to rent in Aiken, but before I could get there, the transmission went out on the car, and I had to pay twenty-five dollars to have it towed. A friend at Murphy Village said he'd look at it, so maybe it won't cost me much to get the car fixed."

Three days later, Jimmy was still not in a good mood. Although his friend at the Village had installed a used transmission in his car and he had picked up food stamps, he had been unable to find a job. "I get so aggravated fillin' out applications and talkin' to people about work. Everybody says we're in the middle of a recession, and there ain't no jobs available. It's especially frustratin' because I know I could make a lot of money shopliftin' or workin' out of a truck."

The writer and his wife offered to loan Jimmy $300 until the young Traveler could find a job. Jimmy tried to express his gratitude but could only sob quietly over the phone. "We're concerned because we know how easy it would be for you to get back into the Traveler life," the writer told him.

"It really would," Jimmy admitted. "It's especially hard for me now because I'm flat broke, and everything keeps going wrong, and then something comes to my mind how easy it would be to do stuff -- the kind of jobs you call scams -- and get some money. I have to fight it off, and also I'm scared about bein' locked up again. I don't want to get back into none of that. If I can get myself together and get a job and some education, that's what I want."

Pat Lynch's visit with lightning rod manufacturer Norman Roberts at Mayville, Missouri, was not very successful. She reported, "We arrived on the scene, and a fellow named Wendall was there. Wendall's Norman's foreman, and Wendall said, 'I have very bad news for you. Norman has the flu.'

"I said, 'Wendall, I just spoke to Norman two hours ago. How could he have the flu?'

"Wendall said, 'He's been coming down with this for two weeks, and it hit him all of a sudden.'

"I said to myself, 'Holy shit. He's probably boozed up.'"

Lynch and her crew filmed a short interview with Wendall, "during which he said how the Williamsons and Irish Travelers were wonderful people and he never had any complaints about them, but that was all he could say because that was all he knew. All of a sudden, I realized some women in the background were trying to get my attention. So I went over to them, and one said, 'Norman's on the phone. He wants you to come over to his office right away.' So I went across the street, and there was Norman wearing a red hat and sunglasses, and he had a bottle of 23-year-old Scotch sitting in front of him. He refused to do the interview and was sort of hostile. But I was able to calm him down, and we got the cameras on, and he was all right. He's no dope. He changed his whole act the minute the camera went on.

"What he said, in effect, was he feels he has the right to do business with anyone he wants to, and he's known the Williamsons since 1945 and doesn't feel they're all that bad, that ninety per cent of them are good and that there are ten per cent who are hustlers and con men who give the rest of them a bad name. He said he knows there is some trouble (with them), but that's the way it is."

Reluctantly, the writer agreed to arrange for Lynch to interview Jimmy Burke in South Carolina, and he suggested that the producer offer the young Traveler compensation. Lynch said she would.

Executives of the RV companies which were selling trailers to Travelers continued to refuse to be interviewed, and Marauder's president threatened to sue NBC if Lynch's crew even filmed his company's property.

Before Jimmy Burke could be interviewed by Lynch, he telephoned the writer again from South Carolina, expressing more frustration with government bureaucracy. "To tell you the truth, if I stay down here, I'm goin' to end up back in prison because they won't leave me alone. I've been tryin' to go straight, but they won't leave me alone."

"Who won't leave you alone? Murphy Village people?"

"No, the cops. After I talked with you last Thursday, I found my birth certificate, so I went to Alabama to get tags for my car. I also tried to get my driver's license, but the place was closed until Tuesday, and I couldn't afford to stay there another couple of nights. I decided to get my license in South Carolina, so I came back and met Johnny McNally. He was goin' out to sell some linoleum, and he asked me to go with him. We sold some and made a little bit of money, so I think I had about $80 because the money you sent me hadn't arrived yet. I figured that on Tuesday, I'd get my car inspected, and with its Alabama tags and a new driver's license and some insurance, everything would be legal."

He continued, "I went to the Department of Motor Vehicles to get my tags. While the clerk was fillin' out papers for that, I went to the next window to get my driver's license. Now, I've never had a driver's license under my real name, and the man asked me, 'Have you ever had a driver's license?'

"I said, 'No.'

"'You're almost twenty-three years old and you've never had a driver's license?' I said no. He said, 'That sounds kind of strange in this day and age?' He gave me some papers with a lot of questions to answer. I was sittin' over at a table fillin' out the papers and answerin' the questions, and he called me back.

"He asked, 'Do you have a Florida I.D. card?' I said I did, and I showed it to him. And he said, 'You've been suspended in Florida.'

"I said, 'How could I be suspended? I've never had a driver's license.'

"He said, 'It's got your I.D. number here, and the state of Florida said you failed to pay a traffic fine in Polk County, so your driving privileges were suspended down there.'

"I said, 'When was that supposed to have been?'

"He said, 'That was back in 1981.'

"I said, 'Well that wasn't me because, to tell you the truth, I was in prison then.'

"And he said, 'Well, all I know is what the computer said. Wait here a minute, and I'll check on it.' So he went into a back room for a minute, and then from out of the back room, four cops came runnin' and grabbed me. They threw me up against the wall and put handcuffs on me and dragged me into the back room. They ran me through a computer system, and it came back that there weren't any warrants out on me. One of the cops called the police station and asked them to send over my rap sheet. A few minutes later, he came back in with a big long rap sheet and said, 'It says you were busted last year in Florida for drugs.'

"I said, 'Wait a minute. I've never used drugs in my life. I don't even smoke pot and only occasionally do I take a drink. That ain't me.'

"He said, 'Well it's your I.D. number. Plus, you've got all these aliases. You're also wanted under John Beechum Young.'

"And then it hit me. Remember last year, I told you my cousin John had gotten locked up in Florida and he was usin' my I.D.? That's what it was. I tried to explain it to them, and they wouldn't believe me. The cop said, 'Come on. Come clean with it.'

"I said, 'I'm not lyin'. I'm telling you everything I know.'

"He said, 'You're being a smartass, and you're goin to jail.'

"I asked, 'For what?'

"He answered, 'For falsifying a statement.'

"I asked, 'What statement did I falsify?'

"He said, 'When you filled out this statement to get your license, it asked if you had ever had a license suspended or revoked, and you marked it no. That's falsifying, so you're going to jail.'

"I said, 'Wait a minute. I just got out of prison. I'm tryin' to go straight and stay out of trouble, and I came in here tryin' to get things done legally. I need to work to stay out of prison. To get a job, I need to drive. To drive, I need a driver's license. So now you're tellin' me you're goin' to take me to jail because I'm tryin' to get a driver's license?'

"He said, 'Well, that's what it adds up to. You're going to jail, and it'll cost you $100 to get out.'

"I said, 'Who has $100? I just bought tags and insurance.'

"He said, 'Well, you'd better find it somewhere or you're goin' to sit in Edgefield County jail, and you might as well bring a Christmas tree with you because you'll need it.'

"So he took me to Edgefield County jail and locked me up. After callin' all over the world, I got hold of Peggy. She scraped up $97, and the cops agreed to let me out for that. They didn't know I was on parole, or they wouldn't have let me out at all."

He added, "It was all a bunch of shit. I didn't deserve to get locked up. I didn't do nothin'. But we paid the bond and then went down to where the car was parked at the department of motor vehicles. As we walked in, I saw that same cop was parked not far from my car, just watchin' it. I said to Peggy, 'He's waitin' for me to come and get the car and drive away with it with no driver's license, and he'll lock me up again.' So we walked and hitchhiked until we found someone with a driver's license who could go back and get the car for me. So now I don't know what in the hell is gonna happen, but I'm gettin' the hell out of here. I can't get no drivers license here, and I can't get a job."

Police told Jimmy he would have to go to Florida, straighten out the identity problem and pay the traffic fines and a twenty-dollar reinstatement fee to get his license reinstated in Florida. Although Jimmy figured his cousin John had acquired a copy of Jimmy's birth certificate from Orange County and was now in jail somewhere, Jimmy had no idea where John was incarcerated.


"The Happy Traveler campground is just loaded with Travelers," Jimmy reported on New Year's Day from Tampa, Florida. He told the writer, "My mom and dad went to Augusta to spend Christmas with me, but I didn't know it, and I'm down here with Wanda and Billy. I worked with Billy for a few days and made about $400. I called Mom and Dad on Christmas Eve, and when I told Mom I was here with Wanda, she flipped out. Her and Wanda and Billy haven't spoken in over a year. They had some kind of big fight in Florida a year ago, and Wanda broke the windows of their van, so Mom filed charges against her and tried to get her arrested. I told Mom, 'Just because y'all aren't speakin' doesn't mean I can't speak to them.' My dad got on the phone and said he was gonna call the Tampa police and have Wanda and Billy locked up. Then he and I got into it over the phone, and I hung up on him."

Jimmy continued, "There was a big blowout Christmas Eve. A lot of Travelers went to a club called The Stable over at University Square Mall. There was a big dance, and the club was so packed with Travelers you couldn't hardly move around. Everything was okay until Jimmy Jigger -- his real name's Jimmy Gorman -- got into a fight with one of the Carrigans, and they both got throwed out. Then somebody else got into it with a bouncer, and it ended up with everybody out on the sidewalk in front of the mall. There were about 200 Travelers and ten bouncers. The Travelers just beat the hell out of the bouncers, and somebody called the cops. I wasn't taking part in any of it, just standin' around, but when the cops came, I hopped into Billy's truck and we all took off.

"Then Christmas night, Billy went to a club on Route 301 called Big Al's, where a bunch of the Traveler men were drinkin' and gamblin'. The bartender told them not to gamble in there, so a bunch of them went behind the bar and beat the hell out of him and then tore up the bar. You know how they get when they're all together!"

Jimmy submitted to an interview for the *Monitor* show after Lynch promised to film him in a shadowed profile and disguise his voice. Then, back on the road once again, pointed toward Murphy Village after leaving Florida, Jimmy telephoned the writer. He still had no driver's license, but said with a light laugh, "I'll get one some way."

Asked about his interview with Lynch, Jimmy said, "She wants me to wear a wire and go out to the Village and talk with some of the Travelers. She said her and her crew will sit nearby in a van and pick up the conversations on tape."

The writer said, "Wow, that could be dangerous."

"Yeah," agreed Jimmy. "I'm not goin' to do that. I'm goin' on to Jamestown, New York, and try to get into the community college there. I'll set up a permanent business sealing and patching driveways. I know how to do a good job even though I never did it, and I know I can make money at it. I made good money at it before and wasn't even doin' half the job I could."

Later, from Murphy Village, Lynch called the writer. "Jimmy Burke has not arrived yet, and I'm a little alarmed," she said. "I don't need him for anything else, but he's been very helpful, and I wanted to let him go with us to Murphy Village since he's seemed so interested in how we do our filming." She did not mention that she had asked Jimmy to wear a wire.

Just before the end of January, Jimmy telephoned from the Chatauqua County jail in Mayville, New York. He had been arrested and charged with driving while intoxicated and criminal mischief. "Me and Bobby (one of his friends from his pre-prison period) went out Tuesday night to have a few drinks. We got pretty well loaded. I asked the barmaid to call me a cab so I could go home and then got into my car to get my cigarettes. Some guy came up behind me. He said he had a gun and told me to get in the car. I got in, and he told me to drive after he got into the back seat. I knew where the police station was, right around the corner, and I had seen a cop car pull in the garage there earlier. So when the guy told me to turn, I just headed for the garage door and ran into it. The cops came out, and I flagged them down and told them the guy was tryin' to rob me. They pulled him out, but they didn't find no gun, so evidently he was just pretendin' like he had one.

"They locked me up for DWI and for runnin' through the garage door. I tried to tell 'em I wouldn't have been DWI if the guy hadn't forced me into he car, and I also wouldn't have run into the garage door if it wasn't for him. I thought he was sittin' in the back seat with a gun on me. Why else would someone run into the door of a police station garage?"

Jimmy paused and then said, "The thing is, you know, I was never able to get a driver's license in my name, so I had another license on me under the name of Thomas Doyle. Today, they found out what my real name is."

Bond on the DWI charge was set at $1,000, but none had yet been determined on the criminal mischief charge. "I've got a public defender," Jimmy told the writer, "but he doesn't know everything that's goin' on. He still thinks my name is Thomas Doyle."

Fortunately for Jimmy, bond money was raised after a series of telephone calls were made, and he was released from jail before he could be accused of violating his probation. He rented an apartment in Jamestown but, before he could buy a used truck and open his driveway paving and sealing business, his parents arrived for a visit. They invited him to go with them to Indiana, where they planned to buy a new trailer. During that trip, Jimmy and the writer met and talked for a few hours. Jimmy admitted he had not yet told his parents he intended to stay in New York.

"They said I should go back to Jamestown and get my stuff together so I can travel with them," he said. "They said they'll buy me a new truck and a trailer so that I can start workin' on the road again."

The writer asked, "You're not going to do that, are you?"

Jimmy did not answer for several seconds. Then he looked away and replied quietly, sadly, almost in a whisper, "I don't know what I'm gonna do."

The TV segment about Irish and Scottish Travelers that Pat Lynch produced for NBC News finally aired on March 19 during the premiere broadcast of the *Monitor* news magazine program. Instead of playing on Sunday evenings opposite *60 Minutes* as originally planned, *Monitor* was moved to Saturday night at ten o'clock.

A dozen years later, Florida police investigator John Wood asked the writer about that program, and the writer said the young Traveler interviewed in silhouette was Jimmy Burke. Wood responded, "I always heard that was an Irish kid. The Scotch said you'd never get a Scotch kid to do that, and they always figured it was one of those Irish twerps."

The *Monitor* program survived only a few episodes, and then both it and host Lloyd Dobbins faded quietly from the network television scene.

# 23

# Death and Taxes

On New Year's Eve following the 1983 Christmas holidays, while the Northern Irish Travelers poured into central Florida for their annual gathering, Jimmy Burke's brother-in-law, 36-year-old Billy O'Roarke, left the Tampa campground where he and his wife Wanda were camped and drove to St. Petersburg. A highly skilled pool player, Billy stopped at a St. Pete bar where he knew he could always find a good game, and he hustled a few games with some local men. The betting was heavy, and within an hour, Billy left the bar with about $200 in winnings.

Four men from the bar followed him outside, and one said, "Hey gypsy, we're not ready for you to leave yet. We want a chance to win our money back."

Billy smiled and replied, "I'd give you another chance, but I'm afraid I'd just take your grocery money from you."

"Well then, why don't you just give us back what you won, and we'll call it square," one of the men said.

"I don't think so," answered Billy.

The four men surrounded the Irish Traveler threateningly and demanded again that he return their money. Billy, a veteran street fighter, refused and prepared for battle. The men closed in on Billy, and fists flew. Badly outnumbered, Billy was pummeled to the ground and then relieved of his wallet, watch and pool winnings. As one of the men attempted to take Billy's saddle-shaped diamond ring from him, Billy struggled to his feet and ran out onto Highway 19 in an attempt to flag down a passing motorist. Instead, he ran into the path of a speeding car and was killed.

Wanda O'Roarke, Jimmy's sister, was a widow at the age of 27.

Jimmy's parents sent him an airline ticket in New York so he could fly to Orlando for the funeral, and while he waited in Florida for Travelers to gather for the funeral, he called the writer. "Wanda is takin' it real bad, and so are her two kids," Jimmy reported. "I feel real bad about it too. Me and Billy were always pretty close."

"My brother Ed flew in from Texas, and everybody else is gonna be here for the funeral -- the whole crowd. Mom and Dad were in South Carolina, and they came down. They'd been having trouble with Wanda and Billy all the last year, and they weren't speakin', so Wanda wouldn't allow them at the funeral home, and they can't go to the funeral. They're really upset about that."

After the funeral, Jimmy reported, "Everybody was there. I mean everybody! There were so many people, mostly Northern Travelers, but some of every group besides -- the Sorries, the Greenhorns, the Mississippi Travelers and even some Scotch. The church was packed. The caravan out to the cemetery was miles long. It was unbelievable. We were only at the cemetery a few minutes, and we had to rush my Mom to the hospital. She's got high blood pressure and reacted to the stress."

Young Wanda Burke was rather well off, financially, after her husband's death. Billy had left her with two trucks, two new trailers and a used one, some property in New Jersey, stocks, bonds and cash. Several weeks after the funeral, Wanda and Peggy were driving around Orlando one night in one of Wanda's trucks when they were stopped by police for a traffic violation. Officers suspected the women were high on drugs, so they searched the truck and found marijuana and amphetamines. Both women faced drug charges, and the truck was impounded. Wanda was released on $25,000 bond -- requiring her to cash in her investments and sell her trailers -- but a check of Peggy's rap sheet revealed she was wanted in Georgia for not returning to prison following her temporary release so she could have her baby.

While awaiting extradition to Georgia, Peggy received a surprise visitor. A cousin, Bridget Carroll (not her real name), told Peggy she had become a lesbian and had fallen in love with Peggy. Bridget said she intended to leave her husband and, if Peggy would live with her, she would hire an expensive lawyer to fight the extradition. Peggy, figuring she had nothing to lose, agreed. Bridget gave several thousand dollars to Florida Gypsy Johnny Johnson, and Johnson found a lawyer to represent Peggy. After two weeks of legal maneuvering, the extradition was rejected, and Peggy was released from jail on only $5,000 bond.

Meanwhile, Traveler Mary Ann Burden left her husband Bill and, with her children and all the cash she could scrape together, she and Wanda moved into Wanda's Uncle Doug's house in Orlando along with Bridget Carroll and Peggy. Bridget's husband, Jim Carroll, learned where his wife was, and one night he broke into Doug's house, slapped and slugged Bridget and then dragged her out to his truck by her hair.

At this point, events became confusing, and several different versions of what happened have been told. The most popular version is that Peggy -- whether alone or accompanied by other family members -- drove to a nearby campground where her father's brother, Jim Burke, was camped with his wife Kathleen. The older Burkes were not in their trailer, so Peggy and her accomplices broke into the coach and stole $80,000 worth of gold jewelry and diamonds.

Following the theft, Wanda and Doug had a serious argument that apparently became physical. Doug, disgusted with his Traveler guests -- and somewhat fearful of his niece's temper -- left his home and went to an aunt's house in Orlando. At that point, Wanda was virtually broke, but Mary Ann Burden had a new Cadillac and about $20,000 in cash. Resentful that Doug had been driven from his own home, Peggy and a friend named Jim took Mary Ann's purse with the $20,000 in it and, after disconnecting all the telephones and gathering up the $80,000 in stolen jewelry, they locked Wanda and Mary Ann in a bedroom with deadbolt locks. Then Jim and Doug took Peggy's baby and flew to Hawaii. Peggy remained in Florida.

Jimmy, reporting on the events, said, "Wanda and Mary Ann were left with only eleven dollars! But Wanda called a used furniture store and sold all of Doug's furniture for $600, and then she and Mary Ann took off in the Cadillac. They didn't get far before the police pulled them over for speeding." Knowing that Mary Ann had drugs in the car with her, Wanda leaped from the vehicle and escaped on foot. Mary Ann was arrested for drug possession, and her car was impounded.

Jimmy said, "Mary Ann's husband Bill bailed her out after she promised she'd go back with him, but as soon as she was out, she took off again and met Wanda. She and Wanda went to a restaurant in Wanda's truck, and while they were there, Bill Burden and another guy came in, snatched Mary Ann and took off with her. Mary Ann had the furniture money on her, so Wanda was left in Orlando by herself without any money except the eleven dollars.

"Wanda went over to the camp where Bill was staying and raised hell, and my Aunt Kathleen called the police and told them the woman who stole her jewelry was there. The police arrived with federal officers who wanted to know why no taxes had been paid on the income that was used to buy $80,000 in jewelry. Aunt Kathleen told them she never had no jewelry, that she'd made it up, but the police didn't believe her, and they impounded Aunt Kathleen and Uncle

Jimmy's Cadillac, their truck and their trailer. After that happened, Aunt Kathleen went into fits, so Uncle Jimmy put her in the nut hospital in Orlando, and he took off.

"Wanda called my brothers Pat and Edward in Columbus, Ohio, where they were paintin' roofs and sellin' trailers and asked them to send her some money. She already owed them about $8,000, but they said they'd come down and help her. But the truth is, they're plottin' against her; they're going to pretend that they're helpin' her, but they're going to have her committed." (In actual fact, Wanda Jessee's older brothers took up a collection for her from among other Travelers and gave her several hundred dollars.)

Jimmy asked the writer, "Can you believe all this? It's gettin' crazier and crazier. I'm glad I've got no part of it. I can't believe a judge let Peggy out on $5,000 bond, especially after she'd skipped from Georgia. That amount of money don't mean nothin' to Peggy! That's cheap for her. But she took her baby into court with her and cried, and the judge felt sorry for her."

After Peggy's uncle Doug returned from Hawaii, he continued to care for her baby.

Jimmy rented a house in the country not far from Stowe, New York, and for two years, he paved and sealed driveways using the names Jamie Linwood Turner and Thomas Doyle. His efforts to settle permanently in that area failed, however, after he and his nephew Michael (brother Edward's son) bought two new pickup trucks but neglected to make bank payments for them. Chatauqua County issued warrants for Jimmy's and Michael's arrests, but Detective Van Ecklund was unable to find them to serve the warrants. Both men had left the state.

Michael finally was located in Columbus, Ohio, and the truck he was using was returned to the dealership where it was purchased. Police in Syracuse, New York, then stepped forward and asked for custody of Michael because the young man had scammed an elderly woman there with a roof repair job. Michael was jailed in Syracuse on that charge, but he was not prosecuted for vehicle theft by Chatauqua County.

Jimmy, who was traveling under another alias -- Kenneth Bradneck -- was traced to Indiana with the help of an anonymous informant. Jimmy was arrested, and that truck also was returned to the dealership. A lenient judge, however, dismissed felony charges against Jimmy after he agreed to pay $2,500 restitution and leave the county.

All Jimmy did, however, was change his name to Jamie Johnson.

He moved to a mobile home near the village of Harmony, New York, and sold a new Kentucky Traveler trailer that he had bought for $8,300. Then, learning about his brother Paul's suicide, he flew to Orlando for Paul's funeral. When he returned, he telephoned police and reported that his trailer -- which he claimed was worth $19,000 -- had been stolen. Then he filed a claim to collect insurance on the stolen trailer.

When the insurance company asked Chautauqua County police to investigate Jimmy's claims, they learned that Jamie Johnson was really James W. Burke, also known as Jamie Turner. He was arrested and went before a judge facing a twelve-count indictment, including grand larceny, issuing false financial statements, criminal impersonation, conspiracy and insurance fraud. He pleaded guilty to the charges but served only a few weeks in jail because he paid the insurance company restitution for its expenses, and charges were dropped.

A few months later, in 1988, Jimmy concocted another insurance scam with his friend Diane's new husband, Mark. At Hamburg, New York, Jimmy reported that Mark seriously damaged Jimmy's new Chrysler automobile in a traffic accident. Jimmy collected $1,700 from Mark's insurance company, and Mark collected $460 for damage to his own car. When police realized the accident was a scam, they arrested Jimmy's accomplice, and Mark told them exactly where Jimmy could be found -- at a motel in Knoxville, Tennessee, where he was trying to sell a new travel trailer. Police in Tennessee nabbed Jimmy a few hours later, and he was extradited to New York. Again, charges against him were dropped after he agreed to return the insurance company's $1,700.

Police were still interested in seeing Jimmy prosecuted for falsifying vehicle registrations and a driver's licenses, but before they could arrest him on those charges, he left the state. He already had acquired a new truck, so once again he started selling travel trailers and operating driveway and roof scams throughout the eastern half of the U.S.

One day while Jimmy was in the Midwest trying to find victims for his roof sealing scam, an elderly prospective victim asked Jimmy if he knew anything about clearing out sewer lines; he said his sewer line appeared to be clogged. Jimmy, whose paternal grandparents had operated a legitimate septic tank cleaning service in Florida before he was born, said he had a great deal of experience unclogging lines. He bought a pistol router from a local discount store, ran the router into the sewer line and charged the old man $300. Then he proceeded to knock on doors all through that neighborhood and, over the next three days, earned more than $12,000 unclogging sewer lines.

Not only did Jimmy use that scam successfully for several years, but he also told other Travelers about it, and the scam became an important part of the Traveler home improvement repertoire. It was so widely practiced, in fact, that the July/August 1992 edition of *Consumers Digest* warned its readers about it. The article noted, "Because your sewer line probably has a diameter of at least six inches, and the pistol router will chew little more than a two-inch hole, your problem can't possibly be resolved. They'll (the con artists) duly tell you that their work won't be enough. Then they'll convince you to spend $1,200 or $2,000 to replace the old pipes. If you don't want the pipes replaced, they'll sell you a service contract to keep coming back, clearing the pipes."

During the late 1980s and early 1990s, Jimmy traveled extensively throughout the East, Midwest and South with a male companion named David. He spent so much time in the South, in fact, that family members began calling him "Dixie." His youngest sister, Wanda Mary, also joined him on the road, and together, they stole dozens of travel trailers from RV dealerships, campground storage lots and other places.

Later, Wanda Mary would tell the writer that as she and Jimmy traveled, they "worked stores" for gasoline money while they searched for trailers they could steal. "We'd see an RV lot, check it out, take a trailer, haul it clear across the country, put it in storage and go somewhere else to get a title for it. A few days later, we'd sell the trailer and be back in the money again. We'd party, entertain, buy nice clothes, stay in nice hotels and go to concerts -- the whole nine yards. Then, when we were flat-assed broke, we'd go work stores and look for more trailers."

At one point, Jimmy, David and Wanda Mary recruited one of Jimmy's nephews to help and, by using three pickup trucks, the quartet stole three trailers at a time. Wanda Mary reported, "Jimmy said, 'Hell, if you're stealin' one, you might as well steal three!'"

Jimmy also became quite selective about which trailers he stole. Once, as Wanda Mary removed a serial number plate from a Coach-Master trailer and prepared to hook it onto a truck, Jimmy stopped her and said, "Wait a minute, kid. That's a 28-footer. It's too small. Go over there and get that 35-footer with the slideout."

Wanda Mary said, "He became so particular about what he was stealin' that he'd use his pass keys to go inside the trailers and check them out before he took them!"

Assigned the job of acquiring new titles for the stolen trailers, Wanda Mary became a familiar figure at vehicle registration bureaus in Georgia and Alabama. "I had so many aliases and so many different IDs that I couldn't keep track of them," she said later. "We were making a trip to Iowa every other week just to get new IDs."

In 1985, Jimmy's father, Edward T. Burke, died. He was sixty-one years old. His death, in effect, split the family apart, although his widow, Wanda, tried to rule the family single-handedly until she died in April 1992. Very little is known about her activities during the last seven years of her life.

Jimmy's brother Edward Thomas, 33 years old when his father died, followed the sun in the Northern Traveler tradition, spending most of his time in the Midwest. He developed a cocaine addiction after reportedly being introduced to the drug by his sister, Jessee. Within a year, apparently due to drugs, he lost virtually everything he owned and was sent to jail on fraud charges. At last report, he was serving two prison terms in Ohio -- one under the name of Edward Daley and the other under his own name. While his family lived on welfare in a Columbus housing project, his 20-year-old son, Danny, started running with a street gang and, in 1995, was arrested for armed robbery and drug possession; he is now serving a 25-year prison term in the same cellblock as his father. Another of Edward and Elizabeth's children, 17-year-old Marty, killed himself in 1995.

Patrick Paul -- The Viking -- was 31 when his father died; among law enforcement agencies, he became the best known member of the Burke family and was sought by police throughout the Midwest and South at one time or another prior to the Disney scam.

Jimmy's sister Wanda O'Roarke -- known to police as "Big Wanda," as opposed to young Wanda Mary, who was called "Little Wanda" -- tried to break away from the Irish Travelers by changing her name legally to Jessee O'Roarke and moving to Maine; the Disney scam attracted her back into the Traveler lifestyle.

Very little is known about the activities of Jimmy's sister Winnie except for a few details that will be mentioned later.

Jimmy's sister Cathy, after divorcing Traveler Tony Robertson, married Ohioan Matt England (not his real name). England was very abusive to Cathy and, on at least two occasions, put a gun to her head and threatened to kill her. About the same time as old Wanda died,

Cathy was found dead from a gunshot wound. In one hand, she was holding a pistol. Although her death was ruled a suicide, family members believe she was murdered by her husband. Her two children are being raised by her ex-husband Tony.

Wanda Mary, the youngest member of the family, married a Western Traveler named John Patrick Normile from San Antonio when she was eighteen; she left him shortly after her baby, Winifred, was born, and by the time the Disney scam was executed, he had seen his daughter only a few times.

Following her Uncle Doug's return to Orlando from Hawaii, Peggy Burke left her son with him and moved to the east coast of Florida. At Delray Beach, she met and married a black man named Martin and gave birth to two children -- Anastasia in 1984 and Clyde Joseph in 1986. Then she left her husband and was later described by police as the best-known prostitute in the Palm Beach area. Two more children followed: Todd Joseph and James Paul, nicknamed J.P.

In April 1987, Peggy reported to Boynton Beach police that her companion of the evening was acting strangely and was in possession of cocaine. When officers searched the man's car, they found 5.7 grams of cocaine and discovered he was a vice unit lieutenant in the Delray Beach police department; Peggy insisted she did not know he was a cop. The lieutenant resigned, entered a drug-treatment program and pleaded guilty to cocaine possession, for which he received eighteen months' probation. Later, he was rehired as the city's code enforcement officer. In March 1991, Peggy told a policeman that a rookie officer asked her for sex after picking her up on the Federal Highway; the rookie, who was still on probation, resigned five days after his supervisors were notified of Peggy's allegations.

By 1992, Peggy had accumulated arrest records in several states. At 33 years old, she weighed 180 pounds and was five-foot-seven inches tall. She had acquired tattoos on both ankles, one breast, her left arm and her right shoulder, and she possessed ten different Social Security numbers and birth dates. Her best known aliases included Star Bakas, Annette Bradshaw, Peggy Betz, Yolanda Bradshaw, Wanda Mary Burke, Theresa Carson, Lisa Clark, Lisa Halsey, Theresa Halsey, Yolanda Halsey, Margaret Hartford, Evelyn Hernandez, Annette Martin, Peggy Ann Martin, Theresa Martin, Peggy McNally, Linda Morgan, Lisa Morgan, Mary Morgan, Peggy Morgan and Lisa Riley. Her given name, which she seldom used, was Margaret Theresa Burke.

Irish, Scottish and English Travelers continued to prey on American homeowners -- focusing especially on the elderly -- during the 1980s and into the 1990s. Law enforcement officials estimated in 1986 that only ten per cent of all home improvement scams were even reported to police. Former Florida Detective Joe Morris explained, "People are embarrassed, or they tell police that are not familiar with the way the (scam artists) work. Or, if they are elderly, they are afraid their family will find out and try to control their lives."

Each winter, Travelers kept their confidence game skills sharp by preying upon elderly Florida residents and vacationers.

During the first six months of 1987, more central Florida residents called the area's Better Business Bureau to check on roofing contractors than on any other type of business -- proof that the Travelers were quite active in Florida following their annual holiday parties. A year later, central Florida businesses were invited to attend special seminars on how to prevent shoplifting in their stores.

Early in 1989, responding to continuing reports of Travelers swindling residents in home repair frauds, the Florida Division of Consumer Services produced a booklet titled *Home Repair -- Before You Start*. It provided tips on how to identify home improvement con artists and how to avoid being cheated by them.

Less than two weeks after the booklet was offered, however, three Irish Travelers posing as carpenters offered to repair the kitchen of an Orlando woman and, during the next six hours, she wrote them checks for $5,020, $6,350 and $8,975. But that wasn't the end of their work. The *Orlando Sentinel* reported, "During the week that followed, the carpenters painted the kitchen cabinets, installed a little linoleum and charged the woman in excess of $20,000 more. The scam ended when her lawyer notified police."

Nearly a month later, police arrested 19-year-old Traveler Peter Gorman when he tried to retrieve an Indiana I.D. that he left at a bank when he tried to cash one of the victim's checks. Gorman identified one of his accomplices as 43-year-old John "Little John" Kent, who was arrested later at the Happy Traveler Campground in Tampa. Charged with grand theft and released on bond, the two men left Florida. Late in 1991, Kent was arrested in South Carolina for skipping bond, but the state attorney general's office there declined to press charges due to insufficient evidence after Kent claimed his identification had been stolen.

Just before Christmas in 1991, two Travelers told an elderly Mount Dora, Florida, woman that the roof of her mobile home needed repaired badly. Then, after inspecting it, they informed her it would require much more work than they originally thought and asked her for several hundred dollars as a down payment. They left with the check she wrote and never returned. Two different men told her a week later that her power meter needed to be repaired, and they charged her $2,000 for that work.

In mid-January 1992, the *Orlando Sentinel* reported that three Travelers, claiming to work for a local roofing company, stopped at the St. Cloud home of a 90-year-old man and his 79-year-old wife and offered them a twenty-dollar rebate on their year-old roofing job. "Less than an hour later," the newspaper said, "after convincing the couple the roof needed repairs, the men started to leave with $1,040 in cash when the wife asked them for her twenty-dollar rebate. The crew boss apologized, peeled off a twenty-dollar bill and left. No repairs were done or needed, police said."

The newspaper warned its readers, "Police throughout central Florida expect more such crimes." Part of the reason for their concerns was that more than 100 families of Travelers were, at that point, camped in parks on West US Highway 192 in western Osceola County.

Some law enforcement agencies questioned by the newspaper said scams such as lightning rod sales, blacktopping and insurance fraud were low-priority economic crimes for police faced with investigating violent and drug-related crimes. One central Florida officer categorized home improvement scams as civil matters, not crimes, because at least some work was performed. Pinellas County Investigator John Wood called such claims excuses not to investigate and prosecute the con artists. "Any time the Travelers do a good job, it's an accident. Trust me," he told the *Sentinel*.

The next month, two Travelers told an 83-year-old Leesburg, Florida, resident that they would repair his roof for just sixteen dollars. The elderly man removed sixteen dollars from a metal box in his home that contained $17,000 and then, while he was on the roof inspecting the repair job, the men went into his home and took the box containing the cash. Travelers also took $8,500 from a Fruitland Park man in a similar manner two weeks later.

Two Irish Travelers convinced an 81-year-old Cuban immigrant in Hialeah that they had purchased a winning Florida lottery ticket but were unable to redeem it because they were illegal Irish aliens. They offered to sell him the ticket for only $25,000. He declined the offer regretfully, saying his life savings amounted to only $7,000. The con artists conversed quietly in whispers with each other and then gave the Cuban some good news: They would accept his $7,000 in return for their ticket. The old man withdrew all his money from a Hialeah bank and gave it to the two Travelers. An hour later, when he tried to cash in the lottery ticket, he was told that the winning numbers on the ticket were for the prior week's lottery, not for the current one. Realizing he had been swindled out of his life savings, the man drove his car into a canal and drowned himself.

During the funeral of Jimmy Burke's mother in April 1992, the stage was unwittingly set for the Disney World scam that Jimmy, Jessee and Wanda Mary would plan several months later. Jessee and her uncle Doug spoke to each other for the first time since she had sold his household furniture in a fit of rage, and they agreed to reconcile the following fall when she intended to visit Orlando during the annual Irish Traveler gathering.

At that point, Peggy had left her husband and was living with an elderly black man in the southwest section of Delray Beach, Florida, a predominantly black neighborhood. On October 20, about the time her sisters and brother were planning their Disney scam, 28-year-old Peggy was stopped in her car during the middle of the night by a Delray police officer. The policeman, a 24-year-old black patrol cop named Adrian Cohen, informed Peggy she was speeding, had run several stop signs, and was driving without headlights. A call to police headquarters also revealed her driver's license had been suspended. Cohen told Peggy to drive her car home, and he would follow her. Then he would decide whether to arrest her.

At her home, Peggy was ordered to get into Cohen's vehicle. "I got in the back of the car, and he told me to lay down," she reported later.

Peggy said Cohen then drove to the rear parking lot of the Florida Power & Light Company building and forced her to have sex with him. After Cohen took her home, Peggy drove to a local hospital and asked to be examined as a rape victim. Then she filed rape charges against Cohen with the Palm Beach County sheriff's office. While being questioned by sheriff's deputies, Peggy admitted that she had consented to have sex with Cohen, that he had not raped her. She told deputies, "He's been bugging me for two months to have sex with him, so I decided to oblige him and then turn him in."

Since no crime had been committed, the sheriff's office turned over investigation of Peggy's complaint to Delray Beach police. "There was nothing for us to investigate," sheriff's spokesman Bob Ferrell said. "It was an ethical or internal matter."

Cohen vehemently denied Peggy's allegations, but his supervisors placed him on administrative leave. They were, however, reluctant to believe Peggy because the young policeman had compiled an excellent record since being hired by the Delray force in 1991. They described him as a good, observant officer who received four patrol commendations in 1992. Cohen also had been named "Officer of the Month" for preventing a burglary and, after checking the tag of a suspicious-looking vehicle, recovering a stolen car and arresting the thieves.

On the other hand, there was some evidence that Cohen had an explosive temper and, perhaps, some personal problems. His department had once investigated him for discharging a firearm at his home after an argument with his wife; Cohen was cleared of wrongdoing when he claimed the weapon fired accidentally, but he was ordered to undergo weapons safety training.

Peggy's earlier complaints against two other Delray officers also caused police to be suspicious of her motives. Additionally, Peggy's extensive police record raised doubts about her credibility; her Florida law enforcement file indicated she had been arrested at least 130 times since 1983. Her credibility suffered another setback the day after filing her complaint against Cohen; she was arrested for trying to steal two bottles of gin from a Walgreen drug store.

Investigation of Peggy's sexual misconduct allegations against Cohen moved slowly, even after blood samples that were taken from him and compared with semen recovered by the hospital revealed that the policeman and Peggy had, indeed, performed sex together.

Peggy consented to take a polygraph test and passed it, and lab reports revealed that her palm print was found on Cohen's patrol car. While the internal affairs office of the Delray Beach police department considered that evidence, Cohen's attorney advised him to check into the Fair Oaks psychiatric hospital for evaluation.

Ten days after entering the hospital, Cohen's well known temper flared, and he claimed members of the city police department were trying to force him out of law enforcement. He threatened to kill those officers and then walked away from the hospital. Ninety minutes later, he returned to answer questions from sheriff's deputies who had been called to the medical facility. The *Palm Beach Post* reported, "Sunday's incident will affect Cohen's return to the city, City Manage David Harden said. The officer would have to be evaluated and found to be fit for duty, he said."

Less than two weeks later, on Monday, April 5, internal affairs investigators concluded that Cohen had performed sex with Peggy while on duty. That report was not made public until five days later.

Meanwhile, Cohen was arrested in Boynton Beach for firing three shots into his girlfriend's car. Circumstances surrounding the shooting were not evident because the woman dropped charges before police could complete their investigation. As Cohen was in custody at the Boynton Beach jail, he punched the bars and threatened to take an officer's gun so he could shoot himself in the head. City Manager Harden immediately fired Cohen "for medical reasons" and a judge ordered Cohen to be admitted to the South County Medical Health Center.

The *Palm Beach Post* reported, "A medical dismissal is not subject to appeal, but Cohen could submit evidence that he is fit for duty. Doctors for the city would then reevaluate him." The newspaper quoted City Manager Harden as saying, "If he were found to be medically fit, then we would have to deal with the (internal affairs investigation) plus the felony charges from the shooting the other night."

The newspaper began its own investigation of Cohen, and in a copyrighted article on May 27, 1993, the *Post* revealed that a week before he had sex with Peggy Burke, he was accused of raping a teenage girl at the same location where he drove Peggy. An internal affairs report acquired by the newspaper indicated the 18-year-old rape victim declined to press charges.

The *Post* stated, "The woman told police Cohen drove her to an office complex. He sat her on the trunk of his patrol car and tried kissing her and licking her legs. When she kicked him and ran, she said, Cohen 'grabbed her around the neck and shoulders...threw her to the ground...then held her down while pulling and ripping her shorts off,' the report says. The woman told a patrol officer about 'various acts of misconduct,' according to the internal affairs report."

Following news reports of Peggy Burke's complaint against Cohen, the *Post* said, the teenager "gave police a sworn statement alleging that Cohen raped her. She declined, though, to press charges. Neither Cohen nor his attorney...could be reached for comment. Cohen has told police he knew the woman, had talked to her and once went to her home to tell her to stop making advances toward him."

The newspaper said internal affairs investigator Lieutenant James Wilson wrote in his report that the teenager's statement "bears several striking, intimate similarities to the complaint filed against Officer Cohen a week later."

Within two weeks of the *Post* article, police in Cohen's home town of Boynton Beach stopped him for a traffic violation and, while searching his car, found a 9-millimeter Smith & Wesson semi-automatic pistol hidden under the seat. He was charged with carrying a concealed weapon, but a judge later ruled the search was improper and ordered charges against the former officer dropped. The gun was returned to Cohen in December.

Two months later, Peggy Burke was found murdered in the cab of a pickup truck. She had been shot six times at point-blank range with a 9-millimeter pistol.

# 24

# The Whistle Blows

Law enforcement agencies in the western Midwest were advised to watch for Irish Traveler Pat "The Viking" Burke during the early summer of 1993. An elderly Iowa man had identified The Viking as the person who robbed him during a home improvement swindle. That state had experienced a rash of strongarmed robberies related to home invasions and home repair fraud, and the primary suspects besides Burke were John and Lloyd Compton. The half-Traveler brothers were also still being sought in connection with a series of similar incidents the year before in Maine. Investigators sought Pat Burke for two reasons: First, descriptions of one robber fit the tall, sandy haired Burke quite well, and secondly, several of the incidents matched The Viking's well known M.O. of using duct tape to incapacitate his victims. Pat's use of duct tape, in fact, was so widely known that he was reported to have once boasted, "I ought to have an investment in 3-M, I've used so much of their tape."

The robbery in Iowa started out as a home improvement scam. Burke and the Comptons stopped at an elderly man's home in Denison and warned the man not to hire some other Travelers who were repairing driveways in the same area.

"They're con artists," Burke told the homeowner.

Then, posing as utility company inspectors, Burke and the Comptons convinced the man to let them repair his home's electrical system. To do the job, however, they needed to be paid in advance. The old fellow said he did not have any cash, so they drove him to his bank in Burke's van so he could withdraw the necessary funds. While returning to the man's home, Burke ordered his victim out of the van and drove away, leaving the old man standing beside the deserted country road.

Iowa police put out a regional bulletin on the van and its occupants. Two days later, a South Dakota Highway Patrol officer stopped the van for a minor traffic violation and, after realizing it was the vehicle wanted in Iowa, he searched the van and found marijuana. The Viking admitted the pot was his, so he was arrested on drug possession charges and then extradited to Iowa for prosecution. Not realizing the Comptons were involved in the Iowa robbery, police detained them briefly and then released them on bond. Immediately, the brothers drove Burke's van to Minnesota. South Dakota police, realizing later they should have held the Comptons, put out a four-state alarm for them, but in the meantime, the brothers stashed Burke's van in the Minneapolis airport parking lot and purchased airline tickets to Cleveland.

At that point, The Viking's FBI rap sheet was impressive, showing warrants or arrests in 1971 for shoplifting in Florida; 1971 for theft in Indiana; 1975 for eluding police and reckless operation in Florida; 1976 for assault and battery in Florida; 1981 for disorderly conduct and resisting arrest in South Carolina, and 1985 as a fugitive from Arkansas.

In February 1989, in an ironic twist of fate, he was arrested for shoplifting at Macon, Georgia, from the same J.C. Penney's store where Officer Neil Godbee had arrested Jimmy Burke nine years earlier for car theft. At that time, Pat and Rose had shoplifted for several days at various stores in Atlanta and Macon. In asking for refunds for their stolen merchandise, Pat identified himself either as Christopher McNally or Patrick McNally, and Rose showed I.D. proving she was Patricia Burke and Rose McNally. Alerted by department stores' security personnel, police watched for Pat to return to the Macon Mall, and when he did, they arrested him. He was fined $150, ordered to pay restitution and sentenced to one year in jail and one year probation. After paying his fines and the restitution, Pat was released from jail.

He and Rose Mary drove to Ohio, where Pat was arrested three different times -- once for falsification of documents and twice for petty theft. He was sought in Rhode Island in 1990 for assault with a knife, and in Tennessee in 1993 for reckless vehicle endangerment and assault on a police officer.

The Viking's overall police record, of course, was much more extensive than his FBI rap sheet. He was known to practice extortion against Murphy Village residents -- who, as a whole, considered him to be a very dangerous individual -- and he was regarded by police as an accomplice of the notorious Johnny "Hook" Mack, both in home repair swindles and counterfeiting.

In 1995, Florida investigator John McMahan would tell the writer about the counterfeiting activity and comment, "Pat will make money wherever he can, and he doesn't much mind who he associates with."

McMahan's associate, Detective John Wood, referred to the counterfeiting as "an aberration" among Travelers. "And for good reason," he emphasized. "Why would the Travelers want to get involved with something as dangerous as counterfeiting or drug selling when they can do what they've done for years and no one ever looks at them? The smart ones are still doing what they've done successfully for the last fifty or sixty years since they gave up horse trading. Some of them are millionaires because of it."

McMahan added, "Drugs are another thing. Pat smokes marijuana constantly, but for the most part, drugs are unheard of among the older Travelers. Drugs are another one of those aberration things with the Burkes. And Pat is a big-time user."

The Viking's sister, Wanda "Jessee" O'Roarke, was well aware of both Pat's reputation and his capabilities when she clashed with him in September 1993 near Youngstown, Ohio, about resolution of the Disney World scam. She knew she was risking a serious beating by opposing Pat's plan to settle with Disney for one or two million dollars. But at the time, Jessee did not believe her brother would try to kill her.

According to police reports, she was wrong.

Jessee was frightened when Pat pinned her to the couch in his trailer and then asked his son for the 9-millimeter pistol that The Viking always kept in the bedroom. That fright turned to horror as Pat put the gun to her head and pulled the trigger three times.

Later, Pat would deny that the events occurred that way, and Wandy Mary would insist that no gun was ever involved in the conflict. But Jessee, in a statement to police officers, claimed Pat tried to kill her, and she theorized that when her nephew retrieved the pistol for his father, he accidentally ejected the clip from it, and the gun was empty.

"I heard the gun go 'click,'" Jessee told investigators. "And when the gun didn't go off, I think it surprised him. He hit me in the head with it. Somehow, in the confusion of being in a 32-foot travel trailer with five children, Wanda Mary and her baby, plus my sister-in-law and my brother, I got loose and out the open front door of the trailer and into my truck as he chased me, yelling to me that I was gonna be killed, that he would kill me."

Wanda Mary's version of events differed considerably from Jessee's. When Jessee first arrived at Pat's trailer, Wanda Mary said, Jessee grabbed her by the hair and dragged her into the bedroom to discuss settlement of the lawsuit against Disney. Wanda Mary said her sister told her that when they arrived in Orlando, she wanted Wanda Mary to inform her attorney that she was mentally incapable of handling her own money and that she wanted the Disney check to be written to Jessee, who would be designated as Wanda Mary's financial advisor. Wanda Mary said she was told if she did not agree to do that, Jessee would beat her and have her arrested.

"When Pat returned to the trailer," Wanda Mary recalled later, "I blurted out what Jessee had said. He flipped out, beat the shit out of her and kicked her out of the trailer."

According to Jessee, Pat warned her not to go to the police. She said Pat announced he intended to contact Wanda Mary's Florida attorney, Ernest H. Eubanks Jr., first and tell him that the Disney scam was Jessee's idea and that Jessee had held Wanda Mary as a captive in Maine and forced her to be a part of the swindle.

When police officers asked Jessee if she really believed Pat tried to kill her, she answered, "Yes, I did. With no hesitation. My brother Pat would do it in a second. He is a very dangerous man. And he would kill somebody because he just goes off, and he wouldn't think twice about it."

She added, "He told me a story just a couple of weeks ago of how he took a gun and put it to a man's head and pulled the trigger three times. It was the man's gun. I guess the man had pulled a gun on him, and he took the gun off the man and held him down and put the gun to (the man's) head and pulled the trigger. He said how fucking stupid (the man) was. He said, 'He pulled an empty gun on me!' But if the gun wouldn't have been empty, he would've killed that man, and he wouldn't have thought twice about it."

Still in possession of the airline ticket to Orlando, Jessee tried to drive to the airport, but she couldn't find it at first. When she finally did find the airport, the early afternoon flight on which she was scheduled had already departed. Certain that her brother would be searching for her, Jessee drove cautiously to the Scottish Inn motel where she had rented a room, and she convinced a friendly house-keeper there to hide her truck. Jessee also described her brother's truck to the motel manager, and the manager volunteered to tell any-one who inquired that Jessee had apparently left without checking out.

"I went back to my room and locked myself in," Jessee said. "They (motel employees) said that Pat's truck had cruised the motel a couple of times. They (her relatives) thought I was gone, so they hooked onto their trailer and left town. They (must have) figured that I was calling the police, or they wasn't gonna take the chance if I was gonna call the police. I would say they headed south to Vir-ginia, the Carolinas or Georgia, but he (Pat) could've been within thirty or forty miles of Youngstown, still figuring to come back and find me. So I laid low until I was able to get out of town." (In actu-al fact, her relatives drove from Youngstown to Dayton, then south to Nashville, where they waited to hear from either Jimmy or Jessee.)

Jessee telephoned Florida attorney Eubanks and told him that she wanted to meet with him earlier than planned. "Does this have any-thing to do with the Disney case?" he asked.

"Well, yes," she answered, "but I need to speak to you in private without Wanda or my brother. I think the Disney case is a scam, and I have information that I need to talk to you or somebody else about."

Eubank responded that he would not be involved in any swindle. "I'm not that kind of attorney," he said, "and any information you have, you should turn over to the sheriff's office." Eubank said he intended to speak with Wanda Mary about Jessee's allegations.

Jessee did not talk with Eubank again. She telephoned her uncle Doug in Orlando and told him about the scam and Pat's alleged attempt to kill her. "What should I do?" she asked, sobbing into the telephone.

Doug, a professional hairdresser, had a client who was an officer with the Orange County sheriff's department, and he offered to arrange for Jessee to meet with with the policewoman -- intelligence analyst Susan Taylor. Jessee agreed and gave Doug the telephone number of her motel room. That evening, Taylor called Jessee, and Jessee consented to meet with sheriff's office investigators in Orlando three days later. Taylor told Jessee she wanted to interview Doug about events surrounding the scam prior to Jessee's arrival. Doug wired money to Jessee so she could drive to Florida.

Two days before Jessee arrived in Orlando, police officers asked her uncle, Doug, what transpired the day of the Disney scam. He said when he arrived home from work that day, Jessee, Jimmy, Wanda Mary and Winnie Burke were there. Jimmy was dressed in an "outlandish" costume with "Halloweenish makeup" on, including "blackish lips, whitish face, dark reddish around the eyes." Jimmy left Doug's home about 6:30 p.m., and soon after that, Doug drove Wanda Mary to the home of a friend named Michael.

An officer asked, "Did Jessee have any conversation with you regarding what Wanda Mary was doing with Michael?"

Doug replied, "She led me to believe that they were going to have sex. She said something like, 'I hope that bitch hurries up and gets finished.'"

Jessee left Doug's house about eight o'clock, and Doug said he did not hear from any of his relatives until the next morning, when they arrived at his home again. Wanda Mary had bandages on her face "and she looked like she had been roughed up," Doug said. "She didn't go into it. She just, like recessed, like a beaten kid."

Later, Doug said, Jessee told him Wanda Mary had been raped. "I asked where, and she said, 'At the motel.'

"I asked, 'What motel?'

"She said, 'At Disney.'"

Doug told police he could not understand why the two women were at a motel when all their clothes and luggage were at his home. Jessee asked Doug for advice on obtaining legal counsel. He presumed it was concerning the rape, he said, "and I figured without a doubt, they were going to try to have some lawsuit going."

Police asked Doug if he knew whether Wanda Mary was actually raped, and he replied, "I presumed she was not."

"Why?"

"After she left here, I do not know what happened, but I do know what supposedly happened at Michael's place." That was where Wanda Mary had obtained the semen sample she needed for the Disney scam.

During a tape-recorded interview with Orange County officers Susan Taylor and Tom Harrison on September 30, 1993, Jessee informed them, "My family are gypsies. Irish Travelers."

Asked if the statement given by her to police almost a year earlier had been accurate, Jessee replied, "No sir, it was not."

"Why is it that now you're here to give us a different story?" Harrison asked.

"Because I've lived with this for almost a year, knowing that it (her earlier statement) was not the truth. What happened at Disney's hotel was all set up," she answered. "I was involved in it, not wanting to be involved in it, and I'm here to clear the air and my conscience and to set things straight. My brother, Jimmy Burke, and my sister, Wanda Mary Normile, had put that plan together. I didn't wanna go along with it, but I ended up going along with it."

Jessee told the officers she wanted to "get my life back where it was before then, and to be straight and honest with the people here at the sheriff's department."

Harrison asked, "Who concocted the idea and where did the concoction take place?"

"The first I heard of this," Jessee answered, "we had went out to dinner at the Cattleman's Steakhouse in Sanford. Over dinner that night, my brother Jimmy started talking of this idea that he had and this plan of suing a large corporation or hotel. He brought up that

Wanda Mary could be used because she was so tiny and young look-ing and innocent looking and could be the perfect victim." She said she believed Jimmy and Wanda Mary had already discussed a plan. Besides Jessee, Jimmy and Wanda Mary, the dinner also was attend-ed by John Holton (not his real name), a non-Traveler friend of Jessee's uncle Doug.

As Jimmy and Wanda Mary discussed how to arrange a lawsuit against a company or hotel, they did not mention Disney World, Jessee said. "They just threw across the ideas of how it could be done. Jimmy, from what I understand, got the idea from seeing a TV show where I guess this had actually happened at a hotel. I really couldn't believe what I was hearing. I thought that it was just talk, or I thought that he may possibly try it (in the future). I did not know that he had plans in the next few days for it to happen and that I was going to be involved, and neither did John Holton."

She added, "John and I spoke afterward, saying how crazy of an idea it was and that Jimmy was crazy and Wanda Mary was even cra-zier for (considering) it and thinking they could get away with it. But I was the most crazy of all, I believe, because I ended up right slap dab in the middle of it."

During the next few days, Jessee said, Jimmy and Wanda put into action their plan to swindle Disney World out of several million dol-lars. Jessee quoted her brother as telling her, "All you have to do is go to the hotel with (Wanda Mary) and say that you are on vacation from Maine."

Jessee emphasized to the investigators, "I was not in agreement with it, and where I made my mistake was, I didn't stand up and say absolutely no, that I didn't want a part of it. Before I knew it, I was in the middle of it. I was there; it happened before I knew it, and it was all too late for...It happened so fast, I had no time to think about it, other than to know it was wrong."

Her original reason for traveling to Florida, Jessee said, was to rec-oncile with her uncle Doug and resolve a dispute between them that occurred several years earlier. She also regarded the visit as a vacation period. "Jimmy had told me a couple of days earlier that they had a room at the Disney World Caribbean Beach Resort that they had *chuckied* -- *chuckied* is a gypsy word for getting something for nothing. I was led to believe that we had a free room and that we were all invited to go out there to enjoy ourselves for the weekend. As it went on, I found out that the room had been rented for this plan."

Harrison asked what Jimmy's role in the scam was to be. "Jimmy's role was the assailant," Jessee replied. "Jimmy was the one who came into the room and supposedly was Wanda's attacker. He was disguised as Dracula."

She laid out details of the scam, and Harrison asked Jessee if she knew what would transpire inside the hotel room during her absence. "Basically, I did," she admitted. "Wanda let Jimmy into the room, and then he was supposed to mess up the room and make it look like a robbery. And supposedly just slap her (Wanda Mary) around. Supposedly."

Harrison asked, "Were you surprised when you got to the hospital to see Wanda Mary in the state that she was in?"

"I was very surprised. I had no idea that it (Wanda Mary's beating) was going to be to that extent. I could not believe that Wanda Mary would let her brother (do that) and agree to go along with it to that extent."

Asked about her own role, Jessee said, "I was supposed to come back to the room and find her, and I was supposed to report it."

"Do you know why it didn't work out that way?"

"Because I didn't come back in time and do what I was supposed to do. Instead, I went to a restaurant and had dinner. I actually didn't eat. I ordered a dinner and sat there and thought and contemplated whether to call and tell (the police). And I didn't do it because I didn't want to turn my family in."

Harrison asked Jessee about her conversations with Wanda Mary at the hospital. She replied, "I think I was kind of in shock when I saw her. Whenever I was alone with her, she didn't really talk to me...She didn't really wanna look at me."

Jessee said she asked Wanda Mary, "Why is it like this? Was it supposed to be like this?" Wanda Mary did not provide a satisfactory reply, Jessee said.

"She just went on and played her part, I guess." Later, Wanda Mary told Jessee the beating she took was part of the plan and that Jimmy had convinced her she must submit to it.

"I have talked to Wanda Mary for almost a year since that (the scam) happened. I have talked to Wanda Mary and talked to Wanda Mary and talked to Wanda Mary. I have asked her to come forward with me. I have asked her to change her life and said that I would go through it with her, and that I would help her as best I could, and if she didn't do it for herself, for her baby. And that this was only gonna come to a very bad end. Wanda Mary does not want to hear any of that. Wanda Mary could see no further than a settlement and money and what she was gonna have and buy and do when it was over." Jessee told police she had talked with Jimmy only a few times since the scam; on those occasions, Jimmy telephoned for information on how the lawsuit and the prospects for settlement were progressing.

Harrison asked, "What involvement has Patrick had in this?"

Jessee replied, "Pat had no involvement, to my knowledge, until the middle of June or first of July. I don't know when Wanda Mary got in contact with Pat and started informing him what was going on and what the plan was. But Wanda grew very unhappy in Maine, and very unhappy with me because I was trying to change her and talk her into dropping the lawsuit."

After providing officers with details of her confrontation with Pat and his alleged attempt to shoot her, Jessee added that her brother and sister probably were not convinced she would blow the whistle on the scam. "I believe they figure that I've done nothing and will do nothing because of it being family and being a code. And because of my part in it, I wouldn't want to spill the beans on myself."

"What do you mean by 'the code'?" Harrison asked.

"The family code that Travelers and gypsies have," she answered. "You don't involve the police in anything. Whatever happens happens among the families. If my brother Pat would've killed me there (in Youngstown) and the police came out, they'd all have said, 'Well, the gun went off, and she got killed,' and everybody would've swore I was killed accidentally."

Susan Taylor asked, "To get out of the Travelers, can you just turn and walk away from it?"

"No. I tried. You're either disowned and thrown out because you've disagreed with them, or if you're talking to the police, as I'm sitting here talking to you now, you won't be accepted and will not be trusted. And either I will be beaten each time I'm seen by certain families or my outfit will be destroyed -- I'm saying outfit as in truck, trailer and car -- each time I am seen. Or, I would be killed by my brother Pat or by somebody that he would have to do it."

"Do you fear that Pat would do that?"

"Pat would do it in a second. Yes, I do fear that."


John Holton, Doug's friend who attended the steakhouse dinner to which Jessee referred in her interview with police, described the event as "a lot of joking around " initially. But, he told investigators, as the evening progressed, "Jimmy kept saying that him and Wanda Mary had a plan that might make them very wealthy. The plan entailed Disney and some type of scam. Of what, I didn't know at that time. It was something in the future that could happen to Wanda Mary, and it could end up being very rewarding to Jimmy and the family. Most of the conversation seemed like (its purpose) was to get Wanda Jessee wound up or excited."

Holton, who had known members of the Burke family for several years, was aware that they were lifetime con artists. But he said Jessee had just started putting her life in order apart from the Traveler lifestyle when "all of a sudden" Jimmy and Wanda Mary appeared and seemed bent on attracting her back into it. Holton said he felt Jessee's younger sister, Winnie, was never involved in planning the scam, although she appeared to be aware of it.

After dinner at the steakhouse, Holton said he and Jessee drove home together, "and we were just amazed at the conversation (about a scam against Disney). We were shocked and said, 'God, they're crazy.'" He admitted to police, however, that the discussion fit the tone of periodic bizarre conversations within the Burke family. He said he tried to dismiss the steakhouse talk as another in a long series of Irish Traveler schemes that would never be implemented.

"When these people are around," he told police, "I just don't take them seriously, and I laugh 'em off. I've learned to shut my ears off when they're around because they're very manipulative."

He added, "They're also very vicious about scheming against each other."

No more discussions about a Disney scam were held in his presence following the dinner, Holton said.

Investigator Harrison asked, "What was the next thing that occurred that raised your suspicions that maybe they did carry out the plan?"

"On Halloween night, I went to a friend's party and took my nine-year-old son. Just before I left, Wanda Mary asked me for my friend Michael's phone number. Well, I don't give 'em my numbers, so I dialed Michael's for her." Minutes later, Wanda Mary asked Doug to drop her off at Michael's house. Then, early the next morning, Jessee and Wanda Mary returned to Doug's house, and Wanda Mary was crying. "She said, 'You won't believe what's happened. I've been raped.' I was shocked. I said, 'Oh, my God. This is awful!'"

The next day, when Holton heard news reports about the rape at a Disney World hotel, he realized what had probably occurred. "I put two and two together," he said. "For a few days, Doug and I were just in a daze. We wanted 'em gone! We wanted 'em out of here without trouble. I could tell Wanda Jessee was distraught. She kept saying over and over to herself, 'Why did I listen to him? Why did I listen to Jimmy? How could he do this? Why did we have to do this?'"

Holton continued, "From that point on, I stayed away from my house as much as possible. I was not raised with that type of people, so any time over the years that there has been a problem, I disappeared, and I stayed away until they were gone. I just knew that this was bad, and it made me very nervous. Doug and I talked later, and we felt like our home had been invaded and abused, that our lives had been invaded -- again!"

Harrison asked, "Did you ever tell anybody -- the authorities, law enforcement, Disney -- what your suspicions were?"

"There were several times that Doug and I wanted to, but we've seen these people -- these kids -- in trouble in the past. Anything that they have done together, they have ended up fighting about and getting themselves into trouble by the commotions that they cause. They turn each other in to the police and that sort of thing." Knowing the tendency of family members to scheme against each other, Holton said, "we just knew it would come out in the wash. And, as usual, we were right."

After learning from Jessee about Pat's attempt to kill her, Holton said, he and Doug had each received phone calls from Wanda Mary and Pat asking if they had heard from Jessee. "Wanda Mary called just yesterday. She said she had heard Jessee was on her way to Florida and that if we heard from Jimmy, he should leave a phone number where they could reach him. She told me she and Pat had contacted the lawyer and dropped the lawsuit because there were too many arguments going on within the family."

John and Doug's friend, Michael, voluntarily submitted to blood and semen tests so that his DNA could be compared with that of the semen recovered from Wanda Mary during the night of her alleged rape. Results of the comparisons were inconclusive.

Based on Jessee's statements to police, arrest warrants were issued for Wanda Mary and Jimmy, charging them with filing a false report, conspiracy to commit grand theft and attempted grand theft. Ninth Judicial Circuit Judge Belvin Perry also authorized $100,000 bonds for them. Police were certain Wanda Mary was traveling with Pat and his family, but none of the family members had seen Jimmy for several months. No charges were filed against Jessee O'Roarke.

No one in the Burke family knew it yet, but the HIV virus Jimmy had acquired in prison had developed into full-blown AIDS. His physical condition had deteriorated significantly, but only a few close friends -- including his companion, David, and a friend named Andre -- knew Jimmy was dying, and he had sworn them to secrecy. Aware that the length of his life was seriously limited, he had decided that before he died, he would build a lasting reputation among the Travelers by pulling off the biggest score in the Irish clan's history. It was for that reason that he had no intention of accepting an offer from Disney for a relatively small settlement figure.

"I'm gonna be more famous than Old Tom Carroll," Jimmy once confided to a friend.

One year and six days after police were called to Wanda Mary's hotel room to investigate her apparent rape, beating and robbery, the *Orlando Sentinel* revealed the scam in a front-page article. The copyrighted report was picked by the nation's newswire services and was broadcast and published all over the world. Commenting about the fake crimes, Orange County Sergeant Ken Cox told reporters, "They made it look very realistic."

The article said, "Last week, an informant angry with the brother and sister called investigators to say the rape had been a hoax." Jessee's role in implicating her brother and sister was not made public until May 7, 1994, when the *Sentinel* mentioned it in an article without identifying her by name; the newspaper called her Wanda Mary's "half sister."

Central Florida police tracked Jimmy Burke to Murphy Village, where he was reported to be visiting his brother, Pat In actual fact, Jimmy had towed his trailer there and was camped not far from Pat's family with his sisters Winnie and Peggy and his two beloved pet Rotweilers. When police officers arrived at his trailer, thin and frail Jimmy hid in the small, narrow space under the coach's rear bed. His sisters placed the two fierce-looking dogs on the bed above their brother, and the policemen merely walked through the trailer and then left.

Afraid they would return, Winnie took Jimmy home to Atlanta with her, and there he checked himself into Mercy Hospital for AIDS treatment. While Jimmy was being treated, police officers who had been trailing him arrived at the hospital and asked that they be allowed to speak with him. Jimmy's doctor refused their request and said the young man was in serious condition and, at that point, heavily sedated. He suggested that the policemen return later that day.

Pat, who had followed Jimmy to Atlanta, learned that the policemen were at the hospital, and he told Jimmy. Jimmy responded by ripping surgically implanted IVs out of his arms and chest and walking out of the hospital. Winnie took him to her home, and he made his sister promise she would let him die there, not in the hospital or jail. When the policemen learned Jimmy had left the hospital, they theorized that Edward and Pat had spirited Jimmy from his room and driven him out of state. They never knew the young Irish Traveler was resting in bed only a few miles from the hospital.

Meanwhile, Peggy had returned to Florida after telling family members she was supposed to testify against a crooked police officer there. She was unaware that death waited for her in the Sunshine State.

On November 22, while police scoured the country for Wanda Mary and Jimmy, the *Orlando Sentinel* reported that, once again, the

Irish, Scottish and English Traveler con artist clans were arriving in central Florida. The article reminded readers in two paragraphs low in the story that the young woman who tried to swindle Disney World was an Irish Traveler, and it noted that Wanda Mary "has disappeared."

Six days later, officers with the Rutherford County sheriff's department near Murphreesboro, Tennessee, were dispatched to Oxley's campground, located just off I-24 at Buchanan, in response to complaints about a domestic dispute. There, a woman who identified herself as Winifred Ann Burke stated she had been struck several times and threatened by her husband, Patrick. The woman agreed to spend the night in a domestic violence shelter. Police left her husband at the family's travel trailer along with an unidentified younger woman and a baby. Winifred Burke was actually Pat's wife, Rose Mary, who regularly used her own nineteen-year-old daughter's name as an alias.

The next day, an anonymous telephone caller to Officer Tom Harrison reported that Wanda Mary was in a campground near Buchanan, Tennessee. The caller even gave Harrison directions to the campground, which was, of course, Oxley's. Once again, Rutherford County deputies were dispatched to the Burke trailer. The door was opened by a pretty young strawberry blonde woman who identified herself as Wanda Mary Normile. Detectives James Harrell and Jack Keisling arrested her and took her and baby Winifred into custody. The baby was turned over to the State of Tennessee Department of Human Services.

In Florida, when he was notified of the arrest by Rutherford Sergeant Chuck Thomas, Harrison requested that Wanda Mary be interviewed immediately, and he gave Thomas specific questions she should be asked. Reporting on that interview later, an Orange County investigator said, "They videotaped Wanda Mary's interview, and she was the most pitiful creature you ever saw. 'I didn't know half of what was going to happen,' she said. 'Big Wanda set this up.' Everything was shucked off on Big Wanda because James was still at large. She wanted to draw some the heat off James. She was really something. She'd cry, boo-hoo and dab her eyes and kind of flirt a little with the detective. She told her version of what she and James had agreed would take place."

Wanda Mary's version of the scam matched Jessee's closely except for one important detail: Although Jessee claimed she knew nothing of the plan to swindle Disney until she was told sketchy details at the steakhouse a few days prior to the crime, Wanda Mary said the plan was hatched while she, Jimmy, sister Winifred and Jessee watched a CBS program -- *48 Hours* -- about hotel security together. And although Wanda Mary later admitted the scam was Jimmy's idea, not Jessee's, she continued to maintain that Jessee took part in the early planning of the crime and argued vehemently against dropping the lawsuit against Disney World.

Wanda Mary's baby was placed in foster care temporarily following her arrest, but the next day, Pat and Rose Mary Burke petitioned for custody. Pat told investigating officers in Tennessee that he knew about the crime Wanda Mary, Jessee and Jimmy had committed, but he had no part in it. He stated that Wanda Mary was forced to participate in the scam by her brother and sister. Because no arrest warrants apparently had been issued for Pat or his wife, the child was turned over to them. They immediately left Tennessee and traveled to Georgia to wait for Wanda Mary's hearing dates to be set.

A Florida officer told the writer, "Although there was a pretty good indication that Pat was involved in some way, at least in trying to swindle money from Disney, there was a jurisdictional problem because there was no convincing evidence as to where the plan had been hatched. So even if he were involved in the planning or execution, where did the planning take place, and who should charge him -- Florida, Georgia, Alabama, Ohio or some other state?"

Late in February 1994, Jimmy Burke's health deteriorated seriously, and he drifted into a coma. Convinced her brother was near
death and committed to making his final hours as comfortable as
possible, Winnie returned Jimmy to Atlanta's Mercy Hospital. He
died there on March 7 unaware that his his favorite sister -- wild and
tempestuous Peggy -- had been murdered two weeks earlier.

Although Orange County, Florida, police officers knew Jimmy's
older brother, Pat, had never actually been to central Florida for execution of the Disney scam or Wanda Mary's lawsuit, they expected
him to use his brother Ed's I.D. and venture into the area for Wanda
Mary's trial. A sixteen-year-old assault warrant for Pat's arrest was
still on the books in Orange County, even though its seven-year
statute of limitations period had expired several years earlier.

John McMahan, who handled investigations of Gypsies and Travelers for the Orange County sheriff's department when Wanda Mary
was arrested, planned a special reception for Pat. He said, "Pat's theory was, you don't go down into central Florida if there are warrants
out for you. You can go into the northern areas and work the Pan-
handle, but you don't go deep into Florida because if something happens and you're identified, the cops can close off all the arteries
before you can get out. You're trapped. He always adopted that men-
tality, and we played on it a little. When he came down for the trial,
we had that sixteen-year-old assault warrant that we whacked him on
right after he walked into the courtroom holding little Winnie Ann
in his arms. We arranged for the prosecutor to take little Winnie into
Wanda Mary's cell for a joyful, tearful reunion with Mother, and
then we whipped Pat out of the courtroom under arrest. He wasn't
real thrilled about that. And he was, just as we figured he would do,
using his brother Edward's identity. Not only did we take Pat into
custody, but we also took his dope -- the marijuana that he smokes
constantly -- from his car and we flushed it."

McMahan said, "Of course, the statute of limitations on the warrant had run out, but the warrant was still on the books, so in effect it was still a 'good' warrant, and it inconvenienced the heck out of Pat. He paid his $500 bond up front, and he's never come back to get his bond money."

On May 6, 1994, Wanda Mary -- then twenty-one years old -- pleaded guilty to grand theft and falsely reporting a crime. As part of a plea-bargain agreement with the prosecutor's office, she was ordered to pay $24,000 in restitution to Disney Security and the Orange County sheriff's office for investigative expenses. She was sentenced to serve up to three and one-half years in the state's minimum-security occupational training program and then twenty years probation. One unique condition of her probation was that she acquire a valid Social Security number. Her attorney attempted to have her probation assigned to the Murphy Village area of South Carolina, but Judge Richard Conrad refused to consider that option after police testified about the Village's Irish Traveler residents.

Wanda Mary's lawyer, Mark O'Mara, told the judge his client became involved with a band of traveling con artists because of her brother, Jimmy. No one mentioned that she had grown up as a member of one of the most notorious con artist families in America.

Ironically, while serving her time in a work-release program near Tampa, Wanda Mary -- the woman who had almost scammed millions of dollars from a major hotel -- was assigned to a local motel as a maid!

Credited with six months for time served, Wanda Mary saw one-third of her incarceration time reduced for good behavior, and she served a total of only eighteen months. All things considered, she was happy with the outcome. "I knew I faced maybe fifteen years in prison if I pleaded not guilty and went to trial," she said following her release late in 1995. "I knew Jessee would be there testifying against me -- and she's a good bullshitter -- and that boy Michael also would testify, as well as probably my uncle Doug and his friend John

Holton. My attorney told me, 'The prosecutor will tear you apart on the stand, and you don't have acting abilities enough to get you out of this one.'"

# 25

# Recipe For Murder

Not long after former Florida policeman Adrian Cohen was arrested for carrying a concealed pistol in his car, Peggy Burke went shopping at a Walgreen's drug store in Delray Beach, Florida, with a friend named Linda Dobard. Peggy, who at the time was using the name Theresa Halsey, told Dobard if she would help Peggy steal a couple bottles of liquor, she would give Dobard some money. Dobard knew her friend had no money, but she consented to help steal the liquor anyway.

Outside the drug store with the liquor safely in her possession, Peggy told Dobard, "Wait here a minute while I make a phone call to get some money."

"Who are you going to call for money?" Dobard asked skeptically.

"Someone who will drive here from Boynton Beach if I ask him to do it," Peggy responded.

About forty minutes after Peggy used a nearby pay phone, a black man arrived in a white Camaro. Peggy walked over to him and engaged him in conversation. Although Dobard could not hear most of what they said, at one point it seemed clear to her that Peggy and the man were arguing, and the man said in a loud voice, "No you won't!"

Peggy answered, "Oh, yes I will! You know I will!" A few minutes later, the man left, and Peggy walked over to Dobard, smiling and waving a twenty-dollar bill.

"Who was that guy?" Dobard asked.

Peggy said, "That was the cop I got caught trickin' with."

Although the weapon found under Adrian Cohen's automobile seat was ordered returned to him on December 2, 1993, the policy of the Boynton Beach police department, which had confiscated the Smith & Wesson pistol, was to retain all ammunition found with confiscated guns. The department retained seventeen rounds of 9-millimeter ammunition belonging to Cohen. That ammunition would later prove to be quite valuable.

Five weeks later, on January 11, 1994, the standards and training division of the Florida Department of Law Enforcement notified Cohen of a hearing to determine whether his state police officer certification should be revoked. At the hearing, scheduled February 24, he would faced charges of making false statements, having sex on duty and aggravated assault with a firearm. Without certification, Cohen would never again be permitted to work in Florida law enforcement. Peggy Burke agreed to testify at that hearing, and she returned to Florida from her visit in South Carolina in order to do so at the same time her brother Jimmy was first admitted to Mercy Hospital in Atlanta.

Adrian Cohen's life was in a shambles. Not only was he facing loss of his police career, but his wife also was threatening to divorce him and a young woman with whom he had had a love affair was pregnant and had filed a paternity suit against him. He had been reduced to working in the kitchen at the First Baptist Church of West Palm Beach. In addition, Cohen was under psychiatric care and was on medication for stress.

He told friends that all the problems in his life could be traced to one person -- the blonde prostitute Theresa Halsey, a well-known drug user who had already been arrested more than 130 times for robbery, larceny, prostitution and cocaine possession.

Faced with a growing anger that he was finding harder and harder to control, Cohen had started spending a great deal of time in a bedroom of his home, studying military tactics. One of his favorite books was titled *Ranger Handbook*. Particular sections of that manual intrigued him, and he underlined certain passages that interested him most. One section explained how to execute an armed ambush and described the importance of stealth and patience. A passage emphasized the value of heavy-volume surprise weapons fire at the time of an attack; it discussed the need for good marksmanship in an ambush; told how to move into ambush positions; recommended foot gear and equipment for an ambush; emphasized the importance of being especially careful while returning to friendly lines, and told how to plan transportation to and from the ambush area.

Cohen was particularly drawn to a chapter of the book that focused on rehearsing and time-scheduling an ambush, and he underlined passages related to what the manual called "the six D's of fire planning": destroy, deceive, deny, defend, direct and delay.

Had any of his former associates on the Delray Beach police department been aware of the selections he had underlined, they probably would have called those passages a recipe for murder.

Cohen also studied the contents of a few other militaristic books that contained details about snipers. Their titles: *Marine Sniper, Dear Mom -- A Sniper's Vietnam; Black Berets and Painted Faces*, and *The Complete Book of U.S. Sniping*. In his bedroom closet, he kept a fully loaded Ruger Ranch .223-caliber semi-automatic rifle -- also known as a Mini-14 -- with a telescopic sight. (The Ruger Ranch is particularly popular among varmint hunters and target shooters. It fires the same ammunition used in the U.S. Army's famous M-16 automatic rifles. Equipped with a telescopic sight, it is a very effective, accurate weapon for long-range shooting.)

Along with the rifle, Cohen kept a shoulder bag containing an extra magazine for the gun, filled with live rounds; three boxes of .223-caliber ammunition; camouflage face paint in a metallic tube; razor blades, and a ceramic pepper shaker capped with a piece of aluminum foil. Inside the pepper shaker, Cohen had poured liquid mercury. A couple of Cohen's books described how to pour mercury into a bullet's hollow point and seal it there with candle wax. Popular among paid assassins, the doctored ammunition would either poison its victim or accelerate infection of the wound.


In agreeing to be a witness at Adrian Cohen's hearing by the Florida Department of Law Enforcement, Peggy knew she held the former policeman's professional future in her hands, but no one familiar with Peggy's bizarre behavior would have been willing to predict what she would say at the hearing.

Peggy lived in a section of Delray Beach where many of the buildings had been condemned but were inhabited by prostitutes, drug dealers and other street people. She shared living quarters with a 68-year-old black man, James Brown, and she often used Brown's blue Chevrolet pickup truck for transportation. The building in which Peggy and Brown lived had no telephone or electricity, and they illuminated their rooms with kerosene lanterns. Drug paraphernalia was scattered throughout the house, in plain view, and any visitors would quickly conclude that Peggy was an avid user of crack cocaine.

Four days before the hearing, Peggy spent the evening with Calvin Spruill, a 37-year-old black neighbor who was known on the streets of Delray Beach as "Fat Calvin." They borrowed Brown's truck and drove to Boynton Beach, then returned about 11 p.m. At that point, a 28-year-old woman named Leslie "Touch" Periord asked them if they would give her a ride to the Federal Highway -- the primary area of the city where local prostitutes exhibited their wares. They did, and Fat Calvin said later that when they returned to Peggy's house just before 11:30, he left her and walked two blocks east to visit a friend.

Meanwhile, Linda Dobard was walking through the neighborhood, and as she approached the intersection of South West 3rd Street and South West 8th Avenue, she saw James Brown's blue truck heading north on South West 8th Avenue. She did not see who was driving or whether there was a passenger in the vehicle. Near the intersection, the truck stopped and then backed into the driveway of the house that Dobard knew was shared by Brown and the prostitute she called Theresa Halsey. While the truck was still in motion, Dobard realized that someone was standing in the shadows of Brown's carport. That person started walking very slowly toward the truck as it continued backing into the driveway. Dobard's attention was distracted from the vehicle momentarily, but then she heard what she thought was a gunshot and immediately looked toward the drive-way again.

Dobard saw a medium-build black man about five-foot-ten or five-foot-eleven standing beside the opened driver's door of Brown's truck. He had a full face and seemed to have "a little fuzz" on his face, but was not bearded. He wore what appeared to be jeans.

The man's right arm was extended into the vehicle, and it was moving in an up-and-down motion. Dobard saw a flash from inside the cab of the truck, along with the sound of another gunshot. Realizing she was witnessing a shooting, Dobard immediately crouched low to the sidewalk. Although Dobard was distracted by the shots, she thought she saw someone running from the area of the truck. When the gunfire stopped and the shooter walked away, Dobard left the area. She knew there was an active warrant for her arrest because she had violated probation on a criminal charge, so she did not inform police what she had seen.

Standing two blocks away, talking with a friend at 11:30 p.m., Fat

Calvin Spruill heard the gunshots and walked back to Brown and Peggy's house. There, he told police, he found Peggy lying on the front seat of the truck. He realized she had been shot, but he saw no sign of her assailant. Later, he would tell reporters, "That person had to be sitting and waiting to catch her by herself."

Brown, who said he had gone to bed after Peggy and Fat Calvin took Touch Periord to the Federal Highway, told police he had heard the shots but did not get out of bed to investigate. The sounds of gunfire were not unusual in that neighborhood.

A few minutes later, however, Fat Calvin banged on Brown's front door and reported that Peggy had been shot. Brown ran outside to the truck. Peggy, sprawled out in the cab of the vehicle, still had the keys to the truck in one hand. Brown took the keys from her and realized for the first time she was dead.


Patrol Officer Philip Dorfman was the first Delray Beach police-man to arrive at the scene of the murder. After speaking with Brown, who had called police, he walked to the blue truck and noticed a "gold-colored casing from a 9-millimeter round" on the driveway near the open driver's door, then later found a second near the rear tire on the driver's side. Crime scene technician Russell Anzalone reported, "I observed the victim lying across the seat. There was blood coming out of both nostrils and there was blood underneath the left side of her head." Officer Craig Hanning dusted the truck for prints and photographed the crime scene. Peggy was lying on her right side, her feet hanging out the open driver's door.

Just after midnight, Detective Robert Stevens arrived at the site. A member of Delray Beach's crimes against persons squad, Stevens was a seventeen-year veteran of the city police force and had already investigated more than a dozen murders. The short 37-year-old detective was a tenacious researcher with a knack for detail -- a skill that would prove invaluable during the months ahead. Although

Stevens had not been told the identity of the shooting victim, he recognized Peggy immediately because of her frequent appearances at the Delray Beach police station.

Peggy had been shot six times from close range -- once, a grazing leg wound, three times in the buttocks, once in the shoulder and once in the head. The fatal head shot, a postmortem later revealed, was fired at point-blank range from quite close to Peggy. That bullet, which exited the top of her head, was never found.

To Stevens' practiced eyes, site of the murder was far from being a perfect crime scene. "The carport directly behind the truck was cluttered with debris," he reported. "The front of the house was in disarray; trash and garbage were scattered throughout the yard." Neighbors told Stevens they had heard the gunshots about a half hour before midnight but did not investigate. One neighbor later told police she had looked out her window after hearing the shots and had seen a black male wearing a white T-shirt walking north along 8th Avenue.

Stevens asked Brown and Spruill to submit to interviews at the police station; they did, but no new information was provided by either man. Leslie "Touch" Periord told Stevens that about ninety minutes after Peggy dropped her off at the Federal Highway, she walked back to Brown's house and, after observing "a lot of police activity" there, learned her friend had been shot and killed. A man living two blocks away confirmed that Spruill was with him when the gunshots were fired. Stevens returned to the scene and, with Brown's permission, searched the house; he found no evidence related to the murder.

Concluding that his best suspect was former police officer Adrian Cohen, Stevens drove to Cohen's home in nearby Boynton Beach. With him was Sergeant Robert Brand, the 44-year-old supervisor of Delray Beach's crimes against persons squad. On the way, Stevens telephoned Cohen with his car phone, and Cohen agreed to meet the two officers outside his home. The former policeman told Stevens and Brand that after dinner with his wife the previous evening, he went to Riviera Beach. "He stated he spent the evening with his friend, Steve Latson, who lives in Boynton Beach but stays at his girl-friend's house in Riviera Beach," Stevens said in his investigative report.

Cohen said he arrived in Riviera Beach about 9:30 on the night of the murder, and about 11:15, he and Latson drove to the corner of Tamarind and 7th Avenue in West Palm Beach to drink beer with friends. Leaving there about 11:45, Cohen said he went to Boynton Beach to check whether his brother's house there was secure, then bought gasoline at the Hypoluxo Seacrest Mobil station before arriving home at about 12:30 a.m.

Cohen insisted he had not seen Peggy since the time she had accused him of raping her and that he had never been to her house or touched any item in the house or any vehicle around the house. He told Stevens he would not have had any contact with her for fear of jeopardizing his upcoming state certification hearings. Stevens reported Cohen said "he would not have killed the victim because he knew that would bring a lot of press reports about what had occurred. He felt this might jeopardize his hearings and therefore he would not commit this murder."

Stevens added, in his investigative report, "He further advised that the only firearm in his house was a Mini-14 rifle and that he present-ly owned no handguns."

Latson confirmed Cohen's statement, but provided a slightly dif-ferent version at first. "Steve Latson advised that he went to the movies with Adrian," Stevens said. "Latson said Adrian arrived in West Palm Beach at approximately 10:30 and left at 11:30. I then advised that Adrian Cohen had told us he was with Latson but had not gone to the movies. Latson then changed his story and advised he was with Cohen, but they had been drinking beer on Tamarind."

Examination of cash register receipts at the service station where Cohen claimed he bought gasoline revealed Cohen had purchased gasoline at about 12:15 a.m. -- about one hour after the murder. The attendant remembered Cohen's white Camaro.

Back at the Delray Beach police department, Stevens and Brand looked over the truck in which Peggy had been killed. It had been towed to the police station and processed for fingerprints. "The vehicle had a gunshot in the interior of the passenger door," Stevens reported. "The trajectory appeared to be in a downward direction from inside toward the outside." Since no spent bullet was found, the two officers returned to the crime scene and, using a metal detector, searched for the bullet that had been fired through the door. None was found.

A Boynton Beach police officer named Deneue reported that on the night of the homicide, while patrolling Cohen's neighborhood shortly after midnight, he saw Cohen's white Camaro stop in front of Cohen's home and back into his driveway.

The morning after the murder, Stevens learned for the first time that the 9-millimeter pistol which had been confiscated from Cohen the previous year had been returned to him in December -- two months earlier.

Efforts to locate members of Peggy's family failed. Brown said he thought she had a brother in the Orlando area and other relatives in Augusta, Georgia, but none could be found.

"Touch" Periord told Stevens she had not heard anything on the streets about who might be responsible for her friend's death, but she had heard that a purse Peggy had lost earlier in the Boynton Beach area was in the possession of a policeman there. Three days later, Stevens would recover that purse and discover it contained Peggy's personal telephone book.

Meanwhile, Stevens spoke with Peggy's estranged husband and was told his and Peggy's two children -- nine-year-old Anastasia and seven-year-old Clyde -- were living with Peggy's brother in Orlando;

he did not know the brother's name or address. In actual fact, as Stevens would later learn, the children were living with Peggy's uncle Doug.

Forensics officers, while searching the interior of the truck in which Peggy had been killed, found a third 9-millimeter shell casing.

The following day, February 23, an article in the *Palm Beach Post* said police called Peggy "the best-known prostitute in the city."

That morning, the girlfriend of Cohen's friend, Steve Latson, confirmed several aspects of the statement Latson had given to police, but she said after Latson and Cohen left her home in Latson's truck on the night of the murder, Cohen's Camaro had remained parked in front of her house until at least 11 p.m. She said Latson telephoned her about 11:25, then returned about midnight, at which time she realized Cohen's car was gone.

Later, Stevens asked Latson for the names of individuals who could verify his claim that he was drinking beer at 7th and Tamarind about the time of the murder. Latson supplied a name and insisted he and Cohen were together until about midnight and that Cohen had never left his sight. Latson agreed to take a polygraph test.

On February 24, Stevens picked up Peggy's purse at the Boynton Beach police department, and an officer there told him Peggy's youngest sister, Wanda Mary Burke, had been arrested in the Orlando area for trying to swindle Disney World. Stevens telephoned police authorities in Orange County and requested that Wanda Mary be notified of her sister's death. Using Peggy's personal phone directory, Stevens also called her uncle Doug with the news.

The following day, Stevens received a valuable piece of news himself: Sergeant Kenneth Herndon, Delray Beach's recognized fingerprint expert, said fingerprint impressions lifted from the driver's door of James Brown's pickup truck were made by the left hand of Adrian Cohen.

Later, Stevens asked Brown when his truck was washed last, and Brown replied that the vehicle had never been washed and that it was constantly exposed to weather. "The vehicle is never parked in the carport and is always parked in front of the house, consistent with the location...at the time of the homicide," Stevens reported.

Interviewed by Stevens once again, Steve Latson continued to insist he and Cohen were together at the time of the homicide. Considering Latson a suspect at that time, Stevens and Lieutenant Robert Musco obtained fingerprints and photographs of Latson from the Boynton Beach police department. They also asked Boynton Beach police to retrieve bullets that Cohen had fired from his 9-millimeter pistol at his girlfriend's automobile the year before.

That evening Sergeant Herndon told Stevens that Latson's fingerprints were not found anywhere on Brown's truck.

On Monday, February 28, Sergeant Brand tried to interview Cohen's wife, but she refused to talk with him. Following that attempt, Cohen made a threatening call to Stevens and stated he was upset "that we are continuing to harass his wife." Brand ordered Stevens to notify road patrols that "Adrian Cohen's demeanor had turned threatening." Brand said later that Cohen's behavior had been so bizarre that he was afraid the former policeman might become violent if confronted by patrol officers over even minor traffic violations. At least once, Sergeant Brand said, Cohen had tried to "bait" patrol officers while driving through the city.

Cohen consented to take a polygraph test the following day and provide any other information Stevens requested.

The next day, Brand and Stevens questioned the man Latson said could confirm he was drinking beer at Tamarind and 7th Avenue between 10:30 and 11:30 on the night Peggy was killed. The man said Latson was with him during that period, along with another black man whose name he did not know. A few days later, when shown photographs of Cohen, the man would tell Stevens that Cohen was not the man who accompanied Latson. The officers were referred to another individual who was part of the beer-drinking group, and that man confirmed Latson was at Tamarind and 7th Avenue the night of the murder, but he was positive Adrian Cohen was not.

Brand and Stevens gave the police polygraph operator questions they wanted Cohen to be asked: "Did you shoot Theresa Halsey? Do you know who shot Theresa Halsey? Did Steve Latson shoot Theresa Halsey? Have you been truthful to the police? Did you conspire to murder Theresa Halsey?"

Cohen did not keep his appointment for the polygraph test.

On March 2, West Palm Beach police department's fingerprint expert informed Brand and Stevens his examination of prints taken from Brown's pickup truck revealed that dried raindrops had been raised by the fingerprint powder and that, because Cohen's fingerprints were on top of the raindrops, the prints had been applied to the truck after the last rainfall. A week later, the Delray Beach Water Department would confirm that although heavy rain fell on Friday, February 18, and a lesser amount was measured on Saturday, February 19, there was no rainfall on Sunday, the day of the murder.

That meant Cohen's fingerprints could have been applied to the truck only during the twenty-four hour period prior to Peggy's death.

Meanwhile, Boynton Beach police provided spent bullets from Cohen's gun that had been recovered from Cohen's girlfriend's car. They had been found in the vehicle's fuel tank. Those bullets were examined by Palm Beach County's firearms expert, John O'Rourke, along with shell casings from the murder scene, bullet fragments recovered from Peggy's body and live rounds from Cohen's gun that had been confiscated when he was arrested several months earlier for carrying a concealed weapon. O'Rourke concluded that the bullets which killed Peggy and the shell casings found at the scene had been cycled through Cohen's Smith & Wesson pistol.

A warrant was issued to search Cohen's home, and Stevens filed another warrant to arrest the former police officer.

Cautious about Cohen's capability for violence, Brand ordered a S.W.A.T. team to put Cohen's house under surveillance until the arrest warrant could be served. As the surveillance was being set up, however, Stevens received a call from Delray Beach Police Chief Richard Overman, who said he had just spotted Cohen. The chief was attending police graduation ceremonies at the Palm Beach Community College in Lake Worth, and Cohen had just appeared in the audience, dressed in a tuxedo, and had taken a seat behind Overman. Cohen's brother was one of the graduates of the police academy program. Accompanied by sheriff's department officers, Stevens arrested Cohen as he exited the auditorium following the evening's ceremonies.

Next, Sergeant Brand, Lieutenant Musco, Lieutenant Ralph J. Phillips and Drug Agent Thomas Brady Myers went to Cohen's bedroom, Phillips recovered newspaper articles about Cohen's suspension, Cohen's former police uniforms and a photograph of Cohen with two armed, unidentified men. Also taken from the room as evidence were Cohen's books on sniping and ambush, the .223-caliber assault rifle and the shoulder bag containing ammunition, camouflage and the pepper shaker of mercury.

Late that evening, Brand and Stevens questioned Cohen about the Smith & Wesson pistol that had been returned to him in December by the Boynton Beach police. "He reported he sold the firearm to a man on the street several months ago and doesn't know who the person was. He said the last contact he had with the victim was on the day she accused him of sexually assaulting her."

When asked if he wanted to comment on events surrounding

Peggy's murder, Cohen told Stevens, "Adrian Cohen didn't do this. Adrian Cohen is a police officer. There's somebody inside Adrian Cohen that's bigger than he is."

Stevens reported, "He further went on to say that he was under a lot of stress lately. He said that when he doesn't take his medication, he acts differently than when he is on his medication. We offered to take a taped statement (but) Cohen refused to cooperate and give us a taped statement."

On March 5, a *Palm Beach Post* article was headlined, "Sex charge shattered Delray's officer's life."

The newspaper reported Cohen's arrest and noted, "Cohen now faces possible decertification as a police officer and a paternity suit he says he can's afford."

The article quoted police spokesman Mike Wright as saying, "Any time we get an arrest on a homicide, it's a good feeling. We feel we have the right person."


Three days later, Steve Latson changed the story he had told police officers during the preceding month. He told Brand and Stevens he went to a movie theater alone at 7:30 on the evening of the murder; at 9 o'clock, he returned a telephone call from Cohen, and then the two men went to Tamarind and 7th Avenue in West Palm Beach at 10 or 10:15 and "drank lots of beer." Latson said Cohen wandered off, and he didn't know how long Cohen was gone because he was intoxicated. He said between 11:30 and 11:45, Cohen returned, and they drove to Latson's girlfriend's house.

Later, Stevens and Musco drove the primary route between Delray Beach and Riviera Beach "in enough time for Adrian Cohen to have committed the murder in Delray Beach, drive with Steven Latson to his girlfriend's house in Riviera Beach and return to the Hypoluxo Mobile gas station in time to make the 12:15 gas stop."

On March 14, Peggy Burke's murder case was presented to the

Palm Beach County Grand Jury. In a prepared statement to the grand jury, Stevens said the fingerprints on the truck "were positioned in such a way that they are consistent with the killer, who held the driver's door open with his left hand and fired with his right." Four days later, the grand jury indicted Cohen and ordered him held without bail.

An article in the *Palm Beach Post* on June 2 reported that Peggy had been buried by the county "because there is no family to bury her."

Legal wrangling over the merits of the case against Cohen dragged on for several months. County prosecutors sought a first-degree murder conviction and the death penalty while Cohen's attorney demanded that charges be dropped because there was no evidence against his client. A trial was scheduled to begin October 17.

On August 29, Assistant State Attorney Kirk Volker notified Sergeant Brand that a female defense witness had come forward with new information about the murder. The woman had confided to Volker that while she was in the county jail, another inmate admitted she had witnessed the murder but had never spoken with police about what she had seen. An investigation by Brand revealed that inmate was Linda Dobard. Not long after she saw a man firing shots into the cab of the truck where Peggy was killed, Dobard had been arrested for violation of probation on a theft conviction. And while Stevens and Brand conducted their investigations into Peggy's murder, Dobard had finished serving her time on that conviction.

Questioned by Brand, Dobard told about the incident at the Walgreen drug store between her friend, Theresa Halsey, and a black male that Halsey had said was a police officer. Brand showed Dobard a photo lineup of six black men, and Dobard pointed to Cohen's photo, saying he looked like the person who gave money to Peggy at the drug store, but she couldn't be certain. Brand said, "I asked Ms. Dobard if she observed any money exchanged between Ms. Halsey and the black male. She stated she did not see any money but was certain the black male gave Ms. Halsey some money because after Ms. Halsey left the black male, she had a twenty-dollar bill which she did not have earlier."

Dobard then told Brand about witnessing the murder, and the sergeant showed her the photo lineup again. She could not positively identify Cohen as the man she saw shoot into the truck where Peggy was found murdered, but she did point to Cohen's photo and said he resembled that man. "I asked Ms. Dobard if she has ever seen a photo of Adrian Cohen either in the newspapers or on television, and she responded she had not," Brand reported. "Ms. Dobard also stated she thought she observed someone else running from the area of the truck, but she was not positive."

At Cohen's trial, his attorney claimed the fingerprints found on James Brown's truck had been applied there by his client several months before the murder when Cohen stopped Peggy for a traffic violation. The attorney also requested that the judge suppress all evidence related to the Smith & Wesson pistol owned by Cohen because that weapon had originally been confiscated illegally by Boynton Beach police, and therefore evidence obtained as a result of that confiscation could not be used against Cohen.

The judge agreed and ordered all ballistics comparisons to be suppressed.

Faced with a possible acquittal of Cohen, the prosecutor's office negotiated a plea bargain with Cohen's attorney: First-degree murder charges would be dropped if Cohen would plead guilty to manslaughter and accept a ten-year prison sentence. Cohen accepted the deal.

Reporting on conclusion of the trial, the *Palm Beach Post* informed its readers, "Adrian Cohen denied killing prostitute Margaret Burke on February 20 and said he accepted the plea bargain because it was 'in his best interest.'"

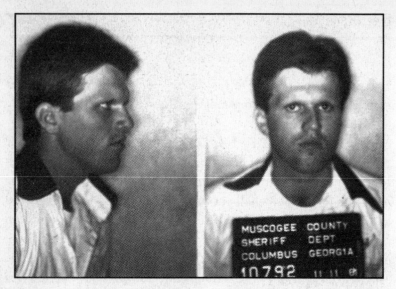

Jimmy Burke at the age of eighteen.

**Left:** Wanda Mary Normile after she was beaten by her brother during the faked rape and robbery at Walt Disney World.

**Right:** Pat "The Viking" Burke as he looked around the time his sisters and brother executed their plot to swindle Walt Disney World for millions.

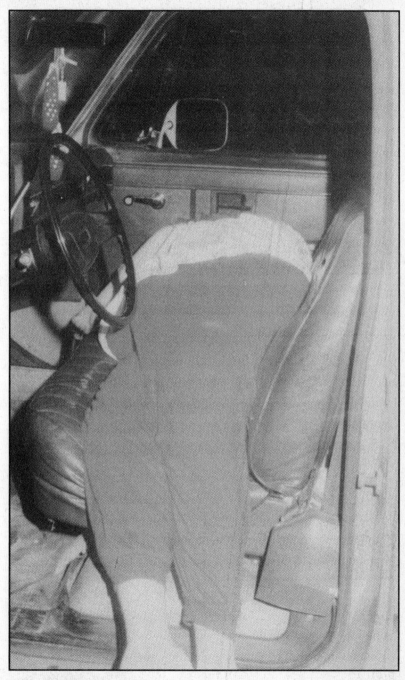

Peggy Burke was shot at point-blank range as she sat behind the steering wheel of this pickup truck.

**Above:** Jimmy Burke's driver's license in 1987 gave him an ID as Jamie L. Johnson.

**Left:** Florida Detective Robert Stevens utilized fine police work in gathering evidence on Cohen, a former fellow police officer.

**Below left:** Thirty-year-old Peggy Burke in 1992 and Adrian Cohen *(below right),* the man convicted in connection with her death in 1994.

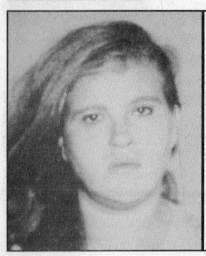

These paving-sealing rigs were parked alongside an Irish Traveler family's campsite in Florida.

Orange County Detective John McMahon checks out a license plate number on a Traveler's truck.

Formerly Travelers Rest, the original South Carolina base of the Southern Travelers is now a campground and mobile home court near North Augusta, SC.

These are just a few of the luxurious homes built in the area around North Augusta, South Carolina, called Murphy Village. Note the mobile homes in upper photos.

Code for lightning protection requires cable to have two-way path to grounding rod; this cable clearly does not.

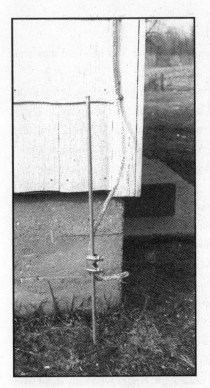

Lightning rod code stipulates grounding rod must be driven completely into ground at least ten feet and not allowed to protrude above ground. Lightning rod work at this house more likely to cause fire, not prevent it.

# EPILOGUE

Jimmy Burke is gone, and so is his wild sister Peggy. Their parents are dead, along with their brother Paul and their sister Cathy. But a new generation of Burkes is at work now in the old Irish Traveler tradition. There are new generations of Scottish Travelers and English Travelers, too. Realizing that, I'm reminded of the observation made to me not long ago by one of the police officers I interviewed. "Travelers are like the Energizer Bunny," he said. "They keep going and going and going..."

Nothing that is written here will change that.

The Travelers themselves are changing, however. I'm not sure they realize it yet.

More and more of them are settling down, buying homes and making certain their children are educated. They're investing in property, in legitimate businesses, in CDs and mutual funds and the stockmarket. Gradually, they're starting to be assimilated into American *country* life. Some of them -- particularly the Travelers of Murphy Village -- are already casting their votes in public elections.

Some of them are even paying taxes!

Not that the Travelers have become model citizens, by any measure. But they *have* become more educated, and they can see the advantage of filing tax returns. As self-employed painters, asphalters, home-repair specialists or lightning rod installers, they can depreciate out their equipment, write off their travel expenses, pay their self-employment taxes and then collect earned income tax credits just like every other qualifying American.

In the final analysis, Travelers are becoming Americanized. The modern Irish Traveler has more in common with the old woman he swindles out of her life savings than he does with the poor Irish Tinker who sells scrap iron on the outskirts of Dublin. Today's Travelers are two or three generations

474

removed from the itinerant horse traders who once haggled with Georgia farmers over a few dollars' profit. And their lives bear little resemblance to those of their clans' founders, Old Tom Carroll and Robert Logan Williamson.

Does that mean the Travelers are well along the path toward giving up their lives as successful con artists?

Not a chance!

Their scams are changing too. Fewer Travelers are content with earning $200 on a roof-sealing job; they know others who have scored $5,000 with state lottery scams, or $20,000 in a fake gold bar swindle, or $30,000 in a condominium sales scheme, or $70,000 in a home-invasion ploy. By now, they've all heard about the multi-million-dollar scam that Jimmy Burke and his sisters almost pulled off against Disney World, and since all the Travelers *know* they're smarter than Jimmy, it's inevitable that some mighty big scores will be planned during the years ahead.

And just consider this: The relatively uneducated Travelers have not even *discovered* white-collar crime yet! Imagine the scams that could be pulled by a Traveler who learns to communicate via the Internet.

As the Twentieth Century was drawing to a close, Traveler scams were being executed in every major city, in every state, in every region of America. During 1995, reports about Traveler activities poured into my office from all over the country.

•A police officer from the sparsely populated section of northwestern Washington telephoned with information about Traveler con artists who were busily swindling tourists and local residents alike.

•Irish and Scottish Travelers moved into Canada's Quebec, Ontario and British Columbia provinces, police officers reported. They also were in the Yukon and Alaska.

•In the northwest suburbs of Chicago during a two-week period, two female Travelers swindled an 88-year-old woman out of $6,000 in a pigeon drop scheme, and six elderly homeowners lost cash savings to men who posed as utility workers.

•Irish Travelers hit the Detroit area hard with driveway, roof, painting and travel trailer scams during the later summer, prompting the local ABC-

TV affiliate, WXYZ, to prepare a three-part news report about the con artists.

During the same time frame, Travelers hit Missoula, Montana; Boise, Idaho; Elkhart, Indiana; Cody, Wyoming; Talladega County, Alabama; Akron, Ohio; Romeo, Michigan; Aurora, Illinois; Aurora, Colorado; Salt Lake City, Utah; Las Vegas, Nevada; San Francisco, California; Syracuse, New York; Aledo, Denton and Lubbock, Texas.

Following publication of two magazine articles about travel trailer scams, I received telephone calls from several Travelers. One refused to identify himself but called the articles "the most absurd, ridiculous collection of racist, pathetic trash I've seen in my life."

A female caller whom I later learned was an English Traveler said, "That piece of paper that you writ is so much untrue, so false that it's unbelievable. Believe me, you will be judged. And I'm talkin' to this phone and tellin' you that. And you will be sorry. Almighty God will judge you."

However, an Irish Traveler from Texas who identified herself as Mary Riley said the articles correctly reported on trailer scams and said, "It's not right for those Travelers to go out there and rob people the way they do."

Another Traveler, who said her name was Mary Sims but later admitted that was not her identity, spoke with me for nearly three hours. Aware that a book focusing on the Burke family was being written, she said, "Jimmy Burke was a pathological liar. Nobody had anything to do with him because he was a low-life."

Calling Jessee Burke "a very bad, abusive woman," she claimed Jessee "used to beat Wanda Mary half to death every chance she got," and she insisted that Jessee intimidated Wanda Mary into participating in the attempted scam against Disney World. The Burkes, she said, "are not real Travelers" because their mother was a non-Traveler. The Burke children, she added, "were not raised, they were drug up. And when they were fifteen years old, they were told to leave."

Their mother, who died in 1992, is "probably being poked with a pitchfork now," Mary insisted. "Nobody that mean and evil could go to heaven."

Mary Sims also did not have many kind words for Irish Travelers living in Murphy Village. "The ones from Murphy Village are looney," she said.

476

She called them "very backward, very clannish people."

As for English Travelers, she said they make no attempt at keeping blood-lines pure and "marry back and forth with country people." Some English Travelers, she added, "are straight-up business people, and others are low-life scum." The English Travelers of Spiro, Oklahoma, she said, "are low-lifes."

Mary called herself "a typical PTA mom."

Jimmy Burke wanted to be remembered as the man who pulled the largest scam in Irish Traveler history. Unfortunately, the Travelers recall him only as the black sheep member of a dysfunctional family who failed to swindle Disney World because the rest of his family couldn't get along with each other long enough to make the scam succeed. Because his bisexual lifestyle was an affront to his family, Jimmy's body was cremated instead of being buried in Florida with his parents.

I miss Jimmy terribly, and I wish he were alive to see the result of our conversations and interviews. But I doubt this book could have been written while Jimmy was still living. For fifteen years, I was careful not to expose Jimmy to prosecution or danger, and publication of this book while Jimmy lived would have done both. In spite of his con artistry, Jimmy was a very trusting person, and he trusted me not to betray him either to law enforcement or to other Travelers.

This book also could not be written until now because it lacked both a focal point and a conclusion. As mentioned earlier, research on the Travelers and their scams is a never-ending process, but it is a repetitive process that, for the most part, involves uncovering particular types of scams over and over, endlessly. Jimmy and his sisters, by attempting to swindle a major American institution, provided this book's focal point. Then Jimmy's unfortunate death, and Peggy's murder, furnished the conclusion.

At the time of Jimmy's death, he was living and traveling with a black man named David; at times they were joined by a third man, Andre. As was his practice before he was arrested and sent to prison, Jimmy carried with him a large assortment of vehicle registration forms, certificates of origin, a stolen notary seal and other paperwork and supplies to assist him in his scams and thefts. When Jimmy admitted himself to the hospital in Atlanta, he left everything in a rented storage space; by the time police learned of it, the storage space had been emptied, presumably by Andre.

Peggy Burke Martin met with me once and talked with me by telephone a few times before moving to Delray Beach, Florida, in the late 1980s. She gave birth to eight children during her active young life. Three died, three of them was placed in foster care, one is being reared by Peggy's Uncle Doug in Orlando, and one is in the care of Peggy's younger sister Winnie. At last report, Peggy's estranged husband lived in Delray Beach; according to police reports, he knew almost nothing about Peggy's early life or about the Irish Travelers. I have been unable to talk with him.

Wanda Jessee Burke O'Roarke and her grown daughter, Lisa, are living in Maine. Her 22-year-old son, Bill, married a 17-year-old girl from Murphy Village late in 1995; the young couple then began traveling with Bill's uncle Pat Burke. Jessee is aggressively shunned by most other Travelers. She refused to be interviewed for this book after being told she would not be paid if she did so. She said she intends to write her own book about the Irish Travelers. I have purposely avoided discussing certain aspects of Jessee's life in the belief that she deserves her privacy.

Wanda Mary Burke Normile, who was incarcerated in Pinellas County, Florida, for her part in the Disney World scam, was released just prior to publication of this book. She regained custody of her daughter, Winifred Ann, from her brother and sister-in-law, Patrick and Rose Mary Burke. Reports within the Traveler community were that Wanda Mary's husband, John Normile, had filed for divorce from her; as of February 1996, she had not been served with divorce papers. Wanda Mary must find some way to reimburse Walt Disney World Security and the Orange County Sheriff's Office a total of $24,000 for the money they spent investigating the Disney World scam. She will be on probation for approximately twenty years. Although she now admits her brother Pat beat Jessee with his fists in Youngstown, Ohio, she said he did that to punish Jessee for demanding that money from the Disney scam be turned over to her. Pat did not attempt to shoot Jessee, she said.

Wanda Mary is currently attending college and has made solid friendships with people who never heard of the Irish Travelers or its criminal heritage. As this was written, she was living in a beautiful home in central Florida and was engaged to be married to a young man -- a former police officer. Although she spoke with members of her family occasionally, she was careful not to let them know where she lived, and she insisted that they contact her, when necessary, through a telephone paging service.

Patrick Paul "The Viking" Burke, now 42, is sought -- although not very aggressively -- for questioning by police agencies in a few states. They would like to ask him questions about his use of duct tape. Although I used the Irish Traveler communication network to inform The Viking I wanted to talk with him so that I could learn his version of the events prior to Wanda Mary's arrest, I did not hear directly from Pat. Through an intermediary, he said Jessee's statements to police that he tried to kill her were false. During the fall of 1995, Pat boasted of reaping enormous rewards with a scam in Ohio; that score provided him with enough money to arrive in Florida with a completely new traveling rig -- trailer, truck and cars. Pat, separated from his wife for several months, announced in January 1995 that he intended to marry Katy Shaw, stepdaughter of infamous Irish Traveler Robert "Bobby D" Daugherty. Pat and Katy spent the winter in central Florida with Pat's children. During that time, four telephone calls were made from Pat's trailer threatening to kill employees of the company publishing this book. The callers appeared to be teenage boys.

Paul Burke, Jimmy's youngest brother, was cremated following his suicide in Erie, Pennsylvania. His ashes were buried in Florida on August 28, 1987 -- his twenty-fifth birthday.

As mentioned earlier, Cathy Burke, Jimmy's sister, apparently committed suicide by shooting herself, although family members believe she was murdered by her husband. Her body, like those of her two brothers, was cremated.

Winifred Burke, Jimmy's younger sister, was less involved in scams than any other member of her family. In fact, all evidence indicates she did not lead the typical life of an Irish Traveler but kept herself apart from it. Although she was present during the initial planning of the Disney World scam, she did not participate. After her sister Peggy died, Winnie took custody one of Peggy's children, James Patrick, and at last report, she was living in Atlanta with Jimmy's friend David. She has four children of her own and is addicted to crack cocaine.

Edward Burke, Jimmy's oldest brother, was serving time in an Ohio prison as this book was being completed. He was not interviewed for this book.

Edward and Wanda Burke, Jimmy's parents, consistently refused to be interviewed by me, although Jimmy's mother frequently said she would consider doing so. Both knew of my meetings with their son. They did not know about my conversations with Peggy.

Doug, Jimmy's non-Traveler uncle, was never part of any scam planned or executed by his sister Wanda's children. Always aware that the Burke siblings were active con artists, Doug kept himself apart from their criminal activities but provided them with food, shelter and emotional support when they needed it. It was always Doug's hope that his nieces and nephews would break away from the Irish Travelers and lead legitimate, productive lives. Doug continues to reside in Orlando, and although he was invaluable in providing personal information about his relatives, he never discussed their criminal activities. I have taken extraordinary steps to ensure Doug's privacy. He is raising one of Peggy's children.

John Holton (not his real name) shares living quarters with Jimmy's uncle Doug and continues to observe Irish Traveler activities with a mixture of interest and disbelief. Wanda Mary Normile told me that Holton had prior knowledge of the Disney scam and, although he did not participate directly in it, it was he who encouraged her to have casual sex with his friend to provide evidence she had been raped. Wanda Mary said Holton threatened to tell his friend about his unwitting involvement in the scam, so she and Jimmy promised to pay Holton and her Uncle Doug $10,000 from the settlement funds if they agreed not to do that. Both Doug and Holton knew Jimmy, Wanda Mary and Jessee had executed a scam against Disney, she added. "Doug said to Jimmy, 'You should have let me beat her (Wanda Mary). I would have made it look more impressive.'" Wanda Mary reported.

Tom Harrison still serves as head of the sex crimes unit at the Orange County sheriff's office in Florida. Although he suspected the Disney World case might have been a scam, he had no evidence to support his suspicions, and he investigated the case with the presumption that a crime had been committed. When it was clear a scam had been attempted, he turned over the investigation to Intelligence Officer John McMahan.

John McMahan spends most of his time in the fall and winter investigating the activities of Gypsies and Travelers throughout central Florida. Like other law enforcement officers who have tracked the con artists, he has developed a personal respect and fondness for the Irish Travelers. John is a deputy with the Orange County sheriff's office.

John Wood continues to be one of the nation's leading authorities on Travelers, and particularly on the Scottish Travelers. He serves in the consumer protection section of the Pinellas County sheriff's office at Clearwater, Florida.

Beatrice Ann Burke, better known as Bridget, raised five children with her non-Traveler husband, Floyd. She died of a heart attack several years ago. Two of Bridget and Floyd's sons have become active con artists in the Irish Traveler tradition, although my evidence indicates they're not very good at it. They have participated in some of Pat "The Viking" Burke's crimes. Bridget's son John, 33, uses several names, including John Compton, John Anderson, John Confer, Joseph Compton, John Donsbach, Joel Taylor, Paul Taylor and John Taylor; he uses three different Social Security numbers. His 31-year-old brother Lloyd uses the names Lloyd Compton, Lloyd Confer, Shaw Confer, David Wells and Shaun Burke. During the winter of 1995-96, Lloyd camped in central Florida with Pat while John traveled to California.

Wayne Johnson, Ohio's "Gypsy Hunter," left his law enforcement post with the state department of motor vehicles and moved to Texas, where he continues to provide consultation to police agencies about Travelers.

Diane, Jimmy's widowed friend from New York, remarried during the mid-1980s but divorced her second husband a few years later. She resides with her children in southwestern New York state. Jimmy visited her periodically during the last years of his life, and she was one of the few persons who knew he had contracted the HIV virus and, later, AIDS. Before his death, he confided to Diane that he had planned and executed the Disney World scam. Diane was informed of Jimmy's death by one of his sisters, and she never heard from any member of the Burke family after that.

Neil Godbee, the off-duty police officer who arrested Jimmy in Macon, Georgia, is still employed by the Bibb County sheriff's office there. He is now a lieutenant. Several years after arresting Jimmy, he stopped at a motel to check out what he thought might be a travel trailer sales scam. There, he met Jimmy again. They had a pleasant conversation, and Jimmy thanked Godbee for the officer's treatment of him following the arrest.

Johnny Johnson is regarded as the *baro* -- head man -- among central Florida's Rom Gypsy community. He continues to earn money by helping Gypsies and Travelers get skillful legal representation when they need it. In recent years, he also became involved in trying to resolve a highly publicized million-dollar swindle of a Hawaiian pineapple heiress, and police uncovered a Gypsy plot either to murder or intimidate him.

Adrian Cohen, the former Delray Beach, Florida, police officer who shot Peggy Burke, is serving ten years in prison for manslaughter.

Robert Stevens, a 17-year veteran with the Delray Beach police department, is a member of his department's crimes against persons unit. He clearly did an excellent job of investigating Peggy's murder, and had it not been for legal technicalities related to confiscation of Adrian Cohen's weapon by Boynton Beach police, the evidence he compiled doubtlessly would have resulted in a first-degree murder conviction of Cohen.

Robert Brand, head of Delray Beach's crimes against persons unit, is serving in his eighteenth year with the city police department. He was Stevens' supervisor during the investigation of Peggy's death.

Beatrice Riley is one of the best known Irish Traveler women in America. Regarded as something as a character, she is sought for questioning by several law enforcement agencies. Now 75 years old, she is the mother of noted "granny man" Tom Riley as well as two daughters, Jane Marie White and Bridget Costello.

Tom Riley, 38 years old, travels with his wife Elizabeth and their four children.

Martha Parks continues to be one of the most active Scottish Travelers in America. As mentioned elsewhere in these pages, she is affectionately referred to by police officers as, simply, "Martha."

Roberts Lightning Protection Company (not its real name) is still supplying lightning rod equipment to Travelers, and during the summer of 1995, lightning rod scams were executed throughout America.

Coachmen Industries is owed a debt of gratitude by the RV industry for filing civil action against against the RV manufacturer I'm calling Federal Traveler. That suit clearly focused attention on Federal's role in supplying trailers to the Irish, Scottish and English Travelers. It was, to the best of my knowledge, the only legal action ever taken against one of the Travelers' RV suppliers, and the judge's decision on Coachmen's behalf underscored the need for a deeper look at how the Travelers acquire the products they misrepresent to consumers.

Federal Traveler has become the primary supplier of travel trailers and fifth-wheels to members of the Irish, English and Scottish Traveler clans. For 1993 and 1994, and through July 1995, the company ranked among the top fifteen travel trailer manufacturers in the nation, with an annual average of more than 700 retailed units per year; it ranked among the top thirty retailers of fifth-wheel trailers during that period.

Kentucky Traveler, once the dominant supplier of RVs for Travelers, still is a major producer of travel trailers and fifth-wheels, although it appears to have difficulty meeting competition from Federal Traveler. In 1993 and 1994 and through July 1995, it was among the top twenty travel trailer manufacturers with an annual average of about 500 retailed units per year.

Renegade Traveler has a small network of bonafide RV dealers and produces only a relatively low number of RVs for sale to Traveler clans. In 1993 and 1994 and through July 1995, its overall retail registrations ranked it among the top twenty trailer manufacturers with an annual average of more than 500 retailed units per year.

Indiana Traveler, located east of Elkhart, Indiana, has not sold trailers to Traveler clans for several years. During the early 1990s, the company experienced an enormous increase in orders for its products and became one of the fastest growing RV manufacturers in America.

Joe Livingston is probably the nation's foremost authority on the Irish Traveler enclave in South Carolina that is called Murphy Village. Livingston is an investigator with South Carolina Law Enforcement Division (SLED) in Columbia. His advice on how to find and arrest Travelers is sought by police forces all over America.

Major Jody Rowland was exposed to the Murphy Village Irish Travelers while he was a rookie deputy in Edgefield County, South Carolina. He now serves as chief deputy for the Aiken County sheriff's office, but rumors are that he will soon seek elective public office.

Jim Penn Sherlock is now one of the most influential members of the Irish Traveler community in Murphy Village, South Carolina.

# ACKNOWLEDGEMENTS

Several members of the Traveler clans were extremely helpful in providing me with information about their lifestyles and their scams. Their identities cannot be revealed for obvious reasons. Besides them, my special appreciation for help in researching this book goes to the following individuals:

Alice Robison, retired editorial director of Trailer Life magazine.

Terry Getsay, former criminal intelligence analyst with the Illinois Department of Law Enforcement.

Bob Cripe, president of Independent Protection Company, the nation's leading producer of lightning rod systems.

Marvin Frydenlund of the Lightning Protection Institute.

Van Ecklund, an officer with the Chautauqua County (New York) Sheriff's Office who successfully tracked Jimmy Burke.

Robert McDowell, south Texas victim of a Traveler roof sealing scam.

Duke Mills, executive director of the Orlando Chamber of Commerce.

Gregg Thomas of the Elkhart, Indiana, police department.

Tom King, former executive director of the Ohio RV Association.

Kay Abrahamson, a South Carolina resident who bought one of the travel trailers Jimmy Burke stole during his odyssey.

Jim Summers, former executive director of the Recreational Vehicle Industry Association.

Jim Moore, retired executive director of the Pennsylvania RV and Camping Association.

Cliff Huoy, retired executive director of the Texas Recreational Vehicle Association.

Tim Keech, co-owner of Estate Manufacturing Company of Elkhart, Indiana.

Bruce Hopkins, vice president of the Recreation Vehicle Industry Association.

Don Dorton, vice president of Starcraft RV Company.

Joe Mohney, owner of Mission RV Center in south Texas.

Dick Bowers, corporate counsel for Coachmen Industries of Elkhart, Indiana.

Tom Corson, co-founder and chairman of Coachmen Industries.

Truman Knox, retired RV dealer from western Missouri.

Delores Delanis, executive of the Better Business Bureau of South Texas.

Joel Young, former officer with the south Texas division of the Department of Public Safety.

Sean Lucy, noted Irish poet.

Churelle Bunton, a Denver resident who conducted her own investigation about Traveler trailer scams.

Joe Kemper of the National Insurance Crime Prevention Institute.

Detective Wayne Marshall of Annapolis, Maryland.

Marshall County, Indiana, patrolman Doug Larrimore.

Bud Lachmann, former executive with the Indiana Manufactured Housing Association.

Former Orange County (Florida) detective Bill Morris.

Alan McCagney, Chicago area insurance fraud investigator and member of Professionals Against Confidence Crime.

Joe G. Murphy Jr., former assistant commander of the Texas Department of Public Safety's criminal intelligence service, now retired.

Bob Kraft, reporter for the Cinncinnati Post-Times Star.

Tom Owens, formerly with the Illinois Secretary of State's office, now retired.

Dave Skinner, Florida Department of Revenue.

Dean Dollison, former registrar with the Ohio Bureau of Motor Vehicles.

Dick Charron, former Florida RV dealer.

Jim Ingram, former district supervisor with Florida's mobile home construction authority.

Lewis Charles, administrator with the Florida Department of Motor Vehicles.

Fran Van Pelt, former president of the Illinois chapter of the Recreational Vehicle Dealers Association, now an RV industry consultant.

Gene Hassett, former Florida campground manager.

Lt. Jerry Posey, Ouachita Parish (Louisiana) sheriff's office.

Walter Lee, Louisiana state police.

Bob Trupe, owner of Mid-State Camper Sales, Rapid City, South Dakota.

Jerry Harrison, former president of the Texas RV Association.

Mike Gleason, formerly with the consumer fraud and protection bureau of the New York attorney general's office.

William Moran, resident of Albany, New York.

Frank Gennusa, Louisiana victim of a travel trailer scam.

Kermit Mishler, investigator with the Indiana Department of Revenue.

Norman Klopp, former detective at Des Moines, Illinois, now retired.

J. Edward Peterson, owner of Lafayette (Indiana) Travel Trailer Sales.

Joseph P. Dalonzo, Ohio victim of travel trailer scam by Edward Burke.